Holt Literature & Language Arts

Third Course

UNIVERSAL ACCESS **Interactive Reading**

- **Word Analysis, Fluency, and Systematic Vocabulary Development**
- **Reading Comprehension**
- **Literary Response and Analysis**

HOLT, RINEHART AND WINSTON

A Harcourt Education Company

Austin • Orlando • Chicago • New York • Toronto • London • San Diego

Credits

Editorial

Project Directors: Kathleen Daniel, Juliana Koenig
Editor: Amy Fleming
Managing Editor: Mike Topp
Manager of Editorial Services: Abigail Winograd
Senior Product Manager: Don Wulbrecht
Editorial Staff: Susan Kent Cakars, Susan Joseph, Brenda Sanabria,
 Sari Wilson, Michael Zakhar
Project Administration: Elizabeth LaManna
Editorial Support: Renée Benitez, Louise Fernandez, Laurie Muir
Editorial Permissions: David Smith, Carrie Jones
Conceptual Framework and Writing: e2 Publishing Services, Inc.

Art, Design, and Production

Director: Athena Blackorby
Senior Design Director: Betty Mintz
Series Design: Proof Positive/Farrowlyne Associates, Inc.
Design and Electronic Files: Bill Smith Studio
Photo Research: Bill Smith Studio
Production Manager: Catherine Gessner
Production Supervisor: Carol Marunas

Printed in the United States of America
ISBN 0-03-065031-3

12   082   09 08 07 06

Contents

• PART ONE •
LITERARY RESPONSE AND ANALYSIS 1

Mastering the California Standards in Reading

CHAPTER 8: LITERARY CRITICISM: EVALUATING STYLE

Reading Standard 1.1 Identify and use the literal and figurative meanings of words and understand word derivations.

Reading Standard 1.2 Distinguish between the denotative and connotative meanings of words and interpret the connotative power of words.

Reading Standard 3.11 Evaluate the aesthetic qualities of style, including the impact of diction and figurative language on tone, mood, and theme, using the terminology of literary criticism. (Aesthetic approach)

CHAPTER 9: LITERARY CRITICISM: BIOGRAPHICAL AND HISTORICAL APPROACH

Reading Standard 1.1 Identify and use the literal and figurative meanings of words and understand word derivations.

Reading Standard 3.7 (Grade 8 Review) Analyze a work of literature, showing how it reflects the heritage, traditions, attitudes, and beliefs of its author. (Biographical approach)

Reading Standard 3.12 Analyze the way in which a work of literature is related to the themes and issues of its historical period. (Historical approach)

CHAPTER 10: EPIC AND MYTH

Reading Standard 1.3 (Grade 8 Review) Use word meanings within the appropriate context and show ability to verify those meanings by definition, restatement, example, comparison, or contrast.

Reading Standard 1.3 Identify Greek, Roman, and Norse mythology and use the knowledge to understand the origin and meaning of new words (e.g., the word *narcissistic* drawn from the myth of Narcissus and Echo).

Reading Standard 3.1 (Grade 8 Review) Determine and articulate the relationship between the purposes and characteristics of different forms of poetry (e.g., ballad, lyric, couplet, epic, elegy, ode, sonnet).

Reading Standard 3.3 Analyze interactions between main and subordinate characters in a literary text (e.g., internal and external conflicts, motivations, relationships, influences) and explain the way those interactions affect the plot.

Reading Standard 3.12 Analyze the way in which a work of literature is related to the themes and issues of its historical period. (Historical approach)

CHAPTER 11: DRAMA

Reading Standard 1.2 (Grade 8 Review) Understand the most important points in the history of the English language and use common word origins to determine the historical influences on English word meanings.

Reading Standard 1.3 Identify Greek, Roman, and Norse mythology and use the knowledge to understand the origin and meaning of new words (e.g., the word *narcissistic* drawn from the myth of Narcissus and Echo).

Reading Standard 3.1 Articulate the relationship between the expressed purposes and the characteristics of different forms of dramatic literature (e.g., comedy, tragedy, drama, dramatic monologue).

Reading Standard 3.10 Identify and describe the function of dialogue, scene designs, soliloquies, asides, and character foils in dramatic literature.

PART TWO: READING COMPREHENSION

Reading Standard 1.1 Identify and use the literal and figurative meanings of words and understand word derivations.

Reading Standard 1.3 (Grade 8 Review) Use word meanings within the appropriate context and show ability to verify those meanings by definition, restatement, example, comparison, or contrast.

Reading Standard 2.1 Analyze the structure and format of functional workplace documents, including the graphics and headers, and explain how authors use the features to achieve their purposes.

Reading Standard 2.2 Prepare a bibliography of reference materials for a report using a variety of consumer, workplace, and public documents.

Reading Standard 2.3 Generate relevant questions about readings on issues that can be researched.

Reading Standard 2.4 Synthesize the content from several sources or works by a single author dealing with a single issue; paraphrase the ideas and connect them to other sources and related topics to demonstrate comprehension.

Reading Standard 2.5 Extend ideas presented in primary or secondary sources through original analysis, evaluation, and elaboration.

Reading Standard 2.6 Demonstrate use of sophisticated learning tools by following technical directions (e.g., those found with graphic calculators and specialized software programs and in access guides to World Wide Web sites on the Internet).

Reading Standard 2.7 Critique the logic of functional documents by examining the sequence of information and procedures in anticipation of possible reader misunderstandings.

Reading Standard 2.8 Evaluate the credibility of an author's argument or defense of a claim by critiquing the relationship between generalizations and evidence, the comprehensiveness of evidence, and the way in which the author's intent affects the structure and tone of the text (e.g., in professional journals, editorials, political speeches, primary source material).

To the Student

A Book for You

....

Teachers open the door, but you must enter by yourself.
—Chinese Proverb

....

Reading is an interactive process. The more you put into it, the more you get out of it. This book is designed to do just that—help you interact with the selections you read by marking them up, asking your own questions, taking notes, recording your own ideas, and responding to the questions of others.

A Book Designed for Your Success

Interactive Reading goes hand-in-hand with *Holt Literature and Language Arts.* It is designed to help you interact with the selections and master the California Language Arts Standards.

To do this, the book has two parts that each follow a simple format:

Part 1 Literary Response and Analysis

Increasing your understanding of literature is a major goal of the California Language Arts Standards. To help you master how to respond to, analyze, evaluate, and interpret literature, *Interactive Reading* provides—

For each chapter:
- The academic vocabulary you need to know to master the literature standards for the chapter, defined for ready reference and use.
- The first selection from the corresponding chapter in *Holt Literature and Language Arts* reprinted in an interactive format to support and guide your reading.
- A new selection for you to read and respond to, enabling you to apply and extend your skills and build toward independence.

For each selection:
- A Before You Read page that preteaches the literary focus and provides a reading skill to help you comprehend the selection.
- A Vocabulary Development page that preteaches selection vocabulary and provides a vocabulary skill to use while reading the prose selections.
- Literature printed in an interactive format to guide your reading and help you respond to text.
- A graphic organizer that helps you understand the literary focus of the selection.
- Standards Review pages that help you practice test-taking skills while applying the standards.

Part 2 Reading Comprehension

Reading informational texts and documents is another major thrust of the California Language Arts Standards. To help you master how to read informational materials, this book contains—

For Informational Materials:
- The academic vocabulary you need to know to master the informational standards, defined for ready reference and use.
- A Before You Read page that preteaches the informational focus and provides a reading skill to help you comprehend the selection.
- New informational selections for each standard in interactive format to guide your reading and help you respond to the text.
- A graphic organizer that helps you understand the informational focus of the selection.
- A Standards Review page that helps you practice test-taking skills while applying the standards.

For Consumer, Workplace, and Public Documents:
- The academic vocabulary you need to know to master the standards, defined for ready reference and use.
- A Before You Read page that preteaches the document focus and defines specialized terms.
- New documents for each standard in interactive format to guide your reading and help you respond to the text.
- A Standards Review page that helps you practice test-taking skills while applying the standard.

A Book for Your Own Thoughts and Feelings

Reading is about *you*. It is about connecting your thoughts and feelings to the thoughts and feelings of the writer. Make this book your own. The more you give of yourself to your reading, the more you will get out of it. We encourage you to write in it. Jot down how you feel about the selection. Question the text. Note details you think need to be cleared up or topics you would like to learn more about.

Keep track of what you have learned and what you have read with the following tools at the back of the book:
- A Word List
- A Checklist for Standards Mastery

A Walk Through the Book

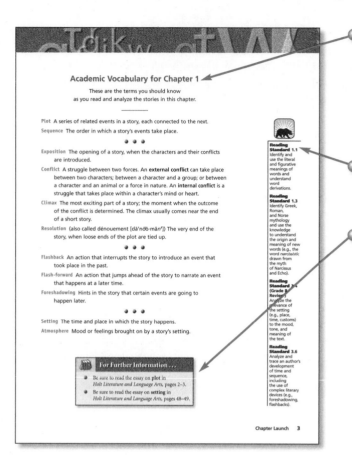

Academic Vocabulary
Academic vocabulary refers to the language of books, tests, and formal writing. Each chapter begins with the terms, or academic language, you need to know to master the standards for that chapter.

Reading Standards
All of the standards covered in the chapter are listed here.

For Further Information
Would you like more information? These are the essays in *Holt Literature and Language Arts* that will help you.

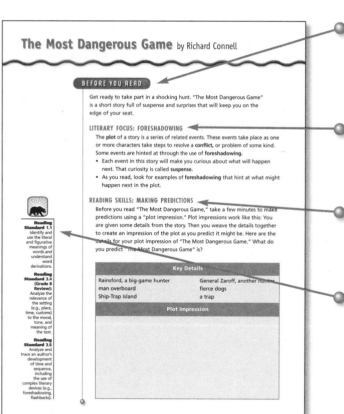

Before You Read
Previewing what you will learn builds success. This page tells you what the selection is about and prepares you to read it.

Literary Focus
This feature introduces the literary focus for the selection. The focus ties into a California literature standard.

Reading Skills
This feature provides a reading skill for you to apply to the selection. It ties into and supports the literary focus.

Reading Standards
The standards covered with the selection are listed here.

Vocabulary Development

Vocabulary words for the selection are pretaught. Each entry gives the pronunciation and definition of the word as well as a context sentence.

Vocabulary Skills

When you read, you not only have to recognize words but also decode them and determine meaning. This feature introduces a vocabulary skill to use to understand words in the selection. It ties into and supports the vocabulary standard.

VOCABULARY DEVELOPMENT

PREVIEW SELECTION VOCABULARY

Preview the following words from the story before you begin reading:

receding (ri·sēd'iŋ) v. used as adj.: becoming more distant.

He could see the ship going away from him, receding in the distance.

disarming (dis·ärm'iŋ) adj.: removing or lessening suspicions or fears.

"Don't be alarmed," said Rainsford, with a smile he hoped was disarming.

prolonged (prō·lôŋd') v. used as adj.: extended.

Zaroff's whole life was one prolonged hunt.

imprudent (im·prōōd'ənt) adj.: unwise.

After the revolution in Russia, Zaroff left the country, for it was imprudent for an officer of the czar to stay there.

surmounted (sər·mount'id) v.: overcame.

The general smiled the quiet smile of one who has faced an obstacle and surmounted it with success.

unruffled (un·ruf'əld) adj.: calm; not disturbed.

Zaroff appeared unruffled, even when Rainsford called him a murderer.

invariably (in·ver'ē·ə·blē) adv.: always; without changing.

Zaroff said that his captives invariably choose the hunt.

diverting (də·vurt'iŋ) adj.: entertaining.

The deadly hunt was a diverting game to Zaroff.

impulse (im'puls') n.: sudden desire to do something.

Rainsford had to control his impulse to run.

protruding (prō·trōōd'iŋ) v. used as adj.: sticking out.

The protruding cliffs blocked Rainsford's sight of the ocean.

PREFIXES: IMPORTANT BEGINNINGS

Prefixes are word parts added to the beginnings of words. Although prefixes consist of just a few letters, they are powerful and can greatly change the meaning of a word. To the right are prefixes you'll come across often in your reading. Recognizing these prefixes will help you figure out the meanings of many words that might be new to you.

Prefix	Meaning	Example
pre–	before	preview, "view before"
inter–	between	interaction, "action between"
un–	not	unpopular, "not popular"
mis–	badly; wrong	mismatch, "bad match"
re–	again	replay, "play again"

The Most Dangerous Game **5**

Side-Column Notes

Each selection is accompanied by notes in the side column that guide your interaction with the selection. Many notes ask you to underline or circle in the text itself. Others provide lines on which you can write your responses to questions.

THE MOST DANGEROUS GAME

Richard Connell

PLOT

Underline the name of the island in line 4. What do you **predict** will happen in the story, based on this name?

_____

_____

_____

_____

_____

_____

_____

"Off there to the right—somewhere—is a large island," said Whitney. "It's rather a mystery—"

"What island is it?" Rainsford asked.

"The old charts call it Ship-Trap Island," Whitney replied. "A suggestive name, isn't it? Sailors have a curious dread of the place. I don't know why. Some superstition—"

"Can't see it," remarked Rainsford, trying to peer through the dank tropical night that was palpable as it pressed its thick warm blackness upon the yacht.

10 "You've good eyes," said Whitney, with a laugh, "and I've seen you pick off a moose moving in the brown fall bush at four hundred yards, but even you can't see four miles or so through a moonless Caribbean night."

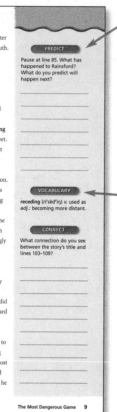

80 He leapt upon the rail and balanced himself there, to get greater elevation; his pipe, striking a rope, was knocked from his mouth. He lunged for it; a short, hoarse cry came from his lips as he realized he had reached too far and had lost his balance. The cry was pinched off short as the blood-warm waters of the Caribbean Sea closed over his head.

He struggled up to the surface and tried to cry out, but the wash from the speeding yacht slapped him in the face and the salt water in his open mouth made him gag and strangle. Desperately he struck out with strong strokes after the **receding**
90 lights of the yacht, but he stopped before he had swum fifty feet. A certain coolheadedness had come to him; it was not the first time he had been in a tight place. There was a chance that his cries could be heard by someone aboard the yacht, but that chance was slender and grew more slender as the yacht raced on. He wrestled himself out of his clothes and shouted with all his power. The lights of the yacht became faint and ever-vanishing fireflies; then they were blotted out entirely by the night.

Rainsford remembered the shots. They had come from the right, and doggedly he swam in that direction, swimming with
100 slow, deliberate strokes, conserving his strength. For a seemingly endless time he fought the sea. He began to count his strokes; he could do possibly a hundred more and then—

Rainsford heard a sound. It came out of the darkness, a high screaming sound, the sound of an animal in an extremity of anguish and terror.

He did not recognize the animal that made the sound; he did not try to; with fresh vitality he swam toward the sound. He heard it again; then it was cut short by another noise, crisp, staccato.

"Pistol shot," muttered Rainsford, swimming on.
110 Ten minutes of determined effort brought another sound to his ears—the most welcome he had ever heard—the muttering and growling of the sea breaking on a rocky shore. He was almost on the rocks before he saw them; on a night less calm he would have been shattered against them. With his remaining strength he

PREDICT
Pause at line 85. What has happened to Rainsford? What do you predict will happen next?

_____
_____
_____
_____
_____
_____

VOCABULARY
receding (ri·sēd′in) v. used as adj.: becoming more distant.

CONNECT
What connection do you see between the story's title and lines 103–109?

_____
_____
_____
_____
_____
_____
_____
_____
_____
_____

The Most Dangerous Game **9**

FLUENCY
Read the boxed passage aloud two times. Try to improve the speed and smoothness of your delivery on your second read.

INFER
When you appraise something, you estimate its value. Why might the general be appraising Rainsford (line 255)?

_____
_____
_____
_____
_____
_____
_____
_____
_____
_____
_____
_____
_____
_____
_____
_____

on, noticed that it came from a London tailor who ordinarily cut and sewed for none below the rank of duke.

The dining room to which Ivan conducted him was in many ways remarkable. There was a medieval magnificence about it; it suggested a baronial hall of feudal times, with its oaken panels, its high ceiling, its vast refectory table where two-score men could sit down to eat. About the hall were the mounted heads of many animals—lions, tigers, elephants, moose, bears; larger or more perfect specimens Rainsford had
240 never seen. At the great table the general was sitting, alone.

"You'll have a cocktail, Mr. Rainsford," he suggested. The cocktail was surpassingly good; and, Rainsford noted, the table appointments were of the finest—the linen, the crystal, the silver, the china.

They were eating borscht, the rich red soup with sour cream so dear to Russian palates. Half apologetically General Zaroff said: "We do our best to preserve the amenities[9] of civilization here. Please forgive any lapses. We are well off the beaten track, you know. Do you think the champagne has suffered from
250 its long ocean trip?"

"Not in the least," declared Rainsford. He was finding the general a most thoughtful and affable host, a true cosmopolite.[10] But there was one small trait of the general's that made Rainsford uncomfortable. Whenever he looked up from his plate he found the general studying him, appraising him narrowly.

"Perhaps," said General Zaroff, "you were surprised that I recognized your name. You see, I read all books on hunting published in English, French, and Russian. I have but one passion in my life, Mr. Rainsford, and it is the hunt."
260 "You have some wonderful heads here," said Rainsford as he ate a particularly well-cooked filet mignon. "That Cape buffalo is the largest I ever saw."

"Oh, that fellow. Yes, he was a monster."

_____
9. amenities (ə·men′ə·tēz) n.: comforts and conveniences.
10. cosmopolite (käz·mäp′ə·līt′) n.: knowledgeable citizen of the world.

14 Part 1 Chapter 1: Plot and Setting

Types of Notes
The different types of notes throughout the selection help you—
- Focus on literary elements
- Apply the reading skill
- Apply the vocabulary skill
- Think critically about the selection
- Develop word knowledge
- Build vocabulary
- Build fluency

Vocabulary
The vocabulary words that were pretaught are defined in the side column and set in boldface in the selection, allowing you to see them in context.

Fluency
Successful readers are able to read fluently—clearly, easily, quickly, and without word identification problems. In most selections, you'll be given an opportunity to practice and improve your fluency.

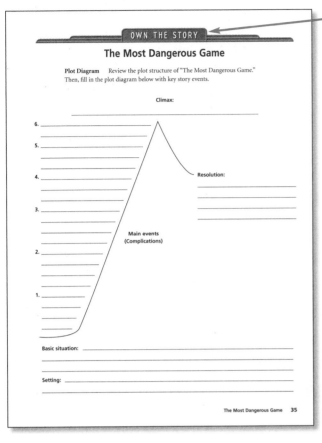

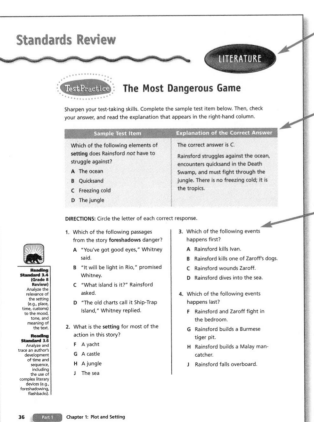

Own the Story
Graphic organizers help reinforce your understanding of the literary focus in a highly visual and creative way.

Standards Review: Literature
This feature helps you practice for the state-wide tests by asking questions about the literary focus.

Sample Test Item
For a multiple-choice question, you have to choose the one—and only one—correct answer. This feature models the thinking involved in making such choices.

Questions
These questions test your mastery of the literary standard, while mirroring the type of questions you will find on the state-wide tests.

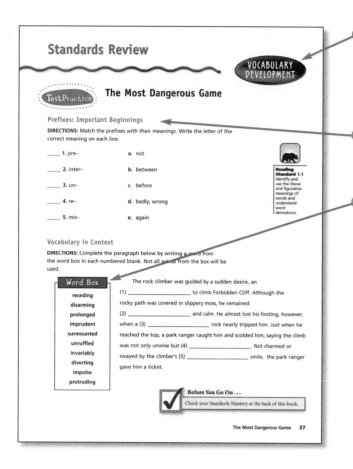

Standards Review

VOCABULARY DEVELOPMENT

TestPractice **The Most Dangerous Game**

Prefixes: Important Beginnings

DIRECTIONS: Match the prefixes with their meanings. Write the letter of the correct meaning on each line.

_____ 1. *pre–*   a. not

_____ 2. *inter–*   b. between

_____ 3. *un–*   c. before

_____ 4. *re–*   d. badly; wrong

_____ 5. *mis–*   e. again

Reading Standard 1.1
Identify and use the literal and figurative meanings of words and understand word derivations.

Vocabulary in Context

DIRECTIONS: Complete the paragraph below by writing a word from the word box in each numbered blank. Not all words from the box will be used.

Word Box

receding
disarming
prolonged
imprudent
surmounted
unruffled
invariably
diverting
impulse
protruding

The rock climber was guided by a sudden desire, an (1) _____ to climb Forbidden Cliff. Although the rocky path was covered in slippery moss, he remained (2) _____ and calm. He almost lost his footing, however, when a (3) _____ rock nearly tripped him. Just when he reached the top, a park ranger caught him and scolded him, saying the climb was not only unwise but (4) _____. Not charmed or swayed by the climber's (5) _____ smile, the park ranger gave him a ticket.

✓ **Before You Go On . . .**
Check your Standards Mastery at the back of this book.

Standards Review: Vocabulary

This feature helps you practice for the state-wide tests by asking questions about the vocabulary skill and the specific vocabulary words taught with the selection.

Questions

The first part of the practice test asks questions about the vocabulary skill.

Vocabulary in Context

The second part of the practice test assesses your mastery of the vocabulary words by asking you to put them in context.

Part One

Literary Response and Analysis

Plot and Setting

Academic Vocabulary for Chapter 1

These are the terms you should know
as you read and analyze the stories in this chapter.

Plot A series of related events in a story, each connected to the next.

Sequence The order in which a story's events take place.

Exposition The opening of a story, when the characters and their conflicts are introduced.

Conflict A struggle between two forces. An **external conflict** can take place between two characters; between a character and a group; or between a character and an animal or a force in nature. An **internal conflict** is a struggle that takes place within a character's mind or heart.

Climax The most exciting part of a story; the moment when the outcome of the conflict is determined. The climax usually comes near the end of a short story.

Resolution (also called dénouement [dā′noō·mä*n*′]) The very end of the story, when loose ends of the plot are tied up.

Flashback An action that interrupts the story to introduce an event that took place in the past.

Flash-forward An action that jumps ahead of the story to narrate an event that happens at a later time.

Foreshadowing Hints in the story that certain events are going to happen later.

Setting The time and place in which the story happens.

Atmosphere Mood or feelings brought on by a story's setting.

Reading Standard 1.1 Identify and use the literal and figurative meanings of words and understand word derivations.

Reading Standard 1.3 Identify Greek, Roman, and Norse mythology and use the knowledge to understand the origin and meaning of new words (e.g., the word *narcissistic* drawn from the myth of Narcissus and Echo).

Reading Standard 3.4 (Grade 8 Review) Analyze the relevance of the setting (e.g., place, time, customs) to the mood, tone, and meaning of the text.

Reading Standard 3.6 Analyze and trace an author's development of time and sequence, including the use of complex literary devices (e.g., foreshadowing, flashbacks).

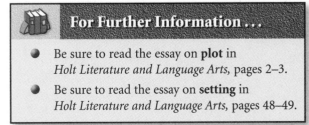

For Further Information . . .

- Be sure to read the essay on **plot** in *Holt Literature and Language Arts*, pages 2–3.
- Be sure to read the essay on **setting** in *Holt Literature and Language Arts*, pages 48–49.

The Most Dangerous Game by Richard Connell

BEFORE YOU READ

Get ready to take part in a shocking hunt. "The Most Dangerous Game" is a short story full of suspense and surprises that will keep you on the edge of your seat.

LITERARY FOCUS: FORESHADOWING

The **plot** of a story is a series of related events. These events take place as one or more characters take steps to resolve a **conflict,** or problem of some kind. Some events are hinted at through the use of **foreshadowing.**
- Each event in this story will make you curious about what will happen next. That curiosity is called **suspense.**
- As you read, look for examples of **foreshadowing** that hint at what might happen next in the plot.

READING SKILLS: MAKING PREDICTIONS

Before you read "The Most Dangerous Game," take a few minutes to make predictions using a "plot impression." Plot impressions work like this: You are given some details from the story. Then you weave the details together to create an impression of the plot as you predict it might be. Here are the details for your plot impression of "The Most Dangerous Game." What do you predict "The Most Dangerous Game" is?

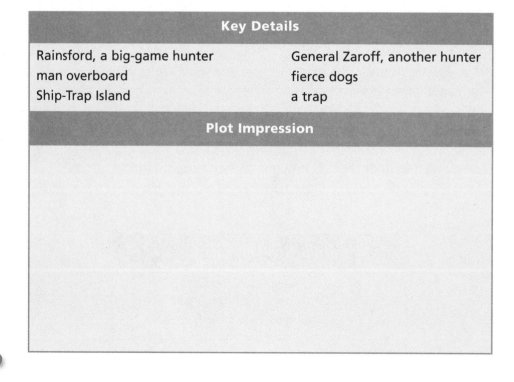

Key Details	
Rainsford, a big-game hunter man overboard Ship-Trap Island	General Zaroff, another hunter fierce dogs a trap
Plot Impression	

Reading Standard 1.1
Identify and use the literal and figurative meanings of words and understand word derivations.

Reading Standard 3.4 (Grade 8 Review):
Analyze the relevance of the setting (e.g., place, time, customs) to the mood, tone, and meaning of the text.

Reading Standard 3.6
Analyze and trace an author's development of time and sequence, including the use of complex literary devices (e.g., foreshadowing, flashbacks).

VOCABULARY DEVELOPMENT

PREVIEW SELECTION VOCABULARY

Preview the following words from the story before you begin reading:

receding (ri·sēd′iŋ) *v.* used as *adj.*: becoming more distant.

> *He could see the ship going away from him, receding in the distance.*

disarming (dis·ärm′iŋ) *adj.*: removing or lessening suspicions or fears.

> *"Don't be alarmed," said Rainsford, with a smile he hoped was disarming.*

prolonged (prō·lôŋd′) *v.* used as *adj.*: extended.

> *Zaroff's whole life was one prolonged hunt.*

imprudent (im·prōōd′ənt) *adj.*: unwise.

> *After the revolution in Russia, Zaroff left the country, for it was imprudent for an officer of the czar to stay there.*

surmounted (sər·mount′id) *v.*: overcame.

> *The general smiled the quiet smile of one who has faced an obstacle and surmounted it with success.*

unruffled (un·ruf′əld) *adj.*: calm; not disturbed.

> *Zaroff appeared unruffled, even when Rainsford called him a murderer.*

invariably (in·ver′ē·ə·blē) *adv.*: always; without changing.

> *Zaroff said that his captives invariably choose the hunt.*

diverting (də·vʉrt′iŋ) *adj.*: entertaining.

> *The deadly hunt was a diverting game to Zaroff.*

impulse (im′puls′) *n.*: sudden desire to do something.

> *Rainsford had to control his impulse to run.*

protruding (prō·trōōd′iŋ) *v.* used as *adj.*: sticking out.

> *The protruding cliffs blocked Rainsford's sight of the ocean.*

PREFIXES: IMPORTANT BEGINNINGS

Prefixes are word parts added to the beginnings of words. Although prefixes consist of just a few letters, they are powerful and can greatly change the meaning of a word. To the right are prefixes you'll come across often in your reading. Recognizing these prefixes will help you figure out the meanings of many words that might be new to you.

Prefix	Meaning	Example
pre–	before	*preview,* "view before"
inter–	between	*interaction,* "action between"
un–	not	*unpopular,* "not popular"
mis–	badly; wrong	*mismatch,* "bad match"
re–	again	*replay,* "play again"

THE MOST DANGEROUS GAME

Richard Connell

PLOT

Underline the name of the island in line 4. What do you **predict** will happen in the story, based on this name?

_____

_____

_____

_____

_____

_____

"Off there to the right—somewhere—is a large island," said Whitney. "It's rather a mystery—"

"What island is it?" Rainsford asked.

"The old charts call it Ship-Trap Island," Whitney replied. "A suggestive name, isn't it? Sailors have a curious dread of the place. I don't know why. Some superstition—"

"Can't see it," remarked Rainsford, trying to peer through the dank tropical night that was palpable as it pressed its thick warm blackness in upon the yacht.

10   "You've good eyes," said Whitney, with a laugh, "and I've seen you pick off a moose moving in the brown fall bush at four hundred yards, but even you can't see four miles or so through a moonless Caribbean night."

"Nor four yards," admitted Rainsford. "Ugh! It's like moist black velvet."

"It will be light in Rio," promised Whitney. "We should make it in a few days. I hope the jaguar guns have come from Purdey's.[1] We should have some good hunting up the Amazon. Great sport, hunting."

20 "The best sport in the world," agreed Rainsford.

"For the hunter," amended Whitney. "Not for the jaguar."

"Don't talk rot, Whitney," said Rainsford. "You're a big-game hunter, not a philosopher. Who cares how a jaguar feels?"

"Perhaps the jaguar does," observed Whitney.

"Bah! They've no understanding."

"Even so, I rather think they understand one thing—fear. The fear of pain and the fear of death."

"Nonsense," laughed Rainsford. "This hot weather is making you soft, Whitney. Be a realist. The world is made up of two 30 classes—the hunters and the huntees. Luckily, you and I are the hunters. Do you think we've passed that island yet?"

"I can't tell in the dark. I hope so."

"Why?" asked Rainsford.

"The place has a reputation—a bad one."

"Cannibals?" suggested Rainsford.

"Hardly. Even cannibals wouldn't live in such a Godforsaken place. But it's gotten into sailor lore, somehow. Didn't you notice that the crew's nerves seemed a bit jumpy today?"

40 "They were a bit strange, now you mention it. Even Captain Nielsen—"

"Yes, even that tough-minded old Swede, who'd go up to the devil himself and ask him for a light. Those fishy blue eyes held a look I never saw there before. All I could get out of him was: 'This place has an evil name among seafaring men, sir.' Then he said to me, very gravely: 'Don't you feel anything?'— as if the air about us was actually poisonous. Now, you mustn't

SETTING

Circle the words in lines 7–15 that describe the **setting**. What mood, or feeling, do these words create in you?

_____

_____

_____

_____

_____

_____

_____

IDENTIFY

Underline the sentences in lines 20–27 that tell how Rainsford feels about hunting animals. Circle the sentences that tell how Whitney feels about hunting animals.

_____

_____

_____

_____

_____

_____

_____

---

1. **Purdey's** (pŭr′dēz): British manufacturer of hunting equipment.

Underline details in lines 42–60 that describe the setting and its effect on Whitney. What **mood** do these details help create?

_____

_____

_____

_____

_____

_____

_____

_____

Pause at line 76. What do you predict will happen?

_____

_____

_____

_____

_____

_____

_____

_____

_____

_____

laugh when I tell you this—I did feel something like a sudden chill.

50   "There was no breeze. The sea was as flat as a plate-glass window. We were drawing near the island then. What I felt was a—a mental chill, a sort of sudden dread."

"Pure imagination," said Rainsford. "One superstitious sailor can taint the whole ship's company with his fear."

"Maybe. But sometimes I think sailors have an extra sense that tells them when they are in danger. Sometimes I think evil is a tangible thing—with wavelengths, just as sound and light have. An evil place can, so to speak, broadcast vibrations of evil. Anyhow, I'm glad we're getting out of this zone. Well, I think
60   I'll turn in now, Rainsford."

"I'm not sleepy," said Rainsford. "I'm going to smoke another pipe on the afterdeck."

"Good night, then, Rainsford. See you at breakfast."

"Right. Good night, Whitney."

There was no sound in the night as Rainsford sat there but the muffled throb of the engine that drove the yacht swiftly through the darkness, and the swish and ripple of the wash of the propeller.

Rainsford, reclining in a steamer chair, indolently[2] puffed
70   on his favorite brier.[3] The sensuous drowsiness of the night was on him. "It's so dark," he thought, "that I could sleep without closing my eyes; the night would be my eyelids—"

An abrupt sound startled him. Off to the right he heard it, and his ears, expert in such matters, could not be mistaken. Again he heard the sound, and again. Somewhere, off in the blackness, someone had fired a gun three times.

Rainsford sprang up and moved quickly to the rail, mystified. He strained his eyes in the direction from which the reports had come, but it was like trying to see through a blanket.

---

2. **indolently** (in′də·lənt·lē) *adv.:* lazily.
3. **brier** (brī′ər) *n.:* tobacco pipe made from the root of a brier bush or tree.

80   He leapt upon the rail and balanced himself there, to get greater
     elevation; his pipe, striking a rope, was knocked from his mouth.
     He lunged for it; a short, hoarse cry came from his lips as
     he realized he had reached too far and had lost his balance.
     The cry was pinched off short as the blood-warm waters of
     the Caribbean Sea closed over his head.

          He struggled up to the surface and tried to cry out, but
     the wash from the speeding yacht slapped him in the face and
     the salt water in his open mouth made him gag and strangle.
     Desperately he struck out with strong strokes after the **receding**
90   lights of the yacht, but he stopped before he had swum fifty feet.
     A certain coolheadedness had come to him; it was not the first
     time he had been in a tight place. There was a chance that his
     cries could be heard by someone aboard the yacht, but that
     chance was slender and grew more slender as the yacht raced on.
     He wrestled himself out of his clothes and shouted with all his
     power. The lights of the yacht became faint and ever-vanishing
     fireflies; then they were blotted out entirely by the night.

          Rainsford remembered the shots. They had come from the
     right, and doggedly he swam in that direction, swimming with
100 slow, deliberate strokes, conserving his strength. For a seemingly
     endless time he fought the sea. He began to count his strokes;
     he could do possibly a hundred more and then—

          Rainsford heard a sound. It came out of the darkness, a
     high screaming sound, the sound of an animal in an extremity
     of anguish and terror.

          He did not recognize the animal that made the sound; he did
     not try to; with fresh vitality he swam toward the sound. He heard
     it again; then it was cut short by another noise, crisp, staccato.

          "Pistol shot," muttered Rainsford, swimming on.

110   Ten minutes of determined effort brought another sound to
     his ears—the most welcome he had ever heard—the muttering
     and growling of the sea breaking on a rocky shore. He was almost
     on the rocks before he saw them; on a night less calm he would
     have been shattered against them. With his remaining strength he

PREDICT

Pause at line 85. What has
happened to Rainsford?
What do you predict will
happen next?

_____

_____

_____

_____

_____

_____

_____

VOCABULARY

receding (ri'sēd'in) _v._ used as
adj.: becoming more distant.

CONNECT

What connection do you see
between the story's title and
lines 103–109?

_____

_____

_____

_____

_____

_____

_____

_____

_____

SETTING

Pause at line 124. Where is Rainsford now?

_____

_____

_____

_____

_____

_____

_____

_____

_____

_____

_____

_____

_____

_____

_____

_____

_____

_____

_____

_____

dragged himself from the swirling waters. Jagged crags appeared to jut into the opaqueness.[4]

He forced himself upward, hand over hand. Gasping, his hands raw, he reached a flat place at the top. Dense jungle came down to the very edge of the cliffs. What perils that tangle

120 of trees and underbrush might hold for him did not concern Rainsford just then. All he knew was that he was safe from his enemy, the sea, and that utter weariness was on him. He flung himself down at the jungle edge and tumbled headlong into the deepest sleep of his life.

When he opened his eyes, he knew from the position of the sun that it was late in the afternoon. Sleep had given him new vigor; a sharp hunger was picking at him. He looked about him, almost cheerfully.

"Where there are pistol shots, there are men. Where there

130 are men, there is food," he thought. But what kind of men, he wondered, in so forbidding a place? An unbroken front of snarled and ragged jungle fringed the shore.

---

4. **opaqueness** (ō·pāk′nis) *n.:* here, darkness. Something opaque does not let light pass through.

He saw no sign of a trail through the closely knit web of weeds and trees; it was easier to go along the shore, and Rainsford floundered along by the water. Not far from where he had landed, he stopped.

Some wounded thing, by the evidence a large animal, had thrashed about in the underbrush; the jungle weeds were crushed down and the moss was lacerated; one patch of weeds was 140 stained crimson. A small, glittering object not far away caught Rainsford's eye and he picked it up. It was an empty cartridge.

"A twenty-two," he remarked. "That's odd. It must have been a fairly large animal too. The hunter had his nerve with him to tackle it with a light gun. It's clear that the brute put up a fight. I suppose the first three shots I heard was when the hunter flushed his quarry[5] and wounded it. The last shot was when he trailed it here and finished it."

He examined the ground closely and found what he had hoped to find—the print of hunting boots. They pointed along 150 the cliff in the direction he had been going. Eagerly he hurried along, now slipping on a rotten log or a loose stone, but making headway; night was beginning to settle down on the island.

Bleak darkness was blacking out the sea and jungle when Rainsford sighted the lights. He came upon them as he turned a crook in the coastline, and his first thought was that he had come upon a village, for there were many lights. But as he forged along, he saw to his great astonishment that all the lights were in one enormous building—a lofty structure with pointed towers plunging upward into the gloom. His eyes made out the shad-160 owy outlines of a palatial château;[6] it was set on a high bluff, and on three sides of it cliffs dived down to where the sea licked greedy lips in the shadows.

"Mirage," thought Rainsford. But it was no mirage, he found, when he opened the tall spiked iron gate. The stone steps

---

5. **flushed his quarry:** drove the animal he was hunting out of its hiding place.
6. **château** (sha·tō′) *n.:* large country house.

PLOT

Lines 137–141 create **suspense** by leaving questions in our minds. What questions would you like answered?

_____

_____

_____

_____

_____

_____

_____

_____

_____

WORD STUDY

Personification is a kind of **figurative language** in which a nonhuman thing or something inanimate (not alive) is talked about as if it were human or alive. Underline the detail in lines 161–162 that gives the sea a human quality. What kind of "person" is this sea?

_____

_____

_____

_____

_____

Here's a conflict in lines 176–178. Is it **external** or **internal**? Explain.

_____

_____

_____

_____

_____

_____

_____

_____

VOCABULARY

disarming (dis·ärm'iŋ) *adj.:* removing or lessening suspicions or fears.

Dis– is a prefix meaning "take away; deprive of." Literally, *disarm* means "take away weapons or arms." What does *discomfort* mean?

_____

_____

_____

_____

_____

_____

_____

were real enough; the massive door with a leering gargoyle for a knocker was real enough; yet about it all hung an air of unreality.

He lifted the knocker, and it creaked up stiffly, as if it had never before been used. He let it fall, and it startled him with its booming loudness.

170　He thought he heard steps within; the door remained closed. Again Rainsford lifted the heavy knocker and let it fall. The door opened then, opened as suddenly as if it were on a spring, and Rainsford stood blinking in the river of glaring gold light that poured out. The first thing Rainsford's eyes discerned was the largest man Rainsford had ever seen—a gigantic creature, solidly made and black-bearded to the waist. In his hand the man held a long-barreled revolver, and he was pointing it straight at Rainsford's heart.

Out of the snarl of beard two small eyes regarded
180　Rainsford.

"Don't be alarmed," said Rainsford, with a smile which he hoped was **disarming.** "I'm no robber. I fell off a yacht. My name is Sanger Rainsford of New York City."

The menacing look in the eyes did not change. The revolver pointed as rigidly as if the giant were a statue. He gave no sign that he understood Rainsford's words or that he had even heard them. He was dressed in uniform, a black uniform trimmed with gray astrakhan.[7]

"I'm Sanger Rainsford of New York," Rainsford began
190　again. "I fell off a yacht. I am hungry."

The man's only answer was to raise with his thumb the hammer of his revolver. Then Rainsford saw the man's free hand go to his forehead in a military salute, and he saw him click his heels together and stand at attention. Another man was coming down the broad marble steps, an erect, slender man in evening clothes. He advanced to Rainsford and held out his hand.

In a cultivated voice marked by a slight accent that gave it added precision and deliberateness, he said: "It is a very great

_____

7. astrakhan (as'trə·kən) *n.:* curly fur of very young lambs.

pleasure and honor to welcome Mr. Sanger Rainsford, the cele-
brated hunter, to my home."

Automatically Rainsford shook the man's hand.

"I've read your book about hunting snow leopards in Tibet,
you see," explained the man. "I am General Zaroff."

Rainsford's first impression was that the man was singularly
handsome; his second was that there was an original, almost
bizarre quality about the general's face. He was a tall man past
middle age, for his hair was a vivid white; but his thick eyebrows
and pointed military moustache were as black as the night from
which Rainsford had come. His eyes, too, were black and very
bright. He had high cheekbones, a sharp-cut nose, a spare, dark
face, the face of a man used to giving orders, the face of an aris-
tocrat. Turning to the giant in uniform, the general made a sign.
The giant put away his pistol, saluted, withdrew.

"Ivan is an incredibly strong fellow," remarked the general,
"but he has the misfortune to be deaf and dumb. A simple
fellow, but, I'm afraid, like all his race, a bit of a savage."

"Is he Russian?"

"He is a Cossack,"[8] said the general, and his smile showed
red lips and pointed teeth. "So am I."

"Come," he said, "we shouldn't be chatting here. We can
talk later. Now you want clothes, food, rest. You shall have them.
This is a most restful spot."

Ivan had reappeared, and the general spoke to him with
lips that moved but gave forth no sound.

"Follow Ivan, if you please, Mr. Rainsford," said the general.
"I was about to have my dinner when you came. I'll wait for
you. You'll find that my clothes will fit you, I think."

It was to a huge, beam-ceilinged bedroom with a canopied
bed big enough for six men that Rainsford followed the silent
giant. Ivan laid out an evening suit, and Rainsford, as he put it

8. Cossack (käs′ak′): member of a group from Ukraine, many of whom served as horsemen to the Russian czars and were famed for their fierceness in battle.

Notes

PREDICT

Circle the word in line 216 that Zaroff uses to describe Cossacks. Now, read on through line 219. What do Zaroff's remarks suggest about how he himself will behave later in the story?

FLUENCY

Read the boxed passage aloud two times. Try to improve the speed and smoothness of your delivery on your second read.

INFER

When you appraise something, you estimate its value. Why might the general be appraising Rainsford (line 255)?

_____

_____

_____

_____

_____

_____

_____

_____

_____

_____

_____

_____

_____

_____

_____

_____

_____

_____

on, noticed that it came from a London tailor who ordinarily cut and sewed for none below the rank of duke.

The dining room to which Ivan conducted him was in many ways remarkable. There was a medieval magnificence about it; it suggested a baronial hall of feudal times, with its oaken panels, its high ceiling, its vast refectory table where two-score men could sit down to eat. About the hall were the mounted heads of many animals—lions, tigers, elephants, moose, bears; larger or more perfect specimens Rainsford had

240 never seen. At the great table the general was sitting, alone.

"You'll have a cocktail, Mr. Rainsford," he suggested. The cocktail was surpassingly good; and, Rainsford noted, the table appointments were of the finest—the linen, the crystal, the silver, the china.

They were eating borscht, the rich red soup with sour cream so dear to Russian palates. Half apologetically General Zaroff said: "We do our best to preserve the amenities[9] of civilization here. Please forgive any lapses. We are well off the beaten track, you know. Do you think the champagne has suffered from

250 its long ocean trip?"

"Not in the least," declared Rainsford. He was finding the general a most thoughtful and affable host, a true cosmopolite.[10] But there was one small trait of the general's that made Rainsford uncomfortable. Whenever he looked up from his plate he found the general studying him, appraising him narrowly.

"Perhaps," said General Zaroff, "you were surprised that I recognized your name. You see, I read all books on hunting published in English, French, and Russian. I have but one passion in my life, Mr. Rainsford, and it is the hunt."

260 "You have some wonderful heads here," said Rainsford as he ate a particularly well-cooked filet mignon. "That Cape buffalo is the largest I ever saw."

"Oh, that fellow. Yes, he was a monster."

---

9. **amenities** (ə·men′ə·tēz) *n.:* comforts and conveniences.
10. **cosmopolite** (käz·mäp′ə·līt′) *n.:* knowledgeable citizen of the world.

Cape buffalo.

"Did he charge you?"

"Hurled me against a tree," said the general. "Fractured my skull. But I got the brute."

"I've always thought," said Rainsford, "that the Cape buffalo is the most dangerous of all big game."

For a moment the general did not reply; he was smiling his curious red-lipped smile. Then he said slowly: "No. You are wrong, sir. The Cape buffalo is not the most dangerous big game." He sipped his wine. "Here in my preserve on this island," he said in the same slow tone, "I hunt more dangerous game."

Rainsford expressed his surprise. "Is there big game on this island?"

The general nodded. "The biggest."

"Really?"

PREDICT

Pause at line 273. What do you **predict** the most dangerous game will be?

"Oh, it isn't here naturally, of course. I have to stock the island."

280   "What have you imported, general?" Rainsford asked. "Tigers?"

The general smiled. "No," he said. "Hunting tigers ceased to interest me some years ago. I exhausted their possibilities, you see. No thrill left in tigers, no real danger. I live for danger, Mr. Rainsford."

The general took from his pocket a gold cigarette case and offered his guest a long black cigarette with a silver tip; it was perfumed and gave off a smell like incense.

"We will have some capital hunting, you and I," said the
290   general. "I shall be most glad to have your society."

"But what game—" began Rainsford.

"I'll tell you," said the general. "You will be amused, I know. I think I may say, in all modesty, that I have done a rare thing. I have invented a new sensation. May I pour you another glass of port, Mr. Rainsford?"

"Thank you, general."

The general filled both glasses and said: "God makes some men poets. Some He makes kings, some beggars. Me He made a hunter. My hand was made for the trigger, my father said.
300   He was a very rich man, with a quarter of a million acres in the Crimea,[11] and he was an ardent sportsman. When I was only five years old, he gave me a little gun, specially made in Moscow for me, to shoot sparrows with. When I shot some of his prize turkeys with it, he did not punish me; he complimented me on my marksmanship. I killed my first bear in the Caucasus[12] when I was ten. My whole life has been one **prolonged** hunt. I went into the army—it was expected of noblemen's sons—and for a time commanded a division of Cossack cavalry, but my real interest was always the hunt. I have hunted every kind of game

---

11. **Crimea** (krī·mē′ə): peninsula in Ukraine jutting into the Black Sea.
12. **Caucasus** (kô′kə·səs): mountainous region between southeastern Europe and western Asia.

PLOT

Notice the sequence of events as Zaroff tells about his past. Underline the words in lines 301–302 that tell when he received his first gun. Underline the words in lines 305–306 that tell when he shot his first bear. Underline the words in line 313 that tell when he left Russia.

VOCABULARY

prolonged (prō·lond′) v. used as adj.: extended.

310 in every land. It would be impossible for me to tell you how
many animals I have killed."

The general puffed at his cigarette.

"After the debacle[13] in Russia I left the country, for it was
imprudent for an officer of the czar to stay there. Many noble
Russians lost everything. I, luckily, had invested heavily in
American securities, so I shall never have to open a tearoom
in Monte Carlo[14] or drive a taxi in Paris. Naturally, I continued
to hunt—grizzlies in your Rockies, crocodiles in the Ganges,[15]
rhinoceroses in East Africa. It was in Africa that the Cape buffalo
320 hit me and laid me up for six months. As soon as I recovered
I started for the Amazon to hunt jaguars, for I had heard they
were unusually cunning. They weren't." The Cossack sighed.
"They were no match at all for a hunter with his wits about him
and a high-powered rifle. I was bitterly disappointed. I was lying
in my tent with a splitting headache one night when a terrible
thought pushed its way into my mind. Hunting was beginning
to bore me! And hunting, remember, had been my life. I have
heard that in America businessmen often go to pieces when they
give up the business that has been their life."

330 "Yes, that's so," said Rainsford.

The general smiled. "I had no wish to go to pieces," he
said. "I must do something. Now, mine is an analytical mind,
Mr. Rainsford. Doubtless that is why I enjoy the problems of
the chase."

"No doubt, General Zaroff."

"So," continued the general, "I asked myself why the hunt
no longer fascinated me. You are much younger than I am,
Mr. Rainsford, and have not hunted as much, but you perhaps
can guess the answer."

340 "What was it?"

---

13. **debacle** (di·bä′kəl) *n.*: overwhelming defeat. Zaroff is referring to the
Russian Revolution of 1917, in which the czar and his government
were overthrown.
14. **Monte Carlo** (mänt′ə kär′lō): gambling resort in Monaco, a country
on the Mediterranean Sea.
15. **Ganges** (gan′jēz): river in northern India and Bangladesh.

VOCABULARY

imprudent (im·prood′ənt)
adj.: unwise.

Im– is a prefix meaning
"not." *Imprudent* means
"not prudent." What does
immature mean?

_____

_____

_____

_____

_____

_____

_____

_____

WORD STUDY

An **idiom** is an expression
that means something different from the literal definitions of its parts. Circle the
idiom in line 328. What does
it mean?

_____

_____

_____

_____

_____

VOCABULARY

surmounted (sər·mount′id) *v.*:
overcame.

PREDICT

Pause at line 357. What
could this "new animal" be?

_____

_____

_____

_____

_____

_____

_____

_____

"Simply this: Hunting had ceased to be what you call a sporting proposition. It had become too easy. I always got my quarry. Always. There is no greater bore than perfection."

The general lit a fresh cigarette.

"No animal had a chance with me anymore. That is no boast; it is a mathematical certainty. The animal had nothing but his legs and his instinct. Instinct is no match for reason. When I thought of this, it was a tragic moment for me, I can tell you."

350 Rainsford leaned across the table, absorbed in what his host was saying.

"It came to me as an inspiration what I must do," the general went on.

"And that was?"

The general smiled the quiet smile of one who has faced an obstacle and **surmounted** it with success. "I had to invent a new animal to hunt," he said.

"A new animal? You're joking."

"Not at all," said the general. "I never joke about hunting.
360 I needed a new animal. I found one. So I bought this island, built this house, and here I do my hunting. The island is perfect for my purposes—there are jungles with a maze of trails in them, hills, swamps—"

"But the animal, General Zaroff?"

"Oh," said the general, "it supplies me with the most exciting hunting in the world. No other hunting compares with it for an instant. Every day I hunt, and I never grow bored now, for I have a quarry with which I can match my wits."

Rainsford's bewilderment showed in his face.

370 "I wanted the ideal animal to hunt," explained the general. "So I said: 'What are the attributes of an ideal quarry?' And the answer was, of course: 'It must have courage, cunning, and, above all, it must be able to reason.'"

"But no animal can reason," objected Rainsford.

"My dear fellow," said the general, "there is one that can."

"But you can't mean—" gasped Rainsford.

"And why not?"

"I can't believe you are serious, General Zaroff. This is a grisly joke."

380   "Why should I not be serious? I am speaking of hunting."

"Hunting? Good God, General Zaroff, what you speak of is murder."

The general laughed with entire good nature. He regarded Rainsford quizzically. "I refuse to believe that so modern and civilized a young man as you seem to be harbors romantic ideas about the value of human life. Surely your experiences in the war—"

"Did not make me condone[16] coldblooded murder," finished Rainsford stiffly.

390   Laughter shook the general. "How extraordinarily droll you are!" he said. "One does not expect nowadays to find a young man of the educated class, even in America, with such a naive, and, if I may say so, mid-Victorian point of view. It's like finding a snuffbox in a limousine. Ah, well, doubtless you had Puritan ancestors. So many Americans appear to have had. I'll wager you'll forget your notions when you go hunting with me. You've a genuine new thrill in store for you, Mr. Rainsford."

"Thank you, I'm a hunter, not a murderer."

"Dear me," said the general, quite **unruffled**, "again that 400 unpleasant word. But I think I can show you that your scruples[17] are quite ill-founded."

"Yes?"

"Life is for the strong, to be lived by the strong, and if need be, taken by the strong. The weak of the world were put here to give the strong pleasure. I am strong. Why should I not use my gift? If I wish to hunt, why should I not? I hunt the scum of the earth—sailors from tramp ships—lascars,[18] blacks, Chinese,

---

16. **condone** (kən·dōn′) v.: overlook an offense; excuse.
17. **scruples** (skrōō′pəlz) n.: feelings of doubt or guilt about a suggested action.
18. **lascars** (las′kərz) n.: East Indian sailors employed on European ships.

PREDICT

Pause at line 382, and confirm your prediction. What is the game that Zaroff hunts?

_____

_____

_____

_____

_____

_____

_____

VOCABULARY

unruffled (un·ruf′əld) adj.: calm; not disturbed.

_Un–_ is a prefix meaning "not." What word in line 400 also uses this prefix? Use _un–_ to give these words the opposite meaning: _kind, necessary, able._

_____

_____

_____

_____

_____

_____

_____

_____

_____

_____

_____

_____

_____

_____

_____

_____

_____

_____

_____

_____

_____

_____

_____

_____

whites, mongrels—a thoroughbred horse or hound is worth more than a score of them."

410   "But they are men," said Rainsford hotly.

    "Precisely," said the general. "That is why I use them. It gives me pleasure. They can reason, after a fashion. So they are dangerous."

    "But where do you get them?"

    The general's left eyelid fluttered down in a wink. "This island is called Ship-Trap," he answered. "Sometimes an angry god of the high seas sends them to me. Sometimes, when Providence is not so kind, I help Providence a bit. Come to the window with me."

420   Rainsford went to the window and looked out toward the sea.

    "Watch! Out there!" exclaimed the general, pointing into the night. Rainsford's eyes saw only blackness, and then, as the

general pressed a button, far out to sea Rainsford saw the flash of lights.

The general chuckled. "They indicate a channel," he said, "where there's none; giant rocks with razor edges crouch like a sea monster with wide-open jaws. They can crush a ship as easily as I crush this nut." He dropped a walnut on the hardwood

430 floor and brought his heel grinding down on it. "Oh, yes," he said, casually, as if in answer to a question, "I have electricity. We try to be civilized here."

"Civilized? And you shoot down men?"

A trace of anger was in the general's black eyes, but it was there for but a second, and he said, in his most pleasant manner: "Dear me, what a righteous young man you are! I assure you I do not do the thing you suggest. That would be barbarous. I treat these visitors with every consideration. They get plenty of good food and exercise. They get into splendid physical con-

440 dition. You shall see for yourself tomorrow."

"What do you mean?"

"We'll visit my training school," smiled the general. "It's in the cellar. I have about a dozen pupils down there now. They're from the Spanish bark *San Lucar* that had the bad luck to go on the rocks out there. A very inferior lot, I regret to say. Poor specimens and more accustomed to the deck than to the jungle."

He raised his hand, and Ivan, who served as waiter, brought thick Turkish coffee. Rainsford, with an effort, held his tongue in check.

450 "It's a game, you see," pursued the general blandly. "I suggest to one of them that we go hunting. I give him a supply of food and an excellent hunting knife. I give him three hours' start. I am to follow, armed only with a pistol of the smallest caliber and range. If my quarry eludes me for three whole days, he wins the game. If I find him"—the general smiled—"he loses."

"Suppose he refuses to be hunted?"

"Oh," said the general, "I give him his option, of course. He need not play that game if he doesn't wish to. If he does not

IDENTIFY

How does Zaroff find men to hunt (lines 422–432)?

_____

_____

_____

_____

_____

_____

_____

_____

WORD STUDY

The word *game* in line 450 means "competition for amusement." What associations come to mind when you hear the word *game*? What impression do you form of Zaroff when he uses this word to describe hunting men?

_____

_____

_____

_____

_____

_____

_____

_____

invariably (in·ver'ē·ə·blē)
adv.: always; without
changing.

PREDICT

Re-read lines 482–490. What
do you **predict** Rainsford will
do next?

460 wish to hunt, I turn him over to Ivan. Ivan once had the honor
of serving as official knouter[19] to the Great White Czar, and he
has his own ideas of sport. **Invariably,** Mr. Rainsford, invariably
they choose the hunt."

"And if they win?"

The smile on the general's face widened. "To date I have not
lost," he said.

Then he added, hastily: "I don't wish you to think me a
braggart, Mr. Rainsford. Many of them afford only the most
elementary sort of problem. Occasionally I strike a tartar.[20] One
almost did win. I eventually had to use the dogs."

470 "The dogs?"

"This way, please. I'll show you."

The general steered Rainsford to a window. The lights from
the windows sent a flickering illumination that made grotesque
patterns on the courtyard below, and Rainsford could see moving about there a dozen or so huge black shapes; as they turned
toward him, their eyes glittered greenly.

"A rather good lot, I think," observed the general. "They
are let out at seven every night. If anyone should try to get
into my house—or out of it—something extremely regrettable
480 would occur to him." He hummed a snatch of song from the
Folies-Bergère.[21]

"And now," said the general, "I want to show you my new
collection of heads. Will you come with me to the library?"

"I hope," said Rainsford, "that you will excuse me tonight,
General Zaroff. I'm really not feeling at all well."

"Ah, indeed?" the general inquired solicitously.[22] "Well, I suppose that's only natural, after your long swim. You need a good,
restful night's sleep. Tomorrow you'll feel like a new man, I'll
wager. Then we'll hunt, eh? I've one rather promising prospect—"

---

19. **knouter** (nout'ər) *n.:* person who beats criminals with a knout, a kind
   of leather whip.
20. **strike a tartar:** get more than one bargained for. A tartar is a violent,
   unmanageable person.
21. **Folies-Bergère** (fô'lē ber·zher'): famous nightclub in Paris.
22. **solicitously** (sə·lis'ə·təs·lē) *adv.:* in a concerned manner.

490　　　　Rainsford was hurrying from the room.

　　　　"Sorry you can't go with me tonight," called the general. "I expect rather fair sport—a big, strong black. He looks resourceful— Well, good night, Mr. Rainsford; I hope you have a good night's rest."

　　　　The bed was good and the pajamas of the softest silk, and he was tired in every fiber of his being, but nevertheless Rainsford could not quiet his brain with the opiate[23] of sleep. He lay, eyes wide open. Once he thought he heard stealthy steps in the corridor outside his room. He sought to throw open the

500　　　door; it would not open. He went to the window and looked out. His room was high up in one of the towers. The lights of the château were out now, and it was dark and silent, but there was a fragment of sallow moon, and by its wan light he could see, dimly, the courtyard; there, weaving in and out in the pattern of shadow, were black, noiseless forms; the hounds heard him at the window and looked up, expectantly, with their green eyes. Rainsford went back to the bed and lay down. By many methods he tried to put himself to sleep. He had achieved a doze when, just as morning began to come, he heard, far off in

510　　　the jungle, the faint report of a pistol.

　　　　General Zaroff did not appear until luncheon. He was dressed faultlessly in the tweeds of a country squire. He was solicitous about the state of Rainsford's health.

　　　　"As for me," sighed the general, "I do not feel so well. I am worried, Mr. Rainsford. Last night I detected traces of my old complaint."

　　　　To Rainsford's questioning glance the general said: "Ennui. Boredom."

　　　　Then, taking a second helping of crêpes suzette,[24] the

520　　　general explained: "The hunting was not good last night. The

---

23. **opiate** (ō′pē·it) *n.:* anything that tends to soothe or calm someone. An opiate may also be a medicine containing opium or a related drug used to relieve pain.
24. **crêpes suzette** (krāp sōō·zet′) *n.:* thin pancakes folded in a hot orange-flavored sauce and served in flaming brandy.

SETTING

Describe the **mood** created by this setting (lines 498–510).

_____

_____

_____

_____

_____

_____

_____

_____

_____

_____

_____

_____

_____

_____

_____

_____

_____

WORD STUDY

What context clue tells you the meaning of *ennui* (än′wē′) in line 517? Underline it.

fellow lost his head. He made a straight trail that offered no problems at all. That's the trouble with these sailors; they have dull brains to begin with, and they do not know how to get about in the woods. They do excessively stupid and obvious things. It's most annoying. Will you have another glass of Chablis, Mr. Rainsford?"

"General," said Rainsford firmly, "I wish to leave this island at once."

The general raised his thickets of eyebrows; he seemed
530 hurt. "But, my dear fellow," the general protested, "you've only just come. You've had no hunting—"

"I wish to go today," said Rainsford. He saw the dead black eyes of the general on him, studying him. General Zaroff's face suddenly brightened.

He filled Rainsford's glass with venerable Chablis from a dusty bottle.

"Tonight," said the general, "we will hunt—you and I."

Rainsford shook his head. "No, general," he said. "I will not hunt."
540 The general shrugged his shoulders and delicately ate a hothouse grape. "As you wish, my friend," he said. "The choice rests entirely with you. But may I not venture to suggest that you will find my idea of sport more **diverting** than Ivan's?"

He nodded toward the corner where the giant stood, scowling, his thick arms crossed on his hogshead of chest.

"You don't mean—" cried Rainsford.

"My dear fellow," said the general, "have I not told you I always mean what I say about hunting? This is really an inspiration. I drink to a foeman worthy of my steel—at last."
550 The general raised his glass, but Rainsford sat staring at him.

"You'll find this game worth playing," the general said enthusiastically. "Your brain against mine. Your woodcraft against mine. Your strength and stamina against mine. Outdoor chess! And the stake is not without value, eh?"

"And if I win—" began Rainsford huskily.

"I'll cheerfully acknowledge myself defeated if I do not find you by midnight of the third day," said General Zaroff. "My sloop will place you on the mainland near a town."

560   The general read what Rainsford was thinking.

"Oh, you can trust me," said the Cossack. "I will give you my word as a gentleman and a sportsman. Of course you, in turn, must agree to say nothing of your visit here."

"I'll agree to nothing of the kind," said Rainsford.

"Oh," said the general, "in that case— But why discuss that now? Three days hence we can discuss it over a bottle of Veuve Clicquot,[25] unless—"

The general sipped his wine.

Then a businesslike air animated him. "Ivan," he said to
570   Rainsford, "will supply you with hunting clothes, food, a knife. I suggest you wear moccasins; they leave a poorer trail. I suggest too that you avoid the big swamp in the southeast corner of the island. We call it Death Swamp. There's quicksand there. One foolish fellow tried it. The deplorable[26] part of it was that Lazarus followed him. You can imagine my feelings, Mr. Rainsford. I loved Lazarus; he was the finest hound in my pack. Well, I must beg you to excuse me now. I always take a siesta after lunch. You'll hardly have time for a nap, I fear. You'll want to start, no doubt. I shall not follow till dusk.
580   Hunting at night is so much more exciting than by day, don't you think? Au revoir[27], Mr. Rainsford, au revoir."

General Zaroff, with a deep, courtly bow, strolled from the room.

From another door came Ivan. Under one arm he carried khaki hunting clothes, a haversack of food, a leather sheath containing a long-bladed hunting knife; his right hand rested on a cocked revolver thrust in the crimson sash about his waist. . . .

---

25. **Veuve Clicquot** (vŏv klē·kô′): brand of fine champagne.
26. **deplorable** (dē·plôr′ə·bəl) *adj.*: regrettable; very bad.
27. **au revoir** (ō′rə·vwär′): French for "goodbye."

IDENTIFY

Pause at line 559. What does Rainsford have to do to win the game?

_____

_____

_____

_____

_____

WORD STUDY

A **sloop** (line 559) is a kind of ship. Circle the context clues that help you figure out the word's meaning.

PLOT

Underline the name of the place in line 573 that Zaroff tells Rainsford to avoid. What might the suggestive name of this place **foreshadow**?

_____

_____

_____

_____

WORD STUDY

Au revoir (line 581) is French for "until we meet again." Read on, and underline the context clues that help you figure out the meaning of the phrase.

PLOT

PLOT

At line 588 the plot **flashes forward.** When do the events beginning in line 588 occur?

Rainsford had fought his way through the bush for two hours.
"I must keep my nerve. I must keep my nerve," he said through
590   tight teeth.

He had not been entirely clearheaded when the château
gates snapped shut behind him. His whole idea at first was to
put distance between himself and General Zaroff, and, to this
end, he had plunged along, spurred on by the sharp rowels[28]
of something very like panic. Now he had got a grip on himself,
had stopped, and was taking stock of himself and the situation.

He saw that straight flight was futile; inevitably it would
bring him face to face with the sea. He was in a picture with
a frame of water, and his operations, clearly, must take place
600   within that frame.

---

28. **rowels** (rou′əlz) *n.:* small wheels with spurs that horseback riders wear on their heels.

PLOT

Re-read lines 601–610. How does Rainsford avoid being captured and killed?

"I'll give him a trail to follow," muttered Rainsford, and he struck off from the rude paths he had been following into the trackless wilderness. He executed a series of intricate loops; he doubled on his trail again and again, recalling all the lore of the fox hunt and all the dodges of the fox. Night found him leg-weary, with hands and face lashed by the branches, on a thickly wooded ridge. He knew it would be insane to blunder on through the dark, even if he had the strength. His need for rest was imperative and he thought: "I have played the fox; now
610   I must play the cat of the fable." A big tree with a thick trunk and outspread branches was nearby, and taking care to leave not the slightest mark, he climbed up into the crotch and stretching out on one of the broad limbs, after a fashion, rested. Rest brought him new confidence and almost a feeling of security. Even so zealous a hunter as General Zaroff could not trace him there, he told himself; only the devil himself could follow that

PREDICT

Pause at line 628. Who is coming through the bush?

_____
_____
_____
_____
_____
_____
_____
_____
_____

VOCABULARY

impulse (im′puls′) *n.*: sudden desire to do something.

PLOT

Underline the details in lines 637–647 that add to the **suspense** of the **plot**. Why does Zaroff smile?

_____
_____
_____
_____
_____
_____
_____
_____

complicated trail through the jungle after dark. But, perhaps, the general was a devil—

An apprehensive night crawled slowly by like a wounded snake, and sleep did not visit Rainsford, although the silence of a dead world was on the jungle. Toward morning, when a dingy gray was varnishing the sky, the cry of some startled bird focused Rainsford's attention in that direction. Something was coming through the bush, coming slowly, carefully, coming by the same winding way Rainsford had come. He flattened himself down on the limb, and through a screen of leaves almost as thick as tapestry, he watched. The thing that was approaching was a man.

It was General Zaroff. He made his way along with his eyes fixed in utmost concentration on the ground before him. He paused, almost beneath the tree, dropped to his knees and studied the ground. Rainsford's **impulse** was to hurl himself down like a panther, but he saw the general's right hand held something metallic—a small automatic pistol.

The hunter shook his head several times, as if he were puzzled. Then he straightened up and took from his case one of his black cigarettes; its pungent incenselike smoke floated up to Rainsford's nostrils.

Rainsford held his breath. The general's eyes had left the ground and were traveling inch by inch up the tree. Rainsford froze there, every muscle tensed for a spring. But the sharp eyes of the hunter stopped before they reached the limb where Rainsford lay; a smile spread over his brown face. Very deliberately he blew a smoke ring into the air; then he turned his back on the tree and walked carelessly away, back along the trail he had come. The swish of the underbrush against his hunting boots grew fainter and fainter.

Then pent-up air burst hotly from Rainsford's lungs. His first thought made him feel sick and numb. The general could

650 follow a trail through the woods at night; he could follow an extremely difficult trail; he must have uncanny powers; only by the merest chance had the Cossack failed to see his quarry.

Rainsford's second thought was even more terrible. It sent a shudder of cold horror through his whole being. Why had the general smiled? Why had he turned back?

Rainsford did not want to believe what his reason told him was true, but the truth was as evident as the sun that had by now pushed through the morning mists. The general was playing with him! The general was saving him for another day's 660 sport! The Cossack was the cat; he was the mouse. Then it was that Rainsford knew the full meaning of terror.

"I will not lose my nerve. I will not."

He slid down from the tree and struck off again into the woods. His face was set and he forced the machinery of his mind to function. Three hundred yards from his hiding place he stopped where a huge dead tree leaned precariously[29] on a smaller living one. Throwing off his sack of food, Rainsford took his knife from its sheath and began to work with all his energy.

The job was finished at last, and he threw himself down 670 behind a fallen log a hundred feet away. He did not have to wait long. The cat was coming again to play with the mouse.

Following the trail with the sureness of a bloodhound came General Zaroff. Nothing escaped those searching black eyes, no crushed blade of grass, no bent twig, no mark, no matter how faint, in the moss. So intent was the Cossack on his stalking that he was upon the thing Rainsford had made before he saw it. His foot touched the **protruding** bough that was the trigger. Even as he touched it, the general sensed his danger and leapt back with the agility of an ape. But he was not quite quick 680 enough; the dead tree, delicately adjusted to rest on the cut living one, crashed down and struck the general a glancing blow on the shoulder as it fell; but for his alertness, he must have been smashed beneath it. He staggered, but he did not fall; nor did he

---

29. **precariously** (prē·ker'ē·əs·lē) *adv.:* unsteadily; in an unstable manner.

PLOT

Pause at line 661. The first stage of the hunt is over. Who has won? What does Rainsford now know that he didn't know at the beginning of the story?

VOCABULARY

protruding (prō·trōod'iŋ) *v.* used as *adj.:* sticking out.

PLOT

Pause at line 692. Who wins
the second stage of this
conflict?

_____

_____

_____

_____

_____

_____

_____

_____

_____

_____

_____

PREDICT

Pause at line 707. What do
you **predict** Rainsford's
"idea" will be?

_____

_____

_____

_____

_____

_____

_____

WORD STUDY

The adjective _placid_ (plas'id)
in line 709 means "calm."

drop his revolver. He stood there, rubbing his injured shoulder, and Rainsford, with fear again gripping his heart, heard the general's mocking laugh ring through the jungle.

"Rainsford," called the general, "if you are within the sound of my voice, as I suppose you are, let me congratulate you. Not many men know how to make a Malay man-catcher. Luckily for me, I too have hunted in Malacca.[30] You are proving interesting, Mr. Rainsford. I am going now to have my wound dressed; it's only a slight one. But I shall be back. I shall be back."

When the general, nursing his bruised shoulder, had gone, Rainsford took up his flight again. It was flight now, a desperate, hopeless flight, that carried him on for some hours. Dusk came, then darkness, and still he pressed on. The ground grew softer under his moccasins; the vegetation grew ranker, denser; insects bit him savagely. Then, as he stepped forward, his foot sank into the ooze. He tried to wrench it back, but the muck sucked viciously at his foot as if it were a giant leech. With a violent effort, he tore loose. He knew where he was now. Death Swamp and its quicksand.

His hands were tight closed as if his nerve were something tangible that someone in the darkness was trying to tear from his grip. The softness of the earth had given him an idea. He stepped back from the quicksand a dozen feet or so, and, like some huge prehistoric beaver, he began to dig.

Rainsford had dug himself in in France,[31] when a second's delay meant death. That had been a placid pastime compared to his digging now. The pit grew deeper; when it was above his shoulders, he climbed out and from some hard saplings cut stakes and sharpened them to a fine point. These stakes he planted in the bottom of the pit with the points sticking up. With flying fingers he wove a rough carpet of weeds and branches and with it he covered the mouth of the pit. Then,

---

30. **Malacca** (mə·lak′ə): state in what is now the nation of Malaysia in southeastern Asia.
31. **dug himself in in France:** dug a hole for shelter from gunfire during World War I (1914–1918).

wet with sweat and aching with tiredness, he crouched behind the stump of a lightning-charred tree.

He knew his pursuer was coming; he heard the padding sound of feet on the soft earth, and the night breeze brought

720 him the perfume of the general's cigarette. It seemed to Rainsford that the general was coming with unusual swiftness; he was not feeling his way along, foot by foot. Rainsford, crouching there, could not see the general, nor could he see the pit. He lived a year in a minute. Then he felt an impulse to cry aloud with joy, for he heard the sharp crackle of the breaking branches as the cover of the pit gave way; he heard the sharp scream of pain as the pointed stakes found their mark. He leapt up from his place of concealment. Then he cowered back. Three feet from the pit a man was standing, with an electric torch in

730 his hand.

"You've done well, Rainsford," the voice of the general called. "Your Burmese tiger pit has claimed one of my best dogs. Again you score. I think, Mr. Rainsford, I'll see what you can do against my whole pack. I'm going home for a rest now. Thank you for a most amusing evening."

At daybreak Rainsford, lying near the swamp, was awakened by the sound that made him know that he had new things to learn about fear. It was a distant sound, faint and wavering, but he knew it. It was the baying of a pack of hounds.

740 Rainsford knew he could do one of two things. He could stay where he was and wait. That was suicide. He could flee. That was postponing the inevitable. For a moment he stood there, thinking. An idea that held a wild chance came to him, and, tightening his belt, he headed away from the swamp.

The baying of the hounds drew nearer, then still nearer, nearer, ever nearer. On a ridge Rainsford climbed a tree. Down a watercourse, not a quarter of a mile away, he could see the bush moving. Straining his eyes, he saw the lean figure of General Zaroff; just ahead of him Rainsford made out another

750 figure whose wide shoulders surged through the tall jungle

PREDICT

Pause at line 730. Who is in the trap? Has Rainsford won?

_____

_____

_____

_____

_____

_____

_____

_____

PLOT

Pause at line 735. Who wins the third stage of this **conflict**? According to Zaroff, what will happen the next day?

_____

_____

_____

_____

_____

_____

_____

Pause at line 761, and recall
Rainsford's earlier ideas
about hunting (lines 19–31).
Why is Rainsford's situation
ironic, or surprising?

weeds. It was the giant Ivan, and he seemed pulled forward by
some unseen force. Rainsford knew that Ivan must be holding
the pack in leash.

They would be on him any minute now. His mind worked
frantically. He thought of a native trick he had learned in
Uganda. He slid down the tree. He caught hold of a springy
young sapling and to it he fastened his hunting knife, with the
blade pointing down the trail; with a bit of wild grapevine he
tied back the sapling. Then he ran for his life. The hounds raised
760 their voices as they hit the fresh scent. Rainsford knew now how
an animal at bay feels.

He had to stop to get his breath. The baying of the hounds stopped abruptly, and Rainsford's heart stopped too. They must have reached the knife.

He shinnied excitedly up a tree and looked back. His pursuers had stopped. But the hope that was in Rainsford's brain when he climbed died, for he saw in the shallow valley that General Zaroff was still on his feet. But Ivan was not. The knife, driven by the recoil of the springing tree, had not wholly failed.

770 "Nerve, nerve, nerve!" he panted, as he dashed along. A blue gap showed between the trees dead ahead. Ever nearer drew the hounds. Rainsford forced himself on toward that gap. He reached it. It was the shore of the sea. Across a cove he could see the gloomy gray stone of the château. Twenty feet below him the sea rumbled and hissed. Rainsford hesitated. He heard the hounds. Then he leapt far out into the sea. . . .

When the general and his pack reached the place by the sea, the Cossack stopped. For some minutes he stood regarding the blue-green expanse of water. He shrugged his shoulders. Then
780 he sat down, took a drink of brandy from a silver flask, lit a perfumed cigarette, and hummed a bit from *Madama Butterfly*.[32]

General Zaroff had an exceedingly good dinner in his great paneled dining hall that evening. With it he had a bottle of Pol Roger and half a bottle of Chambertin. Two slight annoyances kept him from perfect enjoyment. One was the thought that it would be difficult to replace Ivan; the other was that his quarry had escaped him; of course the American hadn't played the game—so thought the general as he tasted his after-dinner liqueur. In his library he read, to soothe himself, from the works
790 of Marcus Aurelius.[33] At ten he went up to his bedroom. He was deliciously tired, he said to himself as he locked himself in. There was a little moonlight, so before turning on his light, he went to the window and looked down at the courtyard.

---

32. *Madama Butterfly:* famous Italian opera by Giacomo Puccini (1858–1924).
33. **Marcus Aurelius** (mär′kəs ô·rē′lē·əs): emperor of Rome from A.D. 161 to 180, who wrote about the philosophy of Stoicism, which held that people should make themselves indifferent to both pain and pleasure.

PLOT

Pause at line 769. What does Rainsford hope to see when he climbs up the tree? What does he actually see?

_____

_____

_____

_____

_____

_____

_____

_____

PREDICT

Pause at line 776. Trapped between his deadly pursuer and the sea, Rainsford jumps. Is the game over? What do you predict will happen next?

_____

_____

_____

_____

_____

_____

_____

_____

PLOT

Underline the passage on this page that reveals the **climax** of this conflict.

PLOT

How is the conflict finally **resolved?**

_____

_____

_____

_____

_____

_____

_____

_____

_____

_____

_____

_____

_____

_____

_____

_____

_____

_____

_____

_____

_____

He could see the great hounds, and he called: "Better luck another time," to them. Then he switched on the light.

A man, who had been hiding in the curtains of the bed, was standing there.

"Rainsford!" screamed the general. "How in God's name did you get here?"

800 "Swam," said Rainsford. "I found it quicker than walking through the jungle."

The general sucked in his breath and smiled. "I congratulate you," he said. "You have won the game."

Rainsford did not smile. "I am still a beast at bay," he said, in a low, hoarse voice. "Get ready, General Zaroff."

The general made one of his deepest bows. "I see," he said. "Splendid! One of us is to furnish a repast[34] for the hounds. The other will sleep in this very excellent bed. On guard, Rainsford. . . ."

810 He had never slept in a better bed, Rainsford decided.

34. **repast** (ri·past′) *n*: meal.

The Most Dangerous Game

Plot Diagram   Review the plot structure of "The Most Dangerous Game."
Then, fill in the plot diagram below with key story events.

Climax:

_____

6. _____

_____

5. _____

_____

_____

4. _____

_____

_____

3. _____

_____

_____

_____

2. _____

_____

_____

_____

1. _____

_____

_____

_____

Resolution:

_____

_____

_____

_____

**Main events
(Complications)**

Basic situation: _____

_____

_____

Setting: _____

_____

Standards Review

 **The Most Dangerous Game**

Sharpen your test-taking skills. Complete the sample test item below. Then, check your answer, and read the explanation that appears in the right-hand column.

Sample Test Item	Explanation of the Correct Answer
Which of the following elements of **setting** does Rainsford *not* have to struggle against? **A** The ocean **B** Quicksand **C** Freezing cold **D** The jungle	The correct answer is C. Rainsford struggles against the ocean, encounters quicksand in the Death Swamp, and must fight through the jungle. There is no freezing cold; it is the tropics.

DIRECTIONS: Circle the letter of each correct response.

Reading Standard 3.4 (Grade 8 Review) Analyze the relevance of the setting (e.g., place, time, customs) to the mood, tone, and meaning of the text.

Reading Standard 3.6 Analyze and trace an author's development of time and sequence, including the use of complex literary devices (e.g., foreshadowing, flashbacks).

1. Which of the following passages from the story **foreshadows** danger?

   A "You've good eyes," Whitney said.

   B "It will be light in Rio," promised Whitney.

   C "What island is it?" Rainsford asked.

   D "The old charts call it Ship-Trap Island," Whitney replied.

2. What is the **setting** for most of the action in this story?

   F A yacht

   G A castle

   H A jungle

   J The sea

3. Which of the following events happens first?

   A Rainsford kills Ivan.

   B Rainsford kills one of Zaroff's dogs.

   C Rainsford wounds Zaroff.

   D Rainsford dives into the sea.

4. Which of the following events happens last?

   F Rainsford and Zaroff fight in the bedroom.

   G Rainsford builds a Burmese tiger pit.

   H Rainsford builds a Malay man-catcher.

   J Rainsford falls overboard.

Standards Review

 **The Most Dangerous Game**

Prefixes: Important Beginnings

DIRECTIONS: Match the prefixes with their meanings. Write the letter of the correct meaning on each line.

_____ **1.** *pre–*   **a.** not

_____ **2.** *inter–*   **b.** between

_____ **3.** *un–*   **c.** before

_____ **4.** *re–*   **d.** badly; wrong

_____ **5.** *mis–*   **e.** again

Reading Standard 1.1 Identify and use the literal and figurative meanings of words and understand word derivations.

Vocabulary in Context

DIRECTIONS: Complete the paragraph below by writing a word from the word box in each numbered blank. Not all words from the box will be used.

Word Box

receding

disarming

prolonged

imprudent

surmounted

unruffled

invariably

diverting

impulse

protruding

The rock climber was guided by a sudden desire, an

(1) _____ to climb Forbidden Cliff. Although the rocky path was covered in slippery moss, he remained

(2) _____ and calm. He almost lost his footing, however, when a (3) _____ rock nearly tripped him. Just when he reached the top, a park ranger caught him and scolded him, saying the climb was not only unwise but (4) _____. Not charmed or swayed by the climber's (5) _____ smile, the park ranger gave him a ticket.

Before You Go On . . .

Check your Standards Mastery at the back of this book.

Crime on Mars by Arthur C. Clarke

BEFORE YOU READ

This mystery takes place in outer space. "Crime on Mars" is a science fiction story about a man who would have stolen Mars's greatest treasure—if it hadn't been for one fact he overlooked!

LITERARY FOCUS: PLOT AND FLASHBACK

Plot is the series of related events that make up a story. A **flashback** is a scene or several scenes that break the time order of the plot in order to tell about a past event.

- Much of this story is told in **flashback.** Be on the lookout for the flashback as you read.
- The **setting** of "Crime on Mars" greatly affects the plot and its outcome. Pay attention to story details that describe Meridian City on the planet Mars.

READING SKILLS: MAKING PREDICTIONS

What do you predict the plot of "Crime of Mars" will be about? Make your predictions by creating a "plot impression." Use the following key details from "Crime on Mars" to create a plot for a mystery. Write your ideas in the space below.

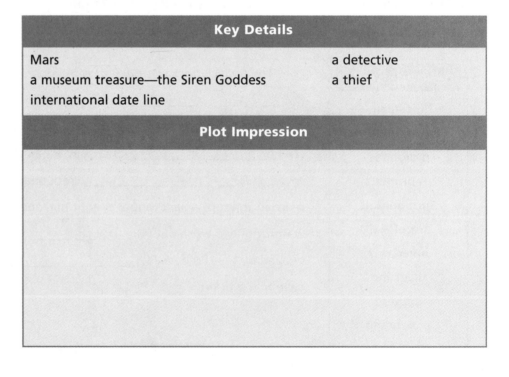

Key Details	
Mars	a detective
a museum treasure—the Siren Goddess	a thief
international date line	
Plot Impression	

Reading Standard 1.3
Identify Greek, Roman, and Norse mythology and use the knowledge to understand the origin and meaning of new words (e.g., the word *narcissistic* drawn from the myth of Narcissus and Echo).

Reading Standard 3.6
Analyze and trace an author's development of time and sequence, including the use of complex literary devices (e.g., foreshadowing, flashbacks).

VOCABULARY DEVELOPMENT

PREVIEW SELECTION VOCABULARY

The following words appear in "Crime on Mars." Become familiar with these words before you read.

replica (rep′li·kə) *n.:* reproduction or copy of a work of art.

*Although he'd never seen the original work of art, like most other departing tourists, he had a **replica** in his baggage.*

enigma (i·nig′mə) *n.:* puzzling matter; mystery.

*The **enigma** was so baffling that it drove a few archaeologists out of their minds.*

aboriginal (ab′ə·rij′ə·nəl) *adj.:* existing from the beginning or from earliest days.

*According to the story the **aboriginal** Martians never achieved space flight, and their civilization died before people existed on Earth.*

WORD ORIGINS

Many words in English have their origins in Greek, Roman, and Norse mythology. For example, in Greek mythology the **sirens** were sea nymphs whose sweet singing lured sailors to turn their ships toward the rocks. How does knowing this fact about mythology give you a clue about the Siren Goddess in "Crime on Mars"? Why would some people call a woman who attracted men a **siren**? What connection do you see to **sirens** at firehouses?

inquisitive (in·kwiz′ə·tiv) *adj.:* inclined to ask many questions or seek information.

*The inspector had to be an **inquisitive** man—it was his profession.*

incredible (in·kred′ə·bəl) *adj.:* seeming too unusual or improbable to be possible.

*The story of the theft was so bizarre it was **incredible.***

Crime on Mars

Arthur C. Clarke

"We don't have much crime on Mars," said Detective-Inspector Rawlings, a little sadly. "In fact, that's the chief reason I'm going back to the Yard.[1] If I stayed here much longer, I'd get completely out of practice."

We were sitting in the main observation lounge of the Phobos Spaceport, looking out across the jagged sun-drenched crags of the tiny moon. The ferry rocket that had brought us up from Mars had left ten minutes ago and was now beginning the long fall back to the ocher-tinted globe hanging there against the stars. In half an hour we would be boarding the liner for Earth—a world on which most of the passengers had never set foot, but which they still called "home."

"At the same time," continued the Inspector, "now and then there's a case that makes life interesting. You're an art dealer, Mr. Maccar; I'm sure you heard about that spot of bother at Meridian City a couple of months ago."

"I don't think so," replied the plump, olive-skinned little man I'd taken for just another returning tourist. Presumably the Inspector had already checked through the passenger list; I wondered how much he knew about me, and tried to reassure myself that my conscience was—well, reasonably clear. After all, everybody took *something* out through Martian Customs—

"It's been rather well hushed up," said the Inspector, "but you can't keep these things quiet for long. Anyway, a jewel thief from Earth tried to steal Meridian Museum's greatest treasure—the Siren Goddess."

---

1. **the Yard:** popular term for "Scotland Yard," headquarters of the London Metropolitan Police.

"But that's absurd!" I objected. "It's priceless, of course—but it's only a lump of sandstone. You couldn't sell it to anyone—you might just as well steal the Mona Lisa."[2]

30 The Inspector grinned, rather mirthlessly. "*That's* happened too," he said. "Maybe the motive was the same. There are collectors who would give a fortune for such an object, even if they could only look at it themselves. Don't you agree, Mr. Maccar?"

"That's perfectly true," said the art dealer. "In my business you meet all sorts of crazy people."

"Well, this chappie—name's Danny Weaver—had been well paid by one of them. And if it hadn't been for a piece of fantastically bad luck, he might have brought it off."

The Spaceport P.A. system apologized for a further slight
40 delay owing to final fuel checks, and asked a number of passengers to report to Information. While we were waiting for the announcement to finish, I recalled what little I knew about the Siren Goddess. Although I'd never seen the original, like most other departing tourists I had a **replica** in my baggage. It bore the certificate of the Mars Bureau of Antiquities, guaranteeing that "this full-scale reproduction is an exact copy of the so-called Siren Goddess, discovered in the Mare Sirenium by the Third Expedition, A.D. 2012 (A.M. 23)."

It's quite a tiny thing to have caused so much controversy.
50 Only eight or nine inches high—you wouldn't look at it twice if you saw it in a museum on Earth. The head of a young woman, with slightly oriental features, elongated earlobes, hair curled in tight ringlets close to the scalp, lips half parted in an expression of pleasure or surprise—that's all.

But it's an **enigma** so baffling that it has inspired a hundred religious sects, and driven quite a few archeologists round the bend. For a perfectly human head has no right whatsoever to be found on Mars, whose only intelligent inhabitants were crustaceans[3]—"educated lobsters," as the newspapers are fond

---

2. **Mona Lisa:** portrait by Leonardo da Vinci, painted from 1503 to 1506.
3. **crustaceans** (krus·tā′shənz) *n.:* arthropods, including shrimps, crabs, and lobsters, that usually live in the water and breathe through gills.

PLOT

Re-read lines 23–29. What two past events does the inspector mention?

_____

_____

_____

_____

_____

_____

_____

WORD STUDY

Mirth comes from Old English and means "merriment; joyfulness." What does *mirthlessly* (line 30) mean?

_____

_____

_____

VOCABULARY

replica (rep′li·kə) *n.:* reproduction or copy of a work of art.

enigma (i·nig′mə) *n.:* puzzling matter; mystery.

Notes

_____

_____

_____

_____

_____

_____

_____

_____

VOCABULARY

aboriginal (ab'ə·rij'ə·nəl) *adj.:*
existing from the beginning
or from earliest days.

PLOT

A **flashback** interrupts a narrative to tell of events that
took place at an earlier time.
Where does this switch in
time occur on this page?
How do you know?

_____

_____

_____

_____

_____

PLOT

Underline the words in lines
69–73 that clarify the time
order of these past events.

The planet Mars.

60   of calling them. The **aboriginal** Martians never came near to
achieving space flight, and in any event, their civilization died
before men existed on Earth.

No wonder the Goddess is the solar system's number-one
mystery. I don't suppose we'll find the answer in my lifetime—
if we ever do.

"Danny's plan was beautifully simple," continued the
Inspector. "You know how absolutely dead a Martian city gets
on Sunday, when everything closes down and the colonists stay
home to watch the TV from Earth. Danny was counting on this
70   when he checked into the hotel in Meridian West, late Friday
afternoon. He'd have Saturday for reconnoitering the museum,
an undisturbed Sunday for the job itself, and on Monday morning he'd be just another tourist leaving town. . . .

"Early Saturday he strolled through the little park and
crossed over into Meridian East, where the museum stands.

In case you don't know, the city gets its name because it's exactly on longitude one hundred and eighty degrees; there's a big stone slab in the park with the Prime Meridian engraved on it, so that visitors can get themselves photographed standing in two hemispheres[4] at once. Amazing what simple things amuse some people.

"Danny spent the day going over the museum, exactly like any other tourist determined to get his money's worth. But at closing time he didn't leave; he'd holed up in one of the galleries not open to the public, where the museum had been arranging a Late Canal Period reconstruction but had run out of money before the job could be finished. He stayed there until about midnight, just in case there were any enthusiastic researchers still in the building. Then he emerged and got to work."

"Just a moment," I interrupted. "What about the night watchman?"

The Inspector laughed.

"My dear chap! They don't have such luxuries on Mars. There weren't even any alarms, for who would bother to steal lumps of stone? True, the Goddess was sealed up neatly in a strong glass-and-metal cabinet, just in case some souvenir hunter took a fancy to her. But even if she were stolen there was nowhere the thief could hide, and of course all outgoing traffic would be searched as soon as the statue was missed."

That was true enough. I'd been thinking in terms of Earth, forgetting that every city on Mars is a closed little world of its own beneath the force-field that protects it from the freezing near-vacuum. Beyond those electronic shields is the utterly hostile emptiness of the Martian Outback, where a man will die in seconds without protection. That makes law enforcement very easy; no wonder there's so little crime on Mars. . . .

"Danny had a beautiful set of tools, as specialized as a watchmaker's. The main item was a microsaw no bigger than a soldering iron; it had a wafer-thin blade, driven at a million cycles a second by an ultrasonic power-pack. It would go

---

4. **hemispheres** (hem′i·sfirz) *n.:* halves of spheres, globes, or celestial bodies.

Pause at line 80. Underline the sentence that tells how the city got its name. On which side of the prime meridian is Danny's hotel? On which side of the prime meridian is the museum? What **prediction** can you make, based on these details?

SETTING

Why does the story's **setting** pose a problem for would-be burglars (lines 99–105)?

Crime on Mars   **43**

VOCABULARY

inquisitive (in·kwiz'ə·tiv) *adj.:*
inclined to ask many ques-
tions or seek information.

WORD STUDY

Circle the two smaller words
you see in *artifacts* in line
122. Artifacts are objects, or
art, crafted by humans. They
help us learn about how
people lived in the past.

VOCABULARY

incredible (in·kred'ə·bəl) *adj.:*
seeming too unusual or
improbable to be possible.

_____

_____

_____

_____

_____

_____

_____

_____

_____

_____

_____

WORD STUDY

Inconspicuous
(in'kən·spik'yōo·əs) in line
142 means "unnoticeable;
not attracting attention."
Circle nearby **context clues**
that help define the word.

110 through glass or metal like butter—and leave a cut only about
as thick as a hair. Which was very important for Danny, since he
had to leave no traces of his handiwork.

"I suppose you've guessed how he intended to operate. He
was going to cut through the base of the cabinet and substitute
one of those souvenir replicas for the genuine Goddess. It might
be a couple of years before some **inquisitive** expert discovered
the awful truth, and long before then the original would have
traveled back to Earth, perfectly disguised as a copy of itself,
with a genuine certificate of authenticity. Pretty neat, eh?

120 "It must have been a weird business, working in that darkened gallery with all those million-year-old carvings and unexplainable artifacts around him. A museum on Earth is bad
enough at night, but at least it's—well, *human.* And Gallery
Three, which houses the Goddess, is particularly unsettling.
It's full of bas-reliefs[5] showing quite **incredible** animals fighting
each other; they look rather like giant beetles, and most
paleontologists[6] flatly deny that they could ever have existed.
But imaginary or not, they belonged to this world, and they
didn't disturb Danny as much as the Goddess, staring at him

130 across the ages and defying him to explain her presence here.
She gave him the creeps. How do I know? He told me.

"Danny set to work on that cabinet as carefully as any
diamond cutter preparing to cleave a gem. It took most of the
night to slice out the trapdoor, and it was nearly dawn when he
relaxed and put down the saw. There was still a lot of work to
do, but the hardest part was over. Putting the replica into the
case, checking its appearance against the photos he'd thought-
fully brought with him, and covering up his traces might take
most of Sunday, but that didn't worry him in the least. He had

140 another twenty-four hours, and would positively welcome
Monday's first visitors so that he could mingle with them and
make his inconspicuous exit.

---

5. **bas-reliefs** (bä'ri·lēfs') *n.:* sculptures in which figures are carved on a
   flat surface so that they project only a little from the background.
6. **paleontologists** (pā'lē·ən·täl'ə·jists) *n.:* scientists who study fossils and
   ancient life forms.

"It was a perfectly horrible shock to his nervous system, therefore, when the main doors were noisily unbarred at eight thirty and the museum staff—all six of them—started to open up for the day. Danny bolted for the emergency exit, leaving everything behind—tools, Goddesses, the lot.

"He had another big surprise when he found himself in the street: it should have been completely deserted at this time of day, with everyone at home reading the Sunday papers. But here were the citizens of Meridian East, as large as life, heading for plant or office on what was obviously a normal working day.

"By the time poor Danny got back to his hotel we were waiting for him. We couldn't claim much credit for deducing that only a visitor from Earth—and a very recent one at that—could have overlooked Meridian City's chief claim to fame. And I presume you know what *that* is."

"Frankly, I don't," I answered. "You can't see much of Mars in six weeks, and I never went east of the Syrtis Major."

"Well, it's absurdly simple, but we shouldn't be too hard on Danny—even the locals occasionally fall into the same trap. It's something that doesn't bother us on Earth, where we've been able to dump the problem in the Pacific Ocean. But Mars, of course, is all dry land; and that means that *somebody* is forced to live with the International Date Line. . . .

IDENTIFY

Pause at line 147. Danny thought it was Sunday and the museum was closed. Why is the museum open?

The word *surveillance*
(sər·vā′lens) in line 179 means
"close watch kept over a
person or place." The word
is formed from *sur–,* meaning
"over," and a Latin form of
vigilare, meaning "to watch."

PLOT

Pause at line 181. Who
becomes the museum guard?
Why is this an unusual
development?

_____

_____

_____

_____

_____

_____

_____

PREDICT

This story's **resolution** leaves
one important question
unanswered: What do you
think will happen next?

_____

_____

_____

_____

_____

_____

_____

"Danny, you see, had worked from Meridian West. It was
Sunday over there all right—and it was still Sunday when we
picked him up back at the hotel. But over in Meridian East, half
a mile away, it was only Saturday. That little trip across the park
170   had made all the difference! I told you it was rotten luck."

There was a long moment of silent sympathy, then I asked,
"What did he get?"

"Three years," said Inspector Rawlings.

"That doesn't seem very much."

"Mars years; that makes it almost six of ours. And a whopping fine which, by an odd coincidence, came to exactly the
refund value of his return ticket to Earth. He isn't in jail, of
course; Mars can't afford that kind of nonproductive luxury.
Danny has to work for a living, under discreet surveillance. I
180   told you that the Meridian Museum couldn't afford a night
watchman. Well, it has one now. Guess who."

"All passengers prepare to board in ten minutes! Please
collect your hand baggage!" ordered the loudspeakers.

As we started to move toward the airlock, I couldn't help
asking one more question.

"What about the people who put Danny up to it? There
must have been a lot of money behind him. Did you get them?"

"Not yet; they'd covered their tracks pretty thoroughly, and
I believe Danny was telling the truth when he said he couldn't
190   give us a lead. Still, it's not my case. As I told you, I'm going back
to my old job at the Yard. But a policeman always keeps his eyes
open—like an art dealer, eh, Mr. Maccar? Why, you look a bit
green about the gills. Have one of my space-sickness tablets."

"No, thank you," answered Mr. Maccar, "I'm quite all right."

His tone was distinctly unfriendly; the social temperature
seemed to have dropped below zero in the last few minutes.
I looked at Mr. Maccar, and I looked at the Inspector. And suddenly I realized that we were going to have a very interesting trip.

Standards Review

 **Crime on Mars**

Word Origins

DIRECTIONS: Greek and Roman names for the gods and other mythological figures have become the names of many things in modern life. Match the origin of the numbered words with gods from mythology. Show how these words and gods match up by writing the correct letter on each numbered line.

_____ **1.** titanic

_____ **2.** panic

_____ **3.** volcano

_____ **4.** phobia

_____ **5.** martial

a. Mars, god of war

b. Phobos, son of Mars; the name means "fear"

c. Pan, god of the woods, a mischief-maker

d. Vulcan, god of fire

e. Titans, powerful gods who ruled before the Olympian gods

Reading Standard 1.3 Identify Greek, Roman, and Norse mythology and use the knowledge to understand the origin and meaning of new words (e.g., the word *narcissistic* drawn from the myth of Narcissus and Echo).

Vocabulary in Context

DIRECTIONS: Complete the paragraph below by writing a word from the word box in each numbered blank.

Word Box

aboriginal

enigma

incredible

replica

inquisitive

"What an (1) _____ find," cried one of the paleontologists who was studying ancient life on the planet. "This is no copy or (2) _____; this is an original piece of art!" "Who made it, when was it made, and how was it made?" questioned the (3) _____ scientist. "If the (4) _____ creatures who lived here from the beginning didn't create it, then who did?" Faced with this (5) _____, the scientists grew silent and thought deeply.

Before You Go On ...

Check your Standards Mastery at the back of this book.

Character

Academic Vocabulary for Chapter 2

These are the terms you should know as you read and analyze the stories in this chapter.

Characterization The way writers create characters in a story. In **direct characterization,** writers tell us directly what a character is like ("good" or "evil" or "lazy"). In **indirect characterization** you use clues in the story to decide what kind of person a character is. Clues may be descriptions of how the character acts, speaks, and thinks and how other people respond to the character.

● ● ●

Protagonist The main character in a story.

Antagonist The character that the main character (protagonist) struggles against.

Subordinate characters Minor characters in the story.

Motivations The reasons behind a character's actions and feelings.

Flat character A character who is not fully developed in the story. A flat character is almost never the main character.

Round character A character who is fully developed, just as a person in actual life is.

Dynamic character A character who changes during the story. The change might involve recognition of some truth about life.

Static character A character who does not change during the story.

● ● ●

Dialogue The conversations characters have with other characters.

First-person narration A story told by an "I" narrator. An "I" narrator is a character in the story.

> **For Further Information ...**
>
> ● Be sure to read the essay on **character** in *Holt Literature and Language Arts,* pages 84–85.
> ● Be sure to read the essay on **character interactions** in *Holt Literature and Language Arts,* pages 116–117.

Reading Standard 1.1 Identify and use the literal and figurative meanings of words and understand word derivations.

Reading Standard 1.3 Identify Greek, Roman, and Norse mythology and use the knowledge to understand the origin and meaning of new words (e.g., the word *narcissistic* drawn from the myth of Narcissus and Echo).

Reading Standard 3.3 Analyze interactions between main and subordinate characters in a literary text (e.g., internal and external conflicts, motivations, relationships, influences) and explain the way those interactions affect the plot.

Reading Standard 3.4 Determine characters' traits by what the characters say about themselves in narration, dialogue, dramatic monologue, and soliloquy.

Thank You, M'am by Langston Hughes

Do you know someone "larger than life"? In "Thank You, M'am," a young boy meets a person who fits that description. Read the story to learn how the boy's outlook on life changes after spending just a few hours in the company of Mrs. Jones.

LITERARY FOCUS: DIALOGUE

- In "Thank You, M'am," two characters, an older woman and a boy, meet in an unusual way. The characters reveal themselves to each other and to the reader through **dialogue,** or conversation. As you read, notice what these characters say to each other—and what they don't say.
- As you read, look for other details that bring the characters to life. For example, what do the characters' actions and appearances tell you about them? What does the setting tell you about one of the characters?

READING SKILLS: MAKING INFERENCES

An **inference** is an educated guess—a guess based on good evidence. When you make an inference, you use details in the text and your own experience to guess about something you don't know for sure.

For example, the writer may say, "When the teacher, Mr. Green, called on the new girl, she smiled." The writer doesn't tell you directly that the new girl is pleased. Based on your own experience, however, you can *infer* that she is pleased to be called on.

To make an inference:
- Look for details in the text.
- Relate the details to what you know about life.
- Make a careful guess.

Make inferences as you read "Thank You, M'am." Look for clues that reveal important information about the characters. Then, read on to see how the characters develop. You might use a chart like this to record your inferences.

Details from Story	My Inferences About Characters

Reading Standard 1.1 Identify and use the literal and figurative meanings of words and understand word derivations.

Reading Standard 3.4 Determine characters' traits by what the characters say about themselves in narration, dialogue, dramatic monologue, and soliloquy.

SHORT STORY

VOCABULARY DEVELOPMENT

PREVIEW SELECTION VOCABULARY

You may be unfamiliar with the following words from "Thank You, M'am." Preview these words before you begin reading.

release (ri·lēs′) *v.:* set free; let go.

*The woman held him and would not **release** him until he promised not to run away.*

frail (frāl) *adj.:* weak; easily broken.

*Although the old woman appeared **frail**, she was actually very strong.*

presentable (prē·zent′ə·bəl) *adj.:* acceptable; suitable.

*Combing his hair would make the boy look **presentable**.*

barren (bar′ən) *adj.:* bare; empty.

*Because no children were playing on it, the stoop looked **barren**.*

SYNONYMS

A **synonym** is a word that has the same or almost the same meaning as another word. Although synonyms sometimes share an exact meaning, often they have different shades of meaning. When writers are dissatisfied with a word, they may replace it with a synonym that expresses the meaning more exactly. When writers feel they have repeated a word too often, they may replace one of its uses with a synonym.

Synonyms/Shades of Meaning	
Original sentence	Synonyms for *surprised*
The boy was **surprised** by the attention.	**shocked,** "extremely surprised" **amazed,** "filled with wonder" **astounded,** "bewildered with sudden surprise" **dumbfounded,** "speechless with amazement" **overwhelmed,** "overcome with emotion"

Replace *surprised* with each of the synonyms to see how the meaning and impact of the original sentence change.

The boy was _____ by the attention.

Thank You, M'am

Langston Hughes

CHARACTER

What does the boy do in lines 1–12? Underline the details that tell you. Then, circle the sentences that tell you how the woman reacts.

_____

_____

_____

_____

_____

_____

She was a large woman with a large purse that had everything in it but a hammer and nails. It had a long strap, and she carried it slung across her shoulder. It was about eleven o'clock at night, dark, and she was walking alone, when a boy ran up behind her and tried to snatch her purse. The strap broke with the sudden single tug the boy gave it from behind. But the boy's weight and the weight of the purse combined caused him to lose his balance. Instead of taking off full blast as he had hoped, the boy fell on his back on the sidewalk and his legs flew up. The large

10 woman simply turned around and kicked him right square in his blue-jeaned sitter. Then she reached down, picked the boy up by his shirt front, and shook him until his teeth rattled.

"Thank You, M'am" from *Short Stories* by Langston Hughes. Copyright © 1996 by Ramona Bass and Arnold Rampersad. Reprinted by permission of **Hill and Wang, a division of Farrar, Straus and Giroux, LLC.**

After that the woman said, "Pick up my pocketbook, boy, and give it here."

She still held him tightly. But she bent down enough to permit him to stoop and pick up her purse. Then she said, "Now ain't you ashamed of yourself?"

Firmly gripped by his shirt front, the boy said, "Yes'm."

The woman said, "What did you want to do it for?"

20 The boy said, "I didn't aim to."

She said, "You a lie!"

By that time two or three people passed, stopped, turned to look, and some stood watching.

"If I turn you loose, will you run?" asked the woman.

"Yes'm," said the boy.

"Then I won't turn you loose," said the woman. She did not release him.

"Lady, I'm sorry," whispered the boy.

"Um-hum! Your face is dirty. I got a great mind to wash

30 your face for you. Ain't you got nobody home to tell you to wash your face?"

"No'm," said the boy.

"Then it will get washed this evening," said the large woman starting up the street, dragging the frightened boy behind her.

He looked as if he were fourteen or fifteen, frail and willow-wild, in tennis shoes and blue jeans.

The woman said, "You ought to be my son. I would teach you right from wrong. Least I can do right now is to wash your

40 face. Are you hungry?"

"No'm," said the being-dragged boy. "I just want you to turn me loose."

"Was I bothering *you* when I turned that corner?" asked the woman.

"No'm."

"But you put yourself in contact with *me*," said the woman. "If you think that that contact is not going to last awhile, you

WORD STUDY

In lines 18–32, the boy answers the woman's questions with "Yes'm" and "No'm." The term *m'am* is a contraction for "madam," a polite way of addressing a woman.

CHARACTER

In lines 18–32, the woman speaks roughly to the boy. Circle what the boy says in response. What do these lines of **dialogue**, or conversation, suggest about the boy's feelings?

_____

_____

_____

_____

_____

_____

_____

CHARACTER

Underline the words in lines 38–40 that tell you what the woman plans to do. What do these words reveal, or show, about her?

_____

_____

_____

_____

_____

_____

_____

In lines 62–65, Roger faces an **internal conflict**—he must make a difficult decision. Underline the words that show his two choices. What is his final decision?

_____

_____

What can you **infer**, or guess, about Roger from what he says about himself in line 74?

_____

_____

_____

Circle the words in line 77 that show the boy's **motivation,** or reason, for trying to steal the pocketbook. Underline Mrs. Jones's response to his reason.

got another thought coming. When I get through with you, sir, you are going to remember Mrs. Luella Bates Washington Jones."

Sweat popped out on the boy's face and he began to struggle. Mrs. Jones stopped, jerked him around in front of her, put a half nelson about his neck, and continued to drag him up the street. When she got to her door, she dragged the boy inside, down a hall, and into a large kitchenette-furnished room at the rear of the house. She switched on the light and left the door open. The boy could hear other roomers laughing and talking in the large house. Some of their doors were open, too, so he knew he and the woman were not alone. The woman still had him by the neck in the middle of her room.

She said, "What is your name?"

"Roger," answered the boy.

"Then, Roger, you go to that sink and wash your face," said the woman, whereupon she turned him loose—at last. Roger looked at the door—looked at the woman—looked at the door—*and went to the sink.*

"Let the water run until it gets warm," she said. "Here's a clean towel."

"You gonna take me to jail?" asked the boy, bending over the sink.

"Not with that face, I would not take you nowhere," said the woman. "Here I am trying to get home to cook me a bite to eat, and you snatch my pocketbook! Maybe you ain't been to your supper either, late as it be. Have you?"

"There's nobody home at my house," said the boy.

"Then we'll eat," said the woman. "I believe you're hungry—or been hungry—to try to snatch my pocketbook."

"I want a pair of blue suede shoes," said the boy.

"Well, you didn't have to snatch *my* pocketbook to get some suede shoes," said Mrs. Luella Bates Washington Jones. "You could've asked me."

INFER

In line 81 Roger says "M'am?" because he is surprised at Mrs. Jones's response. What might he have expected her to say?

_____

_____

_____

_____

_____

CHARACTER

Re-read the sentence in lines 88–89. What does it tell you about Mrs. Jones?

_____

_____

_____

CHARACTER

Pause at line 99. Mrs. Jones avoids saying, "but I didn't snatch people's pocketbooks." Why doesn't she say this?

_____

_____

_____

_____

_____

_____

_____

_____

"M'am?"

The water dripping from his face, the boy looked at her. There was a long pause. A very long pause. After he had dried his face and not knowing what else to do, dried it again, the boy turned around, wondering what next. The door was open. He could make a dash for it down the hall. He could run, run, run, *run!*

The woman was sitting on the daybed. After a while she said, "I were young once and I wanted things I could not get."

90

There was another long pause. The boy's mouth opened. Then he frowned, not knowing he frowned.

The woman said, "Um-hum! You thought I was going to say *but,* didn't you? You thought I was going to say, *but I didn't snatch people's pocketbooks.* Well, I wasn't going to say that." Pause. Silence. "I have done things, too, which I would not tell you, son—neither tell God, if He didn't already know. Everybody's got something in common. So you set down while I fix us something to eat. You might run that comb through your hair so you will look presentable."

CHARACTER

Read the description of Mrs. Jones's home (lines 100–108). What do you learn about her from where she lives?

_____

_____

_____

_____

_____

_____

_____

CHARACTER

Through her **actions** in lines 100–108, Mrs. Jones shows Roger (and the reader) that she trusts him. Underline the details that tell what she does.

FLUENCY

You can learn a lot about the characters' **motivations** from their actions. Read aloud the boxed passage to make each character's motives clear.

_____

_____

_____

_____

_____

_____

_____

100   In another corner of the room behind a screen was a gas plate and an icebox. Mrs. Jones got up and went behind the screen. The woman did not watch the boy to see if he was going to run now, nor did she watch her purse, which she left behind her on the daybed. But the boy took care to sit on the far side of the room, away from the purse, where he thought she could easily see him out of the corner of her eye if she wanted to. He did not trust the woman *not* to trust him. And he did not want to be mistrusted now.

    "Do you need somebody to go the store," asked the boy,
110 "maybe to get some milk or something?"

    "Don't believe I do," said the woman, "unless you just want sweet milk yourself. I was going to make cocoa out of this canned milk I got here."

    "That will be fine," said the boy.

    She heated some lima beans and ham she had in the icebox, made the cocoa, and set the table. The woman did not ask the boy anything about where he lived, or his folks, or anything else that

would embarrass him. Instead, as they ate, she told him about her job in a hotel beauty shop that stayed open late, what the work was like, and how all kinds of women came in and out, blondes, red-heads, and Spanish. Then she cut him a half of her ten-cent cake.

"Eat some more, son," she said.

When they were finished eating, she got up and said, "Now here, take this ten dollars and buy yourself some blue suede shoes. And next time, do not make the mistake of latching onto *my* pocketbook *nor nobody else's*—because shoes got by devilish ways will burn your feet. I got to get my rest now. But from here on in, son, I hope you will behave yourself."

She led him down the hall to the front door and opened it. "Good night! Behave yourself, boy!" she said, looking out into the street as he went down the steps.

The boy wanted to say something other than "Thank you, m'am" to Mrs. Luella Bates Washington Jones, but although his lips moved, he couldn't even say that as he turned at the foot of the barren stoop and looked up at the large woman in the door. Then she shut the door.

120

130

Thank You, M'am

Character Traits Chart In this story much of what you learn about the characters is revealed through their actions and their words. Read the box of character traits below. Which traits apply to Mrs. Jones? Which apply to Roger? List the traits in the correct columns in the chart below, and find details in the story to support your answers.

Character Traits				
self-assured	tough	lonely	generous	young
kindhearted	troubled	timid	strong	scared

Mrs. Jones	Roger
Story Details	**Story Details**

TestPractice ## Thank You, M'am

Complete the sample test item below. Then, read the explanation at the right to understand more about test-taking.

Sample Test Item	Explanation of the Correct Answer
"She was a large woman with a large purse that had everything in it but a hammer and nails." The sentence from the story describes— **A** a character's actions **B** a character's appearance **C** a character's private thoughts **D** a character's motivations	Because the sentence tells you what the character looks like, the correct answer is *B*. The sentence does not describe the character's actions, private thoughts, or motivations (reasons for taking an action); therefore *A*, *C*, and *D* are incorrect.

DIRECTIONS: Circle the letter of the correct response.

1. When Mrs. Jones goes behind the screen, she doesn't keep an eye on the boy. What is her **motivation** for not watching him?

   A She wants him to take her money.

   B She wants to show that she trusts him.

   C She has left her purse in the other room.

   D She has locked the door.

2. The **dialogue** reveals that the relationship between Mrs. Jones and Roger is like the relationship between —

   F a teacher and a student

   G best friends

   H old friends

   J two strangers

3. "He could make a dash for it down the hall. He could run, run, run, *run!*" This sentence from the story is an example of —

   A dialogue

   B a character's speech

   C a character's private thoughts

   D a character's actions

4. When Roger says, "There's nobody home at my house," you can infer that he —

   F has stolen money in the past

   G is confused about whether to go or stay

   H comes from a big family

   J doesn't get much attention

Reading Standard 3.4
Determine characters' traits by what the characters say about themselves in narration, dialogue, dramatic monologue, and soliloquy.

Standards Review

 **Thank You, M'am**

Synonyms

Reading Standard 1.1
Identify and use the literal and figurative meanings of words and understand word derivations.

DIRECTIONS: Match the following words from the story with their synonyms—words that have the same or almost the same meaning.

1. _____ *rattled*   **a.** purse

2. _____ *permit*   **b.** humiliate

3. _____ *sweat*   **c.** allow

4. _____ *pocketbook*   **d.** shook

5. _____ *embarrass*   **e.** perspiration

Vocabulary in Context

DIRECTIONS: Write the word from the box that best completes each sentence.

Word Box

presentable

barren

release

frail

1. We have been caring for an injured bird, and soon we will

_____ it into the forest.

2. The woods are less _____ than in the winter, because during spring many plants grow.

3. The bird is still _____, but with a little more care it will become stronger.

4. In fact, after our good care, the bird should look quite

_____.

 Before You Go On . . .

Check your Standards Mastery at the back of this book.

The White Umbrella by Gish Jen

Many stories (and movies and TV sitcoms) are about families. In "The White Umbrella," a young Asian American girl faces a conflict of divided family loyalties. She tells lies about her family. She is ashamed that her mother has to work. She betrays her mother to get a beautiful white umbrella. What happens to force this girl to recognize her mistakes?

LITERARY FOCUS: CHARACTER

- "The White Umbrella" has a **first-person narrator,** who refers to herself as "I" or "me." This narrator is also the story's **main character** (or **protagonist**). The protagonist is the character in the story whose actions set the plot in motion. The protagonist is the "main actor" in the story.
- In the course of this story, the main character says and does some curious things. Look for clues that help you understand her **motivations**—the reasons for her lies and her actions.

READING SKILLS: MAKING INFERENCES

When you make an **inference** about a character, you use (1) clues from the text and (2) your own experiences. Then you make a good guess about why the character says certain things or acts in a certain way.

Make inferences as you read "The White Umbrella." What **motivates** this girl to do the things she does? You may want to list your inferences in a chart like this one. The first row has been filled in as an example.

Detail from Story	Inference
The parents talk in whispers.	They don't want their daughters to hear.

Reading Standard 1.1 Identify and use the literal and figurative meanings of words and understand word derivations.

Reading Standard 3.3 Analyze interactions between main and subordinate characters in a literary text (e.g., internal and external conflicts, motivations, relationships, influences) and explain the way those interactions affect the plot.

VOCABULARY DEVELOPMENT

PREVIEW SELECTION VOCABULARY

Preview the following words from the story before you begin reading.

lilt (lilt) *n.:* musical quality.

> *My mother's voice had a **lilt,** and her words sounded like notes in a song.*

audible (ô′də·bəl) *adj.:* loud enough to be heard.

> *To keep a secret from us, my parents spoke in barely **audible** voices.*

discreet (di·skrēt′) *adj.:* careful about what one says or does.

> *Please be **discreet** when I give you this information—don't gossip about it.*

credibility (kred′ə·bil′ə·tē) *n.:* believability; trustworthiness.

> *If you aren't always truthful, you may lose **credibility.***

illuminate (i·lōō′mə·nāt′) *v.:* light up.

> *Like a thousand brightly lit candles, the umbrella seemed to **illuminate** the room.*

revelation (rev′ə·lā′shən) *n.:* discovery; surprising news.

> *After the **revelation** about how hard my mother worked, I understood her better.*

maneuver (mə·nōō′vər) *v.:* move (an object) skillfully.

> *Just before the accident, he tried to **maneuver** the car off the road.*

WORD DERIVATIONS

The history, or origin, of a word—where it comes from—is called its **derivation.** Some words come from Old or Middle English; other words may be from Latin, Spanish, or another language. *Audible,* for example, comes from the Latin *audire,* "to hear."

You may want to keep a Word Derivation chart, like the one shown here, to list the word origins you have learned. An example has been provided.

Word	Prefix and Word Root	Meaning of Prefix and Word Root	Definition of Word
constellation	Latin *com–* Latin *stella*	"with; together" "star"	"group of stars"

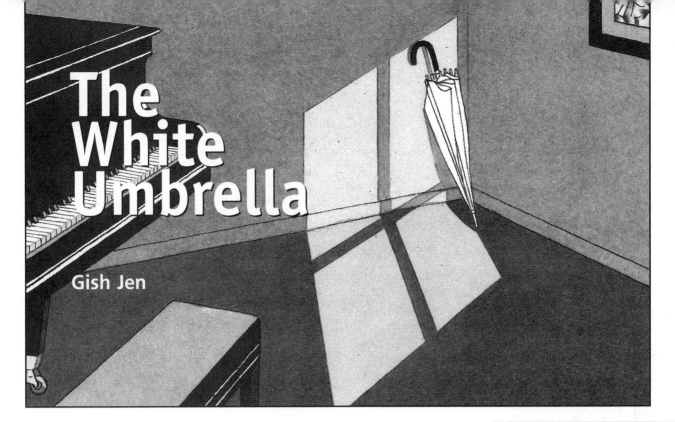

The White Umbrella

Gish Jen

When I was twelve, my mother went to work without telling me or my little sister.

"Not that we need the second income." The **lilt** of her accent drifted from the kitchen up to the top of the stairs, where Mona and I were listening.

"No," said my father, in a barely **audible** voice. "Not like the Lee family."

The Lees were the only other Chinese family in town. I remembered how sorry my parents had felt for Mrs. Lee when she started waitressing downtown the year before; and so when my mother began coming home late, I didn't say anything, and tried to keep Mona from saying anything either.

"But why shouldn't I?" she argued. "Lots of people's mothers work."

"Those are American people," I said.

"So what do you think we are? I can do the pledge of allegiance with my eyes closed."

Nevertheless, she tried to be **discreet**; and if my mother wasn't home by 5:30, we would start cooking by ourselves, to make sure dinner would be on time. Mona would wash the vegetables and put on the rice; I would chop.

"The White Umbrella" by Gish Jen from *The Yale Review,* 1984. Copyright © 1984 by Gish Jen. Reprinted by permission of **Gish Jen c/o Maxine Groffsky Literary Agency.** All rights reserved.

How would you describe a
"cumulus cloud" (lines
32–35)? Circle the **context
clues**.

_____

_____

_____

VOCABULARY

credibility (kred′ə·bil′ə·tē) *n.:*
believability; trustworthiness.

Credibility is from the Latin
word *credere,* meaning "to
believe; to trust." The English
word *incredible* is from the
same Latin word; the **prefix**
(beginning word part) *in–,*
meaning "not," has been
added. What does *incredible*
mean?

_____

INFER

Re-read lines 40–45. Why has
the narrator lied to Miss
Crosman?

_____

_____

_____

_____

_____

_____

_____

_____

For weeks we wondered what kind of work she was doing. I
imagined that she was selling perfume, testing dessert recipes for
the local newspaper. Or maybe she was working for the florist.
Now that she had learned to drive, she might be delivering boxes
of roses to people.

"I don't think so," said Mona as we walked to our piano lesson after school. "She would've hit something by now."

A gust of wind littered the street with leaves.

30   "Maybe we better hurry up," she went on, looking at the
sky. "It's going to pour."

"But we're too early." Her lesson didn't begin until 4:00,
mine until 4:30, so we usually tried to walk as slowly as we
could. "And anyway, those aren't the kind of clouds that rain.
Those are cumulus clouds."

We arrived out of breath and wet.

"Oh, you poor, poor dears," said old Miss Crosman. "Why
don't you call me the next time it's like this out? If your mother
won't drive you, I can come pick you up."

40   "No, that's okay," I answered. Mona wrung her hair out on
Miss Crosman's rug. "We just couldn't get the roof of our car to
close, is all. We took it to the beach last summer and got sand in
the mechanism." I pronounced this last word carefully, as if the
credibility of my lie depended on its middle syllable. "It's never
been the same." I thought for a second. "It's a convertible."

"Well then make yourselves at home." She exchanged looks
with Eugenie Roberts, whose lesson we were interrupting.
Eugenie smiled good-naturedly. "The towels are in the closet
across from the bathroom."

50   Huddling at the end of Miss Crosman's nine-foot
leatherette couch, Mona and I watched Eugenie play. She was a
grade ahead of me and, according to school rumor, had a
boyfriend in high school. I believed it. . . . She had auburn hair,
blue eyes, and, I noted with a particular pang, a pure white folding umbrella.

"I can't see," whispered Mona.

"So clean your glasses."

"My glasses *are* clean. You're in the way."

I looked at her. "They look dirty to me."

60 "That's because *your* glasses are dirty."

Eugenie came bouncing to the end of her piece.

"Oh! Just stupendous!" Miss Crosman hugged her, then looked up as Eugenie's mother walked in. "Stupendous!" she said again. "Oh! Mrs. Roberts! Your daughter has a gift, a real gift. It's an honor to teach her."

Mrs. Roberts, radiant with pride, swept her daughter out of the room as if she were royalty, born to the piano bench. Watching the way Eugenie carried herself, I sat up, and concentrated so hard on sucking in my stomach that I did not realize

70 until the Robertses were gone that Eugenie had left her umbrella. As Mona began to play, I jumped and ran to the window, meaning to call to them—only to see their brake lights flash then fade at the stop sign at the corner. As if to allow them passage, the rain had let up; a quivering sun lit their way.

The umbrella glowed like a scepter on the blue carpet while Mona, slumping over the keyboard, managed to eke out a fair rendition of a catfight. At the end of the piece, Miss Crosman asked her to stand up.

"Stay right there," she said, then came back a minute later

80 with a towel to cover the bench. "You must be cold," she continued. "Shall I call your mother and have her bring over some dry clothes?"

"No," answered Mona. "She won't come because she . . ."

"She's too busy," I broke in from the back of the room.

"I see." Miss Crosman sighed and shook her head a little. "Your glasses are filthy, honey," she said to Mona. "Shall I clean them for you?"

Sisterly embarrassment seized me. Why hadn't Mona wiped her lenses when I told her to? As she resumed abuse of the

90 piano, I stared at the umbrella. I wanted to open it, twirl it around by its slender silver handle; I wanted to dangle it from

INFER

Why is the narrator "sucking in" her stomach (line 69)?

_____

_____

_____

WORD STUDY

In a **simile** a writer uses *like* or *as* to compare two unlike things. Re-read lines 75–77, and circle the simile.

INFER

Finish the sentence Mona is not allowed to complete (line 83). Why does the narrator interrupt Mona?

_____

_____

_____

_____

CHARACTER

Re-read lines 79–87, and underline the two passages where Miss Crosman speaks to the girls. What do Miss Crosman's words reveal about her character?

_____

_____

_____

_____

_____

_____

_____

_____

_____

_____

_____

_____

_____

_____

WORD STUDY

The word *constellation* (line 111) means "group of stars." The narrator is comparing her feelings to the rising of a whole constellation of stars. How does she feel?

_____

_____

_____

_____

_____

my wrist on the way to school the way the other girls did. I wondered what Miss Crosman would say if I offered to bring it to Eugenie at school tomorrow. She would be impressed with my consideration for others; Eugenie would be pleased to have it back; and I would have possession of the umbrella for an entire night. I looked at it again, toying with the idea of asking for one for Christmas. I knew, however, how my mother would react.

"Things," she would say. "What's the matter with a rain-
100   coat? All you want is things, just like an American."

Sitting down for my lesson, I was careful to keep the towel under me and sit up straight.

"I'll bet you can't see a thing either," said Miss Crosman, reaching for my glasses. "And you can relax, you poor dear. This isn't a boot camp."

When Miss Crosman finally allowed me to start playing I played extra well, as well as I possibly could. See, I told her with my fingers. You don't have to feel sorry for me.

"That was wonderful," said Miss Crosman. "Oh! Just won-
110   derful."

An entire constellation rose in my heart.

"And guess what," I announced proudly. "I have a surprise for you."

Then I played a second piece for her, a much more difficult one that she had not assigned.

"Oh! That was stupendous," she said without hugging me. "Stupendous! You are a genius, young lady. If your mother had started you younger, you'd be playing like Eugenie Roberts by now!"

120   I looked at the keyboard, wishing that I had still a third, even more difficult piece to play for her. I wanted to tell her that I was the school spelling bee champion, that I wasn't ticklish, that I could do karate.

"My mother is a concert pianist," I said.

She looked at me for a long moment, then finally, without saying anything, hugged me. I didn't say anything about bringing the umbrella to Eugenie at school.

The steps were dry when Mona and I sat down to wait for my mother.

130 "Do you want to wait inside?" Miss Crosman looked anxiously at the sky.

"No," I said. "Our mother will be here any minute."

"In a while," said Mona.

"Any minute," I said again, even though my mother had been at least twenty minutes late every week since she started working.

According to the church clock across the street we had been waiting twenty-five minutes when Miss Crosman came out again.

140 "Shall I give you ladies a ride home?"

"No," I said. "Our mother is coming any minute."

"Shall I at least give her a call and remind her you're here? Maybe she forgot about you."

"I don't think she *forgot*," said Mona.

"Shall I give her a call anyway? Just to be safe?"

"I bet she already left," I said. "How could she forget about us?"

Miss Crosman went in to call.

"There's no answer," she said, coming back out.

150 "See, she's on her way," I said.

"Are you sure you wouldn't like to come in?"

"No," said Mona.

"Yes," I said. I pointed at my sister. "She meant yes too. She meant no, she wouldn't like to go in."

Miss Crosman looked at her watch. "It's 5:30 now, ladies. My pot roast will be coming out in fifteen minutes. Maybe you'd like to come in and have some then?"

"My mother's almost here," I said. "She's on her way."

INFER

Circle the details in lines 125–126 that tell you what Miss Crosman does when she hears the girl's lie. How does the teacher feel about the girl?

_____

_____

_____

_____

_____

_____

_____

_____

_____

_____

_____

_____

_____

_____

FLUENCY

The **dialogue** in lines 128–158 gives you important information. Read the boxed passage aloud, to show how the sisters and Miss Crosman are feeling.

_____

_____

_____

_____

_____

_____

_____

_____

_____

CHARACTER

In lines 179–195, the narrator faces a hard choice. What is her **internal conflict**?

_____

_____

_____

_____

_____

_____

_____

_____

160   We watched and watched the street. I tried to imagine what my mother was doing; I tried to imagine her writing messages in the sky, even though I knew she was afraid of planes. I watched as the branches of Miss Crosman's big willow tree started to sway; they had all been trimmed to exactly the same height off the ground, so that they looked beautiful, like hair in the wind.

It started to rain.

"Miss Crosman is coming out again," said Mona.

"Don't let her talk you into going inside," I whispered.

"Why not?"

"Because that would mean that Mom isn't really coming
170   any minute."

"But she isn't," said Mona. "She's _working._"

"Shhh! Miss Crosman is going to hear you."

"She's working! She's working! She's working!"

I put my hand over her mouth, but she licked it, and so I was wiping my hand on my wet dress when the front door opened.

"We're getting even _wetter,_" said Mona right away. "Wetter and wetter."

"Shall we all go in?" Miss Crosman pulled Mona to her feet.
180   "Before you young ladies catch pneumonia? You've been out here an hour already."

"We're _freezing._" Mona looked up at Miss Crosman. "Do you have any hot chocolate? We're going to catch _pneumonia._"

"I'm not going in," I said. "My mother's coming any minute."

"Come on," said Mona. "Use your _noggin._"

"Any minute."

"Come on, Mona." Miss Crosman opened the door. "Shall we get you inside first?"

190   "See you in the hospital," said Mona as she went in. "See you in the hospital with _pneumonia._"

I stared out into the empty street. The rain was pricking me all over; I was cold; I wanted to go inside. I wanted to be able to

let myself go inside. If Miss Crosman came out again, I decided, I would go in.

She came out with a blanket and the white umbrella.

I could not believe that I was actually holding the umbrella, opening it. It sprang up by itself as if it were alive, as if that were what it wanted to do—as if it belonged in my hands, above my head. I stared up at the network of silver spokes, then spun the umbrella around and around and around. It was so clean and white that it seemed to glow, to **illuminate** everything around it.

"It's beautiful," I said.

Miss Crosman sat down next to me, on one end of the blanket. I moved the umbrella over so that it covered her too. I could feel the rain on my left shoulder and shivered. She put her arm around me.

"You poor, poor dear."

I knew that I was in store for another bolt of sympathy, and braced myself by staring up into the umbrella.

"You know, I very much wanted to have children when I was younger," she continued.

"You did?"

VOCABULARY

illuminate (i·lōō'mə·nāt') v.: light up.

IDENTIFY

Pause at line 210. What does the narrator *not* want from Miss Crosman?

_____

_____

_____

_____

CHARACTER

Circle the detail in lines 211–212 that hints at why Miss Crosman is so nice to the narrator (and to her other music students).

Pause at line 222. Why does the narrator lie to Miss Crosman about getting a white umbrella for Christmas?

_____

_____

_____

_____

_____

_____

_____

_____

_____

Re-read lines 239–242. Why does the narrator feel bad about what she says to Miss Crosman?

_____

_____

_____

_____

_____

_____

_____

She stared at me a minute. Her face looked dry and crusty, like day-old frosting.

"I did. But then I never got married."

I twirled the umbrella around again.

"This is the most beautiful umbrella I have ever seen," I said. "Ever, in my whole life."

220   "Do you have an umbrella?"

"No. But my mother's going to get me one just like this for Christmas."

"Is she? I tell you what. You don't have to wait until Christmas. You can have this one."

"But this one belongs to Eugenie Roberts," I protested. "I have to give it back to her tomorrow in school."

"Who told you it belongs to Eugenie? It's not Eugenie's. It's mine. And now I'm giving it to you, so it's yours."

"It is?"

230   She hugged me tighter. "That's right. It's all yours."

"It's mine?" I didn't know what to say. "Mine?" Suddenly I was jumping up and down in the rain. "It's beautiful! Oh! It's beautiful!" I laughed.

Miss Crosman laughed too, even though she was getting all wet.

"Thank you, Miss Crosman. Thank you very much. Thanks a zillion. It's beautiful. It's *stupendous!*"

"You're quite welcome," she said.

"Thank you," I said again, but that didn't seem like enough.

240   Suddenly I knew just what she wanted to hear. "I wish you were my mother."

Right away I felt bad.

"You shouldn't say that," she said, but her face was opening into a huge smile as the lights of my mother's car cautiously turned the corner. I quickly collapsed the umbrella and put it up my skirt, holding onto it from the outside, through the material.

"Mona!" I shouted into the house. "Mona! Hurry up! Mom's here! I told you she was coming!"

Then I ran away from Miss Crosman, down to the curb.
250 Mona came tearing up to my side as my mother neared the house. We both backed up a few feet, so that in case she went onto the curb, she wouldn't run us over.

"But why didn't you go inside with Mona?" my mother asked on the way home. She had taken off her own coat to put over me, and had the heat on high.

"She wasn't using her noggin," said Mona, next to me in the back seat.

"I should call next time," said my mother. "I just don't like to say where I am."

260 That was when she finally told us that she was working as a checkout clerk in the A&P. She was supposed to be on the day shift, but the other employees were unreliable, and her boss had promised her a promotion if she would stay until the evening shift filled in.

For a moment no one said anything. Even Mona seemed to find the **revelation** disappointing.

"A promotion already!" she said, finally.

I listened to the windshield wipers.

"You're so quiet." My mother looked at me in the rearview
270 mirror. "What's the matter?"

"I wish you would quit," I said after a moment.

She sighed. "The Chinese have a saying: One beam cannot hold the roof up."

"But Eugenie Roberts's father supports their family."

She sighed once more. "Eugenie Roberts's father is Eugenie Roberts's father," she said.

As we entered the downtown area, Mona started leaning hard against me every time the car turned right, trying to push me over. Remembering what I had said to Miss Crosman, I tried
280 to **maneuver** the umbrella under my leg so she wouldn't feel it.

"What's under your skirt?" Mona wanted to know as we came to a traffic light. My mother, watching us in the rearview mirror again, rolled slowly to a stop.

VOCABULARY

revelation (rev′ə·lā′shən) n.:
discovery; surprising news.
Revelation comes from the
Latin *re–,* meaning "back,"
and *velum,* meaning "veil"
or "curtain." When someone
has a *revelation,* it is as if a
curtain has been pulled back,
uncovering something that
had been hidden.
What commonly used word is
related to *revelation*?

_____

_____

_____

_____

_____

_____

_____

_____

_____

CHARACTER

In lines 260–276, the girls
react badly to the truth
about their mother's job.
Circle the words Mona says
to her mother after she hears
the news. Underline the
words the narrator says.

VOCABULARY

maneuver (mə·noo′vər) v.:
move (an object) skillfully.

IDENTIFY

Underline the words in lines 297–299 that tell what happened to the car and to the narrator, her mother, and her sister.

CHARACTER

Why does the narrator throw the umbrella away at the end of the story?

_____

_____

_____

_____

_____

_____

_____

_____

_____

_____

_____

_____

_____

_____

_____

_____

_____

_____

"What's the matter?" she asked.

"There's something under her skirt!" said Mona, pulling at me. "Under her skirt!"

Meanwhile, a man crossing the street started to yell at us. "Who do you think you are, lady?" he said. "You're blocking the whole crosswalk."

290 We all froze. Other people walking by stopped to watch.

"Didn't you hear me?" he went on, starting to thump on the hood with his fist. "Don't you speak English?"

My mother began to back up, but the car behind us honked. Luckily, the light turned green right after that. She sighed in relief.

"What were you saying, Mona?" she asked.

We wouldn't have hit the car behind us that hard if he hadn't been moving too, but as it was our car bucked violently, throwing us all first back and then forward.

300 "Uh oh," said Mona when we stopped. "Another accident."

I was relieved to have attention diverted from the umbrella. Then I noticed my mother's head, tilted back onto the seat. Her eyes were closed.

"Mom!" I screamed. "Mom! Wake up!"

She opened her eyes. "Please don't yell," she said. "Enough people are going to yell already."

"I thought you were dead," I said, starting to cry. "I thought you were dead."

She turned around, looked at me intently, then put her 310 hand to my forehead.

"Sick," she confirmed. "Some kind of sick is giving you crazy ideas."

As the man from the car behind us started tapping on the window, I moved the umbrella away from my leg. Then Mona and my mother were getting out of the car. I got out after them; and while everyone else was inspecting the damage we'd done, I threw the umbrella down a sewer.

The White Umbrella

Action-Motivation Chart   The narrator in "The White Umbrella" has various motivations, or reasons, for behaving as she does. For each action listed, write the motivation that caused it.

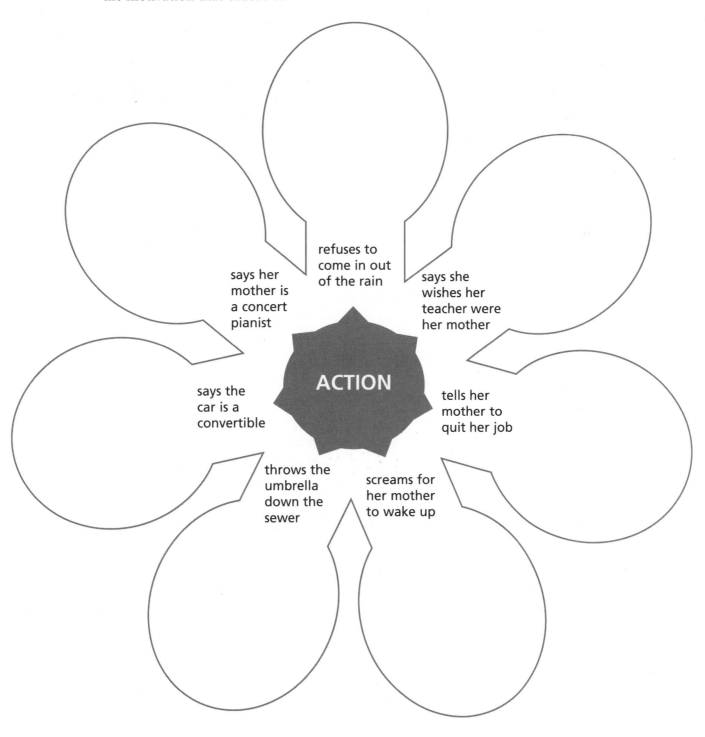

ACTION

- refuses to come in out of the rain
- says she wishes her teacher were her mother
- tells her mother to quit her job
- screams for her mother to wake up
- throws the umbrella down the sewer
- says the car is a convertible
- says her mother is a concert pianist

Standards Review

 **The White Umbrella**

Learning test-taking skills takes practice. Complete the sample test item below; then, check your answer and read the explanation in the right-hand column.

Sample Test Item	Explanation of the Correct Answer
The narrator says to her mother, "I thought you were dead." The comment is an example of which kind of character clue? A appearance B private thoughts C a character's words D a character's action	The correct answer is *C*. Because the narrator is not describing her mother's appearance or an action, *A* and *D* are incorrect. Since she is speaking to her mother, her thoughts are not "private." Therefore, *B* is also wrong.

DIRECTIONS: Circle the letter of the correct response.

1. The narrator doesn't want Miss Crosman to —

   A pity her

   B talk to her

   C teach her

   D praise her

2. The narrator and her sister —

   F are exactly alike

   G respond differently to their problems

   H are both embarrassed by their mother

   J both want the white umbrella

3. The narrator has an **internal conflict** because she —

   A wants to be more "American"

   B has to be home to make dinner

   C secretly hates playing the piano

   D has stolen the white umbrella

4. The narrator's **motivation** for lying is that she —

   F dislikes her sister

   G likes fooling people

   H wants to be pitied

   J is embarrassed that her mother works

Reading Standard 3.3
Analyze interactions between main and subordinate characters in a literary text (e.g., internal and external conflicts, motivations, relationships, influences) and explain the way those interactions affect the plot.

Standards Review

 **The White Umbrella**

Word Derivations

DIRECTIONS: Circle the letter of the correct response.

1. The word *audible* comes from a Latin word meaning "to hear." Which of the following would be an auditory sensation?

   A a sweet taste

   B a loud sound

   C a feeling of coldness

   D an awful smell

2. *Credere* means "to believe." Which of the following words is *not* based on *credere*?

   F credit   **H** credible

   G creed   **J** create

3. The Latin prefix *inter–* means "within." A character's *internal* thoughts are the most —

   A hostile   **C** public

   B private   **D** comical

4. *Diverted* comes from the Latin *dis–*, meaning "away from," and *vertere*, meaning "to turn." When the narrator says she wants attention *diverted* from the umbrella, she means that —

   F she doesn't want the umbrella to be noticed

   G she is proud of the umbrella

   H she loves the umbrella

   J the umbrella is ugly

Reading Standard 1.1 Identify and use the literal and figurative meanings of words and understand word derivations.

Vocabulary in Context

DIRECTIONS: Write the correct word from the box in the numbered blank. Not all words will be used.

Word Box

- lilt
- audible
- discreet
- credibility
- illuminate
- revelation
- maneuver

My secret will be a (1) _____, but Jeri will have to be (2) _____ and keep her mouth shut. Since we met in the library, my voice was barely (3) _____. Jeri kept asking me to speak up because she couldn't hear me. Finally I said, "You know, with all this hush-hush stuff, I've forgotten the secret." I sure lost my (4) _____ as a sharer of secrets.

Before You Go On...

Check your Standards Mastery at the back of this book.

Narrator and Voice

Academic Vocabulary for Chapter 3

These are the terms you should know
as you read and analyze the stories in this chapter.

_____

Narrator The teller of a story. A narrator tells the story from one of three
points of view.

- In a story told from the **omniscient** (äm·nish′ənt) **point of view,** the
  narrator can tell us everything about the characters, including how
  they think and feel. This narrator is not a character in the story.
- A **first-person narrator** is a character in the story who refers to himself
  or herself as *I* or *me.* In a story told from the first-person point of view,
  the reader knows only what this narrator knows and chooses to reveal.
  Some first-person narrators are **credible,** or trustworthy. Others are
  unreliable: They may not always tell the truth about characters or
  events in the story.
- A **third-person-limited narrator** is an omniscient narrator (not someone
  in the story). This narrator, however, focuses on only one character's
  actions and feelings.

Diction The writer's choice of words.

Tone The writer's attitude toward the subject of a story, toward a character,
  or toward the audience (the readers). A story's tone can be described
  by words like *humorous, serious, sad, sarcastic, sympathetic.*

Voice The writer's use of language and overall style, created by tone and
  choice of words.

**Reading
Standard 1.1**
Identify and
use the literal
and figurative
meanings of
words and
understand
word
derivations.

**Reading
Standard 1.3
(Grade 8
Review)**
Use word
meanings within
the appropriate
context and
show ability to
verify those
meanings by
definition,
restatement,
example,
comparison, or
contrast.

**Reading
Standard 3.9**
Explain how
voice, persona, and
the choice of a
narrator affect
characterization
and the tone,
plot, and
credibility of
a text.

For Further Information…

- Be sure to read the essay on **narrator and
  voice** in *Holt Literature and Language Arts,*
  pages 148–149.

The Interlopers by Saki

Imagine you are in a dark forest on a winter night, hunting an enemy—who just happens to be your neighbor. Now suppose that your neighbor is hunting you, too. What makes people who should be friends become fierce enemies? Who is the loser in this story's deadly fight? The answer may shock you.

LITERARY FOCUS: OMNISCIENT NARRATOR

A story's **omniscient narrator** knows everything that happens, and why. This type of narrator is not a character in the story but an outside observer who can tell you what each character is thinking and feeling.

- As you read "The Interlopers," pay special attention to the information the narrator gives you about the two characters' pasts.
- The narrator of "The Interlopers" makes us think that events are leading one way—up until the story's very end. Prepare to be surprised.

READING SKILLS: MONITORING YOUR READING

Some of the words and sentences in "The Interlopers" may seen difficult. The following tips will help you understand this classic story.

- Look for context clues that can help you figure out the meaning of unfamiliar words.
- Break down long sentences into shorter ones.
- Look for the subject and verb in confusing sentences.
- Stop to summarize important passages or scenes.
- Re-read tough passages. Some passages are hard to understand the first time.
- Try to visualize, or picture, the events that are happening.

Reading Standard 1.3 (Grade 8 Review) Use word meanings within the appropriate context and show ability to verify those meanings by definition, restatement, example, comparison, or contrast.

Reading Standard 3.9 Explain how voice, persona, and the choice of a narrator affect characterization and the tone, plot, and credibility of a text.

VOCABULARY DEVELOPMENT

PREVIEW SELECTION VOCABULARY

The following words are from "The Interlopers." Study the words before you begin the story.

precipitous (prē·sip′ə·təs) *adj.:* very steep.

*The wooded slope was **precipitous**—a vertical cliff—and hard to climb.*

acquiesced (ak′wē·est′) *v.* (used with *in*): accepted; agreed; consented.

*They never **acquiesced** in the judgment of the court; instead, they bitterly opposed it.*

marauders (mə·rôd′·ərz) *n.:* people who roam around in search of loot, or goods to steal.

*The man kept a sharp lookout for **marauders** who might be prowling through the woods.*

exasperation (eg·zas′pər·ā′shən) *n.:* great annoyance.

*His **exasperation** at being captured was so great that he cursed aloud.*

pious (pī′əs) *adj.:* showing religious devotion.

*Although not religious, his words were **pious**.*

retorted (ri·tôrt′id) *v.:* replied in a sharp or witty way.

*Feeling insulted, he **retorted** angrily.*

condolences (kən·dō′ləns·iz) *n.:* expressions of sympathy.

*When he heard about his enemy's death, he sent **condolences** to the widow.*

languor (laŋ′gər) *n.:* weakness; weariness.

*After hours of hard work, he felt a great **languor,** and this exhaustion lasted all day.*

reconciliation (rek′ən·sil′ē·ā′shən) *n.:* friendly end to a quarrel.

*The fight could end in one of two ways— **reconciliation** or death.*

succor (suk′ər) *n.:* help given to someone in distress; relief.

*Unable to free themselves, they waited for rescuers to give them **succor**.*

CONTEXT CLUES: SOLVING WORD MYSTERIES

Successful readers are like detectives looking for clues. When good readers see an unfamiliar word, they look at the **context,** the words and sentences around the word, for clues to its meaning. Look at the these examples to learn more.

Type of Context Clue	Example
Definition or restatement	Tito's **languor,** his complete weariness, came when the danger was over.
Example	Tito's **languor** was like the feeling you get after defeat in a basketball game.
Antonym	His cousin was full of pep, but Tito had a feeling of **languor**.
Cause and effect	Because of his **languor,** Tito slept all day.

The Interlopers

Saki

IDENTIFY

Which character are you introduced to in the first paragraph? What is he looking for in the forest?

_____

_____

_____

VOCABULARY

precipitous (prē·sip′ə·təs) *adj.*: very steep.

acquiesced (ak′wē·est′) *v.* (used with *in*): accepted; agreed; consented.

Acquiesce has the same Latin root as *quiet.* Someone who *acquiesces* agrees quietly and without excitement.

In a forest of mixed growth somewhere on the eastern spurs of the Carpathians,[1] a man stood one winter night watching and listening, as though he waited for some beast of the woods to come within the range of his vision and, later, of his rifle. But the game for whose presence he kept so keen an outlook was none that figured in the sportsman's calendar as lawful and proper for the chase; Ulrich von Gradwitz patrolled the dark forest in quest of a human enemy.

The forest lands of Gradwitz were of wide extent and well stocked with game; the narrow strip of **precipitous** woodland that lay on its outskirt was not remarkable for the game it harbored or the shooting it afforded, but it was the most jealously guarded of all its owner's territorial possessions. A famous lawsuit, in the days of his grandfather, had wrested it from the illegal possession of a neighboring family of petty landowners; the dispossessed party had never **acquiesced** in the judgment of the courts, and a long series of poaching affrays[2] and similar scan-

---

1. **Carpathians** (kär·pā′thē·ənz): mountain range that starts in Slovakia and extends through Poland, Ukraine, and Romania.
2. **poaching affrays** (ə·frāz′): noisy quarrels or brawls about poaching, which means "fishing or hunting illegally on private property."

dals had embittered the relationships between the families for three generations. The neighbor feud had grown into a personal one since Ulrich had come to be head of his family; if there was a man in the world whom he detested and wished ill to, it was Georg Znaeym, the inheritor of the quarrel and the tireless game snatcher and raider of the disputed border forest. The feud might, perhaps, have died down or been compromised if the personal ill will of the two men had not stood in the way; as boys they had thirsted for one another's blood, as men each prayed that misfortune might fall on the other, and this wind-scourged winter night Ulrich had banded together his foresters to watch the dark forest, not in quest of four-footed quarry, but to keep a lookout for the prowling thieves whom he suspected of being afoot from across the land boundary. The roebuck,[3] which usually kept in the sheltered hollows during a storm wind, were running like driven things tonight, and there was movement and unrest among the creatures that were wont to sleep through the dark hours. Assuredly there was a disturbing element in the forest, and Ulrich could guess the quarter from whence it came.

He strayed away by himself from the watchers whom he had placed in ambush on the crest of the hill and wandered far down the steep slopes amid the wild tangle of undergrowth, peering through the tree trunks and listening through the whistling and skirling[4] of the wind and the restless beating of the branches for sight or sound of the **marauders.** If only on this wild night, in this dark, lone spot, he might come across Georg Znaeym, man to man, with none to witness—that was the wish that was uppermost in his thoughts. And as he stepped round the trunk of a huge beech he came face to face with the man he sought.

The two enemies stood glaring at one another for a long silent moment. Each had a rifle in his hand, each had hate in his heart and murder uppermost in his mind. The chance had come

---

3. **roebuck** (rō′buk′) *n.*: male (or males) of the roe deer, small deer that live in Europe and Asia.
4. **skirling** (skurl′iŋ) *v.* used as *n.*: shrill, piercing sound.

IDENTIFY

Re-read lines 19–31. Underline what you learn about why the two men continue the fight between the neighboring families. Whom is Ulrich feuding with?

_____

VOCABULARY

marauders (mə·rôd′·ərz) *n.*: people who roam around in search of loot, or goods to steal.

WORD STUDY

In lines 44–45, underline the **compound word**—a word that is made up of two words. What does this compound word mean?

_____

_____

_____

_____

_____

_____

_____

_____

IDENTIFY

In lines 48–49, circle the sentence in which the **omniscient narrator** tells you what each character is thinking and feeling.

IDENTIFY

Circle the important event that happens to the two enemies (lines 56–59).

MONITOR YOUR READING

Draw lines to break down the long sentence in lines 69–72 into shorter units of thought. Then, paraphrase the sentence.

_____

_____

_____

_____

_____

_____

_____

_____

_____

_____

_____

_____

50 to give full play to the passions of a lifetime. But a man who has been brought up under the code of a restraining civilization cannot easily nerve himself to shoot down his neighbor in cold blood and without a word spoken, except for an offense against his hearth and honor. And before the moment of hesitation had given way to action, a deed of Nature's own violence overwhelmed them both. A fierce shriek of the storm had been answered by a splitting crash over their heads, and ere they could leap aside, a mass of falling beech tree had thundered down on them. Ulrich von Gradwitz found himself stretched on

60 the ground, one arm numb beneath him and the other held almost as helplessly in a tight tangle of forked branches, while both legs were pinned beneath the fallen mass. His heavy shooting boots had saved his feet from being crushed to pieces, but if his fractures were not as serious as they might have been, at least it was evident that he could not move from his present position till someone came to release him. The descending twigs had slashed the skin of his face, and he had to wink away some drops of blood from his eyelashes before he could take in a general view of the disaster. At his side, so near that under ordinary cir-

70 cumstances he could almost have touched him, lay Georg Znaeym, alive and struggling, but obviously as helplessly pinioned[5] down as himself. All round them lay a thick-strewn wreckage of splintered branches and broken twigs.

Relief at being alive and **exasperation** at his captive plight brought a strange medley of **pious** thank offerings and sharp curses to Ulrich's lips. Georg, who was nearly blinded with the blood which trickled across his eyes, stopped his struggling for a moment to listen, and then gave a short, snarling laugh.

"So you're not killed, as you ought to be, but you're caught,

80 anyway," he cried, "caught fast. Ho, what a jest, Ulrich von Gradwitz snared in his stolen forest. There's real justice for you!"

And he laughed again, mockingly and savagely.

---

5. **pinioned** (pin′yənd) *v.* used as *adj.*: pinned, as if chained or tied up.

"I'm caught in my own forest land," **retorted** Ulrich. "When my men come to release us, you will wish, perhaps, that you were in a better plight than caught poaching on a neighbor's land, shame on you."

Georg was silent for a moment; then he answered quietly:

"Are you sure that your men will find much to release? I have men, too, in the forest tonight, close behind me, and they will be here first and do the releasing. When they drag me out from under these branches, it won't need much clumsiness on their part to roll this mass of trunk right over on the top of you. Your men will find you dead under a fallen beech tree. For form's sake I shall send my **condolences** to your family."

"It is a useful hint," said Ulrich fiercely. "My men had orders to follow in ten minutes' time, seven of which must have gone by already, and when they get me out—I will remember the hint. Only as you will have met your death poaching on my lands, I don't think I can decently send any message of condolence to your family."

"Good," snarled Georg, "good. We fight this quarrel out to the death, you and I and our foresters, with no cursed interlopers to come between us. Death and damnation to you, Ulrich von Gradwitz."

"The same to you, Georg Znaeym, forest thief, game snatcher."

Both men spoke with the bitterness of possible defeat before them, for each knew that it might be long before his men would seek him out or find him; it was a bare matter of chance which party would arrive first on the scene.

Both had now given up the useless struggle to free themselves from the mass of wood that held them down; Ulrich limited his endeavors to an effort to bring his one partially free arm near enough to his outer coat pocket to draw out his wine flask. Even when he had accomplished that operation, it was long before he could manage the unscrewing of the stopper or get

90

100

110

VOCABULARY

retorted (ri·tôrt′id) *v.*: replied in a sharp or witty way.

condolences (kən·dō′ləns·iz) *n.*: expressions of sympathy. *Condolence* comes from two Latin words: *com–*, a prefix meaning "with," and *dolere*, meaning "to grieve."

CLARIFY

Re-read lines 82–94. What do the enemies threaten to do to each other once they are rescued?

_____

_____

_____

_____

_____

_____

_____

_____

_____

_____

_____

_____

WORD STUDY

In line 113, circle the word that restates the meaning of *endeavors*.

MONITOR
YOUR READING

Re-read the long sentence in
lines 118–124. Then, **summarize** the sentence.

any of the liquid down his throat. But what a heaven-sent draft[6]
it seemed! It was an open winter[7], and little snow had fallen as
yet, hence the captives suffered less from the cold than might
120 have been the case at that season of the year; nevertheless, the
wine was warming and reviving to the wounded man, and he
looked across with something like a throb of pity to where his
enemy lay, just keeping the groans of pain and weariness from
crossing his lips.

"Could you reach this flask if I threw it over to you?" asked
Ulrich suddenly. "There is good wine in it, and one may as well
be as comfortable as one can. Let us drink, even if tonight one of
us dies."

"No, I can scarcely see anything; there is so much blood
130 caked round my eyes," said Georg; "and in any case I don't drink
wine with an enemy."

Ulrich was silent for a few minutes and lay listening to the
weary screeching of the wind. An idea was slowly forming and
growing in his brain, an idea that gained strength every time that
he looked across at the man who was fighting so grimly against
pain and exhaustion. In the pain and **languor** that Ulrich himself
was feeling, the old fierce hatred seemed to be dying down.

"Neighbor," he said presently, "do as you please if your men
come first. It was a fair compact. But as for me, I've changed my
140 mind. If my men are the first to come, you shall be the first to be
helped, as though you were my guest. We have quarreled like
devils all our lives over this stupid strip of forest, where the trees
can't even stand upright in a breath of wind. Lying here tonight,
thinking, I've come to think we've been rather fools; there are
better things in life than getting the better of a boundary dispute. Neighbor, if you will help me to bury the old quarrel, I—I
will ask you to be my friend."

Georg Znaeym was silent for so long that Ulrich thought
perhaps he had fainted with the pain of his injuries. Then he
150 spoke slowly and in jerks.

FLUENCY

Read the boxed passage
aloud several times. Focus on
conveying the different attitudes of Ulrich and Georg.

VOCABULARY

languor (laŋ′gər) *n.*: weakness; weariness.

IDENTIFY

In lines 132–137, the narrator
reveals an important change
in Ulrich's attitude. Circle the
important change the narrator tells you about.

6. **draft** *n.*: drink.
7. **open winter**: mild winter.

"How the whole region would stare and gabble if we rode into the market square together. No one living can remember seeing a Znaeym and a von Gradwitz talking to one another in friendship. And what peace there would be among the forester folk if we ended our feud tonight. And if we choose to make peace among our people, there is none other to interfere, no interlopers from outside. . . . You would come and keep the Sylvester night[8] beneath my roof, and I would come and feast on some high day at your castle. . . . I would never fire a shot on

160   your land, save when you invited me as a guest; and you should come and shoot with me down in the marshes where the wild-fowl are. In all the countryside there are none that could hinder if we willed to make peace. I never thought to have wanted to do other than hate you all my life, but I think I have changed my mind about things too, this last half-hour. And you offered me your wine flask. . . . Ulrich von Gradwitz, I will be your friend."

    For a space both men were silent, turning over in their minds the wonderful changes that this dramatic **reconciliation** would bring about. In the cold, gloomy forest, with the wind

170   tearing in fitful gusts through the naked branches and whistling round the tree trunks, they lay and waited for the help that would now bring release and **succor** to both parties. And each prayed a private prayer that his men might be the first to arrive, so that he might be the first to show honorable attention to the enemy that had become a friend.

---

8. **Sylvester night:** feast day honoring Saint Sylvester (Pope Sylvester I, d. 335), observed on December 31.

VOCABULARY

reconciliation
(rek′ən·sil′ē·ā′shən) *n.:* friendly end to a quarrel.

succor (suk′ər) *n.:* help given to someone in distress; relief.

COMPARE & CONTRAST

Pause at line 175. Earlier in the story (lines 83–100), why did each man hope that his friends would be the first to arrive? What has changed?

Pause at line 203. The **narrator** doesn't reveal who is coming toward the men. What effect does this lack of information create?

_____

_____

IDENTIFY

Read to the end of the story. Underline the one word that reveals the story's **surprise ending.**

ANALYZE

Why is it fitting that the two men, who were hunting each other in the forest that winter night, are discovered by wolves rather than by rescuers?

_____

_____

_____

_____

_____

_____

_____

_____

_____

_____

_____

_____

Presently, as the wind dropped for a moment, Ulrich broke the silence.

"Let's shout for help," he said; "in this lull our voices may carry a little way."

180 "They won't carry far through the trees and undergrowth," said Georg, "but we can try. Together, then."

The two raised their voices in a prolonged hunting call.

"Together again," said Ulrich a few minutes later, after listening in vain for an answering halloo.

"I heard something that time, I think," said Ulrich.

"I heard nothing but the pestilential⁹ wind," said Georg hoarsely.

There was silence again for some minutes, and then Ulrich gave a joyful cry.

190 "I can see figures coming through the wood. They are following in the way I came down the hillside."

Both men raised their voices in as loud a shout as they could muster.

"They hear us! They've stopped. Now they see us. They're running down the hill toward us," cried Ulrich.

"How many of them are there?" asked Georg.

"I can't see distinctly," said Ulrich; "nine or ten."

"Then they are yours," said Georg; "I had only seven out with me."

200 "They are making all the speed they can, brave lads," said Ulrich gladly.

"Are they your men?" asked Georg. "Are they your men?" he repeated impatiently, as Ulrich did not answer.

"No," said Ulrich with a laugh, the idiotic chattering laugh of a man unstrung with hideous fear.

"Who are they?" asked Georg quickly, straining his eyes to see what the other would gladly not have seen.

"*Wolves.*"

---

9. **pestilential** (pes′tə·len′shəl) *adj.*: Strictly speaking, *pestilential* means "deadly; causing disease; harmful." Here, Georg uses the word to mean "cursed."

The Interlopers

Narrator Questionnaire This story is told by an **omniscient narrator,** who knows all the story's secrets. Fill out this chart to examine the way **point of view** affects the plot and characters of "The Interlopers."

1. Does the narrator reveal the thoughts and feelings of the two men? Explain.

2. How would the story be different if it were told from the point of view of *one* of the men?

3. How might the story be different if it were told from the point of view of the wolves?

Standards Review

 **The Interlopers**

Complete the sample test item below. Then, read the explanation at right.

Sample Test Question	Explanation of the Correct Answer
Who is the story's **narrator**? **A** Georg Znaeym **B** Saki **C** Ulrich von Gradwitz **D** an unnamed, all-knowing storyteller	The correct answer is *D*. *A* and *C* are not correct, because the story is told from the omniscient point of view, not the point of view of just one character. *B* is not correct; Saki is the author.

DIRECTIONS: Circle the letter of each correct response.

1. Which passage reveals that the narrator is **omniscient**?

   A "Both men spoke with the bitterness of possible defeat, for each knew that it might be long before his men would seek him out."

   B "The forest lands of Gradwitz were of wide extent and well stocked with game."

   C "The two raised their voices in a prolonged hunting call."

   D "'No,' said Ulrich with a laugh, the idiotic chattering laugh of a man unstrung with hideous fear."

2. The **narrator** tells us the two men—

   F are hunting wolves

   G don't go hunting at night

   H want to kill each other

   J go to hunting parties together

3. The two men decide to become friends because—

   A their men have ordered them to

   B they hate the neighbors

   C they have become tired of being enemies

   D they hope to save themselves by working together

4. The **narrator** creates suspense by waiting until the end to—

   F reveal what is approaching the men

   G tell which man dies first

   H explain what the men were fighting about

   J warn readers against hunting at night

Reading Standard 3.9
Explain how voice, persona, and the choice of a narrator affect characterization and the tone, plot, and credibility of a text.

Standards Review

TestPractice   ## The Interlopers

Context Clues

DIRECTIONS: Read the passage, using context clues to identify the meaning of the boldface word. Then, circle the letter of the definition of that word.

1. The hunter examined his **quarry** after it had been shot.

   A   rifle   C   enemy

   B   land   D   hunted animal

2. No one could stop the bitter **feud** between the two neighbors.

   F   ongoing argument

   G   broken fence

   H   agreement

   J   flooded lands

3. They heard the loud sound when the tree **thundered** down on them.

   A   fell from the sky

   B   was split by lightning

   C   fell with a roaring noise

   D   yelled

4. He felt no pain in his right arm, which was now **numb.**

   F   bandaged   H   painful

   G   without feeling   J   foolish

Reading Standard 1.3 (Grade 8 Review) Use word meanings within the appropriate context and show ability to verify those meanings by definition, restatement, example, comparison, or contrast.

Vocabulary in Context

DIRECTIONS: Complete the paragraph below by writing the correct word from the box in the correct blank. Not all words from the box will be used.

Word Box

- precipitous
- acquiesced
- marauders
- exasperation
- pious
- retorted
- condolences
- languor
- reconciliation
- succor

The two enemies stared at each other. The gray-haired one laughed. "What are you laughing at?" the brown-haired one asked in (1) _____. "I am laughing at two helpless men caught in a trap," the other (2)_____ in anger. "Shall we become friends? No, (3)_____ is not in my plans. I will never make up with you. And don't give me any (4)_____ words about what religion has taught us. We will always be enemies. Our widows can send each other (5)_____ if they wish."

Before You Go On . . .

Check your Standards Mastery at the back of this book.

My Delicate Heart Condition by Toni Cade Bambara

Harriet Watkins loves excitement as much as she loves scaring other kids with her spooky stories. She also loves watching the Fly family perform death-defying feats on the high wire at the circus. Nothing scares Harriet. Or does it?

LITERARY FOCUS: NARRATOR

- The title of this story, "My Delicate Heart Condition," gives you a clue that the tale is told by a **first-person narrator.** The "I" in the story is Harriet Watkins. She is telling us about herself.
- Harriet "speaks" in a distinct, or special, **voice.** The words and sentences she uses are lively and friendly, as if she were talking to her classmates rather than "writing" a story. As you read, "listen" to the voice of Harriet, the storyteller.
- Part of your job as a reader is to decide how **credible,** or believable, the narrator is. Here are questions you can ask yourself to decide whether the narrator is believable:
  1. Does the narrator *exaggerate,* or say that something is bigger or more exciting than it probably is?
  2. Does she misunderstand what adults are saying?
  3. Does the narrator *not* know things that other characters and the reader may know?

READING SKILLS: DRAWING CONCLUSIONS

A **conclusion** is a judgment you make based on *evidence,* or important details. You probably **draw conclusions** about the world around you every day. You pick up bits of information, connect what you've learned with what you already know, and come to a conclusion—about a person, a place, a thing, or an event. For example, one rainy morning your friend arrives at your house, dripping wet and out of breath. You might conclude that he forgot his umbrella and that he has run to your house in an attempt to stay dry.

You also make judgments based on evidence when you read a story. You think about what the narrator tells you and what the story's characters say and do. Then, using what you've learned from the story and from your own life experiences, you put those details together to form a conclusion. As you read, you check to see if your conclusions are correct. One of the pleasures of fiction is that it often surprises us.

Reading Standard 1.1 Identify and use the literal and figurative meanings of words and understand word derivations.

Reading Standard 3.9 Explain how voice, persona, and the choice of a narrator affect characterization and the tone, plot, and credibility of a text.

SHORT STORY

VOCABULARY DEVELOPMENT

PREVIEW SELECTION VOCABULARY

The following words appear in "My Delicate Heart Condition." Look them over before you begin the story.

withstand (with·stand') *v.:* resist; not give in.

> *Harriet's courage and inner strength help her **withstand** fear.*

vacant (vā'kənt) *adj.:* empty; suggesting lack of attention.

> *His **vacant** look made me think he wasn't paying attention.*

suspended (sə·spen'did) *v.* used as *adj.:* hanging by a support from above.

> *The acrobat hung in the air, **suspended** by only a thin rope.*

proportions (prə·pôr'shənz) *n.:* size; dimensions.

> *His hands were small, but his feet had the **proportions** of a giant's.*

LITERAL AND FIGURATIVE MEANING

The **literal** meaning of a word is its dictionary definition. For example, if you say, "The computer is broken," you are using the word *broken* in a literal sense: The computer doesn't work. However, if you say, "My heart is broken," you are using the word *broken* in a **figurative,** or imaginative, sense. Your heart is still pumping blood—it is "working" in the literal sense. What you really mean by "My heart is broken" is that you are feeling deep sorrow or hurt. You *feel* as if your heart is broken into pieces.

Figurative language is based on a comparison between two unlike things. We use figurative language all the time. Writers use figurative language in unusual or interesting ways to create vivid pictures and striking comparisons. When you read a story, be alert to the writer's use of figurative language.

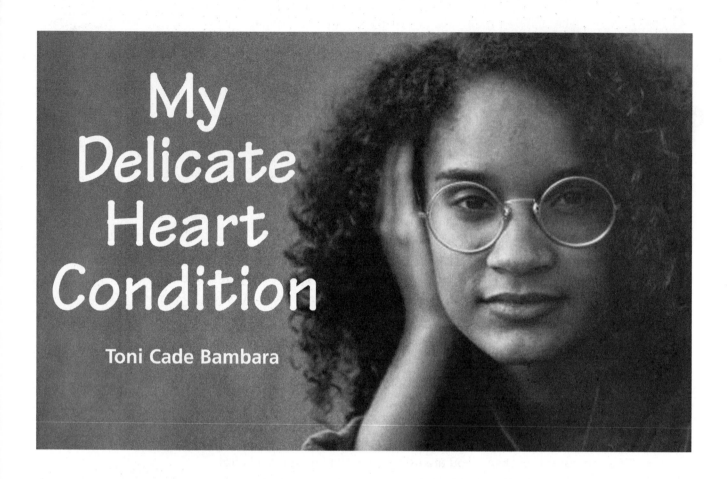

My Delicate Heart Condition

Toni Cade Bambara

My cousin Joanne has not been allowed to hang out with me for some time because she went and told Aunt Hazel that I scare her to death whenever she sleeps over at our house or I spend the weekend at hers. The truth is I sometimes like to tell stories about bloodthirsty vampires or ugly monsters that lurk in clothes closets or giant beetles that eat their way through the shower curtain, like I used to do at camp to entertain the kids in my bunk. But Joanne always cries and that makes the stories even weirder, like background music her crying. And too—I'm

10   not going to lie about it—I get spookier on purpose until all the little crybabies are stuffing themselves under their pillows and throwing their sneakers at me and making such a racket that Mary the counselor has to come in and shine her flashlight around the bunkhouse. I play like I'm asleep. The rest of them are too busy blubbering and finding their way out from under the blankets to tell Mary that it's me. Besides, once they get a load of her standing against the moonlight in that long white

robe of hers looking like a ghost, they just start up again and pretty soon the whole camp is awake. Anyway, that's what I do
20   for fun. So Joanne hasn't been around. And this year I'll have to go to the circus by myself and to camp without her. My mother said on the phone to Aunt Hazel—"Good, keep Jo over there and maybe Harriet'll behave herself if she's got no one to show off to." For all the years my mother's known me, she still doesn't understand that my behaving has got nothing to do with who I hang out with. A private thing between me and me or maybe between me and the Fly family since they were the ones that first got me to sit through monster movies and **withstand** all the terror I could take.

30   For four summers now, me and the Fly family have had this thing going. A battle of nerves, you might say. Each year they raise the rope closer and closer to the very top of the tent—I hear they're going to perform outdoors this year and be even higher—and they stretch the rope further across the rings where the clowns and the pony riders perform. Each year they get bolder and more daring with their rope dancing and the swinging by the legs and flinging themselves into empty space making everyone throw up their hands and gasp for air until Mr. Fly at the very last possible second swings out on his bar to catch them
40   up by the tips of their heels. Everyone just dies and clutches at their hearts. Everybody but me. I sit there calmly. I've trained myself. Joanne used to die and duck her head under the benches and stay there till it was all over.

        Last summer they really got bold. On the final performance just before the fair closed, and some revival-type tent show comes in and all the kids go off to camp, the Fly family performed without a net. I figured they'd be up to something so I made sure my stomach was like steel. I did ten push-ups before breakfast, twenty sit-ups before lunch, skipped dinner altogether.
50   My brother Teddy kidded me all day—"Harriet's trying out for the Olympics." I passed up the ice man on the corner and the pizza and sausage stand by the schoolyard and the cotton candy

NARRATOR

The story's **first-person narrator** does not directly tell readers her name. In lines 20–24, circle the place where you learn her name.

VOCABULARY

withstand (with·stand′) v.: resist; not give in.
Withstand is made up of two words from Old English, the language spoken centuries ago in England. What are the two words?

_____

_____

DRAW CONCLUSIONS

Pause and re-read lines 30–35. Who is the Fly family? What does the family do?

_____

_____

_____

_____

IDENTIFY

Underline the words in lines 40–41 that tell what "everyone" does while watching the Flys. Then, circle the words that tell what Harriet does. What has she trained herself to do?

_____

_____

and jelly-apple lady and the pickle and penny-candy boy, in fact I passed up all the stands that lead from the street down the little roadway to the fair grounds that used to be a swamp when we first moved from Baltimore to Jamaica, Long Island. It wasn't easy, I'm not going to lie, but I was taking no chances. Between the balloon man and the wheel of fortune was the usual clump of ladies from church who came night after night to try to win

60 the giant punch bowl set on the top shelf above the wheel, but had to settle night after night for a jar of gumdrops or salt-and-pepper shakers or some other little thing from the bottom shelf. And from the wheel of fortune to the tent was at least a million stands selling B.B. bats and jawbreakers and gingerbread and sweet potato pie and frozen custard and—like I said it wasn't easy. A million ways to tempt you, to unsettle your stomach, and make you lose the battle to the Fly family.

I sat there almost enjoying the silly clowns who came tumbling out of a steamer trunk no bigger than the one we have in

70 the basement where my mother keeps my old report cards and photographs and letters and things. And I almost enjoyed the fire-eater and the knife-thrower, but I was so close up I could see how there wasn't any real thrill. I almost enjoyed the fat-leg girls who rode the ponies two at a time and standing up, but their costumes weren't very pretty—just an ordinary polo shirt like you get if you run in the PAL meets and short skirts you can wear on either side like the big girls wear at the roller rink. And I almost enjoyed the jugglers except that my Uncle Bubba can juggle the dinner plates better any day of the week so long as Aunt

80 Hazel isn't there to stop him. I was impatient and started yawning. Finally all the clowns hitched up their baggy pants and tumbled over each other out of the ring and into the dark, the jugglers caught all the things that were up in the air and yawning just like me went off to the side. The pony girls brought their horses to a sudden stop that raised a lot of dust, then jumped down into the dirt and bowed. Then the ringmaster stepped into the circle of light and tipped his hat which was a little raggedy

from where I was sitting and said—"And now, Ladieeez and Gentlemen, what you've alll been waiting forrr, the Main aTTRACtion, the FLY FAMILEEE." And everyone jumped up to shout like crazy as they came running out on their toes to stand in the light and then climb the ropes. I took a deep breath and folded my arms over my chest and a kid next to me went into hiding, acting like she was going to tie her shoelaces.

There used to be four of them—the father, a big guy with a bald head and bushy mustache and shoulders and arms like King Kong; a tall lanky mother whom you'd never guess could even climb into a highchair or catch anything heavier than a Ping-Pong ball to look at her; the oldest son who looked like his father except he had hair on his head but none on his face and a big face it was, so that no matter how high up he got, you could always tell whether he was smiling or frowning or counting; the younger boy about thirteen, maybe, had a **vacant** stare like he was a million miles away feeding his turtles or something, any-thing but walking along a tightrope or flying through the air with his family. I had always liked to watch him because he was as cool as I was. But last summer the little girl got into the act. My grandmother says she's probably a midget cause no self-respecting mother would allow her child to be up there acting like a bird. "Just a baby," she'd say. "Can't be more than six years old. Should be home in bed. Must be a midget." My grandfather would give me a look when she started in and we'd smile at her together.

They almost got to me that last performance, dodging around with new routines and two at a time so that you didn't know which one Mr. Fly was going to save at the last minute. But he'd fly out and catch the little boy and swing over to the opposite stand where the big boy was flying out to catch them both by the wrists and the poor woman would be left kind of dangling there, **suspended,** then she'd do this double flip which would kill off everyone in the tent except me, of course, and swing out on the very bar she was on in the first place. And then

90

100

110

120

Underline the words in lines 88–90 where the spelling and capitalization help you "hear" the announcer.

VOCABULARY

vacant (vā′kənt) *adj.*: empty; suggesting lack of attention.

Vacant comes from the Latin word *vacare,* meaning "to be empty."

suspended (sə·spen′did) *v.* used as *adj.*: hanging by a support from above.

The verb *suspend* is from the Latin *sub–,* meaning "under," and *pendere,* meaning "to hang." *Suspend* has the same word origin as *suspense,* which can leave the reader "hanging," or waiting to learn what happens next.

Notes _____

_____

_____

_____

_____

_____

_____

_____

_____

_____

_____

What does Harriet mean when she says, "I almost thought I too had to tie my shoelaces" (line 128)?

_____

_____

_____

_____

_____

_____

_____

_____

_____

they'd mess around two or three flying at once just to confuse you until the big drum roll started and out steps the little girl in a party dress and huge blindfold wrapped around her little head and a pink umbrella like they sell down in Chinatown. And I almost—I won't lie about it—I almost let my heart thump me off the bench. I almost thought I too had to tie my shoelaces. But I sat there. Stubborn. And the kid starts bouncing up and

130   down on the rope like she was about to take off and tear through the canvas roof. Then out swings her little brother and before you know it, Fly Jr. like a great eagle with his arms flapping grabs up the kid, her eyeband in his teeth and swoops her off to the bar that's already got Mrs. Mr. and Big Bro on it and surely there's no room for him. And everyone's standing on their feet clutching at their faces. Everyone but me. Cause I know from the getgo that Mr. and Mrs. are going to leave the bar to give Jr. room and fly over to the other side. Which is exactly what they do. The lady in front of me, Mrs. Perez, who does all

140   the sewing in our neighborhood, gets up and starts shaking her hands like ladies do to get the fingernail polish dry and she says

to me with her eyes jammed shut "I must go finish the wedding gowns. Tell me later who died." And she scoots through the aisle, falling all over everybody with her eyes still shut and never looks up. And Mrs. Caine taps me on the back and leans over and says, "Some people just can't take it." And I smile at her and at her twins who're sitting there with their mouths open. I fold my arms over my chest and just dare the Fly family to do their very worst.

150 The minute I got to camp, I ran up to the main house where all the counselors gather to say hello to the parents and talk with the directors. I had to tell Mary the latest doings with the Fly family. But she put a finger to her mouth like she sometimes does to shush me. "Let's not have any scary stuff this summer, Harriet," she said, looking over my shoulder at a new kid. This new kid, Willie, was from my old neighborhood in Baltimore so we got friendly right off. Then he told me that he had a romantic heart so I quite naturally took him under my wing and decided not to give him a heart attack with any ghost tales. Mary
160 said he meant "rheumatic" heart, but I don't see any difference. So I told Mary to move him out of George's tent and give him a nicer counselor who'd respect his romantic heart. George used to be my play boyfriend when I first came to camp as a little kid and didn't know any better. But he's not a nice person. He makes up funny nicknames for people which aren't funny at all. Like calling Eddie Michaels the Watermelon Kid or David Farmer Charcoal Plenty which I really do not appreciate and especially from a counselor. And once he asked Joanne, who was the table monitor, to go and fetch a pail of milk from the kitchen. And the
170 minute she got up, he started hatching a plot, trying to get the kids to hide her peanut butter sandwich and put spiders in her soup. I had to remind everyone at the table that Joanne was my first cousin by blood, and that I would be forced to waste the

WORD STUDY

In the phrase "took him under my wing" (line 158), the narrator is using language in a **figurative** way. Why can't the phrase be read in a literal way? What does the phrase mean?

_____

_____

_____

_____

_____

_____

_____

_____

_____

WORD STUDY

In lines 157–162, Willie and Harriet confuse the words *romantic* and *rheumatic*. *Romantic* means "full of thoughts and feelings about romance or love." A *rheumatic* heart is a heart that has been damaged by rheumatic fever, a childhood illness. Underline the words that tell what the narrator does to help protect Willie's damaged heart.

DRAW CONCLUSIONS

Re-read lines 178–184. From her actions, how old do you think Harriet is?

_____

_____

VOCABULARY

proportions (prə·pôr′shənz) *n.:* size; dimensions.

Circle a familiar word inside the larger word. What does the smaller word mean?

_____

NARRATOR

Underline the sentence in lines 195–197 where the narrator describes how she treated the kids who laughed at Willie. Is she being **credible,** or honest, or is she exaggerating? Explain.

_____

_____

_____

_____

_____

_____

_____

_____

_____

first bum that laid a hand on her plate. And ole George says, "Oh don't be a dumbhead, Harriet. Jo's so stupid she won't even notice." And I told him right then and there that I was not his play girlfriend anymore and would rather marry the wolfman than grow up and be his wife. And just in case he didn't get the message, that night around campfire when we were all playing

180　Little Sally Walker sittin' in a saucer and it was my turn to shake it to the east and to shake it to the west and to shake it to the very one that I loved the best—I shook straight for Mr. Nelson the lifeguard, who was not only the ugliest person in camp but the arch enemy of ole George.

　　And that very first day of camp last summer when Willie came running up to me to get in line for lunch, here comes George talking some simple stuff about "What a beautiful head you have, Willie. A long, smooth, streamlined head. A sure sign of superior gifts. Definitely genius **proportions**." And poor Willie

190　went for it, grinning and carrying on and touching his head, which if you want to know the truth is a bullet head and that's all there is to it. And he's turning to me every which way, like he's modeling his head in a fashion show. And the minute his back is turned, ole George makes a face about Willie's head and all the kids in the line bust out laughing. So I had to beat up a few right then and there and finish off the rest later in the shower for being so stupid, laughing at a kid with a romantic heart.

One night in the last week of August when the big campfire party is held, it was very dark and the moon was all smoky, and

200　I just couldn't help myself and started in with a story about the great caterpillar who was going to prowl through the tents and nibble off everybody's toes. And Willie started this whimpering in the back of his throat so I had to switch the story real quick to something cheerful. But before I could do that, ole George picked up my story and added a wicked witch who put spells on city kids who come to camp, and a hunchback dwarf that chopped up tents and bunk beds, and a one-eyed phantom giant who gobbled up the hearts of underprivileged kids. And every time he got to the part where the phantom ripped out a heart, poor Willie would get louder and louder until finally he started rolling around in the grass and screaming and all the kids went crazy and scattered behind the rocks almost kicking the fire completely out as they dashed off into the darkness yelling bloody murder. And the counselors could hardly round us all up—me, too, I'm not going to lie about it. Their little circles of flashlight bobbing in and out of the bushes along the patches of pine, bumping into each other as they scrambled for us kids. And poor Willie rolling around something awful, so they took him to the infirmary.

I was sneaking some gingersnaps in to him later that night when I heard Mary and another senior counselor fussing at ole George in the hallway.

"You've been picking on that kid ever since he got here, George. But tonight was the limit—"

"I wasn't picking on him, I was just trying to tell a story—"

"All that talk about hearts, gobblin' up hearts, and underpriv—"

"Yeh, you were directing it all at the little kid. You should be—"

"I wasn't talking about him. They're all underprivileged kids, after all. I mean all the kids are underprivileged."

I huddled back into the shadows and almost banged into Willie's iron bed. I was hoping he'd open his eyes and wink at me and tell me he was just fooling. That it wasn't so bad to have an underprivileged heart. But he just slept. "I'm an underprivileged kid too," I thought to myself. I knew it was a special camp, but I'd never realized. No wonder Aunt Hazel screamed so about my scary stories and my mother flicked off the TV when the monsters came on and Mary was always shushing me. We all had bad hearts. I crawled into the supply cabinet to wait for Willie to wake up so I could ask him about it all. I ate all the

CONNECT

George is using the word *underprivileged* (line 208 and later in lines 226–231) to refer to groups who have suffered from poverty and discrimination, especially in education. The kids in the story do not understand what George means. If they *did* understand, how might the word make them feel?

_____

_____

_____

_____

CLARIFY

Pause to re-read lines 230–240. What has Harriet overheard the counselors say? What does she misunderstand?

_____

_____

_____

_____

_____

_____

_____

_____

IDENTIFY

In lines 255–258, underline the two actions Harriet will take to "help" her heart.

INTERPRET

Pause at line 271. What does Harriet mean when she says she has lost the battle with the Fly family?

_____

_____

_____

INTERPRET

Think about the story's title. What two kinds of "delicate heart condition" are in the story?

_____

_____

_____

_____

_____

_____

gingersnaps but I didn't feel any better. You have a romantic heart, I whispered to myself settling down among the bandages. You will have to be very careful.

It didn't make any difference to Aunt Hazel that I had changed, that I no longer told scary stories or dragged my schoolmates to the latest creature movie, or raced my friends to the edge of the roof, or held my breath, or ran under the train rail when the train was already in sight. As far as she was concerned, I was still
250 the same ole spooky kid I'd always been. So Joanne was kept at home. My mother noticed the difference, but she said over the phone to my grandmother, "She's acting very ladylike these days, growing up." I didn't tell her about my secret, that I knew about my heart. And I was kind of glad Joanne wasn't around 'cause I would have blabbed it all to her and scared her to death. When school starts again, I decided, I'll ask my teacher how to outgrow my underprivileged heart. I'll train myself, just like I did with the Fly family.

"Well, I guess you'll want some change to go to the fair
260 again, hunh?" my mother said coming into my room dumping things in her pocketbook.

"No," I said. "I'm too grown up for circuses."

She put the money on the dresser anyway. I was lying, of course. I was thinking what a terrible strain it would be for Mrs. Perez and everybody else if while sitting there, with the Fly family zooming around in the open air a million miles above the ground, little Harriet Watkins should drop dead with a fatal heart attack behind them.

"I lost," I said out loud.
270 "Lost what?"

"The battle with the Fly family."

She just stood there a long time looking at me, trying to figure me out, the way mothers are always doing but should know better. Then she kissed me goodbye and left for work.

My Delicate Heart Condition

Narrator Profile To fully understand characters in a story, you take note of what they say and what they do, and you draw conclusions about them. Fill in the following chart with the conclusions you draw about Harriet, this story's narrator. Base your conclusions on her words and actions, which are cited in the left-hand column.

Harriet's Words and Actions	My Conclusions
"The truth is I sometimes like to tell stories about bloodthirsty vampires or ugly monsters that lurk in clothes closets or giant beetles that eat their way through the shower curtain. . . ."	
"And from the wheel of fortune to the tent was at least a million stands selling B.B. bats and jawbreakers and gingerbread and sweet potato pie and frozen custard. . . ."	
"I had to remind everyone at the table that Joanne was my first cousin by blood, and that I would be forced to waste the first bum that laid a hand on her plate."	
"So I had to beat up a few right then and there and finish off the rest later in the shower for being so stupid, laughing at a kid with a romantic heart."	
"'I'm an underprivileged kid too.' . . . No wonder Aunt Hazel screamed so about my scary stories and my mother flicked off the TV when the monsters came on and Mary was always shushing me."	

Standards Review

 **My Delicate Heart Condition**

Complete the sample test item below. Then, read the explanation at right.

Sample Test Item	Explanation of the Correct Answer
Who is telling the story? **A** an unnamed narrator **B** Joanne **C** Mary, the counselor **D** Harriet	The correct answer is *D*. Harriet tells the story, using the words *I* and *me* to refer to herself. *A* is not correct because we know who the narrator is. Joanne (*B*) and Mary (*C*) are story characters, but neither one tells the story.

DIRECTIONS: Circle the letter of each correct response.

1. Which of the following is *not* true about Harriet?

   A She is a first-person narrator.

   B She tells us what Willie is thinking.

   C She tells us what she is feeling.

   D She refers to herself as *I* and *me.*

2. Which of the following passages indicates that Harriet is not always a **credible** narrator?

   F "For four summers now, me and the Fly family have had this thing going."

   G "And I almost—I won't lie about it—I almost let my heart thump me off the bench."

   H "Then he told me that he had a romantic heart so I quite naturally took him under my wing. . . ."

   J "I ate all the gingersnaps but I didn't feel any better."

3. At the end of the story, Harriet doesn't want to go to the circus because—

   A her mother is forcing her to go

   B she wants to be more ladylike

   C circuses have become too expensive

   D she knows that she cannot always overcome her fear

4. Harriet's choice of words and her descriptions give the story its special—

   F plot

   G voice

   H ending

   J sadness

Reading Standard 3.9
Explain how voice, persona, and the choice of a narrator affect characterization and the tone, plot, and credibility of a text.

Standards Review

 **My Delicate Heart Condition**

Literal and Figurative Meaning

DIRECTIONS: Circle the letter of each correct response.

Reading Standard 1.1 Identify and use the literal and figurative meanings of words and understand word derivations.

1. The phrase "a battle of nerves"—

   A means that nerve cells are fighting

   B has nothing to do with nerves

   C suggests a mental and not a physical conflict

   D means that people are scared

2. Which of these passages does *not* contain **figurative language?**

   F "Then she'd do this double flip which would kill off everyone in the tent...."

   G "I almost let my heart thump me off the bench...."

   H "Before you know it, Fly Jr. like a great eagle with his arms flapping grabs up the kid...."

   J "And I smile at her and at her twins...."

3. When Harriet says she hopes to outgrow her "underprivileged heart," she is using **figurative language** to suggest that—

   A her heart is too small for her body

   B she wants to be brave and self-confident again

   C she needs money for an operation

   D she may need a heart transplant

Vocabulary in Context

DIRECTIONS: Complete the paragraph below by writing each word from the box in the correct numbered blank.

Word Box

suspended

withstand

proportions

vacant

I'm trying to learn how to (1)_____ the disappointments of life. Recently I went into a dress shop. (2)_____ from the ceiling were hundreds of lights, casting a glow on the clothes below. I wanted to buy everything, but my budget doesn't have the (3)_____ of a millionaire's bank account. Next time I pass the shop, I'll put on a (4)_____ expression, and my thoughts will be far, far away.

 Before You Go On ...

Check your Standards Mastery at the back of this book.

Chapter

4

Comparing Themes

Academic Vocabulary for Chapter 4

These are the terms you should know
as you read and analyze the selections in this chapter.

———————

Subject The topic of a work of literature. The subject can usually be stated in a single word or phrase, such as *love, war, childhood, growing up, aging.*

Theme The general idea or insight about human life that a work of literature reveals. The theme can be stated in one or more sentences. A theme on the subject of love might be: *True love survives all obstacles.* A theme on the subject of war might be: *War destroys the good along with the bad.*

Generalization A broad statement that applies to many individuals, experiences, situations, or observations. A generalization is a kind of conclusion that is drawn after considering as many facts as possible. Themes are expressed as generalizations.

Genres The different forms of literature. Genres include short stories, novels, plays, and poems.

Universal themes Themes that can be found in literature from different times, countries, and cultures. Universal themes cross genres as well as national boundaries, languages, customs, and historic periods. An example of a universal theme is: *A hero often must sacrifice something precious in order to reach a goal.*

Conflict A struggle between opposing characters or opposing forces. In an **external conflict,** a character struggles against an opposing force such as another character, society as a whole, or a force of nature. An **internal conflict** takes place within a character's own mind. It is a struggle between opposing needs, desires, or emotions.

Reading Standard 1.1 Identify and use the literal and figurative meanings of words and understand word derivations.

Reading Standard 3.2 Compare and contrast the presentation of a similar theme or topic across genres to explain how the selection of genre shapes the theme or topic.

Reading Standard 3.3 (Grade 8 Review) Compare and contrast motivations and reactions of literary characters from different historical eras confronting similar situations or conflicts.

Reading Standard 3.5 Compare works that express a universal theme and provide evidence to support the ideas expressed in each work.

For Further Information ...

Be sure to read these essays in *Holt Literature and Language Arts:*

- **Theme,** pages 208–209.
- **Comparing Universal Themes,** page 210.
- **Comparing a Theme Across Genres,** page 244.

The Sniper by Liam O'Flaherty / Thoughts of Hanoi by Nguyen Thi Vinh

The short story "The Sniper" is set in Dublin, Ireland, in the 1920s, during a time of bitter civil war. The Republicans, on one side, wanted all of Ireland to become a republic, totally free from British rule. The Free Staters, on the other side, were willing to allow continued English rule over six counties in the northern part of Ireland. The poem "Thoughts of Hanoi" is set in the Vietnam of the 1960s, when armies from North Vietnam and South Vietnam fought to control the entire country.

LITERARY FOCUS: THEME AND CONFLICT

A **theme** is what a story reveals about life or human nature. One way to discover a theme is to pay close attention to conflict faced by the main character in a short story or by the speaker in a poem. A **conflict** is a struggle between opposing forces. The conflict can be **external**—between two characters or between a character and an outside force such as society or nature—or **internal**—between opposing desires or needs in a character's own mind or heart. In stories and poems about war, the theme may be revealed by how the conflict affects the characters and what they discover as the story or poem ends.

- As you read "The Sniper," ask yourself what the main character has discovered at the end of the story.
- As you read "Thoughts of Hanoi," ask yourself what the speaker is saying to the person he addresses as "Brother."

READING SKILLS: MAKING PREDICTIONS

Predictions are guesses about what will happen. Active readers always make predictions as they read a story. They base their predictions on details in the story and on their own experience.

Before you read "The Sniper," fill in the Predictions Chart below using what you know from the title and from your knowledge of the subject of war. Then, make one or two predictions about what might happen in the story. The first row has been filled in as an example.

What You Know	Predictions
Snipers have guns. In war, people get killed.	One or more people will get killed, maybe including the sniper.

Reading Standard 1.1 Identify and use the literal and figurative meanings of words and understand word derivations.

Reading Standard 3.3 (Grade 8 Review) Compare and contrast motivations and reactions of literary characters from different historical eras confronting similar situations or conflicts.

Reading Standard 3.5 Compare works that express a universal theme and provide evidence to support the ideas expressed in each work.

SHORT STORY/ POEM

VOCABULARY DEVELOPMENT

PREVIEW SELECTION VOCABULARY

The following words appear in "The Sniper." Before you read the story, become familiar with them.

beleaguered (bē·lē′gərd) *v.* used as *adj.*: surrounded and under attack.

*The bullets whizzed by, trapping the **beleaguered** soldier.*

ascetic (ə·set′ik) *adj.*: severe; also, self-disciplined.

*The soldier's **ascetic** lifestyle had prepared him for the hardships of war.*

fanatic (fə·nat′ik) *n.*: person whose extreme devotion to a cause is excessive or unreasonable.

*Only a **fanatic** would enlist in an army that faced certain defeat.*

ruse (ro͞oz) *n.*: trick.

*Using a clever **ruse,** the soldiers fooled their enemy.*

silhouetted (sil′ə·wet′id) *v.* used as *adj.*: outlined.

*The face, **silhouetted** against the wall at sundown, was a living shadow.*

remorse (ri·môrs′) *n.*: deep guilt.

*Did the killer feel **remorse** for his actions?*

WORD HISTORIES

Like people, many words have fascinating pasts. The story behind the word *silhouetted* (see line 96 of "The Sniper") is especially interesting.

By 1759, France was on the brink of bankruptcy. Madame de Pompadour convinced King Louis XV to replace the head of the treasury with a friend of hers, Etienne de Silhouette. He jumped right into the job and began preaching thrift and economy. Meanwhile, the old art form of tracing and cutting out the outline of shadows had become popular again. Because these profiles were the cheapest way to reproduce a person's likeness, they were mocked as being *à la Silhouette.* Etienne de Silhouette lost his job within the year, but his name lives on in the art of creating shadow outlines.

As you read, keep track of words whose histories you'd like to track down.

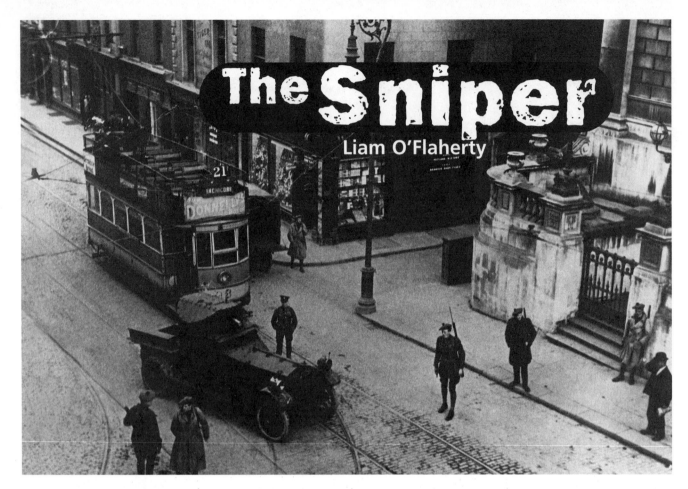

The Sniper

Liam O'Flaherty

The long June twilight faded into night. Dublin lay enveloped in darkness but for the dim light of the moon that shone through fleecy clouds, casting a pale light as of approaching dawn over the streets and the dark waters of the Liffey.[1] Around the **beleaguered** Four Courts[2] the heavy guns roared. Here and there through the city, machine guns and rifles broke the silence of the night, spasmodically, like dogs barking on lone farms. Republicans and Free Staters were waging civil war.

On a rooftop near O'Connell Bridge, a Republican sniper
10 lay watching. Beside him lay his rifle and over his shoulders was slung a pair of field glasses. His face was the face of a student, thin and **ascetic,** but his eyes had the cold gleam of the **fanatic.** They were deep and thoughtful, the eyes of a man who is used to looking at death.

---

1. **Liffey:** river that runs through Dublin.
2. **Four Courts:** government buildings in Dublin.

He was eating a sandwich hungrily. He had eaten nothing since morning. He had been too excited to eat. He finished the sandwich, and, taking a flask of whiskey from his pocket, he took a short draft. Then he returned the flask to his pocket. He paused for a moment, considering whether he should risk a

20 smoke. It was dangerous. The flash might be seen in the darkness, and there were enemies watching. He decided to take the risk.

Placing a cigarette between his lips, he struck a match, inhaled the smoke hurriedly, and put out the light. Almost immediately, a bullet flattened itself against the parapet[3] of the roof. The sniper took another whiff and put out the cigarette. Then he swore softly and crawled away to the left.

Cautiously he raised himself and peered over the parapet. There was a flash and a bullet whizzed over his head. He

30 dropped immediately. He had seen the flash. It came from the opposite side of the street.

He rolled over the roof to a chimney stack in the rear and slowly drew himself up behind it, until his eyes were level with the top of the parapet. There was nothing to be seen—just the dim outline of the opposite housetop against the blue sky. His enemy was under cover.

Just then an armored car came across the bridge and advanced slowly up the street. It stopped on the opposite side of the street, fifty yards ahead. The sniper could hear the dull pant-

40 ing of the motor. His heart beat faster. It was an enemy car. He wanted to fire, but he knew it was useless. His bullets would never pierce the steel that covered the gray monster.

Then round the corner of a side street came an old woman, her head covered by a tattered shawl. She began to talk to the man in the turret[4] of the car. She was pointing to the roof where the sniper lay. An informer.

---

3. **parapet** (par′ə·pet′) *n.:* low wall or railing.
4. **turret** (tʉr′it) *n.:* low, usually revolving structure for guns on a tank or warship.

PREDICT

What do you **predict** the sniper will do, based on the description in lines 9–14?

_____

_____

CONFLICT

Pause at line 31. Does the sniper face an **external conflict** (a struggle against another person, society, or nature) or an **internal conflict** (a struggle within himself)?

_____

_____

PREDICT

Re-read lines 43–46. Circle the word that identifies the woman's role in the war. Underline the sentences that describe her actions. What do you **predict** will happen to the woman?

_____

_____

_____

_____

_____

_____

Pause at line 51. Why does the sniper kill the man in the turret?

_____

_____

_____

Read the boxed passage aloud three times. Improve the speed and the smoothness of your delivery each time you read.

Re-read this page. Think about what has happened. What do you learn about the effects of war?

_____

_____

_____

_____

_____

_____

_____

_____

_____

_____

The turret opened. A man's head and shoulders appeared, looking toward the sniper. The sniper raised his rifle and fired. The head fell heavily on the turret wall. The woman darted
50 toward the side street. The sniper fired again. The woman whirled round and fell with a shriek into the gutter.

Suddenly from the opposite roof a shot rang out and the sniper dropped his rifle with a curse. The rifle clattered to the roof. The sniper thought the noise would wake the dead. He stooped to pick the rifle up. He couldn't lift it. His forearm was dead. "I'm hit," he muttered.

Dropping flat onto the roof, he crawled back to the parapet. With his left hand he felt the injured right forearm. The blood was oozing through the sleeve of his coat. There was no
60 pain—just a deadened sensation, as if the arm had been cut off.

Quickly he drew his knife from his pocket, opened it on the breastwork[5] of the parapet, and ripped open the sleeve. There was a small hole where the bullet had entered. On the other side there was no hole. The bullet had lodged in the bone. It must have fractured it. He bent the arm below the wound. The arm bent back easily. He ground his teeth to overcome the pain.

Then taking out his field dressing, he ripped open the packet with his knife. He broke the neck of the iodine bottle and let the bitter fluid drip into the wound. A paroxysm[6] of pain swept
70 through him. He placed the cotton wadding over the wound and wrapped the dressing over it. He tied the ends with his teeth.

Then he lay still against the parapet, and, closing his eyes, he made an effort of will to overcome the pain.

In the street beneath all was still. The armored car had retired speedily over the bridge, with the machine gunner's head hanging lifeless over the turret. The woman's corpse lay still in the gutter.

The sniper lay still for a long time nursing his wounded arm and planning escape. Morning must not find him wounded

---

5. **breastwork** *n.:* low wall put up as a military defense.
6. **paroxysm** (par′ək·siz′əm) *n.:* sudden attack; fit.

80 on the roof. The enemy on the opposite roof covered his escape. He must kill that enemy and he could not use his rifle. He had only a revolver to do it. Then he thought of a plan.

Taking off his cap, he placed it over the muzzle of his rifle. Then he pushed the rifle slowly upward over the parapet, until the cap was visible from the opposite side of the street. Almost immediately there was a report,[7] and a bullet pierced the center of the cap. The sniper slanted the rifle forward. The cap slipped down into the street. Then, catching the rifle in the middle, the sniper dropped his left hand over the roof and let it hang, life-

90 lessly. After a few moments he let the rifle drop to the street. Then he sank to the roof, dragging his hand with him.

Crawling quickly to the left, he peered up at the corner of the roof. His **ruse** had succeeded. The other sniper, seeing the cap and rifle fall, thought that he had killed his man. He was now standing before a row of chimney pots, looking across, with his head clearly **silhouetted** against the western sky.

The Republican sniper smiled and lifted his revolver above the edge of the parapet. The distance was about fifty yards—a hard shot in the dim light, and his right arm was paining him

100 like a thousand devils. He took a steady aim. His hand trembled with eagerness. Pressing his lips together, he took a deep breath through his nostrils and fired. He was almost deafened with the report and his arm shook with the recoil.

Then when the smoke cleared he peered across and uttered a cry of joy. His enemy had been hit. He was reeling over the parapet in his death agony. He struggled to keep his feet, but he was slowly falling forward, as if in a dream. The rifle fell from his grasp, hit the parapet, fell over, bounded off the pole of a barber's shop beneath, and then clattered on the pavement.

110 Then the dying man on the roof crumpled up and fell forward. The body turned over and over in space and hit the ground with a dull thud. Then it lay still.

---

7. **report** (ri·pôrt') *n.:* loud noise; in this case, from a gunshot.

PREDICT

Pause at line 82. What do you think the sniper's plan will be?

_____

_____

_____

CHARACTER

Re-read lines 83–96. Underline the sentences that describe the sniper's actions.

VOCABULARY

ruse (rōōz) *n.:* trick.

silhouetted (sil'ə·wet'id) *v.* used as *adj.:* outlined.

INFER

Underline the words in line 105 that reveal the sniper's feelings. What has the sniper done that causes these feelings?

_____

_____

_____

_____

_____

_____

THEME

Re-read lines 113–119. How have the sniper's feelings about war changed?

_____

_____

_____

_____

PREDICT

Pause at line 140. Who do you predict the sniper's enemy will be?

_____

_____

_____

THEME

What **theme** does the story's ending reveal? State your answer as a sentence.

_____

_____

_____

_____

_____

_____

_____

The sniper looked at his enemy falling and he shuddered. The lust of battle died in him. He became bitten by **remorse.** The sweat stood out in beads on his forehead. Weakened by his wound and the long summer day of fasting and watching on the roof, he revolted from the sight of the shattered mass of his dead enemy. His teeth chattered, he began to gibber to himself, cursing the war, cursing himself, cursing everybody.

120　　He looked at the smoking revolver in his hand, and with an oath he hurled it to the roof at his feet. The revolver went off with the concussion and the bullet whizzed past the sniper's head. He was frightened back to his senses by the shock. His nerves steadied. The cloud of fear scattered from his mind and he laughed.

Taking the whiskey flask from his pocket, he emptied it at a draft. He felt reckless under the influence of the spirit. He decided to leave the roof now and look for his company commander, to report. Everywhere around was quiet. There was not

130　　much danger in going through the streets. He picked up his revolver and put it in his pocket. Then he crawled down through the skylight to the house underneath.

When the sniper reached the laneway on the street level, he felt a sudden curiosity as to the identity of the enemy sniper whom he had killed. He decided that he was a good shot, whoever he was. He wondered did he know him. Perhaps he had been in his own company before the split in the army. He decided to risk going over to have a look at him. He peered around the corner into O'Connell Street. In the upper part of the street

140　　there was heavy firing, but around here all was quiet.

The sniper darted across the street. A machine gun tore up the ground around him with a hail of bullets, but he escaped. He threw himself face downward beside the corpse. The machine gun stopped.

Then the sniper turned over the dead body and looked into his brother's face.

Thoughts of Hanoi

Nguyen Thi Vinh
translated by **Nguyen Ngoc Bich with Burton Raffel and W. S. Merwin**

The night is deep and chill
as in early autumn. Pitchblack,
it thickens after each lightning flash.
I dream of Hanoi:
5   Co-ngu[1] Road
ten years of separation
the way back sliced by a frontier of hatred.
I want to bury the past
to burn the future
10   still I yearn
still I fear
those endless nights
waiting for dawn.

Brother,
15   how is Hang Dao[2] now?
How is Ngoc Son[3] temple?
Do the trains still run
each day from Hanoi

---

1. **Co-ngu** (kō′nōō′)
2. **Hang Dao** (häŋ′dou′)
3. **Ngoc Son** (nōk′sōn′)

IDENTIFY

Underline the words in lines 4–7 that tell how long it has been since the speaker was last in Hanoi. What is the "frontier of hatred"?

_____

_____

_____

INFER

Pause at line 22. Who is the speaker of the poem? Who is the speaker addressing as "Brother"?

_____

_____

_____

_____

_____

_____

to the neighboring towns?

20 To Bac-ninh, Cam-giang, Yen-bai,[4]

the small villages, islands

of brown thatch in a lush green sea?

The girls
    bright eyes
        ruddy cheeks
25 four-piece dresses
        raven-bill scarves
    sowing harvesting
        spinning weaving
30 all year round,
the boys
    plowing
        transplanting
    in the fields
35   in their shops
    running across
        the meadow at evening
    to fly kites
        and sing alternating songs.

40 Stainless blue sky,
    jubilant voices of children
stumbling through the alphabet,
    village graybeards strolling to the
                    temple,
grandmothers basking in the twilight sun,
45   chewing betel leaves
while the children run—

---

4. **Bac-ninh** (bäk'nin'), **Cam-giang** (käm'gyäŋ'), **Yen-bai** (yēn'bī'): towns near Hanoi.

WORD STUDY

Imagery is language that appeals to the senses. Underline words and phrases in lines 23–46 that help you see, hear, feel, or taste how the speaker remembers village life. Circle the **verbs** that tell you what the villagers are doing.

FLUENCY

Read the boxed passage aloud twice. The first time, decide how you will read the short lines and how you will convey basic meaning. The second time, give emphasis to the words that will help improve your interpretation of the lines.

INFER

Why does the speaker wonder if the village life he remembers has changed (lines 47–49)?

Brother,
how is all that now?
Or is it obsolete?
50 Are you like me,
reliving the past,
imagining the future?
Do you count me as a friend
or am I the enemy in your eyes?
55 Brother, I am afraid
that one day I'll be with the March-North Army
meeting you on your way to the South.
I might be the one to shoot you then
or you me
60 but please
not with hatred.
For don't you remember how it was,
you and I in school together,
plotting our lives together?
65 Those roots go deep!

Brother, we are men,
conscious of more
than material needs.
How can this happen to us
70 my friend
my foe?

CONFLICT

Re-read lines 53–57. What is the conflict between the speaker and the person addressed as "Brother"?

_____

_____

THEME

Underline the speaker's fear in lines 58–59. What **theme** does this fear reveal? How is it similar to a theme from "The Sniper"?

_____

_____

_____

_____

THEME

The speaker reminds Brother of their long friendship and of their values. What message about life do you think he is giving to Brother and to readers?

_____

_____

_____

_____

_____

_____

_____

The Sniper / Thoughts of Hanoi

Theme Chart Both "The Sniper" and "Thoughts of Hanoi" describe the effects of a civil war. Use the following Theme Chart to determine what universal theme the two selections share. Remember that there is no one correct answer.

	The Sniper	Thoughts of Hanoi
Main character / speaker:		
Conflict:		
Character's / speaker's motive:		
What the character discovers / What the speaker says:		
Common Theme(s):		

Standards Review

LITERATURE

 **The Sniper / Thoughts of Hanoi**

Complete the sample test item below. The box at the right explains why three of these choices are not correct.

Sample Test Item	Explanation of the Correct Answer
The title "The Sniper" suggests that — **A** the story takes place in Ireland **B** the story has only one character **C** the sniper will be hurt **D** the story is about a killer	The answer is *D*. A *sniper* is a type of killer, so the story is probably about a killer. *A* is not correct because there may be snipers anywhere, not just in Ireland. *B* is not correct because the title doesn't say how many characters are in the story. *C* is incorrect because the title doesn't say that the sniper will be hurt.

DIRECTIONS: Circle the letter of the best response.

1. The sniper's **external conflict** involves his —

   A sorrow over killing the old woman

   B anger over being spied on

   C struggle with his enemy

   D extreme hunger

2. The sniper experiences an **internal conflict** when —

   F he feels confused sorrow after killing his enemy

   G his enemy shoots at him

   H the armored car comes down the street

   J his arm is broken

3. The speaker in "Thoughts of Hanoi" remembers people in his village as —

   A oppressed by hard work

   B worn out from fighting

   C unaware of the world around them

   D happily working and playing

4. Which sentence best expresses a **theme** the story and poem share?

   F Brothers shouldn't fight each other.

   G All war should be illegal.

   H War can turn friends and families against one another.

   J People should be allowed to enjoy life in peace.

Reading Standard 3.3 (Grade 8 Review) Compare and contrast motivations and reactions of literary characters from different historical eras confronting similar situations or conflicts.

Reading Standard 3.5 Compare works that express a universal theme and provide evidence to support the ideas expressed in each work.

Standards Review

 **The Sniper**

Word Histories

Reading Standard 1.1
Identify and use the literal and figurative meaning of words and understand word derivations.

DIRECTIONS: Match each word with its history by writing the correct letter on the lines provided.

1. _____ bologna

2. _____ snail mail

3. _____ sabotage

4. _____ sofa

a. Compared to the speed of electronic mail, regular mail seems to move very slowly. So letters sent through the post office are sometimes called —

b. French workers, angry at conditions in the factories, threw their wooden shoes, or *sabots*, into the machinery. The act of damaging machinery as a way of reaching a goal is called —

c. For a cozy place to rest, Arabs piled cushions and rugs on a platform called a *suffa*. In English the word became —

d. The city of Bologna, Italy, is famous for its sausages. The city gave its name to —

Vocabulary in Context

DIRECTIONS: Complete the paragraph below by writing the correct word from the box to fit each numbered blank. Not all words will be used.

Word Box

fanatic

ascetic

remorse

beleaguered

ruse

silhouetted

Lisa felt (1) _____ by enemy forces. Her friends and family couldn't understand her (2) _____ lifestyle—the strict training routines and schedules she followed. They thought she was a (3) _____ for her devotion to figure skating. They came up with one (4) _____ after another to encourage her to skip practice and stay out late. They felt (5) _____, however, when Lisa qualified for a national competition.

 Before You Go On . . .

Check your Standards Mastery at the back of this book.

The Moustache by Robert Cormier / Fifteen by William Stafford

BEFORE YOU READ

Seventeen-year-old Mike has grown a moustache, which makes him look older. He resists shaving it off, even though his mother and girlfriend ask him to. Read the story to find out what surprising event finally prompts Mike to get rid of his prized moustache.

The fifteen-year-old speaker of "Fifteen" finds a motorcycle abandoned, but still running, and fantasizes about riding away. This chance event helps guide the boy to adulthood. As you read the story and poem, compare these different works to find what makes them similar.

LITERARY FOCUS: THEME AND GENRE

Theme is an insight about life conveyed in literature. All types of literature can convey a theme. How that theme is conveyed, however, depends on the type of literature. The theme of a short story can often be discovered by noticing how the main character changes and what he or she has discovered by the end of the story. In poems, a theme may be discovered by noting the repetition of key ideas, by looking at word choice, by listening to the sounds of the poem, or by thinking about the poem's title.

- As you read "The Moustache," notice how Mike's experiences change his attitudes. Think about how those changes point to the theme.
- As you read "Fifteen," focus on word choice and the refrain—the repeated lines.

READING SKILLS: MAKING INFERENCES

Themes in literature are usually not stated directly. To discover a theme, you have to think about all the elements of the work and then make an inference. An **inference** is a kind of guess based on clues in the text.

Look for evidence in "The Moustache" that helps you understand what Mike, the narrator and main character, discovers about his grandmother. In "Fifteen," look for clues that help you learn what the speaker is saying about being fifteen years old.

VOCABULARY DEVELOPMENT

PREVIEW SELECTION VOCABULARY

Before you read "The Moustache," become familiar with the following words.

chronic (krä′nik) *adj.:* lasting a long time; constant.

> *Because of her **chronic** illness, the woman lives in a nursing home.*

sterile (ster′əl) *adj.:* free from germs.

> *The **sterile** dressing keeps the wound clean.*

lucid (lo͞o′sid) *adj.:* clearheaded.

> *On her **lucid** days, the woman recognizes her visiting family.*

conspiratorial (kən·spir′ə·tôr′ē·əl) *adj.:* suggesting a secret plot.

> *The nurse tries to draw the visitor in with a **conspiratorial** wink.*

regally (rē′gəl·ē) *adv.:* majestically; in the manner of a queen or king.

> *Although in a hospital bed, the woman spoke **regally** to those who visited her.*

WORD ROOTS

Many English words are based on root words from the classical languages of Greek and Latin. The **root** of every word carries the word's core meaning. When you learn the root of one word, it can often help you to understand the meaning of other words. For instance, the Greek root *chron* or *chronos* means "time." Knowing this, you can probably figure out the meaning of:

  chronic—lasting a long time; constant
  chronicle—a narrative or historical record of events, in time order
  chronological—arranged in time order, the order of occurrence
  chronology—the arrangement of events in order of occurrence

Vocabulary notes in the selection will give you information about word origins.

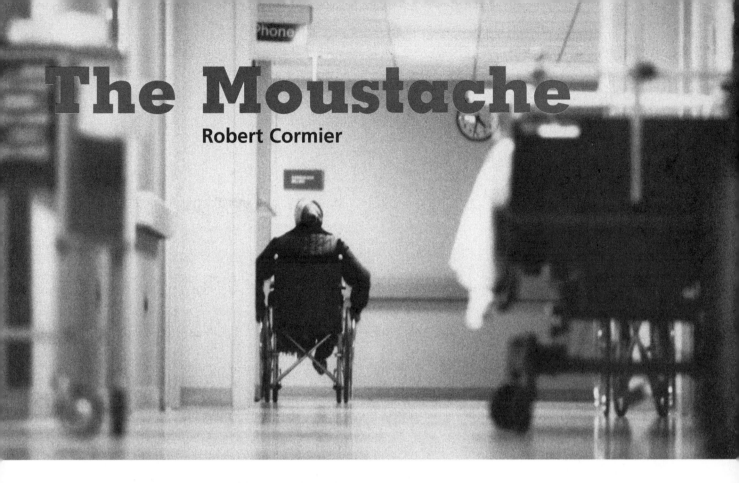

The Moustache

Robert Cormier

At the last minute Annie couldn't go. She was invaded by one of
those twenty-four-hour flu bugs that sent her to bed with a
fever, moaning about the fact that she'd also have to break her
date with Handsome Harry Arnold that night. We call him
Handsome Harry because he's actually handsome, but he's also a
nice guy, cool, and he doesn't treat me like Annie's kid brother,
which I am, but like a regular person. Anyway, I had to go to
Lawnrest alone that afternoon. But first of all I had to stand
inspection. My mother lined me up against the wall. She stood
10   there like a one-man firing squad, which is kind of funny
because she's not like a man at all, she's very feminine, and we
have this great friendship—I mean, I feel as if she really likes
me. I realize that sounds strange, but I know guys whose mothers
love them and cook special stuff for them and worry about them
and all but there's something missing in their relationship.

Anyway. She frowned and started the routine.

"That hair," she said. Then admitted: "Well, at least you
combed it."

WORD STUDY

A **simile** is a comparison,
using the words *like, as,* or
than, of unlike things.
Underline the simile in lines
9–10 the narrator uses to
describe his mom.

IDENTIFY

Pause at line 15. Who is
telling the story? (His name is
not given yet.)

_____

_____

_____

_____

_____

_____

_____

_____

_____

_____

CLARIFY

Why is Mike's moustache costing him money (lines 29–33)?

_____

_____

_____

_____

_____

_____

_____

INFER

Pause at line 46. Why does a shadow fall across Mike's mother's face?

_____

_____

_____

_____

_____

_____

_____

I sighed. I have discovered that it's better to sigh than
20   argue.

"And that moustache." She shook her head. "I still say a seventeen-year-old has no business wearing a moustache."

"It's an experiment," I said. "I just wanted to see if I could grow one." To tell the truth, I had proved my point about being able to grow a decent moustache, but I also had learned to like it.

"It's costing you money, Mike," she said.

"I know, I know."

The money was a reference to the movies. The Downtown
30   Cinema has a special Friday night offer—half-price admission for high school couples seventeen or younger. But the woman in the box office took one look at my moustache and charged me full price. Even when I showed her my driver's license. She charged full admission for Cindy's ticket, too, which left me practically broke and unable to take Cindy out for a hamburger with the crowd afterward. That didn't help matters, because Cindy has been getting impatient recently about things like the fact that I don't own my own car and have to concentrate on my studies if I want to win that college scholarship, for instance.
40   Cindy wasn't exactly crazy about the moustache, either.

Now it was my mother's turn to sigh.

"Look," I said, to cheer her up. "I'm thinking about shaving it off." Even though I wasn't. Another discovery: You can build a way of life on postponement.

"Your grandmother probably won't even recognize you," she said. And I saw the shadow fall across her face.

Let me tell you what the visit to Lawnrest was all about. My grandmother is seventy-three years old. She is a resident—which is supposed to be a better word than *patient*—at the Lawnrest
50   Nursing Home. She used to make the greatest turkey dressing in the world and was a nut about baseball and could even quote batting averages, for crying out loud. She always rooted for the losers. She was in love with the Mets until they started to win.

Now she has arteriosclerosis, which the dictionary says is "a **chronic** disease characterized by abnormal thickening and hardening of the arterial[1] walls." Which really means that she can't live at home anymore or even with us, and her memory has betrayed her, as well as her body. She used to wander off and sometimes didn't recognize people. My mother visits her all the time, driving the thirty miles to Lawnrest almost every day. Because Annie was home for a semester break from college, we had decided to make a special Saturday visit. Now Annie was in bed, groaning theatrically—she's a drama major—but I told my mother I'd go anyway. I hadn't seen my grandmother since she'd been admitted to Lawnrest. Besides, the place is located on the Southwest Turnpike, which meant I could barrel along in my father's new Le Mans. My ambition was to see the speedometer hit seventy-five. Ordinarily, I used the old station wagon, which can barely stagger up to fifty.

Frankly, I wasn't too crazy about visiting a nursing home. They reminded me of hospitals, and hospitals turn me off. I mean, the smell of ether[2] makes me nauseous, and I feel faint at the sight of blood. And as I approached Lawnrest—which is a terrible, cemetery kind of name, to begin with—I was sorry I hadn't avoided the trip. Then I felt guilty about it. I'm loaded with guilt complexes. Like driving like a madman after promising my father to be careful. Like sitting in the parking lot, looking at the nursing home with dread and thinking how I'd rather be with Cindy. Then I thought of all the Christmas and birthday gifts my grandmother had given me and I got out of the car, guilty as usual.

Inside, I was surprised by the lack of hospital smell, although there was another odor or maybe the absence of an odor. The air was antiseptic, **sterile**. As if there was no

---

1. **arterial:** of the arteries, the tubes that carry blood away from the heart.
2. **ether** (ē′thər): strong-smelling anesthetic (substance used to deaden pain or cause unconsciousness).

60

70

80

VOCABULARY

chronic (krä′nik) *adj.:* lasting a long time; constant.

Chronic is derived from the Greek root *chron* or *chronos*, meaning "time."

IDENTIFY CAUSE & EFFECT

Why is Mike going alone to the nursing home (lines 61–69)? Underline the reasons, or causes.

EVALUATE

Re-read lines 70–81. What do you learn about Mike's **character**? Is he a typical teenager?

_____

_____

_____

_____

_____

_____

_____

VOCABULARY

sterile (ster′əl) *adj.:* free from germs.

Sterile comes from the Greek *steira*, meaning "barren."

atmosphere at all or I'd caught a cold suddenly and couldn't taste or smell.

A nurse at the reception desk gave me directions—my grandmother was in East Three. I made my way down the tiled corridor and was glad to see that the walls were painted with

90 cheerful colors like yellow and pink. A wheelchair suddenly shot around a corner, self-propelled by an old man, white-haired and toothless, who cackled merrily as he barely missed me. I jumped aside—here I was, almost getting wiped out by a two-mile-an-hour wheelchair after doing seventy-five on the pike. As I walked through the corridor seeking East Three, I couldn't help glancing into the rooms, and it was like some kind of wax museum—all these figures in various stances and attitudes,[3] sitting in beds or chairs, standing at windows, as if they were frozen forever in these postures. To tell the truth, I began to hurry because I was

100 getting depressed. Finally, I saw a beautiful girl approaching, dressed in white, a nurse or an attendant, and I was so happy to see someone young, someone walking and acting normally, that I gave her a wide smile and a big hello and I must have looked like a kind of nut. Anyway, she looked right through me as if I were a window, which is about par for the course whenever I meet beautiful girls.

I finally found the room and saw my grandmother in bed. My grandmother looks like Ethel Barrymore. I never knew who Ethel Barrymore was until I saw a terrific movie, *None but the*

110 *Lonely Heart,* on TV, starring Ethel Barrymore and Cary Grant. Both my grandmother and Ethel Barrymore have these great craggy faces like the side of a mountain and wonderful voices like syrup being poured. Slowly. She was propped up in bed, pillows puffed behind her. Her hair had been combed out and fell upon her shoulders. For some reason, this flowing hair gave her an almost girlish appearance, despite its whiteness.

She saw me and smiled. Her eyes lit up and her eyebrows arched and she reached out her hands to me in greeting. "Mike,

---

3. **stances and attitudes:** poses and positions.

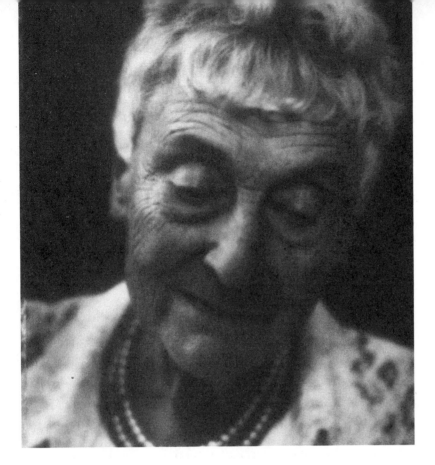

INFER

Pause at line 121. Why do you think Mike is relieved that it is one of his grandmother's good days?

_____

_____

_____

_____

_____

_____

_____

_____

Mike," she said. And I breathed a sigh of relief. This was one of
120   her good days. My mother had warned me that she might not
know who I was at first.

    I took her hands in mine. They were fragile. I could
actually feel her bones, and it seemed as if they would break if I
pressed too hard. Her skin was smooth, almost slippery, as if the
years had worn away all the roughness the way the wind wears
away the surfaces of stones.

    "Mike, Mike, I didn't think you'd come," she said, so happy,
and she was still Ethel Barrymore, that voice like a caress. "I've
been waiting all this time." Before I could reply, she looked away,
130   out the window. "See the birds? I've been watching them at the
feeder. I love to see them come. Even the blue jays. The blue jays
are like hawks—they take the food that the small birds should
have. But the small birds, the chickadees, watch the blue jays and
at least learn where the feeder is."

    She lapsed into silence, and I looked out the window. There
was no feeder. No birds. There was only the parking lot and the
sun glinting on car windshields.

INFER

Re-read lines 127–137. What **inference** can you make about Mike's grandmother from her comments about the birds and bird feeder?

_____

_____

_____

_____

_____

_____

_____

WORD STUDY

The word *radiant* (line 138) comes from the Latin *radius,* meaning "ray." What other words do you know that come from this same root?

_____

_____

_____

WORD ORIGINS

The Chesterfield (line 157), a single-breasted overcoat with a velvet collar, was made popular by a nineteenth-century earl of Chesterfield.

INFER

Re-read lines 156–160. Is Mike's grandmother really all that lucid? Explain.

_____

_____

_____

_____

_____

_____

_____

She turned to me again, eyes bright. Radiant, really. Or was it a medicine brightness? "Ah, Mike. You look so grand, so
140 grand. Is that a new coat?"

"Not really," I said. I'd been wearing my Uncle Jerry's old army-fatigue jacket for months, practically living in it, my mother said. But she insisted that I wear my raincoat for the visit. It was about a year old but looked new because I didn't wear it much. Nobody was wearing raincoats lately.

"You always loved clothes, didn't you, Mike?" she said.

I was beginning to feel uneasy because she regarded me with such intensity. Those bright eyes. I wondered—are old people in places like this so lonesome, so abandoned that they go
150 wild when someone visits? Or was she so happy because she was suddenly **lucid** and everything was sharp and clear? My mother had described those moments when my grandmother suddenly emerged from the fog that so often obscured her mind. I didn't know the answers, but it felt kind of spooky, getting such an emotional welcome from her.

"I remember the time you bought the new coat—the Chesterfield," she said, looking away again, as if watching the birds that weren't there. "That lovely coat with the velvet collar. Black, it was. Stylish. Remember that, Mike? It was hard times,
160 but you could never resist the glitter."

I was about to protest—I had never heard of a Chesterfield, for crying out loud. But I stopped. Be patient with her, my mother had said. Humor her. Be gentle.

We were interrupted by an attendant who pushed a wheeled cart into the room. "Time for juices, dear," the woman said. She was the standard forty- or fifty-year-old woman: glasses, nothing hair, plump cheeks. Her manner was cheerful but a businesslike kind of cheerfulness. I'd hate to be called "dear" by someone getting paid to do it. "Orange or grape or cranberry, dear?
170 Cranberry is good for the bones, you know."

My grandmother ignored the interruption. She didn't even bother to answer, having turned away at the woman's arrival, as if angry about her appearance.

The woman looked at me and winked. A **conspiratorial** kind of wink. It was kind of horrible. I didn't think people winked like that anymore. In fact, I hadn't seen a wink in years.

"She doesn't care much for juices," the woman said, talking to me as if my grandmother weren't even there. "But she loves her coffee. With lots of cream and two lumps of sugar. But this
180 is juice time, not coffee time." Addressing my grandmother again, she said, "Orange or grape or cranberry, dear?"

"Tell her I want no juices, Mike," my grandmother commanded **regally**, her eyes still watching invisible birds.

The woman smiled, patience like a label on her face. "That's all right, dear. I'll just leave some cranberry for you. Drink it at your leisure. It's good for the bones."

She wheeled herself out of the room. My grandmother was still absorbed in the view. Somewhere a toilet flushed. A wheelchair passed the doorway—probably that same old driver fleeing
190 a hit-run accident. A television set exploded with sound somewhere, soap-opera voices filling the air. You can always tell soap-opera voices.

I turned back to find my grandmother staring at me. Her hands cupped her face, her index fingers curled around her cheeks like parenthesis marks.

"But you know, Mike, looking back, I think you were right," she said, continuing our conversation as if there had been no interruption. "You always said, 'It's the things of the spirit that count, Meg.' The spirit! And so you bought the baby-grand
200 piano—a baby grand in the middle of the Depression. A knock came on the door and it was the deliveryman. It took five of them to get it into the house." She leaned back, closing her eyes. "How I loved that piano, Mike. I was never that fine a player, but you loved to sit there in the parlor, on Sunday evenings, Ellie on your lap, listening to me play and sing." She hummed a bit, a

INFER

Why do you think Mike's grandmother is angry at the arrival of the nurse (lines 171–173)?

_____

_____

_____

_____

_____

_____

_____

_____

_____

_____

_____

VOCABULARY

conspiratorial (kən·spir′ə·tôr′ē·əl) *adj.*: suggesting a secret plot.

Conspiratorial is from the Latin *spirare*, meaning "to breathe." Conspirators talk in whispers—low, breathy voices.

regally (rē′gəl·ē) *adv.*: majestically; in the manner of a queen or king.

Regally comes from the Latin *rex, regis*, meaning "king."

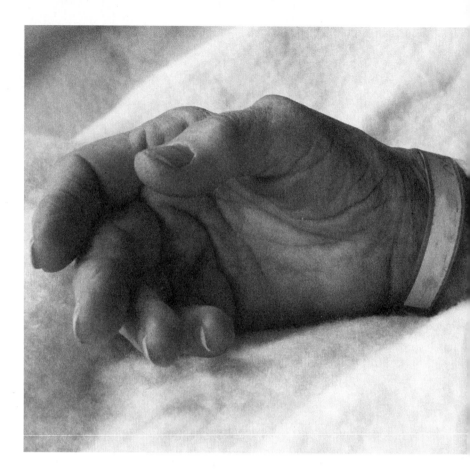

INFER

Pause at line 210. What is it that Mike has just realized?

_____

_____

_____

_____

_____

_____

_____

_____

_____

IDENTIFY CAUSE & EFFECT

Why does Mike's grand-mother mistake him for his grandfather (lines 214–222)?

_____

_____

_____

_____

_____

_____

_____

_____

_____

_____

_____

fragment of melody I didn't recognize. Then she drifted into silence. Maybe she'd fallen asleep. My mother's name is Ellen, but everyone always calls her Ellie. "Take my hand, Mike," my grandmother said suddenly. Then I remembered—my grand-
210 father's name was Michael. I had been named for him.

"Ah, Mike," she said, pressing my hands with all her feeble strength. "I thought I'd lost you forever. And here you are, back with me again. . . ."

Her expression scared me. I don't mean scared as if I were in danger but scared because of what could happen to her when she realized the mistake she had made. My mother always said I favored her side of the family. Thinking back to the pictures in the old family albums, I recalled my grandfather as tall and thin. Like me. But the resemblance ended there. He was thirty-five
220 when he died, almost forty years ago. And he wore a moustache. I brought my hand to my face. I also wore a moustache now, of course.

"I sit here these days, Mike," she said, her voice a lullaby, her hand still holding mine, "and I drift and dream. The days are fuzzy sometimes, merging together. Sometimes it's like I'm not here at all but somewhere else altogether. And I always think of you. Those years we had. Not enough years, Mike, not enough . . ."

Her voice was so sad, so mournful, that I made sounds of sympathy, not words exactly but the kind of soothings that mothers murmur to their children when they awaken from bad dreams.

"And I think of that terrible night, Mike, that terrible night. Have you ever really forgiven me for that night?"

"Listen . . ." I began. I wanted to say: "Nana, this is Mike your grandson, not Mike your husband."

"Sh . . . sh . . ." she whispered, placing a finger as long and cold as a candle against my lips. "Don't say anything. I've waited so long for this moment. To be here. With you. I wondered what I would say if suddenly you walked in that door like other people have done. I've thought and thought about it. And I finally made up my mind—I'd ask you to forgive me. I was too proud to ask before." Her fingers tried to mask her face. "But I'm not proud anymore, Mike." That great voice quivered and then grew strong again. "I hate you to see me this way—you always said I was beautiful. I didn't believe it. The Charity Ball when we led the grand march and you said I was the most beautiful girl there . . ."

"Nana," I said. I couldn't keep up the pretense any longer, adding one more burden to my load of guilt, leading her on this way, playing a pathetic game of make-believe with an old woman clinging to memories. She didn't seem to hear me.

"But that other night, Mike. The terrible one. The terrible accusations I made. Even Ellie woke up and began to cry. I went to her and rocked her in my arms and you came into the room and said I was wrong. You were whispering, an awful whisper, not wanting to upset little Ellie but wanting to make me see the truth. And I didn't answer you, Mike. I was too proud. I've even forgotten the name of the girl. I sit here, wondering now—was it

INFER

Re-read lines 234–235. How does Mike feel about his grandmother's continuing to address him as his grand-father?

_____

_____

_____

_____

What happened to Mike's grandfather (lines 263–264)?

_____

_____

What does Mike come to realize about his grandmother (lines 265–274)? Why does that realization scare him?

_____

_____

_____

_____

_____

Re-read lines 282–288. What has Mike learned about love?

_____

_____

_____

_____

Laura or Evelyn? I can't remember. Later, I learned that you were telling the truth all the time, Mike. That I'd been wrong . . ." Her 260 eyes were brighter than ever as she looked at me now, but tear-bright, the tears gathering. "It was never the same after that night, was it, Mike? The glitter was gone. From you. From us. And then the accident . . . and I never had the chance to ask you to forgive me. . . ."

My grandmother. My poor, poor grandmother. Old people aren't supposed to have those kinds of memories. You see their pictures in the family albums and that's what they are: pictures. They're not supposed to come to life. You drive out in your father's Le Mans doing seventy-five on the pike and all you're 270 doing is visiting an old lady in a nursing home. A duty call. And then you find out that she's a person. She's *somebody.* She's my grandmother, all right, but she's also herself. Like my own mother and father. They exist outside of their relationship to me. I was scared again. I wanted to get out of there.

"Mike, Mike," my grandmother said. "Say it, Mike."

I felt as if my cheeks would crack if I uttered a word.

"Say you forgive me, Mike. I've waited all these years. . . ."

I was surprised at how strong her fingers were.

"Say '*I forgive you, Meg.*'"

280 I said it. My voice sounded funny, as if I were talking in a huge tunnel. "I forgive you, Meg."

Her eyes studied me. Her hands pressed mine. For the first time in my life, I saw love at work. Not movie love. Not Cindy's sparkling eyes when I tell her that we're going to the beach on Sunday afternoon. But love like something alive and tender, asking nothing in return. She raised her face, and I knew what she wanted me to do. I bent and brushed my lips against her cheek. Her flesh was like a leaf in autumn, crisp and dry.

She closed her eyes and I stood up. The sun wasn't glinting 290 on the cars any longer. Somebody had turned on another television set, and the voices were the show-off voices of the panel shows. At the same time you could still hear the soap-opera dialogue on the other television set.

I waited awhile. She seemed to be sleeping, her breathing serene and regular. I buttoned my raincoat. Suddenly she opened her eyes again and looked at me. Her eyes were still bright, but they merely stared at me. Without recognition or curiosity. Empty eyes. I smiled at her, but she didn't smile back. She made a kind of moaning sound and turned away on the bed, pulling the blankets around her.

I counted to twenty-five and then to fifty and did it all over again. I cleared my throat and coughed tentatively. She didn't move; she didn't respond. I wanted to say, "Nana, it's me." But I didn't. I thought of saying, "Meg, it's me." But I couldn't.

Finally I left. Just like that. I didn't say goodbye or anything. I stalked through the corridors, looking neither to the right nor the left, not caring whether that wild old man with the wheelchair ran me down or not.

On the Southwest Turnpike I did seventy-five—no, eighty—most of the way. I turned the radio up as loud as it could go. Rock music—anything to fill the air. When I got home, my mother was vacuuming the living-room rug. She shut off the cleaner, and the silence was deafening. "Well, how was your grandmother?" she asked.

I told her she was fine. I told her a lot of things. How great Nana looked and how she seemed happy and had called me Mike. I wanted to ask her—hey, Mom, you and Dad really love each other, don't you? I mean—there's nothing to forgive between you, is there? But I didn't.

Instead I went upstairs and took out the electric razor Annie had given me for Christmas and shaved off my moustache.

INTERPRET

Re-read lines 309–314. Why might Mike be acting the way he is following his visit?

_____

_____

_____

_____

INFER

Why doesn't Mike tell his mother what really happened (lines 315–319)?

_____

_____

_____

_____

INFER

Why does Mike shave off his moustache?

_____

_____

_____

_____

_____

_____

_____

_____

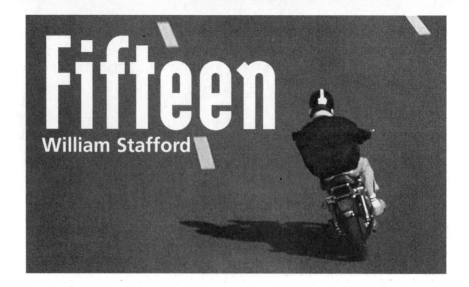

Fifteen
William Stafford

IDENTIFY

Pause at line 5. What does the speaker find? Circle it.

IDENTIFY

In lines 6–10, underline the words that describe what the motorcycle looks like, in the speaker's eyes. Circle the noun that tells how the boy felt about the motorcycle.

CONFLICT

What **internal conflict** does the speaker face (in lines 11–15)?

_____
_____
_____
_____
_____
_____
_____

THEME

Underline the repeated sentence in the poem. What does this repetition suggest about the poem's theme?

_____
_____
_____
_____
_____

South of the Bridge on Seventeenth
I found back of the willows one summer
day a motorcycle with engine running
as it lay on its side, ticking over
5   slowly in the high grass. I was fifteen.

I admired all that pulsing gleam, the
shiny flanks, the demure headlights
fringed where it lay; I led it gently
to the road and stood with that
10   companion, ready and friendly. I was fifteen.

We could find the end of a road, meet
the sky out on Seventeenth. I thought about
hills, and patting the handle got back a
confident opinion. On the bridge we indulged
15   a forward feeling, a tremble. I was fifteen.

Thinking, back farther in the grass I found
the owner, just coming to, where he had flipped
over the rail. He had blood on his hand, was pale—
I helped him walk to his machine. He ran his hand
20   over it, called me a good man, roared away.

I stood there, fifteen.

The Moustache / Fifteen

Genre Chart "The Moustache" and "Fifteen" are different **genres**, or types of literature. One is a short story and the other is a poem, but they both reveal something to us about what it is like to grow up. Use the Genre Chart below to examine how each text reveals its theme. Then, using your own words, state the theme that the two works have in common.

The Moustache	Fifteen
Genre: _____	Genre: _____
Main character: _____ _____	Speaker _____ _____
Setting: _____	Setting: _____
Plot: _____ _____	What happens? _____ _____
Conflict: _____ _____ _____	Conflict: _____ _____ _____
How character changes: _____ _____ _____ _____	Word choice and refrain: _____ _____ _____ _____
Theme: _____ _____ _____	Theme: _____ _____ _____

Universal theme: _____

Standards Review

LITERATURE

TestPractice

The Moustache / Fifteen

Complete the sample test item below. The box at the right explains why three of these choices are not correct.

Sample Test Item	Explanation of the Correct Answer
In "The Moustache," Mike is upset when he learns — A that having a moustache is no fun B a secret from his grandmother's past C that his grandmother doesn't have long to live D that he was speeding on the highway	The answer is *B*. *A* is incorrect because Mike likes his moustache; *C* is incorrect because Mike assumes his grandmother is near death; *D* is incorrect because although Mike speeds, he is not upset about it.

DIRECTIONS: Circle the letter of the best response.

1. In both "The Moustache" and "Fifteen" the main character experiences an —

   A external conflict against another character

   B external conflict against society as a whole

   C internal conflict between good and evil

   D internal conflict between opposing desires

Reading Standard 3.5
Compare works that express a universal theme and provide evidence to support the ideas expressed in each work.

2. The teenage boys in both "The Moustache" and "Fifteen" —

   F learn how to drive

   G face very difficult decisions

   H find motorcycles

   J wish they could stay young forever

3. Which element of literature is *not* shared by the story and the poem?

   A Character

   B Theme

   C Conflict

   D Refrain

4. Which sentence best expresses a **universal theme** shared by the story and the poem?

   F It is great to be a teenager.

   G Growing up is hard to do.

   H There is no escape from reality.

   J Life is just a bowl of cherries.

Standards Review

 The Moustache

Reading Standard 1.1
Identify and use the literal and figurative meanings of words and understand word derivations.

Word Roots

DIRECTIONS: Write the words from the box next to their roots.

Word Box

chronic

sterile

lucid

conspiratorial

regally

Greek Roots

1. *chron, chronos,* "time" _____

2. *steira,* "barren" _____

Latin Roots

3. *lucere,* "to shine" _____

4. *rex; regis,* "king" _____

5. *spirare,* "to breathe" _____

Vocabulary in Context

DIRECTIONS: Complete the paragraph below by writing the correct word from the word box above to fit each numbered blank. Use each word only once.

Samuel Martin Maddington's (1)_____ back pain was gone, for the moment, and he was able to stand straight and walk (2)_____ down the street. As usual, though, he wore a (3)_____ bandage across his forehead, which he believed made his thoughts clear and perfectly (4)_____. He had great plans for the day. In a (5)_____ whisper, he said to everyone he met, "Let me tell you the true secret of the universe." Samuel was definitely having a very good day.

Before You Go On...

Check your Standards Mastery at the back of this book.

Irony and
Ambiguity

Academic Vocabulary for Chapter 5

These are the terms you should know
as you read and analyze the stories in this chapter.

Irony The difference between what we expect or what seems suitable and what actually happens. There are three main types of irony.

- **Verbal irony** occurs when someone *says* something but *means* the opposite. "Nice day," you say as you slog through flood water up to your waist.
- **Situational irony** refers to an event that is *contrary to,* or the opposite of, what we expected. The firehouse burns. The winner of the wrestling match is the weakest team member.
- **Dramatic irony** takes place when *we* know what is going to happen to a character but the character does not know. Margo opens the door to a garage we know is filled with snakes. We know, but the robbers do not know, that the hotel they plan to rob is host to a police convention.

● ● ●

Ambiguity A quality that allows something to be interpreted in several different or conflicting ways. For example, if you and a friend have completely different ideas about an ambiguous character or the ambiguous ending of a story, you both might be "right." There is no single way to interpret an ambiguous story. That is part of its fun.

Reading Standard 1.1
Identify and use the literal and figurative meanings of words and understand word derivations.

Reading Standard 1.3 (Grade 8 Review)
Use word meanings within the appropriate context, and show ability to verify those meanings by definition, restatement, example, comparison, or contrast.

Reading Standard 3.8
Interpret and evaluate the impact of ambiguities, subtleties, contradictions, ironies, and incongruities in a text.

 For Further Information . . .

- Be sure to read the essay on **irony and ambiguity** in *Holt Literature and Language Arts*, pages 284–285.

The Gift of the Magi by O. Henry

BEFORE YOU READ

The Magi referred to in the title of this story are the three wise men, who, according to the Bible (Matthew 2:1–13), brought gifts to the infant Jesus. In O. Henry's "The Gift of the Magi," see if you can predict what Della and Jim, a young couple very much in love, will give each other for Christmas.

LITERARY FOCUS: SITUATIONAL IRONY

A story with a surprise ending has an outcome, or conclusion, that most readers would not have predicted. A writer may create a surprise ending by withholding, or not giving, important information to readers. In a well-written story, the conclusion may surprise us, but once we think about it, we realize that it "fits" all the details in the plot.

Surprise endings often create **irony**—the difference between what we expected would happen and what really happens. Sometimes the ending is not just *different* from what we had expected but *contrary* to it. Outcomes that are contrary to our expectations are examples of **situational irony.**

- As you read "The Gift of the Magi," think about what Della and Jim *were expecting* to happen—and what *really* happens. In what way is the ending an example of **situational irony**?

- Like many of O. Henry's stories, "The Gift of the Magi" has a **surprise ending.** What ending does O. Henry seem to be leading you to? What important information does he withhold from you?

READING SKILLS: MAKING PREDICTIONS

Successful readers **make predictions** as they read. This means that they make a series of guesses about what will happen next. Become involved in the lives of Jim and Della by making predictions as you read "The Gift of the Magi." Keep asking: What is going to happen next?

To make a prediction:
- Look for clues in the story that suggest what might happen next.
- Make a prediction about future events based on clues in the story and on what you know from your own experiences.
- Read on to confirm your prediction—to see if it is correct. If necessary, revise your prediction.

Reading Standard 1.1 Identify and use the literal and figurative meanings of words and understand word derivations.

Reading Standard 3.8 Interpret and evaluate the impact of ambiguities, subtleties, contradictions, ironies, and incongruities in a text.

VOCABULARY DEVELOPMENT

PREVIEW SELECTION VOCABULARY

Get to know these words before you read "The Gift of the Magi."

instigates (in'stə·gāts') v.: gives rise to; causes.

*When Jim and Della fight, it is usually money that **instigates** the argument.*

agile (aj'əl) adj.: moving with ease.

*Della's movements were graceful and **agile**, like a cat's.*

depreciate (dē·prē'shē·āt') v.: make something seem less important; lower the value of.

*Will the value of the jewels **depreciate**, or will their worth increase?*

cascade (kas·kād') n.: waterfall.

*Like a **cascade**, tears ran down Della's cheeks.*

ransacking (ran'sak'iŋ) v.: searching thoroughly.

*Della was **ransacking** her purse, looking in every pocket for a coin.*

discreet (di·skrēt') adj.: showing good judgment in words or actions, especially in being silent or careful.

*To Jim, the **discreet** thing to do was not to mention the gift.*

scrutiny (skrōōt''n·ē) n.: close inspection.

*Careful **scrutiny** of the jacket showed many worn spots.*

nimble (nim'bəl) adj.: quickly moving.

*With **nimble** hands she untied the carefully wrapped package.*

coveted (kuv'it·id) v. used as adj.: longed-for.

*Della's wishes were granted when she received the **coveted** treasure.*

singed (sinjd) v. used as adj.: slightly burned.

*Della looked at her **singed** hair, which she had burned while using the curling iron.*

DICTION: PLAIN OR FANCY?

Diction means "word choice." Diction is an important aspect of a writer's style. For instance, look at this sentence from "The Gift of the Magi":

"For ten seconds let us regard with discreet scrutiny some inconsequential object in the other direction."

This fancy, or *ornate,* language may sound old-fashioned to you. Here is the same sentence rewritten in a simple style that sounds very modern.

"Okay, let's pretend we don't see them."

The two sentences have pretty much the same meaning, but their diction— their choice of words—differs. As you read "The Gift of the Magi," be aware of O. Henry's special style. You'll have a chance to practice rewriting his sentences in simpler language.

The Gift of the Magi

O. Henry

CLARIFY

Pause at line 11. Why does Della flop down on the couch and howl?

_____

_____

_____

_____

_____

VOCABULARY

instigates (in'stə·gāts') *v.:* gives rise to; causes.

WORD STUDY

Beggar, in line 14, is a verb meaning "make useless." The passage suggests that the unattractive apartment wasn't worth describing.

One dollar and eighty-seven cents. That was all. And sixty cents of it was in pennies. Pennies saved one and two at a time by bulldozing the grocer and the vegetable man and the butcher until one's cheeks burned with the silent imputation of parsimony[1] that such close dealing implied. Three times Della counted it. One dollar and eighty-seven cents. And the next day would be Christmas.

There was clearly nothing to do but flop down on the shabby little couch and howl. So Della did it. Which **instigates** the
10 moral reflection that life is made up of sobs, sniffles, and smiles, with sniffles predominating.

While the mistress of the home is gradually subsiding from the first stage to the second, take a look at the home. A furnished flat[2] at $8 per week. It did not exactly beggar description, but it certainly had that word on the lookout for the mendicancy squad.[3]

---

1. **imputation** (im'pyo͞o·tā'shən) **of parsimony** (pär'sə·mō'nē): suggestion of stinginess.
2. **flat** *n.:* apartment.
3. **mendicancy** (men'di·kən·sē) **squad:** police who arrested beggars and homeless people.

In the vestibule[4] below was a letter box into which no letter would go, and an electric button from which no mortal finger could coax a ring. Also appertaining[5] thereunto was a card bearing the name "Mr. James Dillingham Young."

The "Dillingham" had been flung to the breeze during a former period of prosperity when its possessor was being paid $30 per week. Now, when the income was shrunk to $20, the letters of "Dillingham" looked blurred, as though they were thinking seriously of contracting to a modest and unassuming D. But whenever Mr. James Dillingham Young came home and reached his flat above, he was called Jim and greatly hugged by Mrs. James Dillingham Young, already introduced to you as Della. Which is all very good.

Della finished her cry and attended to her cheeks with the powder rag. She stood by the window and looked out dully at a gray cat walking a gray fence in a gray back yard. Tomorrow would be Christmas Day and she had only $1.87 with which to buy Jim a present. She had been saving every penny she could for months, with this result. Twenty dollars a week doesn't go far. Expenses had been greater than she had calculated. They always are. Only $1.87 to buy a present for Jim. Her Jim. Many a happy hour she had spent planning for something nice for him. Something fine and rare and sterling—something just a little bit near to being worthy of the honor of being owned by Jim.

There was a pier glass[6] between the windows of the room. Perhaps you have seen a pier glass in an $8 flat. A very thin and very **agile** person may, by observing his reflection in a rapid sequence of longitudinal strips, obtain a fairly accurate conception of his looks. Della, being slender, had mastered the art.

Suddenly she whirled from the window and stood before the glass. Her eyes were shining brilliantly, but her face had lost its color within twenty seconds. Rapidly she pulled down her hair and let it fall to its full length.

---

4. **vestibule** (ves′tə·byo͞ol′) *n.*: small entrance hall.
5. **appertaining** (ap′ər·tān′iŋ) *v.* used as *adj.*: belonging.
6. **pier glass** *n.*: tall mirror hung between two windows.

INFER

Pause at line 29. How would you describe Jim and Della's relationship?

IDENTIFY

Pause at line 40. Why does Della want more money?

VOCABULARY

agile (aj′əl) *adj.*: moving with ease.

Now, there were two possessions of the James Dillingham Youngs in which they both took a mighty pride. One was Jim's gold watch that had been his father's and his grandfather's. The other was Della's hair. Had the Queen of Sheba lived in the flat across the air shaft,[7] Della would have let her hair hang out the window some day to dry just to **depreciate** Her Majesty's jewels and gifts. Had King Solomon been the janitor, with all his treasures piled up in the basement, Jim would have pulled out his watch every time he passed, just to see him pluck at his beard from envy.

So now Della's beautiful hair fell about her rippling and shining like a **cascade** of brown waters. It reached below her knee and made itself almost a garment for her. And then she did it up again nervously and quickly. Once she faltered for a minute and stood still while a tear or two splashed on the worn red carpet.

On went her old brown jacket; on went her old brown hat. With a whirl of skirts and with the brilliant sparkle still in her eyes, she fluttered out the door and down the stairs to the street.

Where she stopped, the sign read: "Mme. Sofronie. Hair Goods of All Kinds." One flight up Della ran, and collected herself, panting. Madame, large, too white, chilly, hardly looked the "Sofronie."

"Will you buy my hair?" asked Della.

"I buy hair," said Madame. "Take yer hat off and let's have a sight at the looks of it."

Down rippled the brown cascade.

"Twenty dollars," said Madame, lifting the mass with a practiced hand.

"Give it to me quick," said Della.

Oh, and the next two hours tripped by on rosy wings. Forget the hashed metaphor. She was **ransacking** the stores for Jim's present.

---

7. **air shaft** n.: narrow gap between two buildings.

IDENTIFY

Lines 51–53 name the two possessions that make Jim and Della proudest. Circle the word that names Jim's possession. Underline the word that names Della's. Why are the two items so important to the couple?

VOCABULARY

depreciate (dē·prē′shē·āt′) v.: make something seem less important; lower the value of.

cascade (kas·kād′) n.: waterfall.

ransacking (ran′sak′iŋ) v.: searching thoroughly.

PREDICT

Pause at line 79. What do you **predict** Della will do with the money?

144 Part 1 Chapter 5: Irony and Ambiguity

She found it at last. It surely had been made for Jim and no one else. There was no other like it in any of the stores, and she had turned all of them inside out. It was a platinum fob chain,[8] simple and chaste in design, properly proclaiming its value by substance alone and not by meretricious[9] ornamentation—as all good things should do. It was even worthy of The Watch. As soon as she saw it she knew that it must be Jim's. It was like him.

90 Quietness and value—the description applied to both. Twenty-one dollars they took from her for it, and she hurried home with the 87 cents. With that chain on his watch, Jim might be properly anxious about the time in any company. Grand as the watch was, he sometimes looked at it on the sly on account of the old leather strap that he used in place of a chain.

When Della reached home, her intoxication gave way a little to prudence and reason. She got out her curling irons and lighted the gas and went to work repairing the ravages[10] made by generosity added to love. Which is always a tremendous task,

100 dear friends—a mammoth task.

Within forty minutes her head was covered with tiny, close-lying curls that made her look wonderfully like a truant school-boy. She looked at her reflection in the mirror long, carefully, and critically.

"If Jim doesn't kill me," she said to herself, "before he takes a second look at me, he'll say I look like a Coney Island chorus girl. But what could I do—oh! what could I do with a dollar and eighty-seven cents?"

At 7 o'clock the coffee was made and the frying pan was on

110 the back of the stove hot and ready to cook the chops.

Jim was never late. Della doubled the fob chain in her hand and sat on the corner of the table near the door that he always entered. Then she heard his step on the stair away down on the first flight, and she turned white for just a moment. She had a

---

8. **fob chain:** short chain meant to be attached to a pocket watch.
9. **meretricious** (mer′ə·trish′əs) *adj.:* attractive in a cheap, flashy way.
10. **ravages** (rav′ij·iz) *n.:* terrible damage.

IDENTIFY

Re-read lines 83–89. Locate and circle the item that Della buys for Jim.

INTERPRET

The sentence in lines 93–95 is an example of O. Henry's ornate (fancy) **diction,** or word choice. What does the sentence mean, in simpler language?

_____
_____
_____
_____
_____

CLARIFY

Pause at line 108. What reaction does Della think Jim will have to her short hair?

_____
_____
_____
_____
_____
_____
_____

INTERPRET

Re-read lines 122–127. To create a **surprise ending,** a writer may withhold important information. What information does O. Henry *not* give us here?

_____

_____

_____

_____

_____

INTERPRET

Re-read lines 136–143. How would you describe Jim's reaction to Della's haircut?

_____

_____

_____

_____

_____

_____

_____

_____

_____

_____

_____

_____

habit of saying little silent prayers about the simplest everyday things, and now she whispered: "Please God, make him think I am still pretty."

The door opened and Jim stepped in and closed it. He looked thin and very serious. Poor fellow, he was only twenty-two—and to be burdened with a family! He needed a new overcoat and he was without gloves.

Jim stepped inside the door, as immovable as a setter at the scent of quail. His eyes were fixed upon Della, and there was an expression in them that she could not read, and it terrified her. It was not anger, nor surprise, nor disapproval, nor horror, nor any of the sentiments that she had been prepared for. He simply stared at her fixedly with that peculiar expression on his face.

Della wriggled off the table and went for him.

"Jim, darling," she cried, "don't look at me that way. I had my hair cut off and sold it because I couldn't have lived through Christmas without giving you a present. It'll grow out again—you won't mind, will you? I just had to do it. My hair grows awfully fast. Say 'Merry Christmas!' Jim, and let's be happy. You don't know what a nice—what a beautiful, nice gift I've got for you."

"You've cut off your hair?" asked Jim, laboriously, as if he had not arrived at that patent[11] fact yet even after the hardest mental labor.

"Cut it off and sold it," said Della. "Don't you like me just as well, anyhow? I'm me without my hair, ain't I?"

Jim looked about the room curiously.

"You say your hair is gone?" he said, with an air almost of idiocy.

"You needn't look for it," said Della. "It's sold, I tell you— sold and gone, too. It's Christmas Eve, boy. Be good to me, for it went for you. Maybe the hairs on my head were numbered," she went on with a sudden serious sweetness, "but nobody could ever count my love for you. Shall I put the chops on, Jim?"

---

11. **patent** (pāt″nt) *adj.:* obvious.

Out of his trance Jim seemed quickly to wake. He enfolded
his Della. For ten seconds let us regard with **discreet scrutiny**
some inconsequential object in the other direction. Eight dollars
a week or a million a year—what is the difference? A mathe-
matician or a wit would give you the wrong answer. The Magi
brought valuable gifts, but that was not among them. This dark
assertion will be illuminated later on.

Jim drew a package from his overcoat pocket and threw it
upon the table.

"Don't make any mistake, Dell," he said, "about me. I don't
think there's anything in the way of a haircut or a shave or a
shampoo that could make me like my girl any less. But if you'll
unwrap that package, you may see why you had me going awhile
at first."

White fingers and **nimble** tore at the string and paper. And
then an ecstatic scream of joy; and then, alas! a quick feminine
change to hysterical tears and wails, necessitating the immediate
employment of all the comforting powers of the lord of the flat.

For there lay The Combs—the set of combs, side and back,
that Della had worshiped for long in a Broadway window.

VOCABULARY

discreet (di·skrēt′) *adj.:* showing good judgment in words
or actions, especially in being
silent or careful.

scrutiny (skrōōt′n·ē) *n.:* close
inspection.

nimble (nim′bəl) *adj.:* quickly
moving.

PREDICT

Pause at line 157. What do
you **predict** the package
contains?

_____

_____

_____

_____

IDENTIFY

What has Jim bought for
Della (lines 167–168)? Circle
the text that tells you so.

IRONY

Pause at line 174. **Situational irony** occurs when an event is the *opposite* of what you expected or of what would be appropriate. How does Jim's gift to Della create situational irony?

_____

_____

_____

VOCABULARY

coveted (kuv'it·id) *v.* used as *adj.:* longed-for.

singed (sinjd) *v.* used as *adj.:* slightly burned.

IRONY

Re-read lines 188–191. Describe the **situational irony** you find there.

_____

_____

_____

_____

FLUENCY

Read the boxed passage aloud two times. Focus on conveying the narrator's message and expressing his tone simply and clearly.

170 Beautiful combs, pure tortoise shell, with jeweled rims—just the shade to wear in the beautiful vanished hair. They were expensive combs, she knew, and her heart had simply craved and yearned over them without the least hope of possession. And now, they were hers, but the tresses that should have adorned the **coveted** adornments were gone.

But she hugged them to her bosom, and at length she was able to look up with dim eyes and a smile and say: "My hair grows so fast, Jim!"

And then Della leaped up like a little **singed** cat and cried, "Oh, oh!"

180 Jim had not yet seen his beautiful present. She held it out to him eagerly upon her open palm. The dull precious metal seemed to flash with a reflection of her bright and ardent spirit.

"Isn't it a dandy, Jim? I hunted all over town to find it. You'll have to look at the time a hundred times a day now. Give me your watch. I want to see how it looks on it."

Instead of obeying, Jim tumbled down on the couch and put his hands under the back of his head and smiled.

"Dell," said he, "let's put our Christmas presents away and keep 'em a while. They're too nice to use just at present. I sold
190 the watch to get the money to buy your combs. And now suppose you put the chops on."

The Magi, as you know, were wise men—wonderfully wise men—who brought gifts to the Babe in the manger. They invented the art of giving Christmas presents. Being wise, their gifts were no doubt wise ones, possibly bearing the privilege of exchange in case of duplication. And here I have lamely related to you the uneventful chronicle of two foolish children in a flat who most unwisely sacrificed for each other the greatest treasures of their house. But in a last word to the wise of these days,
200 let it be said that of all who give gifts, these two were the wisest. Of all who give and receive gifts, such as they are wisest. Everywhere they are wisest. They are the Magi.

The Gift of the Magi

Irony Map "The Gift of the Magi" is famous for its **situational irony.** Fill in the Irony Map below to understand how the story's events create situational irony. Then, explain what the irony shows us about the characters.

Della	Jim
What Della Sells: _____ _____	What Jim Sells: _____ _____
What Della Buys: _____ _____	What Jim Buys: _____ _____
Why Della Buys It: _____ _____	Why Jim Buys Them: _____ _____
What Della Receives: _____ _____	What Jim Receives: _____ _____
Situational Irony/Why the Gift Is Useless: _____ _____	Situational Irony/Why the Gift Is Useless: _____ _____
What We Learn About Della: _____ _____	What We Learn About Jim: _____ _____

Standards Review

 **The Gift of the Magi**

Complete the sample test item below. Then, check your answer, and read the explanation at right.

Sample Test Item	Explanation of the Correct Answer
To create a **surprise ending** in "The Gift of the Magi," O. Henry — **A** keeps one character hidden **B** withholds important information **C** does not let the characters meet **D** explains right away what the characters know	The correct answer is *B*. *A* and *C* are incorrect because Jim and Della are not hidden and they do meet. *D* is not correct because O. Henry does not tell us right away what Jim is thinking when he sees Della's hair.

DIRECTIONS: Circle the letter of each correct response.

1. Della buys a watch fob for Jim because —

   A he lost his watch

   B he treasures his watch

   C he doesn't know how to tell time

   D his watch has a new strap

2. When Jim sees Della's short hair, he realizes —

   F she has been to a beauty parlor

   G he likes the new look

   H she couldn't always have long hair

   J his gift to her will be useless

3. O. Henry suggests that Della and Jim's "greatest treasure" is —

   A a watch fob and a comb

   B their foolishness

   C their sacrifices

   D their love for each other

4. Which statement best describes the **situational irony** in the story?

   F The watch fob is as useless to Jim as the combs are to Della.

   G Jim and Della bought each other expensive gifts.

   H Della's combs were bought with the money she received for her hair.

   J Jim and Della are as wise as the Magi.

Reading Standard 3.8
Interpret and evaluate the impact of ambiguities, subtleties, contradictions, ironies, and incongruities in a text.

Standards Review

Diction

DIRECTIONS: Write the letter of the type of **diction** from the right column next to its example in the left column.

Reading Standard 1.1 Identify and use the literal and figurative meanings of words and understand word derivations.

___ 1. Jed knew that an enormous task had befallen him; nevertheless he forged ahead and proceeded to locate the volumes of learning that would help him.

___ 2. "What a chore, but someone has to get this work done," mumbled Jed. He grabbed his bookbag.

___ 3. For Jed it was a huge task, but he knew he would have to finish the project. He picked up his school-books with a sense of purpose.

a. fancy diction

b. simpler diction

c. simplest diction

Vocabulary in Context

DIRECTIONS: Complete the passage with words from the box. Not all words from the box will be used.

Word Box

instigates

agile

depreciate

cascade

ransacking

discreet

scrutiny

nimble

coveted

singed

We were trying to avoid (1) _____ , to keep our work a secret. (2) We were _____ the enemy's files, checking everywhere, to find what we really wanted, the

(3) _____ Monster File. We were

(4) _____ enough not to tell anyone about our project, but we were constantly on the lookout for Agent X, a spy whose

(5) _____ body and (6) _____ fingers could cause us real trouble.

Before You Go On . . .

Check your Standards Mastery at the back of this book.

August Heat by William Fryer Harvey

Are some things foretold in the stars? Do we all march to our destinies, helpless to change the course of our lives? Reading "August Heat" will give you lots to think—and wonder—about.

LITERARY FOCUS: AMBIGUITY

A story that contains **ambiguity** can be interpreted in different ways. This "open-endedness" is deliberate; ambiguity is intended to make you think about what's happened. "August Heat" tells the story of a painter caught up in a horrifying series of events that lead him to an uncertain—or ambiguous—fate.

- As you read, pay close attention to details describing the situation the main character finds himself in.
- Read the story through, and then think about how *you* would interpret what has happened to the painter.

READING SKILLS: DRAWING CONCLUSIONS

A **conclusion** is a judgment based on evidence. You draw conclusions all the time. You draw conclusions about why your favorite team lost the series. You draw conclusions about why you didn't get a part in the play. You draw conclusions about why so many people like you. As you read a story, you draw all kinds of conclusions about the characters and what happens to them. You base your conclusions on the clues the author gives and on what you already know from life.

You might find it helpful to fill in a chart like this as you read. The first row is done as an example.

Detail from Story	My Inferences About Characters
"By profession I am an artist, not a very successful one, but I earn enough money by my black-and-white work to satisfy my necessary wants."	The narrator sounds pretty honest.

Reading Standard 1.3 (Grade 8 Review) Use word meanings within the appropriate context and show ability to verify those meanings by definition, restatement, example, comparison, or contrast.

Reading Standard 3.8 Interpret and evaluate the impact of ambiguities, subtleties, contradictions, ironies, and incongruities in a text.

VOCABULARY DEVELOPMENT

PREVIEW SELECTION VOCABULARY

The following words appear in "August Heat." You may want to learn these words before you start reading.

oppressively (ə·pres′iv·lē) *adv.:* hard to put up with; weighing heavily on the mind, spirits, or senses.

*Though the windows were open, the room was **oppressively** stuffy.*

sustain (sə·stān′) *v.:* carry the weight or burden of; support.

*The heavy man did not seem strong enough to **sustain** the weight of his body.*

palpable (pal′pə·bəl) *adj.:* able to be touched, felt, or held.

*In the tiny room, the heat was **palpable**—you could feel it in the air.*

plausible (plô′zə·bəl) *adj.:* believable.

*His explanation for the odd work was at least **plausible**, even if it wasn't true.*

CONTEXT CLUES: LOOKING FOR SIGNS

When you come across an unfamiliar word while reading, look at the word's context, that is, its surrounding words and sentences. See if you can find a definition, a restatement, an example, or a comparison or contrast that helps you guess at the meaning of the unfamiliar word. In the examples below, the italicized context clues help define the meanings of the boldface words.

Definition: We sat beneath the **eaves,** *where the roof juts out from the building.*

Restatement: After my *interruption* he stopped work; I apologized later for the **intrusion.**

Example: Atkinson was handy with *tools,* such as the **chisel** he was sharpening.

Comparison: I'm not good at **self-deception:** *it's like trying to fool your innermost being.*

Contrast: His business was **prosperous,** *but the man didn't have a penny in his pocket.*

As you read "August Heat," use context clues to help you figure out the meanings of unfamiliar words.

August Heat

William Fryer Harvey

PENISTONE ROAD, CLAPHAM

20th August, 19—.

INFER

Re-read lines 1–3. Circle the words the narrator uses to describe the kind of day he has had. At roughly what time of day is he writing these words?

_____

_____

_____

_____

_____

_____

_____

IDENTIFY

In lines 4–12, underline the information the narrator gives about himself.

I have had what I believe to be the most remarkable day in my life, and while the events are still fresh in my mind, I wish to put them down on paper as clearly as possible.

Let me say at the outset that my name is James Clarence Withencroft.

I am forty years old, in perfect health, never having known a day's illness.

By profession I am an artist, not a very successful one, but I earn enough money by my black-and-white work to satisfy my

10 necessary wants.

My only near relative, a sister, died five years ago, so that I am independent.

I breakfasted this morning at nine, and after glancing through the morning paper I lighted my pipe and proceeded to let my mind wander in the hope that I might chance upon some subject for my pencil.

The room, though door and windows were open, was **oppressively** hot, and I had just made up my mind that the coolest and most comfortable place in the neighborhood would

20 be the deep end of the public swimming bath, when the idea came.

I began to draw. So intent was I on my work that I left my lunch untouched, only stopping work when the clock of St. Jude's struck four.

The final result, for a hurried sketch, was, I felt sure, the best thing I had done.

It showed a criminal in the dock[1] immediately after the judge had pronounced sentence. The man was fat—enormously fat. The flesh hung in rolls about his chin; it creased his huge,

30 stumpy neck. He was cleanshaven (perhaps I should say a few days before he must have been cleanshaven) and almost bald. He stood in the dock, his short, stumpy fingers clasping the rail, looking straight in front of him. The feeling that his expression conveyed was not so much one of horror as of utter, absolute collapse.

There seemed nothing in the man strong enough to **sustain** that mountain of flesh.

I rolled up the sketch, and without quite knowing why, placed it in my pocket. Then with the rare sense of happiness

40 which the knowledge of a good thing well done gives, I left the house.

I believe that I set out with the idea of calling upon Trenton, for I remember walking along Lytton Street and turning to the right along Gilchrist Road at the bottom of the hill where the men were at work on the new tram lines.[2]

From there onward I have only the vaguest recollections of where I went. The one thing of which I was fully conscious was the awful heat, that came up from the dusty asphalt pavement as

---

1. **dock:** in English criminal courts, the place where a defendant sits or stands.
2. **tram lines:** tracks for a streetcar.

VOCABULARY

oppressively (ə·pres′iv·lē) *adv.:* hard to put up with; weighing heavily on the mind, spirits, or senses.

sustain (sə·stān′) *v.:* carry the weight or burden of; support.

DRAW CONCLUSIONS

Pause at line 24. What conclusion can you draw about the narrator?

_____

_____

_____

IDENTIFY

What has the narrator been drawing (lines 27–35)? Underline the details the narrator uses to describe the picture.

_____

_____

_____

IDENTIFY

Re-read lines 38–41. Underline what the narrator does that he cannot explain.

VOCABULARY

palpable (pal′pə·bəl) adj.: able to be touched, felt, or held.

WORD STUDY

Locate and circle the **context clue** that helps you guess at the meaning of *reverie* in line 53.

CLARIFY

Re-read the inscription (lines 60–62). *Monumental* here means "pertaining to a monument to the dead; of a tombstone." What does Atkinson do for a living?

_____

_____

IDENTIFY

Pause at line 70. Whom does the narrator meet? Why is this meeting so surprising?

_____

_____

_____

_____

_____

_____

_____

an almost **palpable** wave. I longed for the thunder promised by 50 the great banks of copper-colored cloud that hung low over the western sky.

I must have walked five or six miles, when a small boy roused me from my reverie by asking the time.

It was twenty minutes to seven.

When he left me I began to take stock of my bearings. I found myself standing before a gate that led into a yard bordered by a strip of thirsty earth, where there were flowers, purple stock and scarlet geranium. Above the entrance was a board with the inscription—

60
CHAS. ATKINSON

MONUMENTAL MASON

WORKER IN ENGLISH AND ITALIAN MARBLES

From the yard itself came a cheery whistle, the noise of hammer blows, and the cold sound of steel meeting stone.

A sudden impulse made me enter.

A man was sitting with his back toward me, busy at work on a slab of curiously veined marble. He turned round as he heard my steps and stopped short.

It was the man I had been drawing, whose portrait lay in 70 my pocket.

He sat there, huge and elephantine,³ the sweat pouring from his scalp, which he wiped with a red silk handkerchief. But though the face was the same, the expression was absolutely different.

He greeted me smiling, as if we were old friends, and shook my hand.

I apologized for my intrusion.

"Everything is hot and glary outside," I said. "This seems an oasis in the wilderness."

---

3. **elephantine** (el′ə·fan′tēn′): enormous; like an elephant in size.

80   "I don't know about the oasis," he replied, "but it certainly is hot. Take a seat, sir!"

    He pointed to the end of the gravestone on which he was at work, and I sat down.

    "That's a beautiful piece of stone you've got hold of," I said.

    He shook his head. "In a way it is," he answered; "the surface here is as fine as anything you could wish, but there's a big flaw at the back, though I don't expect you'd ever notice it. I could never make really a good job of a bit of marble like that. It would be all right in a summer like this; it wouldn't mind the

90 blasted heat. But wait till the winter comes. There's nothing quite like frost to find out the weak points in stone."

    "Then what's it for?" I asked.

    The man burst out laughing.

    "You'd hardly believe me if I was to tell you it's for an exhibition, but it's the truth. Artists have exhibitions: so do grocers and butchers; we have them too. All the latest little things in headstones, you know."

    He went on to talk of marbles, which sort best withstood wind and rain, and which were easiest to work; then of his gar-

100 den and a new sort of carnation he had bought. At the end of every other minute he would drop his tools, wipe his shining head, and curse the heat.

    I said little, for I felt uneasy. There was something unnatural, uncanny, in meeting this man.

    I tried at first to persuade myself that I had seen him before, that his face, unknown to me, had found a place in some out-of-the-way corner of my memory, but I knew that I was practicing little more than a **plausible** piece of self-deception.

    Mr. Atkinson finished his work, spat on the ground, and

110 got up with a sigh of relief.

    "There! What do you think of that?" he said, with an air of evident pride.

    The inscription which I read for the first time was this—

CLARIFY

Pause at line 97. What is the man making the gravestone for?

_____

_____

IDENTIFY

In lines 103–104, circle the two words that provide the **context clues** for *uncanny*. Why does the narrator feel odd about meeting the man?

_____

_____

_____

_____

_____

_____

_____

_____

_____

VOCABULARY

plausible (plô′zə·bəl) *adj.*: believable.

Notes _____

_____

_____

_____

_____

_____

_____

Re-read lines 114–120. Underline the name on the tombstone and the date of death. Why does this information frighten the narrator? (For a clue, look at similar information at the story's beginning.)

_____

_____

_____

_____

Pause at line 137. At this point in the story, do you find both men believable? Why or why not?

_____

_____

_____

_____

Why does Atkinson ask the narrator if he'd ever been to Clacton (lines 139–140)?

_____

_____

_____

_____

_____

_____

SACRED TO THE MEMORY

OF

JAMES CLARENCE WITHENCROFT.

BORN, JAN. 18TH, 1860.

HE PASSED AWAY VERY SUDDENLY

ON AUGUST 20TH, 190—

120   *"In the midst of life we are in death."*

For some time I sat in silence. Then a cold shudder ran down my spine. I asked him where he had seen the name.

"Oh, I didn't see it anywhere," replied Mr. Atkinson. "I wanted some name, and I put down the first that came into my head. Why do you want to know?"

"It's a strange coincidence, but it happens to be mine."

He gave a long, low whistle.

"And the dates?"

"I can only answer for one of them, and that's correct."

130   "It's a rum go!"[4] he said.

But he knew less than I did. I told him of my morning's work. I took the sketch from my pocket and showed it to him. As he looked, the expression of his face altered until it became more and more like that of the man I had drawn.

"And it was only the day before yesterday," he said, "that I told Maria there were no such things as ghosts!"

Neither of us had seen a ghost, but I knew what he meant.

"You probably heard my name," I said.

"And you must have seen me somewhere and have forgot-

140   ten it! Were you at Clacton-on-Sea last July?"

I had never been to Clacton in my life. We were both silent for some time. We were both looking at the same thing, the two dates on the gravestone, and one was right.

"Come inside and have some supper," said Mr. Atkinson.

---

4. **It's a rum go:** British slang for "It's an odd thing."

His wife is a cheerful little woman, with the flaky red cheeks of the country-bred. Her husband introduced me as a friend of his who was an artist. The result was unfortunate, for after the sardines and watercress had been removed, she brought out a Doré[5] Bible, and I had to sit and express my admiration for nearly half an hour.

I went outside, and found Atkinson sitting on the gravestone smoking.

We resumed the conversation at the point we had left off.

"You must excuse my asking," I said, "but do you know of anything you've done for which you could be put on trial?"

He shook his head.

"I'm not a bankrupt, the business is prosperous enough. Three years ago I gave turkeys to some of the guardians[6] at Christmas, but that's all I can think of. And they were small ones, too," he added as an afterthought.

150

160

---

5. **Doré:** Gustave Doré (dô·rā′), a French artist and illustrator (1832–1883).
6. **guardians** *n.:* members of a board that cares for poor people within a district.

INFER

Pause at line 155. Why does the narrator ask Atkinson if he's ever done anything criminal?

IDENTIFY
CAUSE & EFFECT

Re-read lines 167–176, and underline reasons Atkinson gives for the narrator to stay at his house until midnight.

FLUENCY

Read the boxed passage aloud two times. On your first read, focus on conveying basic meaning and on your reading rate. During the second read, experiment with the tone and volume of your voice to bring the passage to life for your listeners.

IDENTIFY

Re-read lines 178–181. Underline what the narrator says Atkinson is doing. Why would Atkinson's actions increase the narrator's fear of being killed?

_____

_____

_____

AMBIGUITY

What might the narrator mean by the word *gone* in line 186? In what two ways can this word be interpreted?

_____

_____

_____

He got up, fetched a can from the porch, and began to water the flowers. "Twice a day regular in the hot weather," he said, "and then the heat sometimes gets the better of the delicate ones. And ferns, they could never stand it. Where do you live?"

I told him my address. It would take an hour's quick walk to get back home.

"It's like this," he said. "We'll look at the matter straight. If you go back home tonight, you take your chance of accidents. A cart may run over you, and there's always banana skins and
170 orange peel, to say nothing of fallen ladders."

He spoke of the improbable with an intense seriousness that would have been laughable six hours before. But I did not laugh.

"The best thing we can do," he continued, "is for you to stay here till twelve o'clock. We'll go upstairs and smoke; it may be cooler inside."

To my surprise I agreed.

We are sitting now in a long, low room beneath the eaves. Atkinson has sent his wife to bed. He himself is busy sharpening
180 some tools at a little oilstone, smoking one of my cigars the while.

The air seems charged with thunder. I am writing this at a shaky table before the open window. The leg is cracked, and Atkinson, who seems a handy man with his tools, is going to mend it as soon as he has finished putting an edge on his chisel.

It is after eleven now. I shall be gone in less than an hour. But the heat is stifling.

It is enough to send a man mad.

August Heat

Ambiguity Chart   "August Heat" contains plenty of **ambiguity:** The events in it can be interpreted in different, even conflicting ways. The chart below contains story details that are ambiguous. Next to each detail from the story, provide a reasonable interpretation that conflicts with the one already filled in.

Details from Story	Interpretation 1	Interpretation 2
Narrator reads the newspaper, then thinks about a subject to draw.	Newspaper reading is just an unimportant detail.	
The narrator says Atkinson is the man he sketched, only he has a different expression.		He is the man the narrator sketched, but he is now looking relaxed.
Atkinson says he is making the tombstone for a special show.		He is lying; he is making the tombstone for some other reason.
The tombstone has the narrator's name and birthdate and today as date of death.	Information is a coincidence— a chance happening.	
Atkinson says he has done nothing criminal.		He is lying; maybe the narrator did see him at trial or in the newspaper.
Atkinson invites the narrator to stay till twelve o'clock, to avoid a deadly accident before midnight.		Atkinson wants the narrator to stay so he can kill him by midnight.
Atkinson is sharpening his tools.	He is sharpening them for work.	
The narrator says the heat is bad enough to make a man go crazy.	The heat has made him crazy; Atkinson is harmless.	

Standards Review

LITERATURE

August Heat

Complete the sample test item below. Then, read the explanation in the right-hand column.

Sample Test Item	Explanation of the Correct Answer
What reason does Atkinson give for putting the narrator's name on the tombstone? **A** He saw it in the newspaper. **B** The name popped into his head. **C** It's also the name of his friend. **D** He wanted to honor the narrator.	The correct answer is *B*. *A* is not correct, because Atkinson doesn't read a paper in the story. Atkinson mentions no other friends in the story, so *C* is incorrect. Atkinson and the narrator never met before, so *D* is also incorrect.

DIRECTIONS: Circle the letter of the correct response.

1. The narrator can hardly remember where he walked because he —

   A knew where he was going

   B was carrying his sketch

   C was interrupted by a small boy

   D was in a daze because of the awful heat

2. What surprises the narrator when he first sees Atkinson?

   F Atkinson is a small man.

   G Atkinson is very friendly to him.

   H Atkinson is the man in the narrator's drawing.

   J Atkinson is wiping sweat from his face.

3. The story's ending is **ambiguous** because —

   A the narrator is sworn to secrecy

   B we don't know what will happen to the narrator

   C the tombstone breaks

   D Atkinson is killed by the heat

4. Which **interpretation** of the story below is most valid?

   F It was all a bad dream.

   G Atkinson is really the narrator's twin brother.

   H The narrator has an overactive imagination.

   J Atkinson and the narrator are really the same person.

Reading Standard 3.8
Interpret and evaluate the impact of ambiguities, subtleties, contradictions, ironies, and incongruities in a text.

Standards Review

TestPractice   **August Heat**

Context Clues

DIRECTIONS: Write the word from the box that best completes the sentence. Use the context clues in italics to help you.

remarkable	inscription	recollections	exhibition

1. The _____ on the tombstone *gave the name, birth, and death dates* of the dead person.

2. I have unclear _____ of that day; my *memory* is not as good as it used to be.

3. The *big show* of tombstones opens tomorrow; he is getting his work ready for the _____.

4. Was your day _____, or was it *ordinary*?

Reading Standard 1.3 (Grade 8 Review) Use word meanings within the appropriate context and show ability to verify those meanings by definition, restatement, example, comparison, or contrast.

Vocabulary in Context

DIRECTIONS: Complete the paragraph below by writing each word from the box in the correct numbered blank. Use each word once.

Word Box

sustain

palpable

plausible

oppressively

Where we live, some days are so hot you can hardly breathe. The temperature rises (1) _____, chasing us inside. The heat waves are almost (2) _____, weighing heavily on our skin. To people in cool-weather areas, this description may not sound (3) _____. "It can't be true," they say. In fact, the heat can be hazardous to good health. For people who are overweight, for example, the heat may make it hard to (4) _____ the extra pounds. The solution: People should take it easy and stay out of the sun.

Before You Go On . . .

Check your Standards Mastery at the back of this book.

Chapter 6

Symbolism and Allegory

Moby Dick (1930) by Rockwell Kent. Pen-and-ink drawing.
The Granger Collection, New York.

Academic Vocabulary for Chapter 6

These are the terms you should know
as you read and analyze the stories in this chapter.

———————

Symbol An object, a person, an animal, or an event that stands for something more than itself. For example, a blindfolded woman who is holding up scales is often used to symbolize justice, which is supposed to be fair in weighing the fate of the accused.

Public symbol A symbol that has become widely recognized, such as the bald eagle (a symbol of the United States) or the olive branch (a symbol of peace).

Invented symbol A symbol invented by a writer, which usually stands for something abstract, such as evil, innocence, or love. The meanings of literary symbols must be interpreted by the reader. Use these guidelines when you are trying to interpret the meaning of a symbol:

- Symbols are often visual.
- When an object or event is used as a symbol, it usually appears several times in a text.
- A symbol is a type of figurative language. Like a metaphor, a symbol is identified with something that is very different but that shares some of the same qualities. When you are thinking about whether something is used symbolically, ask yourself: "Does this character, object, or event stand for something?" In Herman Melville's novel *Moby-Dick*, for example, readers begin to sense that the white whale being hunted by Captain Ahab is more than just a whale. From the many descriptions of the whale in the novel, readers come to see it as a symbol of random, unexplainable evil.

Allegory A story in which characters and settings stand for something beyond themselves, usually virtues and vices. Sometimes the characters in an allegory are given names that indicate what they stand for. For example, a woman who stands for goodness may be named Mrs. Kind.

● ● ●

For Further Information ...

- Be sure to read the essay on **symbolism and allegory** in *Holt Literature and Language Arts*, page 340–341.

Reading Standard 1.1 Identify and use the literal and figurative meanings of words and understand word derivations.

Reading Standard 1.1 (Grade 8 Review) Analyze idioms, analogies, metaphors, and similes to infer the literal and figurative meanings of phrases.

Reading Standard 1.2 Distinguish between the denotative and connotative meanings of words and interpret the connotative power of words.

Reading Standard 3.7 Recognize and understand the significance of various literary devices, including figurative language, imagery, allegory, and symbolism, and explain their appeal.

The Scarlet Ibis by James Hurst

Sometimes we act in ways we later regret. Imagine that you could go back in time and change the way you treated someone you love. What would you change—and how? The narrator of "The Scarlet Ibis" remembers a time he was cruel and selfish. He thought he was doing the right thing, but pride clouded his judgment. As you read the story, decide how you would have acted in the narrator's place.

LITERARY FOCUS: SYMBOLS

A **symbol** is a person, a place, a thing, or an event that stands both for itself and for something beyond itself. For example, you may find that a writer mentions a mirror many times in a story. A mirror is an actual object, but the writer may be using it to stand for vanity or for an unreal world. Writers invent symbols to deepen the meaning of their stories. As you read "The Scarlet Ibis," you'll notice that the writer keeps drawing similarities and connections between one character and the scarlet ibis. The ibis is a rare water bird with long legs; a long, slender, curved bill; and brilliant orange-red feathers.

- As you read, look for clues that suggest that the ibis stands for something more than itself.

READING SKILLS: MAKING INFERENCES

An **inference** is an intelligent guess you make about the meaning of something. You form inferences by putting together several related details and then generalizing about what they might mean. In making inferences about characters, you also draw on your own experiences. For example, if you observe a character who speaks harshly to her dog, slams the door, and won't speak to her classmates, you can make an inference that this character is upset about something. You make that inference based on story details and on your own experience with people.

To make inferences about the meaning of a symbol, follow these steps:

- Pay careful attention to details. Does the writer repeat something, such as a color, an animal, or an object, throughout the story?
- Think about what the color, animal, or object represents to *you*. If the object is a ring, for example, it may represent love or faithfulness.
- Then, combine your own experience and the evidence in the story to make an inference about what this object or animal or color might signify.
- Be prepared to revise your inferences about symbols. You might have to re-read the story to be sure your inference holds up.

Reading Standard 1.1 Identify and use the literal and figurative meanings of words and understand word derivations.

Reading Standard 1.1 (Grade 8 Review) Analyze idioms, analogies, metaphors, and similes to infer the literal and figurative meanings of phrases.

Reading Standard 3.7 Recognize and understand the significance of various literary devices, including figurative language, imagery, allegory, and symbolism, and explain their appeal.

VOCABULARY DEVELOPMENT

PREVIEW SELECTION VOCABULARY

The following words appear in the story you're about to read. You may
want to become familiar with them before you begin reading.

sullenly (sul'ən·lē) *adv.:* resentfully; gloomily.

Sullenly, the narrator took Doodle with him, all the while resenting the task.

imminent (im'ə·nənt) *adj.:* near; about to happen.

When thunder boomed and the sky darkened, they could tell the storm was imminent.

iridescent (ir'i·des'ənt) *adj.:* rainbowlike; displaying a shifting range of colors.

The bird's wings glowed with iridescent color.

serene (sə·rēn') *adj.:* peaceful; calm.

The serene lake was as smooth and calm as a mirror.

infallibility (in·fal'ə·bil'ə·tē) *n.:* inability to make a mistake.

Because of his belief in his infallibility, the narrator never doubted the success of his project.

blighted (blīt'id) *v.* used as *adj.:* suffering from conditions that destroy or prevent growth.

The blighted fields would never produce any corn or cotton.

doggedness (dôg'id·nis) *n.:* stubbornness; persistence.

Because of his doggedness, Doodle did learn to walk.

reiterated (rē·it'ə·rāt'id) *v.:* repeated.

Several times, the narrator reiterated his desire to teach Doodle to swim.

precariously (pri·ker'ē·əs·lē) *adv.:* unsteadily; insecurely.

Doodle balanced precariously on his thin legs.

mar (mär) *v.:* damage; spoil.

The storm could mar the cotton and other crops, causing the loss of acres of profits.

FIGURATIVE LANGUAGE

Figurative language helps you see familiar things in new ways. The simplest
type of figurative language, the **simile,** uses comparisons to create fresh,
new meaning. A simile is a comparison between two dissimilar things linked
by a word such as *like, as,* or *resembles.* For example:

> The storm was as fierce as an angry lion.

In this simile, a storm is compared to a lion. Comparing a fierce storm to an
angry lion helps readers see how violent and dangerous the storm was.

As you read "The Scarlet Ibis," look for other similes. Figure out what is
being compared. Ask yourself: "What does this simile help me *see*? How
does it help me understand the story more fully?"

The Scarlet Ibis

James Hurst

CLARIFY

A *clove* (klōv) is a division or split of some kind. During what time of year does this story take place?

_____

_____

_____

_____

IDENTIFY

Re-read the narrator's description of the garden (lines 1–9). Underline the words and phrases that bring to mind death or dying.

Notes _____

_____

_____

_____

It was in the clove of seasons, summer was dead but autumn had not yet been born, that the ibis lit in the bleeding tree. The flower garden was stained with rotting brown magnolia petals, and ironweeds grew rank[1] amid the purple phlox. The five o'clocks by the chimney still marked time, but the oriole nest in the elm was untenanted and rocked back and forth like an empty cradle. The last graveyard flowers were blooming, and their smell drifted across the cotton field and through every room of our house, speaking softly the names of our dead.

10   It's strange that all this is still so clear to me, now that that summer has long since fled and time has had its way. A grindstone stands where the bleeding tree stood, just outside the kitchen door, and now if an oriole sings in the elm, its song seems to die up in the leaves, a silvery dust. The flower garden is prim, the house a gleaming white, and the pale fence across the yard stands straight and spruce. But sometimes (like right now), as I sit in the cool, green-draped parlor, the grindstone begins to turn, and time with all its changes is ground away—and I remember Doodle.

---

1. **rank** (raŋk) *adj.:* thick and wild. *Rank* also means "smelly."

"The Scarlet Ibis" by **James R. Hurst** from *The Atlantic Monthly,* July 1960. Copyright © 1960 by The Atlantic Monthly. Reprinted by permission of the author.

20   Doodle was just about the craziest brother a boy ever had.
Of course, he wasn't a crazy crazy like old Miss Leedie, who was
in love with President Wilson and wrote him a letter every day,
but was a nice crazy, like someone you meet in your dreams. He
was born when I was six and was, from the outset, a disappoint-
ment. He seemed all head, with a tiny body which was red and
shriveled like an old man's. Everybody thought he was going to
die—everybody except Aunt Nicey, who had delivered him. She
said he would live because he was born in a caul[2] and cauls were
made from Jesus' nightgown. Daddy had Mr. Heath, the carpen-
30   ter, build a little mahogany coffin for him. But he didn't die, and
when he was three months old, Mama and Daddy decided they
might as well name him. They named him William Armstrong,
which was like tying a big tail on a small kite. Such a name
sounds good only on a tombstone.

I thought myself pretty smart at many things, like holding
my breath, running, jumping, or climbing the vines in Old
Woman Swamp, and I wanted more than anything else someone
to race to Horsehead Landing, someone to box with, and someone to perch with in the top fork of the great pine behind the
40   barn, where across the fields and swamps you could see the sea.
I wanted a brother. But Mama, crying, told me that even if
William Armstrong lived, he would never do these things with
me. He might not, she sobbed, even be "all there." He might, as
long as he lived, lie on the rubber sheet in the center of the bed
in the front bedroom where the white marquisette[3] curtains bil-
lowed out in the afternoon sea breeze, rustling like palmetto
fronds.[4]

It was bad enough having an invalid brother, but having
one who possibly was not all there was unbearable, so I began to
50   make plans to kill him by smothering him with a pillow.

---

2. **caul** (kôl) *n.:* membrane (thin, skinlike material) that sometimes
   covers a baby's head at birth.
3. **marquisette** (mär′ki·zet′) *adj.:* made of a thin, netlike fabric.
4. **palmetto fronds:** fanlike leaves of a palm tree.

IDENTIFY

Re-read lines 20–23.
Underline the detail that tells
you that the story takes
place in the past.

INTERPRET

In lines 32–33, the narrator
compares his brother's given
name to a "big tail on a
small kite." What does this
simile tell you about the narrator's opinion of his brother's name?

_____

_____

_____

_____

_____

_____

_____

_____

_____

_____

_____

_____

IDENTIFY

Re-read lines 35–41. What
does the narrator want?
Underline what you find out.

Why is it so important to the
narrator that his brother is
"all there" (lines 54–55)?

_____

_____

_____

_____

_____

What does the description in
lines 59–61 tell you about
Doodle?

_____

_____

_____

Pause at line 79. Why doesn't
Aunt Nicey like Doodle's
nickname?

_____

_____

_____

_____

_____

_____

_____

_____

_____

However, one afternoon as I watched him, my head poked between the iron posts of the foot of the bed, he looked straight at me and grinned. I skipped through the rooms, down the echoing halls, shouting, "Mama, he smiled. He's all there! He's all there!" and he was.

When he was two, if you laid him on his stomach, he began to try to move himself, straining terribly. The doctor said that with his weak heart this strain would probably kill him, but it didn't. Trembling, he'd push himself up, turning first red, then a soft

60 purple, and finally collapse back onto the bed like an old worn-out doll. I can still see Mama watching him, her hand pressed tight across her mouth, her eyes wide and unblinking. But he learned to crawl (it was his third winter), and we brought him out of the front bedroom, putting him on the rug before the fireplace. For the first time he became one of us.

As long as he lay all the time in bed, we called him William Armstrong, even though it was formal and sounded as if we were referring to one of our ancestors, but with his creeping around on the deerskin rug and beginning to talk, something

70 had to be done about his name. It was I who renamed him. When he crawled, he crawled backward, as if he were in reverse and couldn't change gears. If you called him, he'd turn around as if he were going in the other direction, then he'd back right up to you to be picked up. Crawling backward made him look like a doodlebug[5] so I began to call him Doodle, and in time even Mama and Daddy thought it was a better name than William Armstrong. Only Aunt Nicey disagreed. She said caul babies should be treated with special respect since they might turn out to be saints. Renaming my brother was perhaps the

80 kindest thing I ever did for him, because nobody expects much from someone called Doodle.

_____

5. **doodlebug** (dōōd'l·bug') *n.:* larva of a type of insect that moves backward.

Although Doodle learned to crawl, he showed no signs of walking, but he wasn't idle. He talked so much that we all quit listening to what he said. It was about this time that Daddy built him a go-cart, and I had to pull him around. At first I just paraded him up and down the piazza,[6] but then he started crying to be taken out into the yard and it ended up by my having to lug him wherever I went. If I so much as picked up my cap, he'd start crying to go with me, and Mama would call from wherever she was, "Take Doodle with you."

He was a burden in many ways. The doctor had said that he mustn't get too excited, too hot, too cold, or too tired and that he must always be treated gently. A long list of don'ts went with him, all of which I ignored once we got out of the house. To discourage his coming with me, I'd run with him across the ends of the cotton rows and careen him around corners on two wheels. Sometimes I accidentally turned him over, but he never told Mama. His skin was very sensitive, and he had to wear a big straw hat whenever he went out. When the going got rough and he had to cling to the sides of the go-cart, the hat slipped all the way down over his ears. He was a sight. Finally, I could see I was licked. Doodle was my brother, and he was going to cling to me forever, no matter what I did, so I dragged him across the burning cotton field to share with him the only beauty I knew, Old Woman Swamp. I pulled the go-cart through the sawtooth fern, down into the green dimness where the palmetto fronds whispered by the stream. I lifted him out and set him down in the soft rubber grass beside a tall pine. His eyes were round with wonder as he gazed about him, and his little hands began to stroke the rubber grass. Then he began to cry.

"For heaven's sake, what's the matter?" I asked, annoyed.

"It's so pretty," he said. "So pretty, pretty, pretty."

After that day Doodle and I often went down into Old Woman Swamp. I would gather wildflowers, wild violets,

---

6. **piazza** (pē·az′ə) *n.:* large covered porch.

IDENTIFY

What does the narrator transport Doodle in (lines 82–90)? Underline the sentence where you find out.

VISUALIZE

Re-read lines 91–101. In your own words, describe the narrator and his brother as they might look to an observer.

_____

_____

_____

_____

_____

_____

_____

_____

_____

_____

_____

_____

INFER

Re-read lines 108–112, and circle the details that help you infer Doodle's character traits. What are they?

_____

_____

CLARIFY

Re-read the long sentence in lines 122–125. What is the narrator saying about the relationship between love and cruelty?

_____

_____

_____

VOCABULARY

sullenly (sul′ən·lē) *adv.:* resentfully; gloomily.

INFER

Pause at line 144. Why do you think the narrator shows Doodle the coffin? What might this event **foreshadow**?

_____

_____

_____

_____

_____

_____

_____

_____

_____

_____

_____

honeysuckle, yellow jasmine, snakeflowers, and waterlilies, and with wire grass we'd weave them into necklaces and crowns. We'd bedeck ourselves with our handiwork and loll about thus beautified, beyond the touch of the everyday world. Then when the slanted rays of the sun burned orange in the tops of the
120   pines, we'd drop our jewels into the stream and watch them float away toward the sea.

    There is within me (and with sadness I have watched it in others) a knot of cruelty borne by the stream of love, much as our blood sometimes bears the seed of our destruction, and at times I was mean to Doodle. One day I took him up to the barn loft and showed him his casket, telling him how we all had believed he would die. It was covered with a film of Paris green[7] sprinkled to kill the rats, and screech owls had built a nest inside it.

130   Doodle studied the mahogany box for a long time, then said, "It's not mine."

    "It is," I said. "And before I'll help you down from the loft, you're going to have to touch it."

    "I won't touch it," he said **sullenly.**

    "Then I'll leave you here by yourself," I threatened, and made as if I were going down.

    Doodle was frightened of being left. "Don't go leave me, Brother," he cried, and he leaned toward the coffin. His hand, trembling, reached out, and when he touched the casket, he
140   screamed. A screech owl flapped out of the box into our faces, scaring us and covering us with Paris green. Doodle was paralyzed, so I put him on my shoulder and carried him down the ladder, and even when we were outside in the bright sunshine, he clung to me, crying, "Don't leave me. Don't leave me."

    When Doodle was five years old, I was embarrassed at having a brother of that age who couldn't walk, so I set out to teach him.

---

7. **Paris green** *n.:* poisonous green powder used to kill insects.

We were down in Old Woman Swamp and it was spring and the sick-sweet smell of bay flowers hung everywhere like a mournful song. "I'm going to teach you to walk, Doodle," I said.

150   He was sitting comfortably on the soft grass, leaning back against the pine. "Why?" he asked.

I hadn't expected such an answer. "So I won't have to haul you around all the time."

"I can't walk, Brother," he said.

"Who says so?" I demanded.

"Mama, the doctor—everybody."

"Oh, you can walk," I said, and I took him by the arms and stood him up. He collapsed onto the grass like a half-empty flour sack. It was as if he had no bones in his little legs.

160   "Don't hurt me, Brother," he warned.

"Shut up. I'm not going to hurt you. I'm going to teach you to walk." I heaved him up again, and again he collapsed.

WORD STUDY

Re-read lines 147–149. Underline the **simile,** and explain what two things are being compared.

_____

_____

_____

_____

_____

_____

_____

_____

_____

_____

_____

_____

_____

_____

_____

_____

This time he did not lift his face up out of the rubber grass. "I just can't do it. Let's make honeysuckle wreaths."

"Oh yes you can, Doodle," I said. "All you got to do is try. Now come on," and I hauled him up once more.

It seemed so hopeless from the beginning that it's a miracle I didn't give up. But all of us must have something or someone to be proud of, and Doodle had become mine. I did not know then that pride is a wonderful, terrible thing, a seed that bears two vines, life and death. Every day that summer we went to the pine beside the stream of Old Woman Swamp, and I put him on his feet at least a hundred times each afternoon. Occasionally I too became discouraged because it didn't seem as if he was trying, and I would say, "Doodle, don't you want to learn to walk?"

He'd nod his head, and I'd say, "Well, if you don't keep trying, you'll never learn." Then I'd paint for him a picture of us as old men, white-haired, him with a long white beard and me still pulling him around in the go-cart. This never failed to make him try again.

Finally, one day, after many weeks of practicing, he stood alone for a few seconds. When he fell, I grabbed him in my arms and hugged him, our laughter pealing through the swamp like a ringing bell. Now we knew it could be done. Hope no longer hid in the dark palmetto thicket but perched like a cardinal in the lacy toothbrush tree, brilliantly visible. "Yes, yes," I cried, and he cried it too, and the grass beneath us was soft and the smell of the swamp was sweet.

With success so **imminent,** we decided not to tell anyone until he could actually walk. Each day, barring rain, we sneaked into Old Woman Swamp, and by cotton-picking time Doodle was ready to show what he could do. He still wasn't able to walk far, but we could wait no longer. Keeping a nice secret is very hard to do, like holding your breath. We chose to reveal all on October eighth, Doodle's sixth birthday, and for weeks ahead we mooned around the house, promising everybody a most spectacular surprise. Aunt Nicey said that, after so much talk, if we produced anything less tremendous than the Resurrection,[8] she was going to be disappointed.

200   At breakfast on our chosen day, when Mama, Daddy, and Aunt Nicey were in the dining room, I brought Doodle to the door in the go-cart just as usual and had them turn their backs, making them cross their hearts and hope to die if they peeked. I helped Doodle up, and when he was standing alone I let them look. There wasn't a sound as Doodle walked slowly across the room and sat down at his place at the table. Then Mama began to cry and ran over to him, hugging him and kissing him. Daddy hugged him too, so I went to Aunt Nicey, who was thanks-praying in the doorway, and began to waltz her around. We danced

210   together quite well until she came down on my big toe with her brogans,[9] hurting me so badly I thought I was crippled for life.

Doodle told them it was I who had taught him to walk, so everyone wanted to hug me, and I began to cry.

"What are you crying for?" asked Daddy, but I couldn't answer. They did not know that I did it for myself; that pride, whose slave I was, spoke to me louder than all their voices; and that Doodle walked only because I was ashamed of having a crippled brother.

Within a few months Doodle had learned to walk well and

220   his go-cart was put up in the barn loft (it's still there) beside his little mahogany coffin. Now, when we roamed off together, resting often, we never turned back until our destination had been reached, and to help pass the time, we took up lying. From the beginning Doodle was a terrible liar, and he got me in the habit. Had anyone stopped to listen to us, we would have been sent off to Dix Hill.

My lies were scary, involved, and usually pointless, but Doodle's were twice as crazy. People in his stories all had wings and flew wherever they wanted to go. His favorite lie was about a

---

8. **Resurrection:** reference to the Christian belief in the rising of Jesus from the dead after his burial.
9. **brogans** (brō′gənz) *n.:* heavy, ankle-high shoes.

INTERPRET

Re-read lines 215–218. Is the narrator describing pride that brings something wonderful or something terrible?

_____

_____

_____

_____

_____

_____

_____

_____

_____

CLARIFY

Re-read lines 225–226. Dix Hill is a state mental hospital in Raleigh, North Carolina. What does the narrator mean by this statement?

_____

_____

_____

_____

_____

_____

VISUALIZE

Re-read lines 231–236. Underline the details that help you visualize Doodle's lie. Why is the peacock important in his lie?

_____

_____

_____

_____

_____

_____

VOCABULARY

iridescent (ir′i·des′ənt) _adj._: rainbowlike; displaying a shifting range of colors.

serene (sə·rēn′) _adj._: peaceful; calm.

infallibility (in·fal′ə·bil′ə·tē) _n._: inability to make a mistake.

EVALUATE

Pause at line 260. Do you think the narrator's "development program" is a good idea? Briefly explain.

_____

_____

_____

_____

_____

_____

230 boy named Peter who had a pet peacock with a ten-foot tail. Peter wore a golden robe that glittered so brightly that when he walked through the sunflowers they turned away from the sun to face him. When Peter was ready to go to sleep, the peacock spread his magnificent tail, enfolding the boy gently like a closing go-to-sleep flower, burying him in the gloriously **iridescent,** rustling vortex.[10] Yes, I must admit it. Doodle could beat me lying.

Doodle and I spent lots of time thinking about our future. We decided that when we were grown, we'd live in Old Woman

240 Swamp and pick dog's-tongue[11] for a living. Beside the stream, he planned, we'd build us a house of whispering leaves and the swamp birds would be our chickens. All day long (when we weren't gathering dog's-tongue) we'd swing through the cypresses on the rope vines, and if it rained we'd huddle beneath an umbrella tree and play stickfrog. Mama and Daddy could come and live with us if they wanted to. He even came up with the idea that he could marry Mama and I could marry Daddy. Of course, I was old enough to know this wouldn't work out, but the picture he painted was so beautiful and **serene** that all I

250 could do was whisper yes, yes.

Once I had succeeded in teaching Doodle to walk, I began to believe in my own **infallibility** and I prepared a terrific development program for him, unknown to Mama and Daddy, of course. I would teach him to run, to swim, to climb trees, and to fight. He, too, now believed in my infallibility, so we set the deadline for these accomplishments less than a year away, when, it had been decided, Doodle could start to school.

That winter we didn't make much progress, for I was in school and Doodle suffered from one bad cold after another. But

260 when spring came, rich and warm, we raised our sights again. Success lay at the end of summer like a pot of gold, and our

---

10. **vortex** (vôr′teks′) _n._: something resembling a whirlpool.
11. **dog's-tongue** _n._: wild vanilla.

campaign got off to a good start. On hot days, Doodle and I went down to Horsehead Landing, and I gave him swimming lessons or showed him how to row a boat. Sometimes we descended into the cool greenness of Old Woman Swamp and climbed the rope vines or boxed scientifically beneath the pine where he had learned to walk. Promise hung about us like leaves, and wherever we looked, ferns unfurled and birds broke into song.

270   That summer, the summer of 1918, was **blighted.** In May and June there was no rain and the crops withered, curled up, then died under the thirsty sun. One morning in July a hurricane came out of the east, tipping over the oaks in the yard and splitting the limbs of the elm trees. That afternoon it roared back out of the west, blew the fallen oaks around, snapping their roots and tearing them out of the earth like a hawk at the entrails[12] of a chicken. Cotton bolls were wrenched from the stalks and lay like green walnuts in the valleys between the rows, while the cornfield leaned over uniformly so that the tassels

280   touched the ground. Doodle and I followed Daddy out into the cotton field, where he stood, shoulders sagging, surveying the ruin. When his chin sank down onto his chest, we were frightened, and Doodle slipped his hand into mine. Suddenly Daddy straightened his shoulders, raised a giant knuckly fist, and with a voice that seemed to rumble out of the earth itself began cursing heaven, hell, the weather, and the Republican party.[13] Doodle and I, prodding each other and giggling, went back to the house, knowing that everything would be all right.

        And during that summer, strange names were heard

290   through the house: Château-Thierry, Amiens, Soissons, and in her blessing at the supper table, Mama once said, "And bless the Pearsons, whose boy Joe was lost in Belleau Wood."[14]

---

12. **entrails** (en′trālz) *n.:* inner organs; guts.
13. **Republican party:** At this time most southern farmers were loyal Democrats.
14. **Château-Thierry** (sha′tō′ tē·er′·ē), **Amiens** (a·myan′), **Soissons** (swä·sôn′), **Belleau** (be·lô′) **Wood:** World War I battle sites in France.

VOCABULARY

blighted (blīt′id) *v.* used as *adj.:* suffering from conditions that destroy or prevent growth.

INTERPRET

Re-read lines 274–277. Underline the **simile** the narrator uses to describe the destruction of the oak trees. Why do you think the writer chose this comparison?

_____

_____

_____

_____

SYMBOLISM

Pause at line 288. If the "blighted" summer, including the violent hurricane, is a **symbol** of what is to come, what might lie in Doodle's future?

_____

_____

_____

_____

_____

_____

_____

PREDICT

Underline the details in lines 309–313 that suggest Doodle is becoming increasingly ill and weak. Based on these details, what do you **predict** will happen to Doodle?

_____

_____

_____

_____

_____

_____

_____

_____

_____

_____

So we came to that clove of seasons. School was only a few weeks away, and Doodle was far behind schedule. He could barely clear the ground when climbing up the rope vines, and his swimming was certainly not passable. We decided to double our efforts, to make that last drive and reach our pot of gold. I made him swim until he turned blue and row until he couldn't lift an oar. Wherever we went, I purposely walked fast, and

300 although he kept up, his face turned red and his eyes became glazed. Once, he could go no further, so he collapsed on the ground and began to cry.

"Aw, come on, Doodle," I urged. "You can do it. Do you want to be different from everybody else when you start school?"

"Does it make any difference?"

"It certainly does," I said. "Now, come on," and I helped him up.

As we slipped through the dog days,[15] Doodle began to

310 look feverish, and Mama felt his forehead, asking him if he felt

---

15. **dog days** *n.:* hot days in July and August, named after the Dog Star (Sirius), which rises and sets with the sun during this period.

ill. At night he didn't sleep well, and sometimes he had night-mares, crying out until I touched him and said, "Wake up, Doodle. Wake up."

It was Saturday noon, just a few days before school was to start. I should have already admitted defeat, but my pride wouldn't let me. The excitement of our program had now been gone for weeks, but still we kept on with a tired **doggedness.** It was too late to turn back, for we had both wandered too far into a net of expectations and had left no crumbs behind.

320   Daddy, Mama, Doodle, and I were seated at the dining-room table having lunch. It was a hot day, with all the windows and doors open in case a breeze should come. In the kitchen Aunt Nicey was humming softly. After a long silence, Daddy spoke. "It's so calm, I wouldn't be surprised if we had a storm this afternoon."

"I haven't heard a rain frog," said Mama, who believed in signs, as she served the bread around the table.

"I did," declared Doodle. "Down in the swamp."

"He didn't," I said contrarily.

330   "You did, eh?" said Daddy, ignoring my denial.

"I certainly did," Doodle **reiterated,** scowling at me over the top of his iced-tea glass, and we were quiet again.

Suddenly, from out in the yard came a strange croaking noise. Doodle stopped eating, with a piece of bread poised ready for his mouth, his eyes popped round like two blue buttons. "What's that?" he whispered.

I jumped up, knocking over my chair, and had reached the door when Mama called, "Pick up the chair, sit down again, and say excuse me."

340   By the time I had done this, Doodle had excused himself and had slipped out into the yard. He was looking up into the bleeding tree. "It's a great big red bird!" he called.

The bird croaked loudly again, and Mama and Daddy came out into the yard. We shaded our eyes with our hands against the hazy glare of the sun and peered up through the still leaves.

VOCABULARY

doggedness (dôg′id·nis) *n.:* stubbornness; persistence.

reiterated (rē·it′ə·rāt′id) *v.:* repeated.

INTERPRET

In your own words, explain what the narrator means by lines 316–319.

SYMBOLISM

Re-read lines 346–351. In
what ways does the bird
remind you of Doodle?

_____

_____

INTERPRET

Pause at line 364. Like
Doodle, the scarlet ibis is
described as being uncoordinated, delicate, and unique.
How might the death of the
ibis foreshadow the story's
ending?

_____

_____

_____

_____

_____

_____

_____

_____

_____

_____

_____

_____

On the topmost branch a bird the size of a chicken, with scarlet feathers and long legs, was perched **precariously.** Its wings hung down loosely, and as we watched, a feather dropped away and floated slowly down through the green leaves.

350   "It's not even frightened of us," Mama said.

"It looks tired," Daddy added. "Or maybe sick."

Doodle's hands were clasped at his throat, and I had never seen him stand still so long. "What is it?" he asked.

Daddy shook his head. "I don't know, maybe it's—"

At that moment the bird began to flutter, but the wings were uncoordinated, and amid much flapping and a spray of fly-ing feathers, it tumbled down, bumping through the limbs of the bleeding tree and landing at our feet with a thud. Its long, graceful neck jerked twice into an S, then straightened out, and

360 the bird was still. A white veil came over the eyes, and the long white beak unhinged. Its legs were crossed and its clawlike feet were delicately curved at rest. Even death did not **mar** its grace, for it lay on the earth like a broken vase of red flowers, and we stood around it, awed by its exotic beauty.

"It's dead," Mama said.

"What is it?" Doodle repeated.

"Go bring me the bird book," said Daddy.

I ran into the house and brought back the bird book. As we watched, Daddy thumbed through its pages. "It's a scarlet ibis,"

370 he said, pointing to a picture. "It lives in the tropics—South America to Florida. A storm must have brought it here."

Sadly, we all looked back at the bird. A scarlet ibis! How many miles it had traveled to die like this, in *our* yard, beneath the bleeding tree.

"Let's finish lunch," Mama said, nudging us back toward the dining room.

"I'm not hungry," said Doodle, and he knelt down beside the ibis.

"We've got peach cobbler for dessert," Mama tempted from

380 the doorway.

Doodle remained kneeling. "I'm going to bury him."

"Don't you dare touch him," Mama warned. "There's no telling what disease he might have had."

"All right," said Doodle. "I won't."

Daddy, Mama, and I went back to the dining-room table, but we watched Doodle through the open door. He took out a piece of string from his pocket and, without touching the ibis, looped one end around its neck. Slowly, while singing softly "Shall We Gather at the River," he carried the bird around to the front yard and dug a hole in the flower garden, next to the petunia bed. Now we were watching him through the front window, but he didn't know it. His awkwardness at digging the hole with a shovel whose handle was twice as long as he was made us laugh, and we covered our mouths with our hands so he wouldn't hear.

When Doodle came into the dining room, he found us seriously eating our cobbler. He was pale and lingered just inside the screen door. "Did you get the scarlet ibis buried?" asked Daddy.

Doodle didn't speak but nodded his head.

"Go wash your hands, and then you can have some peach cobbler," said Mama.

"I'm not hungry," he said.

"Dead birds is bad luck," said Aunt Nicey, poking her head from the kitchen door. "Specially *red* dead birds!"

As soon as I had finished eating, Doodle and I hurried off to Horsehead Landing. Time was short, and Doodle still had a long way to go if he was going to keep up with the other boys when he started school. The sun, gilded with the yellow cast of autumn, still burned fiercely, but the dark green woods through which we passed were shady and cool. When we reached the landing, Doodle said he was too tired to swim, so we got into a skiff and floated down the creek with the tide. Far off in the marsh a rail was scolding, and over on the beach locusts were singing in the myrtle trees. Doodle did not speak and kept his head turned away, letting one hand trail limply in the water.

INFER

Pause at line 395. Why is Doodle so fascinated by the scarlet ibis? Why does he take such pains to bury it?

FLUENCY

The description of Doodle's burial of the scarlet ibis in lines 385–399 is a very moving passage. Read the boxed passage aloud twice. Focus on conveying meaning the first time you read. The second time you read, try to convey the passage's emotional overtones.

Notes

INTERPRET

Re-read lines 416–425. Circle the details describing the approaching storm. What do you think the storm **foreshadows**?

_____

_____

_____

INTERPRET

Underline line 441. Then, underline the parts of the story where you have heard this before—Doodle's begging his brother not to leave him or not to hurt him. What could these words **foreshadow**?

_____

_____

_____

_____

_____

INFER

Pause at line 447. Why does the narrator leave Doodle behind?

_____

_____

_____

_____

_____

_____

After we had drifted a long way, I put the oars in place and made Doodle row back against the tide. Black clouds began to gather in the southwest, and he kept watching them, trying to pull the oars a little faster. When we reached Horsehead
420 Landing, lightning was playing across half the sky and thunder roared out, hiding even the sound of the sea. The sun disappeared and darkness descended, almost like night. Flocks of marsh crows flew by, heading inland to their roosting trees, and two egrets, squawking, arose from the oyster-rock shallows and careened away.

Doodle was both tired and frightened, and when he stepped from the skiff he collapsed onto the mud, sending an armada[16] of fiddler crabs rustling off into the marsh grass. I helped him up, and as he wiped the mud off his trousers, he
430 smiled at me ashamedly. He had failed and we both knew it, so we started back home, racing the storm. We never spoke (what are the words that can solder[17] cracked pride?), but I knew he was watching me, watching for a sign of mercy. The lightning was near now, and from fear he walked so close behind me he kept stepping on my heels. The faster I walked, the faster he walked, so I began to run. The rain was coming, roaring through the pines, and then, like a bursting Roman candle, a gum tree ahead of us was shattered by a bolt of lightning. When the deafening peal of thunder had died, and in the moment before the
440 rain arrived, I heard Doodle, who had fallen behind, cry out, "Brother, Brother, don't leave me! Don't leave me!"

The knowledge that Doodle's and my plans had come to naught was bitter, and that streak of cruelty within me awakened. I ran as fast as I could, leaving him far behind with a wall of rain dividing us. The drops stung my face like nettles, and the wind flared the wet, glistening leaves of the bordering trees. Soon I could hear his voice no more.

16. **armada** (är·mä′də) *n.:* group. *Armada* is generally used to mean "fleet, or group, of warships."
17. **solder** (säd′ər) *v.:* patch or repair. Solder is a mixture of metals melted and used to repair metal parts.

I hadn't run too far before I became tired, and the flood of childish spite evanesced[18] as well. I stopped and waited for

450 Doodle. The sound of rain was everywhere, but the wind had died and it fell straight down in parallel paths like ropes hanging from the sky. As I waited, I peered through the downpour, but no one came. Finally I went back and found him huddled beneath a red nightshade bush beside the road. He was sitting on the ground, his face buried in his arms, which were resting on his drawn-up knees. "Let's go, Doodle," I said.

He didn't answer, so I placed my hand on his forehead and lifted his head. Limply, he fell backward onto the earth. He had been bleeding from the mouth, and his neck and the front of his

460 shirt were stained a brilliant red.

"Doodle! Doodle!" I cried, shaking him, but there was no answer but the ropy rain. He lay very awkwardly, with his head thrown far back, making his vermilion[19] neck appear unusually long and slim. His little legs, bent sharply at the knees, had never before seemed so fragile, so thin.

I began to weep, and the tear-blurred vision in red before me looked very familiar. "Doodle!" I screamed above the pounding storm, and threw my body to the earth above his. For a long, long time, it seemed forever, I lay there crying, sheltering my

470 fallen scarlet ibis from the heresy[20] of rain.

---

18. **evanesced** (ev′ə·nest′) *v.*: faded away; disappeared.
19. **vermilion** (vər·mil′yən) *adj.*: bright red.
20. **heresy** (her′ə·sē) *n.*: here, mockery. *Heresy* generally means "denial of what is commonly believed to be true" or "rejection of a church's teaching."

SYMBOLISM

What do the details in the description of Doodle in the last two paragraphs remind you of? Why do you think the writer makes this association?

_____

_____

_____

_____

_____

_____

_____

_____

_____

SYMBOLISM

In lines 468–470, what does the narrator call his dead brother?

_____

_____

_____

_____

_____

_____

The Scarlet Ibis

Symbol Chart In "The Scarlet Ibis," some of the people, places, things, and events stand both for themselves and for something beyond themselves. Fill out the symbol chart below to see how symbols convey meaning in the story. In the first column are passages from the story. Locate a symbol from each passage, and write it in the second column. Then, write the meaning of the symbol in the third column. The first row is done for you. Fill in the bottom row with a symbolic story passage that you find on your own.

Story Passage	Symbol	Meaning
That winter we didn't make much progress, for I was in school and Doodle suffered from one bad cold after another. But when spring came, rich and warm, we raised our sights again (lines 258–260).	spring	new start; rebirth
When Peter was ready to go to sleep, the peacock spread his magnificent tail, enfolding the boy gently like a closing go-to-sleep flower, burying him in the gloriously iridescent, rustling vortex (lines 233–236).		
Sadly, we all looked back at the bird. A scarlet ibis! How many miles it had traveled to die like this, in *our* yard, beneath the bleeding tree (lines 372–374).		

 **The Scarlet Ibis**

Complete the sample test item below. Then, read the explanation at the right.

Sample Test Question	Explanation of the Correct Answer
Which of the following are recurring **symbols** in "The Scarlet Ibis"? **A** birds **B** flowers **C** bees **D** tombstones	The correct answer is *A;* the writer uses birds as symbols all through the story. *B* and *D* are not correct because they are used only once. *C* is not correct because bees aren't mentioned in the story.

DIRECTIONS: Circle the letter of each correct answer.

1. The description of Doodle's last summer as "blighted" **foreshadows** —

   A Doodle's birth

   B Doodle's coming death

   C the scarlet ibis

   D life in the South

2. The scarlet ibis **symbolizes** Doodle in that both the child and bird are —

   F able to move very quickly

   G trying to learn to fly

   H rare, beautiful, and fragile

   J very fond of being outside

3. The **setting** of the story as presented in the opening paragraph could best be described as—

   A sad and suggestive of death

   B cheerful and suggestive of life

   C peaceful and suggestive of heaven

   D haunted and suggestive of danger

4. Which of these details is *not* an example of **foreshadowing** in the story?

   F "'Don't hurt me, Brother,' he warned."

   G "The oriole nest . . . rocked back and forth like an empty cradle."

   H "One day I took him up to the barn loft and showed him his casket. . . ."

   J "Keeping a nice secret is very hard to do. . . ."

Reading Standard 3.7 Recognize and understand the significance of various literary devices, including figurative language, imagery, allegory, and symbolism, and explain their appeal.

Standards Review

 **The Scarlet Ibis**

Reading Standard 1.1
Identify the literal and figurative meanings of words and understand word derivations.

Reading Standard 1.1 (Grade 8 Review)
Analyze idioms, analogies, metaphors, and similes to infer the literal and figurative meanings of phrases.

Similes

DIRECTIONS: Circle the letter of the correct response.

1. What does this **simile** indicate?
   They named him William Armstrong, which was like tying a big tail on a small kite.

   A The baby's abilities are amazing.

   B Babies do not need decoration.

   C The baby's name is too grand.

   D Coming up with names is tricky.

2. Which of the following sentences contains a **simile**?

   F He collapsed onto the grass like a half-empty flour sack.

   G For the first time he became one of us.

   H He was a burden in many ways.

   J Finally, I could see I was licked.

3. Which of the following sentences contains a **simile**?

   A The flower garden was brown.

   B A grindstone stands where the bleeding tree stood.

   C The oriole nest rocked back and forth like an empty cradle.

   D The pale fence across the yard stands straight.

Vocabulary in Context

DIRECTIONS: Complete the paragraph below by writing words from the box in the correct blanks. Not all words from the box will be used.

Word Box

- sullenly
- imminent
- iridescent
- serene
- infallibility
- blighted
- doggedness
- reiterated
- precariously
- mar

Tony stared (1) _____ out the window. He was unhappy about the weather. The vacation brochure had showed a (2) _____ lake, calm and blue. Another photograph featured a waterfall that sparkled, (3) _____ and colorful. Here, however, Tony saw nothing but a (4) _____ landscape, brown, bare, and damp. He said to the empty room, "Nothing is going to (5) _____ my vacation! I'm going to enjoy myself, rain or shine."

 Before You Go On . . .
Check your Standards Mastery at the back of this book.

The Skull and the Arrow by Louis L'Amour

In many tales an underdog overcomes great odds to conquer a much more powerful enemy. What qualities do you think it takes to beat the odds? Read "The Skull and the Arrow" to learn of one man's desperate struggle for survival.

LITERARY FOCUS: ALLEGORY

An **allegory** is a story that has two meanings—a literal meaning and a symbolic meaning. Allegories are sometimes written to teach lessons. For example, in L. Frank Baum's allegory *The Wonderful Wizard of Oz,* Dorothy literally meets a scarecrow who wants a brain, a tinman who wants a heart, and a cowardly lion who wants to be courageous. On a symbolic level, however, she learns the value of wisdom, compassion, and bravery. Allegories tend to tell about simple situations, using characters that have only one or two distinct traits.

- Read this story on a literal level to find out what happens to whom.
- Then, consider story elements that may be symbolic—that may represent larger ideas.

READING SKILLS: IDENTIFY CAUSE AND EFFECT

A **cause** explains why something happens. An **effect** is the result of something that has happened. It is a good idea, when you are reading a story, to question why things happen.

To help you identify cause-and-effect relationships as you read "The Skull and the Arrow":

- Watch for words and phrases that signal cause-and-effect relationships, such as *because, for, since, so, as a result*, and *therefore*.
- Pay attention to the main character's decisions and actions. If a character changes his mind, ask yourself "Why?"
- As an event takes place, try to predict its effect.

Reading Standard 1.1 Identify and use the literal and figurative meanings of words and understand word derivations.

Reading Standard 3.7 Recognize and understand the significance of various literary devices, including figurative language, imagery, allegory, and symbolism, and explain their appeal.

SHORT STORY

PREVIEW SELECTION VOCABULARY

The following words appear in the story you're about to read. You may want to become familiar with them before you begin reading.

tentative (ten'tə·tiv) *adj.:* gently probing; uncertain.

*His fingers were **tentative** as they touched his painful wound.*

inert (in·urt') *adj.:* without the power to move.

*Wounded, the man lay **inert.***

anguish (aŋ'gwish) *n.:* great suffering or pain.

*The pain and **anguish** were so great that the man passed out.*

principle (prin'sə·pəl) *n.:* fundamental truth.

*He fought for the **principle** that a man's property was his alone.*

CONNOTATION AND DENOTATION

Every word has a **denotation,** which is its dictionary meaning. In addition, some words have **connotations,** associations and emotions that have come to be attached to the word beyond its literal meaning. You can figure out a word's connotation by its context. For example, *grief, pain, distress,* and *anguish* all have the same denotation: "suffering." However, these words' connotations are not the same, since they represent different degrees of suffering.

Study this chart to understand the different connotations of these words:

strong suffering		stronger suffering		strongest suffering
distress	→	pain →	grief	→ anguish

The Skull and the Arrow

Louis L'Amour

Heavy clouds hung above the iron-colored peaks, and lancets of lightning[1] flashed and probed. Thunder rolled like a distant avalanche in the mountain valleys. . . . The man on the rocky slope was alone.

He stumbled, staggering beneath the driving rain, his face hammered and raw. Upon his skull a wound gaped wide, upon his cheek the white bone showed through. It was the end. He was finished, and so were they all . . . they were through.

Far-off pines made a dark etching along the skyline, and that horizon marked a crossing. Beyond it was security, a life outside the reach of his enemies, who now believed him dead. Yet, in this storm, he knew he could go no further. Hail laid a

10

Pay careful attention to the notes about **allegory**. By adding up the information, you will come to understand the allegorical meaning of this story.

ALLEGORY

Writers sometimes introduce **symbols** in a story's title. What are the two symbols in this title? What does each object usually symbolize?

_____

_____

_____

---

1. **lancets of lightning:** A lancet is a small, pointed knife used in surgery. The author is creating an image of lightning slicing the sky.

IDENTIFY
CAUSE & EFFECT

Why is the man giving up?
Underline the causes of the
man's decision to quit (lines
15–19).

INTERPRET

In line 24 the narrator says
that "man always returns to
the cave." Briefly explain
what you think this statement means.

_____

_____

_____

_____

_____

_____

_____

_____

VOCABULARY

tentative (ten′tə·tiv) *adj.:*
gently probing; uncertain.

IDENTIFY
CAUSE & EFFECT

Re-read lines 36–37. *So* is a
transitional word that signals
the effect of the man's
defeat. Circle the effect of
the man's defeat.

volley of musketry[2] against the rock where he leaned, so he
started on, falling at times.

He had never been a man to quit, but now he had. They
had beaten him, not man to man but a dozen to one. With fists
and clubs and gun barrels they had beaten him. . . and now he
was through. Yes, he would quit. They had taught him how to
quit.

20   The clouds hung like dark, blowing tapestries[3] in the gaps
of the hills. The man went on until he saw the dark opening of a
cave. He turned to it for shelter then, as men have always done.
Though there are tents and wickiups,[4] halls and palaces, in his
direst need man always returns to the cave.

He was out of the rain but it was cold within. Shivering, he
gathered sticks and some blown leaves. Among the rags of his
wet and muddy clothing, he found a match, and from the
match, a flame. The leaves caught, the blaze stretched **tentative,**
exploring fingers and found food to its liking.

30   He added fuel; the fire took hold, crackled, and gave off
heat. The man moved closer, feeling the warmth upon his hands,
his body. Firelight played shadow games upon the blackened
walls where the smoke from many fires had etched their memories . . . for how many generations of men?

This time he was finished. There was no use going back.
His enemies were sure he was dead, and his friends would accept
it as true. So he was free. He had done his best, so now a little
rest, a little healing, and then over the pine-clad ridge and into
the sunlight. Yet in freedom there is not always contentment.

40   He found fuel again, and came upon a piece of ancient pot-
tery. Dipping water from a pool, he rinsed the pot, then filled it
and brought it back to heat. He squeezed rain from the folds of

---

2. **volley of musketry:** simultaneous discharge of a number of muskets
    or other large-barreled firearms.
3. **tapestries** (tap′əs·trēz) *n.:* heavy, woven cloths with decorative
    designs used as wall hangings.
4. **wickiups** (wik′ē·ups′) *n.:* small, temporary houses or shelters made of
    grass or brush over a frame, used by Indian peoples of the
    Southwest.

his garments, then huddled between the fire and the cave wall, holding tight against the cold.

There was no end to the rain . . . gusts of wind whipped at the cave mouth and dimmed the fire. It was insanity to think of returning. He had been beaten beyond limit. When he was down they had taken turns kicking him. They had broken ribs . . . he could feel them under the cold, a raw pain in his side.

50 Long after he had lain **inert** and helpless, they had bruised and battered and worried at him. Yet he was a tough man, and he could not even find the relief of unconsciousness. He felt every blow, every kick. When they were tired from beating him, they went away.

He had not moved for hours, and only the coming of night and the rain revived him. He moved, agony in every muscle, **anguish** in his side, a mighty throbbing inside his skull, but somehow he managed distance. He crawled, walked, staggered, fell. He fainted, then revived, lay for a time mouth open to the
60 rain, eyes blank and empty.

By now his friends believed him dead. . . . Well, he was not dead, but he was not going back. After all, it was their fight, had always been their fight. Each of them fought for a home, perhaps for a wife, children, parents. He had fought for a **principle,** and because it was his nature to fight.

With the hot water he bathed his head and face, eased the pain of his bruises, washed the blood from his hair, bathed possible poison from his cuts. He felt better then, and the cave grew warmer. He leaned against the wall and relaxed. Peace came to
70 his muscles. After a while he heated more water and drank some of it.

Lightning revealed the frayed trees outside the cave, revealed the gray rain before the cave mouth. He would need more fuel. He got up and rummaged in the further darkness of the cave. He found more sticks and carried them back to his fire. And then he found the skull.

inert (in·urt') *adj.:* without the power to move.

anguish (aŋ'gwish) *n.:* great suffering or pain.

principle (prin'sə·pəl) *n.:* fundamental truth.

COMPARE & CONTRAST

Pause at line 65. What is the difference between the main character's reason for fighting and his friends' reasons for fighting?

_____

_____

_____

_____

_____

_____

_____

_____

_____

_____

_____

_____

_____

_____

_____

_____

_____

_____

_____

_____

FLUENCY

Read aloud the boxed pas-sage two times. Try to improve the speed and smoothness of your delivery on your second read.

Notes _____

_____

_____

_____

_____

_____

_____

_____

_____

He believed its whiteness to be a stick, imbedded as it was in the sandy floor. He tugged to get it loose, becoming more curious as its enormous size became obvious. It was the skull of
80 a gigantic bear, without doubt from prehistoric times. From the size of the skull, the creature must have weighed well over a ton.

Crouching by the firelight he examined it. Wedged in the eye socket was a bit of flint. He broke it free, needing all his strength. It was a finely chipped arrowhead.

The arrow could not have killed the bear. Blinded him, yes, enraged him, but not killed him. Yet the bear had been killed. Probably by a blow from a stone ax, for there was a crack in the skull, and at another place, a spot near the ear where the bone was crushed.

90 Using a bit of stick he dug around, finding more bones. One was a shattered foreleg of the monster, the bone fractured by a blow. And then he found the head of a stone ax. But nowhere did he find the bones of the man.

Despite the throbbing in his skull and the raw pain in his side, he was excited. Within the cave, thousands of years ago, a lone man fought a battle to the death against impossible odds . . . and won.

Fought for what? Surely there was easier game? And with the bear half blinded the man could have escaped, for the cave mouth was wide. In the whirling fury of the fight there must have been opportunities. Yet he had not fled. He had fought on against the overwhelming strength of the wounded beast, pitting against it only his lesser strength, his primitive weapons, and his man-cunning.

Venturing outside the cave for more fuel, he dragged a log within, although the effort made him gasp with agony. He drew the log along the back edge of his fire so that it was at once fuel and reflector of heat.

Burrowing a little in the now warm sand of the cave floor, he was soon asleep.

For three weeks he lived in the cave, finding berries and nuts, snaring small game, always conscious of the presence of the pine-clad ridge, yet also aware of the skull and the arrowhead. In all that time he saw no man, either near or far . . . there was, then, no search for him.

Finally it was time to move. Now he could go over the ridge to safety. Much of his natural strength had returned; he felt better. It was a relief to know that his fight was over.

ALLEGORY

Re-read lines 98–104, which describe a long-ago battle. Circle the clues that suggest that the story's main character admires the man from long ago.

WORD STUDY

The word *man-cunning* in line 104 is a combination of the words *man* and *cunning*, which means "skill" or "cleverness." The writer is using the word *man* here in a traditional way to mean "all humans." By combining the words, he is distinguishing the man's intelligence from that of the bear, which was not able to survive.

IDENTIFY

Underline the phrase in lines 113–114 that suggests the skull and arrowhead have a special meaning for the man.

PREDICT

Pause at line 118. What do you think the man will do now?

_____

_____

_____

_____

_____

_____

_____

_____

What causes the man's enemies to abandon the fight
(lines 125–129)?

_____

_____

_____

_____

_____

_____

_____

_____

ALLEGORY

The man has taken the
arrowhead from the cave
and keeps it with him. What
do you think the arrowhead
symbolizes to the man?

_____

_____

_____

_____

_____

_____

_____

_____

_____

At noon of the following day he stood in the middle of a heat-
120 baked street and faced his enemies again. Behind him were silent
ranks of simple men.

"We've come back," he said quietly. "We're going to stay.
You had me beaten a few weeks ago. You may beat us today, but
some of you will die. And we'll be back. We'll always be back."

There was silence in the dusty street, and then the line
before them wavered, and from behind it a man was walking
away, and then another, and their leader looked at him and said,
"You're insane. Completely insane!" And then he, too, turned
away and the street before them was empty.

130 And the quiet men stood in the street with the light of vic-
tory in their eyes, and the man with the battered face tossed
something and caught it again, something that gleamed for a
moment in the sun.

"What was that?" someone asked.

"An arrowhead," the man said. "Only an arrowhead."

The Skull and the Arrow

Allegory Chart "The Skull and the Arrow" is an allegory: It is meant to be read on both a literal and symbolic level. It also offers readers some lessons about life. Use the following chart to explore the allegorical meanings of the story events. The left-hand column summarizes the literal story events. In the right-hand column, write the allegorical meaning of those events. The first one is done for you.

Literal Story Event	Allegorical Meaning
The man enters the cave.	The man returns to his origins.
The man makes a fire.	
The man finds evidence of an ancient fight between a cave man and a bear.	
The man returns to face his enemies.	
The man displays the arrowhead.	

Standards Review

 **The Skull and the Arrow**

Complete the sample test item below. The box at the right explains why three of these choices are not correct.

Sample Test Question	Explanation of the Correct Answer
We can assume that the man in the story was — A breaking some local law B attacked by a violent group of men C discovered to have a dangerous disease D hunting on someone else's property	The correct answer is *B*; the man has been beaten nearly to death for doing something a group of men did not like. *A* is not correct because there is no mention of local laws. *C* and *D* are not correct because there is no evidence in the story of either.

DIRECTIONS: Circle the letter of the best response.

1. "The Skull and the Arrow" is an **allegory** because —

   A its main character hides in a cave

   B the conclusion of the story is strange

   C it has a simple and unusual setting

   D characters and objects have symbolic meaning

2. Since "The Skull and the Arrow" is an allegory, it —

   F has only one fixed meaning

   G can be read on a literal level and a symbolic level

   H contains dead animals as well as people

   J shows that good always wins over evil

3. What does the man mean when he says, "And we'll be back. We'll always be back"?

   A He has rejected nonviolence.

   B He has many supporters outside the cave.

   C There will always be people who fight against evil.

   D He is a superhero.

4. What **moral lesson** does "The Skull and the Arrow" teach?

   F If your cause is just, don't give in.

   G People don't always beat the odds.

   H True friends never desert you.

   J Be kind to your enemies as well as your friends.

Reading Standard 3.7 Recognize and understand the significance of various literary devices, including figurative language, imagery, allegory, and symbolism, and explain their appeal.

Standards Review

 **The Skull and the Arrow**

Connotation/Denotation

DIRECTIONS: Read each set of words. Write the symbol "+" in front of the word in each pair that seems stronger. Write "−" in front of the word that seems weaker.

1. _____ cried _____ sobbed

2. _____ discomfort _____ agony

3. _____ disgusting _____ disagreeable

4. _____ timid _____ modest

Reading Standard 1.1 Identify and use the literal and figurative meanings of words and understand word derivations.

Vocabulary in Context

DIRECTIONS: Complete the paragraph below by writing a word from the word box to fit each numbered blank.

Word Box
tentative
inert
anguish
principle

The bear ran into the cave, looking for a hiding place. She felt terrible (1) _____ over the cub caught by the hunters, but she had to run with her other cub, which lay (2) _____ from exhaustion on the cave floor. She made a (3) _____ attempt to go outside, but the sound of men's voices drove her back into the cave. In (4) _____ , she should be hibernating by now, but the human predators made her future uncertain at best.

Before You Go On . . .

Check your Standards Mastery at the back of this book.

Poetry

Academic Vocabulary for Chapter 7

These are the terms you should know
as you read and analyze the poems in this chapter.

Imagery Language that appeals to one or more of the five senses: sight, hearing, taste, touch, and smell. For example, this image—"the fish's slippery, shiny scales"—appeals to the senses of sight and touch. The words help us to picture the fish and to imagine how it would feel if we touched it.

Figurative language A word or phrase that creates an imaginative comparison. Figurative language is not meant to be taken literally. There are several types of figures of speech.

- A **simile** compares two unlike things by using a word such as *like* or *as:* "The many-colored fish is like a rainbow."
- A **metaphor** compares two unlike things without using a word such as *like* or *as.* "The fish is a rainbow."
- **Personification** is a type of metaphor in which an object, animal, or idea is talked about as if it were human: "The fish smiles happily."

Reading Standard 3.1 (Grade 8 Review) Determine and articulate the relationship between the purposes and characteristics of different forms of poetry (e.g., ballad, lyric, couplet, epic, elegy, ode, sonnet).

Reading Standard 3.7 Recognize and understand the significance of various literary devices, including figurative language, imagery, allegory, and symbolism, and explain their appeal.

Rhyme The repetition of the sound of the stressed vowel and the rest of the word (*thinking, linking*).

- Words that have **approximate rhyme** repeat some sounds but are not exact echoes (*mean, fine*).
- Most rhymes—called **end rhymes**—come at the end of lines: "Where in this *book* / Do you think I should *look*?"
- Some rhymes—called **internal rhymes**—occur within a line of poetry: "I set my *hat* on the *mat.*"

(continued on next page)

Rhythm A musical quality based on the pattern of stressed and unstressed syllables.

Meter The regular pattern of stressed and unstressed syllables in each line of poetry.

Free verse Poetry that does not follow a regular pattern of rhyme and meter. Free verse sounds like ordinary conversation.

● ● · ●

Onomatopoeia (än′ō·mat′ō·pē′ə) The use of words that sound like what they mean. The words *hiss, crackle, gurgle,* and *pow* sound like what they mean.

Alliteration (ə·lit′ər·ā′shən) The repetition of consonant sounds (usually in the beginnings of words) in words that appear close together: "**H**e **h**ad **h**orse and **h**arness for them all" (from "Johnny Armstrong").

For Further Information . . .

Be sure to read these essays on the elements of poetry in *Holt Literature and Language Arts:*

· **Imagery,** pages 402–403
· **Figures of Speech,** pages 428–429
· **The Sounds of Poetry,** pages 454–455

A Blessing by James Wright

POEM

A realization that someone you love also loves you, a perfect vault in gymnastics, sudden and complete understanding of a math concept that always gave you problems: These may be among the best moments in life, when everything works out well and you feel happy. In "The Blessing," James Wright captures such a moment of joy.

LITERARY FOCUS: IMAGERY

Poets help us share their experiences by using **imagery**—language that appeals to one or more of our fives senses: sight, hearing, touch, smell, and taste.

- The **images** in "A Blessing" appeal mostly to two senses, sight and touch. As you read, think about how these images help you share the speaker's experience.

READING SKILLS: READING A POEM

When you're reading a poem, keep the following strategies in mind:

1. **Look for punctuation in the poem telling you where sentences begin and end.** Most poems—though not all of them—are written in full sentences.
2. **Do not make a full stop at the end of a line if there is no period, comma, colon, semicolon, or dash.** If there is no punctuation at the end of a line of poetry, most poets intend us to read right on to the next line to complete the sense of the sentence.
3. **If a passage of a poem is difficult to understand, look for the subject, verb, and complement of each sentence.** Decide what words the clauses and phrases modify.
4. **Be alert for comparisons—for figures of speech.** Try to visualize what the poet is describing for you.
5. **Read the poem aloud.** Poets are not likely to work in silence. The sound of a poem is very important.
6. **After you have read the poem, talk about it with someone and read it again.** This time, you'll see things in the poem you didn't see before.
7. **Read the poem a third time.** This time, the poem's meaning should become clear.

Reading Standard 3.7 Recognize and understand the significance of various literary devices, including figurative language, imagery, allegory, and symbolism, and explain their appeal.

A Blessing

James Wright

READING A POEM

Use punctuation clues to locate the poem's first sentence. Draw a box around the sentence.

IMAGERY

Circle the **images** in the poem—the words that help you see, touch, hear, smell, or taste something.

INTERPRET

In lines 22–24, the speaker creates a surprising **image**. What is he comparing himself to?

_____

_____

_____

_____

_____

_____

FLUENCY

Read the poem aloud twice. The first time you read, focus on where you pause in your reading and where you come to a full stop. The second time you read, focus on conveying the emotions of the speaker.

Just off the highway to Rochester, Minnesota,

Twilight bounds softly forth on the grass,

And the eyes of those two Indian ponies

Darken with kindness.

5   They have come gladly out of the willows

To welcome my friend and me.

We step over the barbed wire into the pasture

Where they have been grazing all day, alone.

They ripple tensely, they can hardly contain their happiness

10   That we have come.

They bow shyly as wet swans. They love each other.

There is no loneliness like theirs.

At home once more,

They begin munching the young tufts of spring in the

darkness.

15   I would like to hold the slenderer one in my arms,

For she has walked over to me

And nuzzled my left hand.

She is black and white,

Her mane falls wild on her forehead,

20   And the light breeze moves me to caress her long ear

That is delicate as the skin over a girl's wrist.

Suddenly I realize

That if I stepped out of my body I would break

Into blossom.

A Blessing

Imagery Chart   Imagery is language that appeals to the senses of sight, hearing, smell, taste, or touch. To analyze the imagery in "A Blessing," fill in the chart that follows with images you find in the poem and the sense or senses each image appeals to.

Image	Sense or senses it appeals to

LITERATURE

TestPractice **A Blessing**

Complete the sample test item below. Then, read the explanation in the right-hand column.

Sample Test Item	Explanation of the Correct Answer
Which **image** describes the ponies' excitement at seeing the visitors? A young tufts of spring B She is black and white. C twilight bounds D They ripple tensely	The correct answer is *D*. *A* describes the grass. *B* describes one pony's color. *C* describes the sunset.

DIRECTIONS: Circle the letter of each correct response.

1. What can you **infer** about the poem's speaker?

    A He is a horse.

    B He turns into a flower.

    C Horses frighten him.

    D He loves horses.

2. The speaker uses an **image** when he says that the horse's ear is "as delicate as the skin over a girl's wrist." He means that the ear is —

    F stiff

    G coarse

    H soft

    J bony

3. The last three lines of the poem use vivid **imagery** to describe —

    A the speaker's feeling of being blessed

    B the horses' devotion to each other

    C the mane of the black and white horse

    D the highway to Rochester, Minnesota

4. How does the speaker feel about his experience?

    F It has made him sad.

    G He regrets it has happened.

    H It has given him great joy.

    J He feels guilty.

Reading Standard 3.7
Recognize and understand the significance of various literary devices, including figurative language, imagery, allegory, and symbolism, and explain their appeal.

The Sacred by Stephen Dunn; Mooring by Cathy Song

POEMS

BEFORE YOU READ

When you have a deep love for something, you may find that ordinary speech just can't explain that feeling. Instead, you may need to express that love by comparing what you love to something else.

LITERARY FOCUS: FIGURES OF SPEECH

A **figure of speech** is based on a comparison between two unlike things; it is not meant to be taken literally. Several figures of speech are central to poetry. As you read the poems that follow, look for figures of speech. Several types of figurative speech are defined below.

- A **simile** compares two unlike things by using a word such as *like* or *as:* "A scooter ride is like a Frisbee toss on wheels."

- A **metaphor** compares two unlike items without using any specific word of comparison. Metaphors are often **direct;** the two items being compared are linked by *is* or *are:* "The moon is a ghostly galleon." Other metaphors are **implied;** the comparison is suggested rather than stated: "The moon sailed away on the clouds."

- **Personification** is a special type of metaphor in which objects, animals, or ideas are given human qualities or abilities: "The tennis balls arranged themselves to form a grin under the net."

Reading Standard 3.1 (Grade 8 Review) Determine and articulate the relationship between the purposes and characteristics of different forms of poetry (e.g., ballad, lyric, couplet, epic, elegy, ode, sonnet).

Reading Standard 3.7 Recognize and understand the significance of various literary devices, including figurative language, imagery, allegory, and symbolism, and explain their appeal.

The Sacred
Stephen Dunn

After the teacher asked if anyone had
   a sacred place
and the students fidgeted and shrank

in their chairs, the most serious of them all
5   said it was his car,
being in it alone, his tape deck playing

things he'd chosen, and others knew the truth
   had been spoken
and began speaking about their rooms,

10   their hiding places, but the car kept coming up,
   the car in motion,
music filling it, and sometimes one other person

who understood the bright altar of the dashboard
   and how far away
15   a car could take him from the need

to speak, or to answer, the key
   in having a key
and putting it in, and going

Mooring

Cathy Song

My daughter's long black
hair touches the water

where she sits, waist deep in the warm
bath to receive her baby brother.

5   I cup the running water,
precious in the summer of drought,

and enter the cool porcelain tub,
my arms weighed with the sturdy

cargo of my infant son.
10   He lies on his back

and calmly gazes into the faces
of those who love him.

We adore him,
delight in the kernel of toes,

15   like the youngest corn,
the bracelets of flesh,

the apricot glow of skin.
His sister anoints him with the sweetest soap.

"Mooring" from *School Figures* by Cathy Song. Copyright © 1994 by Cathy Song. Reprinted by permission of the **University of Pittsburgh Press.**

CLARIFY

Who is speaking in this poem?

_____

_____

CLARIFY

Pause at line 9. **Paraphrase**, or restate in your own words, what is happening in the poem.

_____

_____

_____

_____

_____

_____

_____

_____

_____

_____

FIGURES OF SPEECH

Re-read lines 13–16. Circle the **simile,** or comparison using *like* or *as*. Underline the **metaphor** in line 16.

_____

_____

_____

_____

CONNECT

Lines 21–25 contain an **allusion**, or reference, to the biblical story of Moses. Moses, a Hebrew baby, was hidden by his mother in the reeds by a river in order to save him from Pharaoh's decree that all male Hebrew babies be killed. Pharaoh's daughter found Moses and raised him. Moses's sister, Miriam, had waited in secret at the river and offered to bring the baby's mother to care for the baby. (Exodus 1:8–22; 2:1–10). Who is Moses in the poem? Who is Miriam?

_____

_____

_____

_____

_____

_____

_____

_____

FIGURES OF SPEECH

Underline the **metaphor** in lines 26–27. What does it suggest about the sister?

_____

_____

_____

_____

_____

_____

20 And love passes like this,
cloudless in the face of a thousand years—

for the mother who parts the water
and sends

the baby in the reeds
upstream

25 to a young girl who waits,
arms and legs

a small harbor.

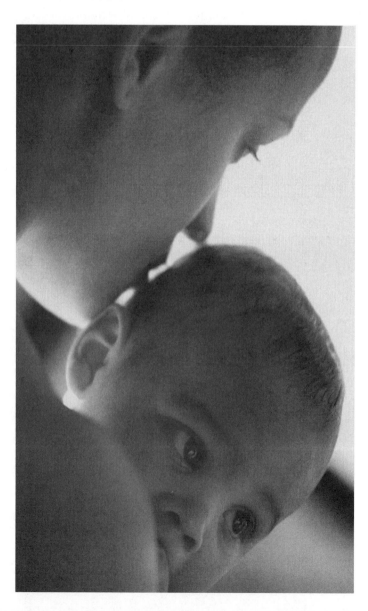

The Sacred; Mooring

Figure of Speech Chart   **Figures of speech** are comparisons between two unlike things; figures of speech provide imaginative ways of thinking about ordinary things. Fill in the chart below as you analyze the use of figurative speech in these poems. The first row has been filled in as an example.

Figure of Speech	Things Being Compared	What Comparison Suggests
"the bright altar of the dashboard" ("The Sacred," line 13)	Dashboard is compared to an altar.	Dashboards are as important to cars as altars are to religious places.
"the sturdy / cargo of my infant son" ("Mooring," lines 8–9)		
"kernel of toes" ("Mooring," line 14)		
"bracelets of flesh" ("Mooring," line 16)		
"to a young girl who waits, / arms and legs / a small harbor" ("Mooring," lines 25–27)		

Standards Review

 **The Sacred; Mooring**

Complete the sample test item below. Then, read the explanation in the right-hand column.

Sample Test Item	Explanation of the Correct Answer
Which of the following is true of the speaker in "The Sacred"? **A** He is a student. **B** He is an outside observer. **C** He has a sacred place. **D** He just got his license.	The correct answer is *B*. *A* is incorrect because he refers to the class as "students," not as "we." *C* is incorrect because the speaker never mentions a sacred place of his own. No one in the poem just got a license, so *D* is also incorrect.

DIRECTIONS: Circle the letter of each correct response.

1. In "The Sacred," the comparison between the dashboard and an altar —

   A warns passengers not to spill their drinks

   B suggests the special, sacred nature of the car

   C explains the importance of music

   D is not a metaphor

2. In Dunn's poem, why is the car so "sacred"?

   F It was a special gift.

   G It gives students freedom.

   H It looks like an altar.

   J It had survived an accident.

3. The lines "to a young girl who waits, / arms and legs / a small harbor" in "Mooring" create a —

   A simile

   B metaphor

   C pun

   D paraphrase

4. The baby in "Mooring" is compared to —

   F sweet soap

   G his sister

   H baby Moses

   J a small harbor

Reading Standard 3.7 Recognize and understand the significance of various literary devices, including figurative language, imagery, allegory, and symbolism, and explain their appeal.

BEFORE YOU READ

Some people mistakenly think that poetry has to be about grand, "poetic" subjects. Look at the titles of these poems, above, to preview the very ordinary subjects they deal with.

LITERARY FOCUS: THE SOUNDS OF POETRY

Two special elements—rhyme and rhythm—give poetry a musical quality.

- **Rhyme** is the repetition of a stressed vowel (one that is strongly pronounced) and any sounds that follow: *phone* and *loan; station* and *nation*. **End rhyme** is created when the sound-alike words come at the ends of lines. **Internal rhyme** occurs when the sound-alike words come within a line or within a line and at the end of the line. Here's an example that has both end rhyme and internal rhyme:

> Walk with *me*, by *tree* and *glen*:
> The sun is on *high*; not a cloud's in the *sky*:
> We'll stop to rest; we know not *when*;
> *Then* like the birds, we'll homeward *fly*.

- **Rhythm** also creates a musical quality. Rhythm is created by a pattern of stressed and unstressed syllables. Some poems have a regular pattern of stressed and unstressed syllables, called **meter.** This line from a poem by John Keats, for example, has a pattern of unstressed and stressed syllables: "I set her on my pacing steed."
- **Free-verse** poems do not contain regular rhyme or meter. Instead, these poems sound more like everyday conversation. Poems written in free verse, however, may contain special sound effects. One effect is **onomatopoeia,** the use of words that sound like their meanings (for example, *meow* and *arf*). Another effect is **alliteration,** the repetition of consonant sounds in words occurring close together (for example, in this line by Henry Wadsworth Longfellow: "The day is done, and the darkness").

Reading Standard 3.1 (Grade 8 Review) Determine and articulate the relationship between the purposes and characteristics of different forms of poetry (e.g., ballad, lyric, couplet, epic, elegy, ode, sonnet).

Reading Standard 3.7 Recognize and understand the significance of various literary devices, including figurative language, imagery, allegory, and symbolism, and explain their appeal.

The Bat
Theodore Roethke

By day the bat is cousin to the mouse.

He likes the attic of an aging house.

His fingers make a hat about his head.

His pulse beat is so slow we think him dead.

5   He loops in crazy figures half the night

Among the trees that face the corner light.

But when he brushes up against a screen,

We are afraid of what our eyes have seen:

For something is amiss or out of place

10   When mice with wings can wear a human face.

"The Bat" from *The Collected Poems of Theodore Roethke*. Copyright 1938 by Theodore Roethke. Reprinted by permission of **Doubleday, a division of Random House, Inc.**

IDENTIFY

Pause at line 2. Where does the bat live in daytime?

_____

IDENTIFY

Pause at line 6. What does the bat do at night? Underline the answer.

INTERPRET

In lines 7–10, underline what the speaker is afraid of.

SOUNDS OF POETRY

Re-read the poem, and circle the words that **rhyme**.

SOUNDS OF POETRY

Scan the poem by marking the strongly stressed syllables like this (′). Mark the unstressed syllables like this (˘). Is the poem built on a regular meter?

_____

_____

_____

FLUENCY

Read the poem aloud twice. Focus on the poem's rhythm on your first read. Then, focus on creating an eerie tone.

this morning
Lucille Clifton

(For the girls of Eastern High School)

this morning
this morning
       i met myself
coming in

5   a bright
jungle girl
shining
quick as a snake
a tall
10   tree girl a
me girl
       i met myself
this morning
coming in

15   and all day
i have been
a black bell
ringing
i survive
20   survive
survive

FORM/FLUENCY

The poem does not contain any punctuation. Read the poem aloud, using spacing to help you decide when to pause and when to read on.

IDENTIFY

Pause at line 11. Who is the speaker?

_____

SOUNDS OF POETRY

Lines 12–14 and 16–17 contain **alliteration.** Underline the repeated sounds.

INTERPRET

What does the **metaphor** "I have been / a black bell / ringing" in lines 16–18 suggest about the speaker?

_____
_____
_____
_____
_____
_____
_____

INTERPRET

What do you think is the most important word in the poem? Circle it.

How I Learned English

Gregory Djanikian

CLARIFY

Re-read lines 1–8. Describe what is happening.

_____

_____

_____

It was in an empty lot
Ringed by elms and fir and honeysuckle.
Bill Corson was pitching in his buckskin jacket,
Chuck Keller, fat even as a boy, was on first,
5   His t-shirt riding up over his gut,
Ron O'Neill, Jim, Dennis, were talking it up
In the field, a blue sky above them
Tipped with cirrus.

SOUNDS OF POETRY

Plopped in line 10 is an example of **onomatopoeia**. Find other examples of onomatopoeia in lines 14 and 23. Circle them.

          And there I was,
10   Just off the plane and plopped in the middle
Of Williamsport, Pa. and a neighborhood game,
Unnatural and without any moves,
My notions of baseball and America
Growing fuzzier each time I whiffed.

CLARIFY

Pause at the end of line 14. What do you know about the speaker?

_____

_____

_____

_____

_____

_____

_____

_____

_____

_____

"How I Learned English" from *Falling Deeply into America* by Gregory Djanikian, Carnegie-Mellon University Press, 1989. Copyright © 1989 by **Gregory Djanikian**. First published in *Poetry*, 1986. Reprinted by permission of the author.

15 So it was not impossible that I,

Banished to the outfield and daydreaming

Of water, or a hotel in the mountains,

Would suddenly find myself in the path

Of a ball stung by Joe Barone.

20 I watched it closing in

Clean and untouched, transfixed

By its easy arc before it hit

My forehead with a thud.

                        I fell back,

25 Dazed, clutching my brow,

Groaning, "Oh my shin, oh my shin,"

And everybody peeled away from me

And dropped from laughter, and there we were,

All of us writhing on the ground for one reason

30 Or another.

                        Someone said "shin" again,

There was a wild stamping of hands on the ground,

A kicking of feet, and the fit

Of laughter overtook me too,

35 And that was important, as important

As Joe Barone asking me how I was

Through his tears, picking me up

And dusting me off with hands like swatters,

And though my head felt heavy,

40 I played on till dusk

Missing flies and pop-ups and grounders

And calling out in desperation things like

"Yours" and "take it," but doing all right,

Tugging at my cap in just the right way,

45 Crouching low, my feet set,

"Hum baby" sweetly on my lips.

PREDICT

Pause at line 19. What do you think will happen next?

_____

_____

IDENTIFY CAUSE & EFFECT

Re-read lines 24–30. Why are the boys laughing at the speaker?

_____

_____

_____

_____

IDENTIFY

Underline the two events in lines 31–38 that are "important" to the speaker. How do these events make him feel?

_____

_____

_____

_____

_____

FLUENCY

Read the boxed stanza aloud twice. The first time, focus on where you should come to a full stop and when you should only pause. The second time, concentrate on conveying the boys' and the speaker's feelings.

The Bat; this morning; How I Learned English

Sounds of Poetry Diagram   Some poems get their sound from **rhyme** and **meter.** In other poems, musical quality comes from the **repetition** of words and lines, **onomatopoeia**, and **alliteration.** Read each passage in the left column. Then, decide which of the four sound devices the passage illustrates. Place an *X* in the appropriate column or columns.

Passage	Repetition	Rhyme & Meter	Alliteration	Onomatopoeia
"Hum, baby" sweetly on my lips. ("How I Learned English," line 46)				
But when he brushes up against a screen, / We are afraid of what our eyes have seen: ("The Bat," lines 7–8)				
this morning / this morning / I met myself / coming in ("this morning," lines 1–4)				
His fingers make a hat about his head. / His pulse beat is so slow we think him dead. ("The Bat," lines 3–4)				

Standards Review

LITERATURE

TestPractice

The Bat; this morning; How I Learned English

Complete the sample test item below. The box at the right explains why three of these choices are not correct.

Sample Test Item	Explanation of the Correct Answer
Which of the following is *not* a word for a type of sound device? **A** metaphor **B** rhythm **C** rhyme **D** alliteration	The correct answer is *A*. A metaphor is a type of comparison. All the other choices are types of sound devices.

DIRECTIONS: Circle the letter of each correct response.

1. In "The Bat," what is the bat compared to?

   A A rat

   B A mouse with wings

   C A demon

   D An aging attic

2. Which of the following contains an example of **onomatopoeia**?

   F "it hit / My forehead with a thud."

   G "quick as a snake"

   H "the bat is cousin to the mouse"

   J "the attic of an aging house"

3. In "this morning" the line "i met myself" contains —

   A rhyme

   B onomatopoeia

   C alliteration

   D repetition

4. The **rhythm** in "How I Learned English"—

   F has a regular beat

   G follows the pattern of a baseball game

   H helps the speaker learn English

   J sounds like conversation

Reading Standard 3.7 Recognize and understand the significance of various literary devices, including figurative language, imagery, allegory, and symbolism, and explain their appeal.

Chapter 8

LITERARY CRITICISM
Evaluating Style

Academic Vocabulary for Chapter 8

These are the terms you should know
as you read and analyze the stories in this chapter.

Style The particular way a writer uses language. Style is revealed chiefly
through diction (word choice), sentence structure, and tone. The use or
avoidance of specialized language such as figurative language also has
an impact on style.

Diction The writer's choice of words—an essential element of a writer's
style. Diction has a major effect on the tone of a piece of writing.

Connotations Meanings and emotions associated with a word that go
beyond its dictionary definition, or **denotation.** Words that have similar
meanings may have different connotations. For example, you could
describe someone who rarely changes his mind as *determined* or *pigheaded.* The two words have similar denotations, but *determined* has
positive connotations and *pigheaded* has negative connotations.

Figures of speech Imaginative comparisons in which one thing is described in
terms of another. Figures of speech are not meant to be understood on
a literal level. Common examples are **metaphor** (*The bird's song is an
aria on wing*), **simile** (*The bird sings like a piccolo*), and **personification**
(*The bird wished its song would make the world happy*).

Imagery Language that appeals to the five senses—sight, hearing, smell,
taste, touch.

Tone The writer's attitude toward a subject or a character, or toward the
audience. When people speak, their tone of voice gives added meaning to what they say. Writers must use written language to create similar effects.

Mood The overall feeling or atmosphere of a work of literature. Diction and
figures of speech both contribute to mood. The setting of a story also
helps to create mood.

**Reading
Standard 1.1**
Identify and use
the literal and
figurative
meanings of
words and
understand word
derivations.

**Reading
Standard 1.2**
Distinguish
between the
denotative and
connotative
meanings of
words and
interpret the
connotative
power of words.

**Reading
Standard 3.11**
Evaluate the
aesthetic qualities
of style, including
the impact
of diction and
figurative
language on tone,
mood, and theme,
using the
terminology of
literary criticism.
(Aesthetic
approach)

For Further Information . . .

- Be sure to read the essay on **evaluating style**
  in *Holt Literature and Language Arts,* pages
  496–497.

A Sound of Thunder by Ray Bradbury

BEFORE YOU READ

Imagine being able to travel back in time. Many writers have explored this idea in science fiction stories and movies. You are about to read one of the most popular—and thought-provoking—stories about time travel ever written.

LITERARY FOCUS: STYLE AND MOOD

A writer's diction, or word choice, greatly defines a work's **style.** Style is also determined by sentence length and complexity. A story that is written in brief simple sentences, for example, is different in style from a story written in long complex sentences. See below:

Style: Simple	Style: More Complex
The sun rose. The air was warm, my coffee was hot. Nothing stirred. Nothing breathed except for the lizard. That lizard could outstare a rock.	"It was Miss Murdstone who was arrived, and a gloomy-looking lady she was: dark, like her brother, whom she greatly resembled in face and voice . . ." (from *David Copperfield*, by Charles Dickens)

The use (or non-use) of imagery and figurative language also has an effect on style. In the story you're about to read, Ray Bradbury uses vivid imagery and figurative language to create a style that is as lush as its prehistoric setting. **Mood,** like style, is also created by diction, sentence length, imagery, and figurative language. A story's mood, or atmosphere, can be described using adjectives like *scary, calm,* and *mysterious.*

- As you read "A Sound of Thunder," notice how Bradbury's choice of words, imagery, and figurative language creates a unique style.
- As Bradbury describes the ancient jungle, think about the words you'd use to describe the story's mood.

READING SKILLS: CAUSE AND EFFECT

The events in a story are connected by a chain of **causes and effects.** One event causes another, which causes another, and so on. A **cause** is the reason something happens. An **effect** is the result. Certain words—like *because, consequently, for, so, since,* and *therefore*—can alert you to cause-and-effect relationships.

As you read "A Sound of Thunder," look for causes and effects. There are plenty to find. In fact, the whole story is about how one event causes another—and another, and another, and . . .

Reading Standard 1.1 Identify and use the literal and figurative meaning of words and understand word derivations.

Reading Standard 3.11 Evaluate the aesthetic qualities of style, including the impact of diction and figurative language on tone, mood, and theme, using the terminology of literary criticism. (Aesthetic approach)

SHORT STORY

VOCABULARY DEVELOPMENT

PREVIEW SELECTION VOCABULARY

The following words appear in the story you are about to read. You may want to become familiar with them before you begin reading.

annihilate (ə·nī′ə·lāt′) *v.*: destroy; wipe out.

*If we continue to destroy the region's forests, we may also **annihilate** the wildlife that lives there.*

expendable (ek·spen′də·bəl) *adj.*: worth sacrificing to gain an objective.

*The officers regretted the loss but considered the ground troops **expendable**.*

depression (dē·presh′ən) *n.*: major economic downturn. (*Depression* also means "sadness.")

*A **depression** hit the country, resulting in widespread unemployment and homelessness.*

paradox (par′ə·däks′) *n.*: something that has or seems to have contradictory qualities.

*The **paradox** is that sometimes we are loneliest when we are in a crowd of people.*

delirium (di·lir′ē·əm) *n.*: extreme mental disturbance, often accompanied by hallucinations (seeing things that are not there).

*In his **delirium,** he imagined he was seeing giant insects.*

resilient (ri·zil′yənt) *adj.*: able to return to its original shape quickly after being stretched or compressed; elastic.

*This **resilient** fabric springs back to its original shape no matter how you stretch it.*

remit (ri·mit′) *v.*: return payment.

*The company will **remit,** or return, full payment if the consumers are not satisfied.*

revoke (ri·vōk′) *v.*: cancel; withdraw.

*They can **revoke** your club membership if you fail to attend meetings.*

primeval (prī·mē′vəl) *adj.*: primitive; of the earliest times.

*In the prehistoric world, giant lizards crashed through the **primeval** forest.*

subliminal (sub·lim′ə·nəl) *adj.*: below the level of awareness.

*Unaware of the movie's **subliminal** message to buy food, the audience flocked to buy snacks.*

PREFIXES AND WORD ROOTS

A **prefix** is a word part that comes before a word root and affects its meaning. A knowledge of prefixes can help you figure out the meanings of unfamiliar words. It can also help you use and understand a wider variety of words. The word *remit,* for example, contains the prefix *re–,* which means "back." It also contains the word root *mit,* which means "send." When you *remit* something, you send it back.

When you come across an unfamiliar word, look for a prefix or word root you recognize to help you figure out the word's meaning.

A Sound of Thunder

Ray Bradbury

INFER

Pause after you read the sign (lines 4–5). Underline the information that seems unusual. Based on this information, when do you think the story takes place?

_____

_____

INFER

Pause at line 16. Why do you think there is such a stiff penalty for disobeying instructions?

_____

_____

_____

_____

_____

The sign on the wall seemed to quaver under a film of sliding warm water. Eckels felt his eyelids blink over his stare, and the sign burned in this momentary darkness:

> TIME SAFARI, INC. SAFARIS TO ANY YEAR IN THE PAST.
> YOU NAME THE ANIMAL. WE TAKE YOU THERE. YOU SHOOT IT.

A warm phlegm gathered in Eckels's throat; he swallowed and pushed it down. The muscles around his mouth formed a smile as he put his hand slowly out upon the air, and in that hand waved a check for ten thousand dollars to the man behind the desk.

10 "Does this safari guarantee I come back alive?"

"We guarantee nothing," said the official, "except the dinosaurs." He turned. "This is Mr. Travis, your Safari Guide in the Past. He'll tell you what and where to shoot. If he says no shooting, no shooting. If you disobey instructions, there's a stiff penalty of another ten thousand dollars, plus possible government action, on your return."

Eckels glanced across the vast office at a mass and tangle, a snaking and humming of wires and steel boxes, at an aurora[1] that flickered now orange, now silver, now blue. There was

20 a sound like a gigantic bonfire burning all of Time, all the years and all the parchment calendars, all the hours piled high and set aflame.

A touch of the hand and this burning would, on the instant, beautifully reverse itself. Eckels remembered the wording in the advertisements to the letter. Out of chars and ashes, out of dust and coals, like golden salamanders, the old years, the green years, might leap; roses sweeten the air, white hair turn Irish-black, wrinkles vanish; all, everything fly back to seed, flee death, rush down to their beginnings, suns rise in western skies

30 and set in glorious easts, moons eat themselves opposite to the custom, all and everything cupping one in another like Chinese boxes[2], rabbits into hats, all and everything returning to the fresh death, the seed death, the green death, to the time before the beginning. A touch of a hand might do it, the merest touch of a hand.

"Unbelievable." Eckels breathed, the light of the Machine on his thin face. "A real Time Machine." He shook his head. "Makes you think. If the election had gone badly yesterday, I might be here now running away from the results. Thank God

40 Keith won. He'll make a fine President of the United States."

"Yes," said the man behind the desk. "We're lucky. If Deutscher had gotten in, we'd have the worst kind of dictatorship. There's an anti-everything man for you, a militarist, anti-Christ, anti-human, anti-intellectual. People called us up, you know, joking but not joking. Said if Deutscher became President they wanted to go live in 1492. Of course it's not our business to conduct Escapes, but to form Safaris. Anyway, Keith's President now. All you got to worry about is—"

---

1. **aurora** (ô·rôr′ə) *n.:* Bradbury is comparing the glow coming from the time machine to an aurora, a colorful display of light that appears at night in the skies near the North and South Poles.
2. **Chinese boxes:** set of boxes, each of which fits into the next-largest one.

STYLE

Re-read lines 17–35, and underline examples of **figurative language** (simile, metaphor, personification).

IDENTIFY

Pause at line 43. Who were the two candidates for president of the United States? Circle their names. Which one won the election?

_____

_____

_____

_____

_____

_____

_____

WORD STUDY

Anti– is a prefix meaning "against." According to the description of Deutscher in lines 43–44, what is he "against"?

_____

_____

_____

_____

_____

_____

IDENTIFY

Pause at line 52. What animal is Eckels hunting? Circle the answer.

INTERPRET

Re-read lines 54–58. What do these details suggest about Time Safari, Inc.?

_____

_____

_____

_____

_____

_____

_____

INTERPRET

Circle the words in lines 76–77 that mean "Eckels said." What does this phrase reveal about Eckels?

_____

_____

_____

_____

_____

_____

_____

_____

_____

"Shooting my dinosaur," Eckels finished it for him.

50 "A *Tyrannosaurus rex*. The Tyrant Lizard, the most incredible monster in history. Sign this release. Anything happens to you, we're not responsible. Those dinosaurs are hungry."

Eckels flushed angrily. "Trying to scare me!"

"Frankly, yes. We don't want anyone going who'll panic at the first shot. Six Safari leaders were killed last year, and a dozen hunters. We're here to give you the severest thrill a real hunter ever asked for. Traveling you back sixty million years to bag the biggest game in all of Time. Your personal check's still there. Tear it up."

Mr. Eckels looked at the check. His fingers twitched.

60 "Good luck," said the man behind the desk. "Mr. Travis, he's all yours."

They moved silently across the room, taking their guns with them, toward the Machine, toward the silver metal and the roaring light.

First a day and then a night and then a day and then a night, then it was day-night-day-night-day. A week, a month, a year, a decade! A.D. 2055. A.D. 2019. 1999! 1957! Gone! The Machine roared.

They put on their oxygen helmets and tested the intercoms.

70 Eckels swayed on the padded seat, his face pale, his jaw stiff. He felt the trembling in his arms, and he looked down and found his hands tight on the new rifle. There were four other men in the Machine. Travis, the Safari Leader; his assistant, Lesperance; and two other hunters, Billings and Kramer. They sat looking at each other, and the years blazed around them.

"Can these guns get a dinosaur cold?" Eckels felt his mouth saying.

"If you hit them right," said Travis on the helmet radio. "Some dinosaurs have two brains, one in the head, another far

80 down the spinal column. We stay away from those. That's stretching luck. Put your first two shots into the eyes, if you can, blind them, and go back into the brain."

The Machine howled. Time was a film run backward. Suns fled and ten million moons fled after them. "Think," said Eckels. "Every hunter that ever lived would envy us today. This makes Africa seem like Illinois."

The Machine slowed; its scream fell to a murmur. The Machine stopped.

The sun stopped in the sky.

90 The fog that had enveloped the Machine blew away and they were in an old time, a very old time indeed, three hunters and two Safari Heads with their blue metal guns across their knees.

"Christ isn't born yet," said Travis. "Moses has not gone to the mountain to talk with God. The Pyramids are still in the earth, waiting to be cut out and put up. *Remember* that. Alexander, Caesar, Napoleon, Hitler—none of them exists."

The men nodded.

"That"—Mr. Travis pointed—"is the jungle of sixty million 100 two thousand and fifty-five years before President Keith."

He indicated a metal path that struck off into green wilderness, over streaming swamp, among giant ferns and palms.

"And that," he said, "is the Path, laid by Time Safari for your use. It floats six inches above the earth. Doesn't touch so much as one grass blade, flower, or tree. It's an anti-gravity metal. Its purpose is to keep you from touching this world of the Past in any way. Stay on the Path. Don't go off it. I repeat. *Don't go off*. For *any* reason! If you fall off, there's a penalty. And don't shoot any animal we don't okay."

110 "Why?" asked Eckels.

They sat in the ancient wilderness. Far birds' cries blew on a wind, and the smell of tar and an old salt sea, moist grasses, and flowers the color of blood.

"We don't want to change the Future. We don't belong here in the Past. The government doesn't like us here. We have to pay big graft[3] to keep our franchise. A Time Machine is finicky

---

3. **graft** *n.*: bribes.

IDENTIFY

Underline the sentence in lines 103–107 that tells you the purpose of "the Path." Why do you think the term is capitalized?

_____

_____

_____

_____

_____

ANALYZE

Re-read lines 111–113, which are full of **imagery**. To what senses do these images appeal?

_____

_____

_____

_____

_____

_____

_____

_____

_____

_____

_____

_____

_____

_____

_____

_____

_____

_____

_____

VOCABULARY

annihilate (ə·nī′ə·lāt′) v.:
destroy; wipe out.

expendable (ek·spen′də·bəl)
adj.: worth sacrificing to gain
an objective.

**IDENTIFY
CAUSE & EFFECT**

In this long paragraph (lines
130–155), Travis explains the
possible effects of stepping
off the path and killing a
mouse. Each effect, in turn,
becomes the cause of another event. What is the final
effect Travis mentions?

_____

_____

_____

_____

_____

_____

business. Not knowing it, we might kill an important animal, a
small bird, a roach, a flower even, thus destroying an important
link in a growing species."

120   "That's not clear," said Eckels.

"All right," Travis continued, "say we accidentally kill one
mouse here. That means all the future families of this one particular mouse are destroyed, right?"

"Right."

"And all the families of the families of the families of that
one mouse! With a stamp of your foot, you **annihilate** first one,
then a dozen, then a thousand, a million, a billion possible
mice!"

"So they're dead," said Eckels. "So what?"

130   "So what?" Travis snorted quietly. "Well, what about the
foxes that'll need those mice to survive? For want of ten mice, a
fox dies. For want of ten foxes, a lion starves. For want of a lion,
all manner of insects, vultures, infinite billions of life forms are
thrown into chaos and destruction. Eventually it all boils down to
this: Fifty-nine million years later, a cave man, one of a dozen in
the *entire world*, goes hunting wild boar or saber-toothed tiger
for food. But you, friend, have *stepped* on all the tigers in that
region. By stepping on *one* single mouse. So the cave man starves.
And the cave man, please note, is not just *any* **expendable** man,

140   no! He is an *entire future nation*. From his loins would have
sprung ten sons. From *their* loins one hundred sons, and thus
onward to a civilization. Destroy this one man, and you destroy a
race, a people, an entire history of life. It is comparable to slaying
some of Adam's grandchildren. The stomp of your foot, on one
mouse, could start an earthquake, the effects of which could
shake our earth and destinies down through Time, to their very
foundations. With the death of that one cave man, a billion others yet unborn are throttled in the womb. Perhaps Rome never
rises on its seven hills. Perhaps Europe is forever a dark forest,

150   and only Asia waxes healthy and teeming.[4] Step on a mouse and

4. **teeming** (tēm′iŋ) adj.: swarming; overflowing.

you crush the Pyramids. Step on a mouse and you leave your print, like a Grand Canyon, across Eternity. Queen Elizabeth might never be born, Washington might not cross the Delaware, there might never be a United States at all. So be careful. Stay on the Path. *Never* step off!"

"I see," said Eckels. "Then it wouldn't pay for us even to touch the *grass*?"

"Correct. Crushing certain plants could add up infinitesimally.[5] A little error here would multiply in sixty million years,
160 all out of proportion. Of course maybe our theory is wrong. Maybe Time *can't* be changed by us. Or maybe it can be changed only in little subtle ways. A dead mouse here makes an insect imbalance there, a population disproportion later, a bad harvest further on, a **depression**, mass starvation, and, finally, a change in social temperament in far-flung countries. Something much more subtle, like that. Perhaps only a soft breath, a whisper, a hair, pollen on the air, such a slight, slight change that unless you looked close you wouldn't see it. Who knows? Who really can say he knows? We don't know. We're guessing. But until we
170 do know for certain whether our messing around in Time *can* make a big roar or a little rustle in history, we're being careful.

---

5. **infinitesimally** (in′fin·i·tes′i·məl·ē) *adv.:* in amounts too small to be measured.

VOCABULARY

depression (dē·presh′ən) *n.:* major economic downturn.

CLARIFY

What does Travis mean when he says he's not sure whether "messing around in Time *can* make a big roar or a little rustle in history" (lines 169–171)?

IDENTIFY
CAUSE & EFFECT

Pause at line 175. Why do the travelers wear sterilized clothing and oxygen helmets?

_____

_____

_____

_____

IDENTIFY
CAUSE & EFFECT

Pause at line 190. Why are only animals that are about to die anyway chosen for hunting?

_____

_____

_____

PREDICT

Re-read lines 195–202. What do *you* think? Will the expedition be a success or will it end in tragedy?

_____

_____

_____

VOCABULARY

paradox (par'ə·däks') *n.:* something that has or seems to have contradictory qualities.

This Machine, this Path, your clothing and bodies, were sterilized, as you know, before the journey. We wear these oxygen helmets so we can't introduce our bacteria into an ancient atmosphere."

"How do we know which animals to shoot?"

"They're marked with red paint," said Travis. "Today, before our journey, we sent Lesperance here back with the Machine. He came to this particular era and followed certain animals."

180 "Studying them?"

"Right," said Lesperance. "I track them through their entire existence, noting which of them lives longest. Very few. How many times they mate. Not often. Life's short. When I find one that's going to die when a tree falls on him, or one that drowns in a tar pit, I note the exact hour, minute, and second. I shoot a paint bomb. It leaves a red patch on his side. We can't miss it. Then I correlate our arrival in the Past so that we meet the Monster not more than two minutes before he would have died anyway. This way, we kill only animals with no future, that are

190 never going to mate again. You see how *careful* we are?"

"But if you came back this morning in Time," said Eckels eagerly, "you must've bumped into us, our Safari! How did it turn out? Was it successful? Did all of us get through—alive?"

Travis and Lesperance gave each other a look.

"That'd be a **paradox**," said the latter. "Time doesn't permit that sort of mess—a man meeting himself. When such occasions threaten, Time steps aside. Like an airplane hitting an air pocket. You felt the Machine jump just before we stopped? That was us passing ourselves on the way back to the Future. We saw noth-

200 ing. There's no way of telling *if* this expedition was a success, *if we* got our monster, or whether all of us—meaning *you*, Mr. Eckels—got out alive."

Eckels smiled palely.

"Cut that," said Travis sharply. "Everyone on his feet!"

They were ready to leave the Machine.

The jungle was high and the jungle was broad and the jungle was the entire world forever and forever. Sounds like music and sounds like flying tents filled the sky, and those were pterodactyls soaring with cavernous gray wings, gigantic bats of

210   **delirium** and night fever. Eckels, balanced on the narrow Path, aimed his rifle playfully.

"Stop that!" said Travis. "Don't even aim for fun, blast you! If your guns should go off—"

Eckels flushed. "Where's our *Tyrannosaurus*?"

Lesperance checked his wristwatch. "Up ahead. We'll bisect his trail in sixty seconds. Look for the red paint! Don't shoot till we give the word. Stay on the Path. *Stay on the Path!*"

They moved forward in the wind of morning.

"Strange," murmured Eckels. "Up ahead, sixty million years,

220   Election Day over. Keith made President. Everyone celebrating. And here we are, a million years lost, and they don't exist. The things we worried about for months, a lifetime, not even born or thought of yet."

"Safety catches off, everyone!" ordered Travis. "You, first shot, Eckels. Second, Billings. Third, Kramer."

"I've hunted tiger, wild boar, buffalo, elephant, but now, this is *it*," said Eckels. "I'm shaking like a kid."

"Ah," said Travis.

Everyone stopped.

230   Travis raised his hand. "Ahead," he whispered. "In the mist. There he is. There's His Royal Majesty now."

The jungle was wide and full of twitterings, rustlings, murmurs, and sighs.

Suddenly it all ceased, as if someone had shut a door.

Silence.

A sound of thunder.

Out of the mist, one hundred yards away, came *Tyrannosaurus rex*.

"It," whispered Eckels. "It . . ."

240   "Sh!"

VOCABULARY

delirium (di·lir′ē·əm) *n.:* extreme mental disturbance, often accompanied by hallucinations (seeing things that are not there).

STYLE

Re-read lines 206–211, and circle repeated words. Then, underline the imaginative description of pterodactyls. How would you describe the style of the writing here?

_____

_____

_____

_____

PREDICT

Pause at line 217. The guides keep telling Eckels, "Stay on the Path!" What do their warnings lead you to predict?

_____

_____

_____

INFER

Pause at line 231. Whom might Travis be referring to as "His Royal Majesty"?

_____

_____

_____

VOCABULARY

resilient (ri·zil′yənt) *adj.:* able to return to its original shape quickly after being stretched or compressed; elastic.

STYLE

The author uses rich **figurative language** in lines 241–259. Underline at least four metaphors or similes that help you visualize the fearsome dinosaur.

FLUENCY

Read the boxed passage aloud twice. Focus on reading the figures of speech clearly and dramatically.

Notes _____

_____
_____
_____
_____
_____
_____
_____
_____
_____
_____

It came on great oiled, **resilient**, striding legs. It towered thirty feet above half of the trees, a great evil god, folding its delicate watchmaker's claws close to its oily reptilian chest. Each lower leg was a piston, a thousand pounds of white bone, sunk in thick ropes of muscle, sheathed over in a gleam of pebbled skin like the mail[6] of a terrible warrior. Each thigh was a ton of meat, ivory, and steel mesh. And from the great breathing cage of the upper body those two delicate arms dangled out front, arms with hands which might pick up and examine men like

250 toys, while the snake neck coiled. And the head itself, a ton of sculptured stone, lifted easily upon the sky. Its mouth gaped, exposing a fence of teeth like daggers. Its eyes rolled, ostrich eggs, empty of all expression save hunger. It closed its mouth in a death grin. It ran, its pelvic bones crushing aside trees and bushes, its taloned feet clawing damp earth, leaving prints six inches deep wherever it settled its weight. It ran with a gliding ballet step, far too poised and balanced for its ten tons. It moved into a sunlit arena warily, its beautifully reptilian hands feeling the air.

260 "Why, why," Eckels twitched his mouth. "It could reach up and grab the moon."

"Sh!" Travis jerked angrily. "He hasn't seen us yet."

"It can't be killed." Eckels pronounced this verdict quietly, as if there could be no argument. He had weighed the evidence and this was his considered opinion. The rifle in his hands seemed a cap gun. "We were fools to come. This is impossible."

"Shut up!" hissed Travis.

"Nightmare."

"Turn around," commanded Travis. "Walk quietly to the

270 Machine. We'll **remit** one half your fee."

"I didn't realize it would be this *big*," said Eckels. "I miscalculated, that's all. And now I want out."

"It *sees* us!"

"There's the red paint on its chest!"

---

6. **mail** *n.:* here, flexible metal armor.

The Tyrant Lizard raised itself. Its armored flesh glittered like a thousand green coins. The coins, crusted with slime, steamed. In the slime, tiny insects wriggled, so that the entire body seemed to twitch and undulate,[7] even while the monster itself did not move. It exhaled. The stink of raw flesh blew down the wilderness.

"Get me out of here," said Eckels. "It was never like this before. I was always sure I'd come through alive. I had good guides, good safaris, and safety. This time, I figured wrong. I've met my match and admit it. This is too much for me to get hold of."

"Don't run," said Lesperance. "Turn around. Hide in the Machine."

"Yes." Eckels seemed to be numb. He looked at his feet as if trying to make them move. He gave a grunt of helplessness.

"Eckels!"

He took a few steps, blinking, shuffling.

"Not *that* way!"

The Monster, at the first motion, lunged forward with a terrible scream. It covered one hundred yards in six seconds. The rifles jerked up and blazed fire. A windstorm from the beast's mouth engulfed them in the stench of slime and old blood. The Monster roared, teeth glittering with sun.

Eckels, not looking back, walked blindly to the edge of the Path, his gun limp in his arms, stepped off the Path, and walked, not knowing it, in the jungle. His feet sank into green moss. His legs moved him, and he felt alone and remote from the events behind.

The rifles cracked again. Their sound was lost in shriek and lizard thunder. The great level of the reptile's tail swung up, lashed sideways. Trees exploded in clouds of leaf and branch. The Monster twitched its jeweler's hands down to fondle at the men, to twist them in half, to crush them like berries, to cram them into its teeth and its screaming throat. Its boulder-stone

---

7. **undulate** (un′jə·lāt′) v.: move in waves.

IDENTIFY

How does Eckels react when he sees the dinosaur (lines 260–287)? What do the guides tell him to do?

_____

_____

_____

_____

_____

_____

_____

IDENTIFY CAUSE & EFFECT

Pause at line 302. What causes Eckels to step off the path? What effect might this action have?

_____

_____

_____

_____

_____

_____

_____

_____

eyes leveled with the men. They saw themselves mirrored. They fired at the metallic eyelids and the blazing black iris.

Like a stone idol, like a mountain avalanche, *Tyrannosaurus* fell. Thundering, it clutched trees, pulled them with it. It wrenched and tore the metal Path. The men flung themselves back and away. The body hit, ten tons of cold flesh and stone. The guns fired. The Monster lashed its armored tail, twitched its snake jaws, and lay still. A fount of blood spurted from its throat. Somewhere inside, a sac of fluids burst. Sickening gushes drenched the hunters. They stood, red and glistening.

The thunder faded.

The jungle was silent. After the avalanche, a green peace. After the nightmare, morning.

Billings and Kramer sat on the pathway and threw up. Travis and Lesperance stood with smoking rifles, cursing steadily.

In the Time Machine, on his face, Eckels lay shivering. He had found his way back to the Path, climbed into the Machine.

Travis came walking, glanced at Eckels, took cotton gauze from a metal box, and returned to the others, who were sitting on the Path.

"Clean up."

They wiped the blood from their helmets. They began to curse too. The Monster lay, a hill of solid flesh. Within, you could hear the sighs and murmurs as the furthest chambers of it died, the organs malfunctioning, liquids running a final instant from pocket to sac to spleen, everything shutting off, closing up forever. It was like standing by a wrecked locomotive or a steam shovel at quitting time, all valves being released or levered tight. Bones cracked; the tonnage of its own flesh, off balance, dead weight, snapped the delicate forearms, caught underneath. The meat settled, quivering.

Another cracking sound. Overhead, a gigantic tree branch broke from its heavy mooring, fell. It crashed upon the dead beast with finality.

310

320

330

340

IDENTIFY

What two things is the dinosaur compared to in line 311? What type of figurative language is each comparison?

_____

_____

_____

_____

VISUALIZE

Circle the words in lines 311–318 that help you visualize the violent death of the giant dinosaur.

WORD STUDY

The prefix *mal–* means "not" or "bad." What do you think *malfunctioning* (line 334) means?

_____

_____

"There." Lesperance checked his watch. "Right on time. That's the giant tree that was scheduled to fall and kill this animal originally." He glanced at the two hunters. "You want the trophy picture?"

"What?"

"We can't take a trophy back to the Future. The body has to stay right here where it would have died originally, so the insects, birds, and bacteria can get at it, as they were intended to. Everything in balance. The body stays. But we *can* take a picture of you standing near it."

The two men tried to think, but gave up, shaking their heads.

They let themselves be led along the metal Path. They sank wearily into the Machine cushions. They gazed back at the ruined Monster, the stagnating mound, where already strange reptilian birds and golden insects were busy at the steaming armor.

A sound on the floor of the Time Machine stiffened them. Eckels sat there, shivering.

"I'm sorry," he said at last.

"Get up!" cried Travis.

Eckels got up.

"Go out on that Path alone," said Travis. He had his rifle pointed. "You're not coming back in the Machine. We're leaving you here!"

Lesperance seized Travis's arm. "Wait—"

"Stay out of this!" Travis shook his hand away. "This fool nearly killed us. But it isn't *that* so much, no. It's his *shoes*! Look at them! He ran off the Path. That *ruins* us! We'll forfeit! Thousands of dollars of insurance! We guarantee no one leaves the Path. He left it. Oh, the fool! I'll have to report to the government. They might **revoke** our license to travel. Who knows *what* he's done to Time, to History!"

INFER

Pause at line 355. Why do you think the two hunters, Billings and Kramer, do not want to take "trophy pictures"?

_____

_____

_____

_____

_____

_____

_____

_____

_____

_____

_____

_____

IDENTIFY CAUSE & EFFECT

Re-read lines 369–376. Underline what Travis fears might happen because Eckels stepped off the path.

VOCABULARY

revoke (ri·vōk´) *v.:* cancel; withdraw.

CLARIFY

Pause at line 388. What does Travis want Eckels to do as punishment?

_____

_____

_____

_____

_____

_____

VOCABULARY

primeval (prī·mē′vəl) *adj.:* primitive; of the earliest times.

Notes _____

_____

_____

_____

_____

_____

_____

_____

_____

_____

_____

_____

"Take it easy, all he did was kick up some dirt."

"How do we know?" cried Travis. "We don't know anything! It's all a mystery! Get out of here, Eckels!"

380 Eckels fumbled his shirt. "I'll pay anything. A hundred thousand dollars!"

Travis glared at Eckels's checkbook and spat. "Go out there. The Monster's next to the Path. Stick your arms up to your elbows in his mouth. Then you can come back with us."

"That's unreasonable!"

"The Monster's dead, you idiot. The bullets! The bullets can't be left behind. They don't belong in the Past; they might change anything. Here's my knife. Dig them out!"

The jungle was alive again, full of the old tremorings and
390 bird cries. Eckels turned slowly to regard the **primeval** garbage dump, that hill of nightmares and terror. After a long time, like a sleepwalker he shuffled out along the Path.

He returned, shuddering, five minutes later, his arms soaked and red to the elbows. He held out his hands. Each held a number of steel bullets. Then he fell. He lay where he fell, not moving.

"You didn't have to make him do that," said Lesperance.

"Didn't I? It's too early to tell." Travis nudged the still body. "He'll live. Next time he won't go hunting game like this. Okay."
400 He jerked his thumb wearily at Lesperance. "Switch on. Let's go home."

1492. 1776. 1812.

They cleaned their hands and faces. They changed their caking shirts and pants. Eckels was up and around again, not speaking. Travis glared at him for a full ten minutes.

"Don't look at me," cried Eckels. "I haven't done anything."

"Who can tell?"

"Just ran off the Path, that's all, a little mud on my shoes—what do you want me to do—get down and pray?"
410 "We might need it. I'm warning you, Eckels, I might kill you yet. I've got my gun ready."

"I'm innocent. I've done nothing!"

1999. 2000. 2055.

The Machine stopped.

"Get out," said Travis.

The room was there as they had left it. But not the same as they had left it. The same man sat behind the same desk. But the same man did not quite sit behind the same desk.

Travis looked around swiftly. "Everything okay here?" he snapped.

"Fine. Welcome home!"

Travis did not relax. He seemed to be looking at the very atoms of the air itself, at the way the sun poured through the one high window.

"Okay, Eckels, get out. Don't ever come back."

Eckels could not move.

"You heard me," said Travis. "What're you *staring* at?"

Eckels stood smelling of the air, and there was a thing to the air, a chemical taint so subtle, so slight, that only a faint cry of his **subliminal** senses warned him it was there. The colors, white, gray, blue, orange, in the wall, in the furniture, in the sky beyond the window, were . . . were . . . And there was a *feel*. His flesh twitched. His hands twitched. He stood drinking the oddness with the pores of his body. Somewhere, someone must have been screaming one of those whistles that only a dog can hear. His body screamed silence in return. Beyond this room, beyond this wall, beyond this man who was not quite the same man seated at this desk that was not quite the same desk . . . lay an entire world of streets and people. What sort of world it was now, there was no telling. He could feel them moving there, beyond the walls, almost, like so many chess pieces blown in a dry wind. . . .

But the immediate thing was the sign painted on the office wall, the same sign he had read earlier today on first entering.

Somehow, the sign had changed:

PREDICT

Pause at line 415. Do you think that Eckels will find that he has "done nothing" when he gets back to the future?

_____

_____

_____

_____

IDENTIFY

Underline clues in lines 416–418 that indicate that Eckels's actions have had an effect on life in his present.

VOCABULARY

subliminal (sub·lim′ə·nəl) *adj.*: below the level of awareness.

INTERPRET

Circle the sensory images in lines 428–442 that describe Eckels's feeling that something is not right. Why does he compare people to chess pieces?

_____

_____

_____

_____

_____

Tyme Sefari, Inc.

Sefaris tu any yeer en the past.

Yu naim the animall.
Wee taekyuthair.

Yu shoot itt.

COMPARE & CONTRAST

Compare this sign with the one at the beginning of the story. How are they the same or different?

_____

_____

_____

IDENTIFY CAUSE & EFFECT

What was the main effect of Eckels's killing of the butterfly?

_____

_____

_____

_____

_____

_____

_____

_____

INTERPRET

What is the "sound of thunder" in line 471?

_____

_____

_____

_____

_____

Eckels felt himself fall into a chair. He fumbled crazily at the thick slime on his boots. He held up a clod of dirt, trembling, "No, it can't be. Not a *little* thing like that. No!"

450 Embedded in the mud, glistening green and gold and black, was a butterfly, very beautiful and very dead.

"Not a little thing like *that*! Not a butterfly!" cried Eckels.

It fell to the floor, an exquisite thing, a small thing that could upset balances and knock down a line of small dominoes and then big dominoes and then gigantic dominoes, all down the years across Time. Eckels's mind whirled. It couldn't change things. Killing one butterfly couldn't be that important! Could it?

His face was cold. His mouth trembled, asking: "Who— who won the presidential election yesterday?"

The man behind the desk laughed. "You joking? You know 460 very well. Deutscher, of course! Who else? Not that fool weakling Keith. We got an iron man now, a man with guts!" The official stopped. "What's wrong?"

Eckels moaned. He dropped to his knees. He scrabbled at the golden butterfly with shaking fingers. "Can't we," he pleaded to the world, to himself, to the officials, to the Machine, "can't we take it *back*, can't we *make* it alive again? Can't we start over? Can't we—"

He did not move. Eyes shut, he waited, shivering. He heard Travis breathe loud in the room; he heard Travis shift his rifle, 470 click the safety catch, and raise the weapon.

There was a sound of thunder.

A Sound of Thunder

Style Chart Ray Bradbury uses language to re-create a lush prehistoric setting. We see and feel the vast jungle and its huge inhabitant, the *Tyrannosaurus rex*. The boxed passages below contain some of Bradbury's stylistic devices:

- **figures of speech**—metaphors, similes, personification
- **imagery**—words that appeal to sight, hearing, taste, touch, smell

Underline figures of speech, circle the images, and draw boxes around examples of repetition. Then, in the space provided, describe the writer's **style** and the **mood** of the story.

Passage One	Passage Two
The jungle was high and the jungle was broad and the jungle was the entire world forever and forever. Sounds like music and sounds like flying tents filled the sky, and those were pterodactyls, soaring with cavernous gray wings, gigantic bats of delirium and night fever.	The Tyrant Lizard raised itself. Its armored flesh glittered like a thousand green coins. The coins, crusted with slime, steamed. In the slime, tiny insects wriggled, so that the entire body seemed to twitch and undulate, even while the monster itself did not move. It exhaled. The stink of raw flesh blew down the wilderness.

Describe Bradbury's Style

_____

_____

_____

Describe the Story's Mood

_____

_____

_____

Standards Review

 **A Sound of Thunder**

Complete the sample test item below. Then, check your answer, and read the explanation that appears in the right-hand box.

Sample Test Item	Explanation of the Correct Answer
In "A Sound of Thunder," Bradbury's **style** is created by all the following elements *except* — **A** regional dialect **B** diction, or word choice **C** sentence length and pattern **D** figurative language	The correct answer is *A*. The word *except* tells you that the correct answer is the one that does *not* fit. The story does not include any characters who speak in a regional dialect. *B* and *C* are not correct because word choice and sentence length are elements of style. *D* is wrong because this story is full of figurative language, another component of style.

DIRECTIONS: Circle the letter of each correct answer.

1. Which passage from the story contains a **figure of speech**?

    A "Stay on the Path."

    B "They were ready to leave the Machine."

    C "That'd be a paradox."

    D "Each lower leg was a piston . . ."

2. In this story, Bradbury's **diction,** or word choice, can *best* be described as —

    F flat

    G vivid

    H everyday

    J technical

3. Overall, Bradbury's **style** can *best* be described as —

    A humorous

    B matter-of-fact

    C sparse

    D richly descriptive

4. Which of the following words *best* describes the **mood** of "A Sound of Thunder"?

    F relaxed

    G quiet

    H terrifying

    J evil

Reading Standard 3.11
Evaluate the aesthetic qualities of style, including the impact of diction and figurative language on tone, mood, and theme, using the terminology of literary criticism.

Standards Review

 **A Sound of Thunder**

Prefixes and Word Roots

Prefixes and Meanings	
in-, *im-*, or *un-*, meaning "not"	*re-*, meaning "back; again"
ex-, meaning "out"	*sub-*, meaning "below"
extra-, meaning "outside; beyond"	*pre-*, meaning "came before"

Reading Standard 1.1 Identify and use the literal and figurative meanings of words and understand word derivations.

DIRECTIONS: Read each sentence carefully. Then, write the definition of each boldface word on the line below. Refer to the chart above for help.

1. Eckels took an **extraordinary** journey into the past.

   _____

2. To keep the world **unchanged**, they were ordered to stay on the Path.

   _____

3. The dinosaur seemed **immortal**, like a terrifying pagan god.

   _____

4. After their adventure, the travelers had no desire to **revisit** the past.

   _____

Vocabulary in Context

DIRECTIONS: Complete the paragraph below by writing a word from the word box to fit each numbered blank. Not all words from the box will be used.

Word Box

- annihilate
- expendable
- depression
- paradox
- delirium
- resilient
- remit
- revoke
- primeval
- subliminal

I have been wanting to go to the (1) _____ forest, the oldest place open to time travelers. I have money to pay the hefty fee, though the world is in an economic (2) _____. Besides, Historic Travels, Inc., will (3) _____ my fee if the authorities (4) _____ the company's license and cancel the trip.

Before You Go On . . .

Check your Standards Mastery at the back of this book.

The Blue Jar by Isak Dinesen

Isak Dinesen keeps you spellbound in this tale about a woman's quest for a particular shade of blue. Instead of relying on plot to hold your interest—the plot of this story is very simple—the author works her magic through style. Dinesen uses the language of a fairy tale to give her story a timeless, hypnotic quality that mirrors the story's theme.

LITERARY FOCUS: IDENTIFYING STYLE

Every writer has a style, though some styles are more distinctive than others. **Style** refers to the way a writer uses language. You can identify a writer's style by examining his or her word choice (diction), use of figurative language and imagery, and sentence patterns and structures. When you describe a writer's style, you talk about how the writer's use of language affects the mood and tone of the story.

To describe the style of "The Blue Jar":
- Read the story once, for enjoyment and basic comprehension.
- Read the story a second time, and pay attention to Dinesen's word choice, sentence length and patterns, imagery, and figures of speech.
- Ask yourself how Dinesen's use of language contributes to the mood of the story.
- Then, think about the words you'd use to describe Dinesen's style.

READING SKILLS: VISUALIZING THE STORY

Writers use words to help you **visualize,** or imagine, a story's setting and characters. When you visualize, you use the writer's words to create a mental picture of what's going on—almost as if you were watching a movie. Visualizing makes it easier to "enter into" a story and to understand what you are reading.

To visualize a story:
- Pay special attention to descriptions and word choices.
- Pause at the end of a paragraph or any other logical stopping point to imagine the scene.
- Look for sensory details, ones that appeal to any or all of your senses. Re-read the passage to catch any details you might have missed.

Reading Standard 1.2
Distinguish between the denotative and connotative meanings of words and interpret the connotative power of words.

Reading Standard 3.11
Evaluate the aesthetic qualities of style, including the impact of diction and figurative language on tone, mood, and theme, using the terminology of literary criticism. (Aesthetic approach)

SHORT STORY

VOCABULARY DEVELOPMENT

PREVIEW VOCABULARY

The following words appear in the story you are about to read. You may want to become familiar with them before you begin reading.

fugitives (fyōō′ji·tivz) *n.:* people fleeing from danger or oppression.

*The **fugitives** escaped from the burning ship.*

hemisphere (hem′i·sfir′) *n.:* half of a sphere; specifically, half of the Earth.

*Europe and Asia are in the eastern **hemisphere**, while the Americas are in the western hemisphere.*

implored (im·plôrd′) *v.:* begged; pleaded.

*Her aunts **implored** Lady Helena to return, but she refused.*

plunder (plun′dər) *n.:* the act of robbery or of taking property by force.

*During the **plunder** of the castle, the Emperor lost his precious jade collection.*

contemplation (kän′təm·plā′shən) *n.:* thoughtful observation.

*Following her rescue, Lady Helena spent many hours in **contemplation** of the color blue.*

DENOTATION AND CONNOTATION

Denotations are the literal meanings of words—the meanings you find in the dictionary. **Connotations** are the associations and emotions that have come to be attached to a word. For example, *slender, skinny, scrawny,* and *svelte* could all be used to describe a thin person, but they have very different connotations. *Slender* and *svelte* suggest a lovely and graceful person. *Skinny* and *scrawny* imply that the person is too thin and perhaps unattractive.

Writers choose words carefully for their connotations. They look for the connotation that will help them create a certain **mood** or set the right **tone**. As you read "The Blue Jar," notice how the connotations of Isak Dinesen's words make her writing precise and powerful.

The Blue Jar

Isak Dinesen

The Bridgeman Art Library.

STYLE

Notice how the first words of the story are similar to "Once upon a time," the traditional opening of fairy tales. Underline other words in the first sentence that remind you of a fairy tale.

VOCABULARY

fugitives (fyōō′ji·tivz) *n.:* people fleeing from danger or oppression.

IDENTIFY

Pause at line 17. Who saves Lady Helena from the burning ship?

_____

_____

_____

_____

There was once an immensely rich old Englishman who had been a courtier and a councilor to the Queen and who now, in his old age, cared for nothing but collecting ancient blue china. To that end he traveled to Persia, Japan, and China, and he was everywhere accompanied by his daughter, the Lady Helena. It happened, as they sailed in the Chinese Sea, that the ship caught fire on a still night, and everybody went into the lifeboats and left her. In the dark and the confusion the old peer was separated from his daughter. Lady Helena got up on deck late, and

10 found the ship quite deserted. In the last moment a young English sailor carried her down into a lifeboat that had been forgotten. To the two **fugitives** it seemed as if fire was following them from all sides, for the phosphorescence[1] played in the dark sea, and, as they looked up, a falling star ran across the sky, as if it was going to drop into the boat. They sailed for nine days, till they were picked up by a Dutch merchantman,[2] and came home to England.

---

1. **phosphorescence** (fäs′fə·res′əns) *n.:* light given off by tiny organisms in the sea.
2. **merchantman:** ship used in commerce.

The old lord had believed his daughter to be dead. He now
wept with joy, and at once took her off to a fashionable watering
place³ so that she might recover from the hardships she had gone
through. And as he thought it must be unpleasant to her that a
young sailor, who made his bread in the merchant service, should
tell the world that he had sailed for nine days alone with a peer's
daughter, he paid the boy a fine sum, and made him promise to
go shipping in the other **hemisphere** and never come back. "For
what," said the old nobleman, "would be the good of that?"

When Lady Helena recovered, and they gave her the news of the
Court and of her family, and in the end also told her how the
young sailor had been sent away never to come back, they found
that her mind had suffered from her trials, and that she cared for
nothing in all the world. She would not go back to her father's castle in its park, nor go to Court, nor travel to any gay town of the
continent. The only thing which she now wanted to do was to go,
like her father before her, to collect rare blue china. So she began to
sail, from one country to the other, and her father went with her.

In her search she told the people, with whom she dealt, that
she was looking for a particular blue color, and would pay any
price for it. But although she bought many hundred blue jars
and bowls, she would always after a time put them aside and say:
"Alas, alas, it is not the right blue." Her father, when they had
sailed for many years, suggested to her that perhaps the color
which she sought did not exist. "O God, Papa," said she, "how
can you speak so wickedly? Surely there must be some of it left
from the time when all the world was blue."

Her two old aunts in England **implored** her to come back,
still to make a great match. But she answered them: "Nay, I have
got to sail. For you must know, dear aunts, that it is all nonsense
when learned people tell you that the seas have got a bottom to
them. On the contrary, the water, which is the noblest of the
elements, does, of course, go all through the earth, so that our
planet really floats in the ether, like a soapbubble. And there, on

---

3. **watering place:** spa; health center with a mineral spring.

IDENTIFY

Re-read lines 18–26.
Underline the actions the
lord takes when his daughter
returns.

FLUENCY

Read the boxed passage
aloud twice. The first time,
focus on conveying the basic
meaning of the passage. The
second time you read, allow
the writer's word choice to
guide your reading rate and
tone of voice.

VOCABULARY

hemisphere (hem'i·sfir') n.:
half of a sphere; specifically,
half of the Earth.

implored (im·plôrd') v.:
begged; pleaded.

CLARIFY

Re-read lines 27–35. In what
ways has Lady Helena
changed?

_____

_____

_____

_____

_____

VISUALIZE

Underline the words in lines
49–51 that help you visualize
Lady Helena's ideas about
the sea and earth.

Pause at line 66. Whom is Lady Helena imagining on the "opposite side of the globe"? How will they finally be together?

_____

_____

_____

_____

VOCABULARY

plunder (plun′dər) *n.:* the act of robbery or of taking property by force.

contemplation (kän′təm·plā′shən) *n.:* thoughtful observation.

INFER

Pause at line 81. Why does Lady Helena want her heart placed in the blue jar after her death (lines 77–78)?

_____

_____

_____

_____

_____

_____

_____

_____

_____

the other hemisphere, a ship sails, with which I have got to keep pace. We two are like the reflection of one another, in the deep sea, and the ship of which I speak is always exactly beneath my own ship, upon the opposite side of the globe. You have never seen a big fish swimming underneath a boat, following it like a dark-blue shade in the water. But in that way this ship goes, like the shadow of my ship, and I draw it to and fro wherever I go, as the moon draws the tides, all through the bulk of the earth. If I

60 stopped sailing, what would these poor sailors who make their bread in the merchant service do? But I shall tell you a secret," she said. "In the end my ship will go down, to the center of the globe, and at the very same hour the other ship will sink as well—for people call it sinking, although I can assure you that there is no up and down in the sea—and there, in the midst of the world, we two shall meet."

Many years passed, the old lord died, and Lady Helena became old and deaf, but she still sailed. Then it happened, after the **plunder** of the summer palace[4] of the Emperor of China, that a

70 merchant brought her a very old blue jar. The moment she set eyes on it she gave a terrible shriek. "There it is!" she cried. "I have found it at last. This is the true blue. Oh, how light it makes one. Oh, it is as fresh as a breeze, as deep as a deep secret, as full as I say not what." With trembling hands she held the jar to her bosom, and sat for six hours sunk in **contemplation** of it. Then she said to her doctor and her lady-companion: "Now I can die. And when I am dead you will cut out my heart and lay it in the blue jar. For then everything will be as it was then. All shall be blue round me, and in the midst of the blue world my heart will

80 be innocent and free, and will beat gently, like a wake[5] that sings, like the drops that fall from an oar blade." A little later she asked them: "Is it not a sweet thing to think that, if only you have patience, all that has ever been, will come back to you?" Shortly afterwards the old lady died.

---

4. **plunder of the summer palace:** In 1860, British and French soldiers plundered and burned the summer residence of the Chinese royal family.
5. **wake:** trail left in the water by a moving boat.

The Blue Jar

Style Analysis Chart Fill in the chart below as you examine the style of "The Blue Jar." Be sure to provide examples of imagery and figures of speech from the story. Use quotation marks when you quote directly from the story.

Elements of Style
1. Describe the imagery in the story and give examples.
2. Give examples of the writer's use of figurative language.
3. Describe the writer's sentence structures (long? short? simple? complex?).
4. Write at least one sentence describing the general mood of the story.
5. Write at least one sentence describing the story's style.

Standards Review

 **The Blue Jar**

Complete the sample test item below. Then, check your answer, and read the explanation that appears in the right-hand column.

Sample Test Item	Explanation of the Correct Answer
The **diction,** or word choice, of "The Blue Jar" can *best* be described as — A humorous B formal C informal D factual	The answer is *B*. The story is not funny, so *A* is incorrect. The language used is exact and proper; therefore, *C* is incorrect. Since the story focuses on experiences and feelings, *D* is not correct, either.

DIRECTIONS: Circle the letter of each correct answer.

1. Which of the following passages makes this story seem like a fairy tale?

   A "There was once"

   B "They sailed for nine days"

   C "So she began to sail"

   D "Shortly afterwards"

2. The description of the "true blue" color—"Oh, it is as fresh as a breeze"—uses which **figure of speech**?

   F personification

   G metaphor

   H simile

   J none of the above

3. The narrator's **tone** is *best* described as —

   A irritated

   B commanding

   C lecturing

   D sincere

4. The **style** of "The Blue Jar" can *best* be characterized as —

   F direct

   G dreamlike

   H joyous

   J scary

Reading Standard 3.11 Evaluate the aesthetic qualities of style, including the impact of diction and figurative language on tone, mood, and theme, using the terminology of literary criticism. (Aesthetic approach)

Standards Review

 **The Blue Jar**

Connotations

Connotations are the feelings associated with a word that go beyond its strict definition, or **denotation**. Connotations often show shades of meaning or intensity.

DIRECTIONS: Answer "true" or "false" by checking the correct item.

Reading Standard 1.2 Distinguish between the denotative and connotative meanings of words and interpret the connotative power of words.

1. *Lady Helena's aunts **implored** her to return home.* Replacing the boldface word with "asked" would make the sentence stronger. ___ True ___ False

2. *The old peer **wept** when he discovered that Lady Helena was safe.* Replacing the boldface word with "blubbered" would portray the old peer more positively. ___ True ___ False

3. *Lady Helena was sent to a watering place to recover from her **hardships**.* Replacing the boldface word with "ordeal" would make her experience seem more difficult. ___ True ___ False

Vocabulary in Context

DIRECTIONS: Complete the paragraph below by writing a word from the word box to fit each numbered blank.

Word Box

- fugitives
- hemisphere
- implored
- plunder
- contemplation

The (1) _____ from the bloody battle stowed their booty from the (2) _____ of the castle in the sailboat and cast off. Their plan was to be far away, in the other (3) _____ of the earth, before they were missed. The older man was very tired and hungry, and (4) _____ his friend to stop to get supplies. The young man didn't hear him, however. He was lost in (5) _____, imagining all the wonderful things the money would buy.

 Before You Go On...

Check your Standards Mastery at the back of this book.

LITERARY CRITICISM
Biographical and Historical Approach

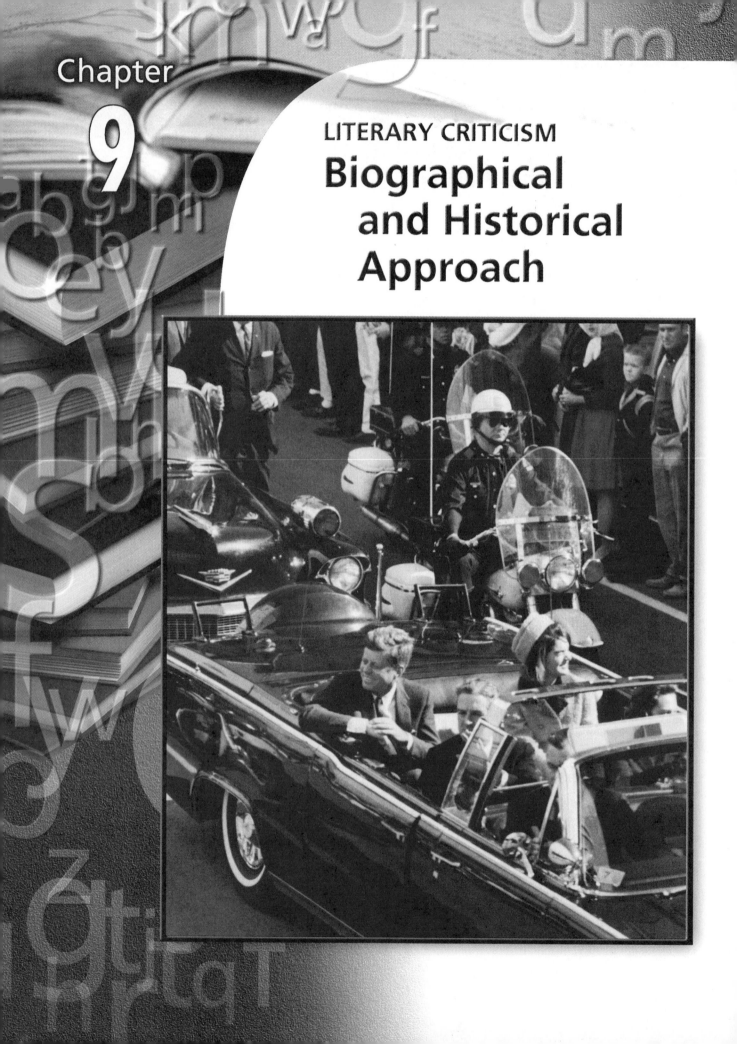

Academic Vocabulary for Chapter 9

These are the terms you should know
as you read and analyze the stories in this chapter.

———————

Historical setting or historical context The historical period that shapes a
work of literature. Understanding the historical setting helps us grasp
the issues that were important in a given time period.

Historical approach The use of historical context to help analyze and
respond to a text.

• • •

Biographical knowledge Information about a writer's life experiences.
Understanding a writer's life, including his or her attitudes, heritage,
and traditions, adds meaning to what we are reading.

Biographical approach The use of a writer's life experiences to help analyze
and respond to a text.

**Reading
Standard 1.1**
Identify and use
the literal and
figurative
meanings of
words and
understand
word
derivations.

**Reading
Standard 3.7
(Grade 8
Review)**
Analyze a work
of literature
showing how it
reflects the
heritage,
traditions,
attitudes, and
beliefs of its
author.
(Biographical
approach)

**Reading
Standard 3.12**
Analyze the way
in which a work
of literature is
related to the
themes and
issues of its
historical period.
(Historical
approach)

> ### For Further Information . . .
>
> • Be sure to read the essay on **literary roots** in
> *Holt Literature and Language Arts*, pages
> 562–563.

American History by Judith Ortiz Cofer

Sometimes our personal feelings are so overwhelming that they can minimize even the most tragic events. At least, that's how it seems to Elena, the narrator and main character of "American History." Elena's story is set against the backdrop of the Kennedy assassination, a time when the whole country was in shock. As you read, notice how the author uses historical details and her own life experience to give her story and its historical setting focus and depth.

LITERARY FOCUS: BIOGRAPHICAL AND HISTORICAL APPROACH

- **Historical setting** is the time and place that shapes a work of literature. "American History" is set in urban New Jersey in the 1960s, on the day of President Kennedy's assassination. President Kennedy's assassination caused widespread shock and grief. To many people, the young president with his forward-looking ideas represented hope for a better future. As you read, look for **historical details** from the story that give you insight into Elena's world.

- Look for details from the author's life. In "American History," Cofer tells a story that mirrors her own experience growing up Puerto Rican in 1960s America. Notice how she uses **biographical details** to make her characters and the events of the story seem realistic and true.

- **Theme** is the central idea or insight revealed by a story. As you read "American History," look for **historical** and **biographical details** that contribute to the story's underlying theme.

READING SKILLS: SUMMARIZING

A **summary** is a short restatement of the important ideas in a work. When you summarize a story, you retell just the main events. Summarizing helps you keep track of the characters and the plot. It also increases your ability to understand and remember what you read.

To summarize *as you read:*	To summarize *after you read:*
• Pause occasionally. • Review who the characters are. • Retell what has happened to them so far.	• Briefly describe the story's beginning, middle, and end. • Focus on the main characters and events.

Reading Standard 1.1
Identify and use the literal and figurative meanings of words and understand word derivations.

Reading Standard 3.7 (Grade 8 Review)
Analyze a work of literature, showing how it reflects the heritage, traditions, attitudes, and beliefs of its author. (Biographical approach)

Reading Standard 3.12
Analyze the way in which a work of literature is related to the themes and issues of its historical period. (Historical approach)

SHORT STORY

VOCABULARY DEVELOPMENT

PREVIEW SELECTION VOCABULARY

The following words appear in the story you are about to read. Become familiar with them before you begin reading.

literally (lit′ər·əl·ē) *adv.:* actually; in fact.

Elena went to the fire escape to think, feeling **literally** *suspended in time and place.*

discreet (di·skrēt′) *adj.:* careful; showing good judgment.

Elena was so **discreet** *about her feelings for Eugene, even her best friends were clueless.*

linger (liŋ′gər) *v.:* continue to stay; be reluctant to leave.

It felt so good in the warm sun that Elena decided to **linger** *there as long as possible.*

infatuated (in·fach′oo·āt′id) *adj.:* carried away by shallow or foolish love.

She decided not to become so **infatuated,** *and tried not to act "moony" all the time.*

vigilant (vij′ə·lənt) *adj.:* watchful.

Elena's mother became increasingly **vigilant** *about her comings and goings, often locking the front door to prevent Elena from going out.*

enthralled (en·thrôld′) *v.:* fascinated.

The dancers **enthralled** *Elena with their skill and grace.*

elation (ē·lā′shən) *n.:* great joy.

Elena had a feeling of **elation** *when the boy she admired smiled at her.*

distraught (di·strôt′) *adj.:* deeply troubled, as with worry or grief.

Elena's parents were so **distraught** *that she put off seeing Eugene in order to calm them down.*

dilapidated (də·lap′ə·dāt′id) *adj.:* in poor condition; shabby and neglected.

The broken-down, **dilapidated** *building depressed Elena.*

solace (säl′is) *n.:* comfort; easing of grief.

In the awful days that followed, Elena's mother went from friend to friend, seeking the **solace** *she needed.*

ANALOGIES: WORD PAIRS

A **word analogy** is a word puzzle based on two pairs of words that have the same relationship. The words in each pair might have the same meaning or an opposite meaning, or they might share some other relationship, such as cause and effect or whole to part. Follow this example for completing analogies:

    START is to STOP as_____is to love.

    Start and *stop* are opposites, so the word that would show the same relationship in the second pair is *hate,* the opposite of *love.*

The analogy above is spelled out. Sometimes analogies are written like this:

    HUGE : ELEPHANT :: tiny : flea.

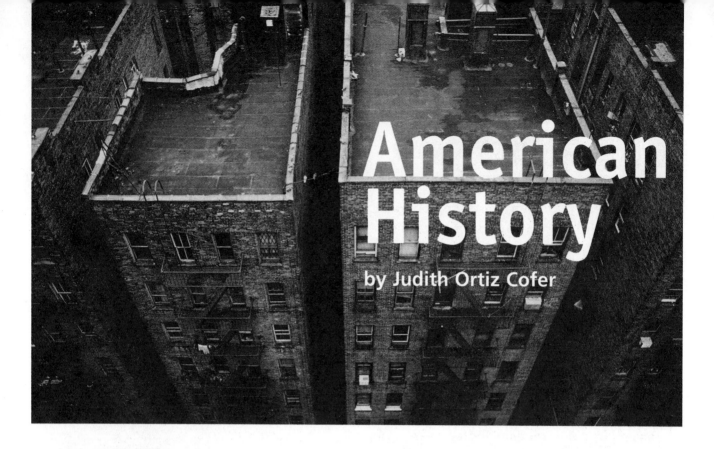

American History
by Judith Ortiz Cofer

VISUALIZE

Pause at line 10. Underline details that help you picture El Building.

HISTORICAL DETAILS

Re-read lines 10–16. Circle the world-shaking event that occurred on November 22, 1963. What effect did this event have on the people of El Building?

_____

_____

_____

_____

I once read in a "Ripley's Believe It or Not" column that Paterson, New Jersey, is the place where the Straight and Narrow (streets) intersect. The Puerto Rican tenement known as El Building was one block up on Straight. It was, in fact, the corner of Straight and Market; not "at" the corner, but *the* corner. At almost any hour of the day, El Building was like a monstrous jukebox, blasting out salsas[1] from open windows as the residents, mostly new immigrants just up from the island, tried to drown out whatever they were currently enduring with loud

10 music. But the day President Kennedy was shot, there was a profound silence in El Building; even the abusive tongues of viragoes,[2] the cursing of the unemployed, and the screeching of small children had been somehow muted. President Kennedy was a saint to these people. In fact, soon his photograph would be hung alongside the Sacred Heart and over the spiritist altars[3] that many women kept in their apartments. He would become

---

1. **salsas** (säl′səz) *n.:* lively dance music from Latin America.
2. **viragoes** (vi·rä′gōz) *n.:* quarrelsome women.
3. **the Sacred Heart . . . altars:** The Sacred Heart is an image depicting the wounded heart of Jesus, often encircled by a crown of thorns. "Spiritist altars" most likely refers to memorials for dead relatives.

part of the hierarchy of martyrs[4] they prayed to for favors that only one who had died for a cause would understand.

On the day that President Kennedy was shot, my ninth-grade class had been out in the fenced playground of Public School Number 13. We had been given "free" exercise time and had been ordered by our PE teacher, Mr. DePalma, to "keep moving." That meant that the girls should jump rope and the boys toss basketballs through a hoop at the far end of the yard. He in the meantime would "keep an eye" on us from just inside the building.

It was a cold gray day in Paterson. The kind that warns of early snow. I was miserable, since I had forgotten my gloves and my knuckles were turning red and raw from the jump rope. I was also taking a lot of abuse from the black girls for not turning the rope hard and fast enough for them.

"Hey, Skinny Bones, pump it, girl. Ain't you got no energy today?" Gail, the biggest of the black girls who had the other end of the rope yelled, "Didn't you eat your rice and beans and pork chops for breakfast today?"

The other girls picked up the "pork chop" and made it into a refrain: "Pork chop, pork chop, did you eat your pork chop?" They entered the double ropes in pairs and exited without tripping or missing a beat. I felt a burning on my cheeks and then my glasses fogged up so that I could not manage to coordinate the jump rope with Gail. The chill was doing to me what it always did: entering my bones, making me cry, humiliating me. I hated the city, especially in winter. I hated Public School Number 13. I hated my skinny, flat-chested body, and I envied the black girls, who could jump rope so fast that their legs became a blur. They always seemed to be warm, while I froze.

There was only one source of beauty and light for me that school year—the only thing I had anticipated at the start of the

---

4. **hierarchy** (hī′ər·är′kē) **of martyrs** (märt′ərz): *Hierarchy* means "ranking in order of importance." Martyrs are people who have suffered or died rather than give up their faith or principles.

Notes

INFER

Re-read lines 32–35. Circle the words the girls say to taunt Elena, the narrator. What are they making fun of?

IDENTIFY

Pause at line 49. What is the one source of beauty in Elena's world?

_____

_____

_____

_____

_____

_____

_____

IDENTIFY

Re-read lines 61–74. Elena draws conclusions based on the details she observes about the old couple's life. Underline the conclusion Elena makes about what happened to the man. Then, circle the details she observes that led her to that conclusion.

COMPARE & CONTRAST

Re-read lines 75–85. Underline details that show how Eugene's family is different from the old couple that previously lived in the house.

semester. That was seeing Eugene. In August, Eugene and his

50 family had moved into the only house on the block that had a yard and trees. I could see his place from my window in El Building. In fact, if I sat on the fire escape I was **literally** suspended above Eugene's backyard. It was my favorite spot to read my library books in the summer. Until that August the house had been occupied by an old Jewish couple. Over the years I had become part of their family, without their knowing it, of course. I had a view of their kitchen and their backyard, and though I could not hear what they said, I knew when they were arguing, when one of them was sick, and many other things. I knew all

60 this by watching them at mealtimes. I could see their kitchen table, the sink, and the stove. During good times, he sat at the table and read his newspapers while she fixed the meals. If they argued, he would leave and the old woman would sit and stare at nothing for a long time. When one of them was sick, the other would come and get things from the kitchen and carry them out on a tray. The old man had died in June. The last week of school I had not seen him at the table at all.   Then one day I saw that there was a crowd in the kitchen.   The old woman had finally emerged from the house on the arm of a stocky middle-

70 aged woman, whom I had seen there a few times before, maybe her daughter. Then a man had carried out suitcases. The house had stood empty for weeks. I had had to resist the temptation to climb down into the yard and water the flowers the old lady had taken such good care of.

By the time Eugene's family moved in, the yard was a tangled mass of weeds. The father had spent several days mowing, and when he finished, from where I sat I didn't see the red, yellow, and purple clusters that meant flowers to me. I didn't see this family sit down at the kitchen table together. It was just the

80 mother, a redheaded, tall woman who wore a white uniform—a nurse's, I guessed it was; the father was gone before I got up in the morning and was never there at dinner time. I only saw him on weekends, when they sometimes sat on lawn chairs under the

oak tree, each hidden behind a section of the newspaper; and there was Eugene. He was tall and blond, and he wore glasses. I liked him right away because he sat at the kitchen table and read books for hours. That summer, before we had even spoken one word to each other, I kept him company on my fire escape.

Once school started, I looked for him in all my classes, but
90 PS 13 was a huge, overpopulated place and it took me days and many **discreet** questions to discover that Eugene was in honors classes for all his subjects, classes that were not open to me because English was not my first language, though I was a straight-A student. After much maneuvering I managed to "run into him" in the hallway where his locker was—on the other side of the building from mine—and in study hall at the library, where he first seemed to notice me but did not speak, and finally, on the way home after school one day when I decided to approach him directly, though my stomach was doing
100 somersaults.

I was ready for rejection, snobbery, the worst. But when I came up to him, practically panting in my nervousness, and blurted out: "You're Eugene. Right?" He smiled, pushed his glasses up on his nose, and nodded. I saw then that he was blushing deeply. Eugene liked me, but he was shy. I did most of the talking that day. He nodded and smiled a lot. In the weeks that followed, we walked home together. He would **linger** at the corner of El Building for a few minutes, then walk down to his two-story house. It was not until Eugene moved into that house that
110 I noticed that El Building blocked most of the sun and that the only spot that got a little sunlight during the day was the tiny square of earth the old woman had planted with flowers.

I did not tell Eugene that I could see inside his kitchen from my bedroom. I felt dishonest, but I liked my secret sharing of his evenings, especially now that I knew what he was reading since we chose our books together at the school library.

One day my mother came into my room as I was sitting on the windowsill staring out. In her abrupt way she said: "Elena,

COMPARE & CONTRAST

What similarity do you see between Eugene and Elena (lines 85–87)?

_____

_____

_____

VOCABULARY

discreet (di·skrēt') *adj.:* careful; showing good judgment.

linger (liŋ'gər) *v.:* continue to stay; be reluctant to leave.

IDENTIFY CAUSE & EFFECT

Pause at line 94. How does Elena's background keep her apart from Eugene, even at school?

_____

_____

_____

_____

_____

CONNECT

People's feelings can influence the way that they see their environment. What new details does Elena notice about her surroundings as a result of her feelings for Eugene (lines 109–112)? Underline what you find out.

IDENTIFY

Re-read lines 117–124. Circle the words that describe how Elena's mother *doesn't* want her to behave. What words do you think describe how a "señorita" should behave?

_____

_____

_____

_____

_____

VOCABULARY

infatuated (in·fach′oo·āt′id) *adj.:* carried away by shallow or foolish love.

vigilant (vij′ə·lənt) *adj.:* watchful.

IDENTIFY

Re-read lines 125–132. Underline details that describe the father's dream for their life in America.

BIOGRAPHICAL CONTEXT

The author, whose family came to the United States when she was young, went on to master English, attend college, and become a teacher. Circle the sentence in lines 144–145 that suggests Elena's experience is similar to the writer's.

you are acting 'moony.'" "Enamorada" was what she really said, that is—like a girl stupidly **infatuated**. Since I had turned fourteen, my mother had been more **vigilant** than ever. She acted as if I was going to go crazy or explode or something if she didn't watch me and nag me all the time about being a señorita[5] now. She kept talking about virtue, morality, and other subjects that did not interest me in the least. My mother was unhappy in Paterson, but my father had a good job at the bluejeans factory in Passaic and soon, he kept assuring us, we would be moving to our own house there. Every Sunday we drove out to the suburbs of Paterson, Clifton, and Passaic, out to where people mowed grass on Sundays in the summer and where children made snowmen in the winter from pure white snow, not like the gray slush of Paterson, which seemed to fall from the sky in that hue. I had learned to listen to my parents' dreams, which were spoken in Spanish, as fairy tales, like the stories about life in the island paradise of Puerto Rico before I was born. I had been to the island once as a little girl, to Grandmother's funeral, and all I remembered was wailing women in black, my mother becoming hysterical and being given a pill that made her sleep two days, and me feeling lost in a crowd of strangers all claiming to be my aunts, uncles, and cousins. I had actually been glad to return to the city. We had not been back there since then, though my parents talked constantly about buying a house on the beach someday, retiring on the island—that was a common topic among the residents of El Building. As for me, I was going to go to college and become a teacher.

But after meeting Eugene I began to think of the present more than of the future. What I wanted now was to enter that house I had watched for so many years. I wanted to see the other rooms where the old people had lived and where the boy spent his time. Most of all I wanted to sit at the kitchen table with Eugene like two adults, like the old man and his wife had done,

---

5. **señorita** (se′nyô·rē′tä) *n.:* Spanish for "unmarried woman."

maybe drink some coffee and talk about books. I had started reading *Gone with the Wind*. I was **enthralled** by it, with the daring and the passion of the beautiful girl living in a mansion, and with her devoted parents and the slaves who did everything for them. I didn't believe such a world had ever really existed, and I wanted to ask Eugene some questions since he and his parents, he had told me, had come up from Georgia, the same place where the novel was set. His father worked for a company that had transferred him to Paterson. His mother was very unhappy, Eugene said, in his beautiful voice that rose and fell over words in a strange, lilting way. The kids at school called him "the Hick" and made fun of the way he talked. I knew I was his only friend so far, and I liked that, though I felt sad for him sometimes. "Skinny Bones and the Hick" was what they called us at school when we were seen together.

The day Mr. DePalma came out into the cold and asked us to line up in front of him was the day that President Kennedy was shot. Mr. DePalma, a short, muscular man with slicked-down black hair, was the science teacher, PE coach, and disciplinarian at PS 13. He was the teacher to whose homeroom you got assigned if you were a troublemaker, and the man called out to break up playground fights and to escort violently angry teenagers to the office. And Mr. DePalma was the man who called your parents in for "a conference."

That day, he stood in front of two rows of mostly black and Puerto Rican kids, brittle from their efforts to "keep moving" on a November day that was turning bitter cold. Mr. DePalma, to our complete shock, was crying. Not just silent adult tears, but really sobbing. There were a few titters from the back of the line where I stood shivering.

"Listen," Mr. DePalma raised his arms over his head as if he were about to conduct an orchestra. His voice broke, and he covered his face with his hands. His barrel chest was heaving. Someone giggled behind me.

160

170

180

VOCABULARY

enthralled (en·thrôld') v.: fascinated.

COMPARE & CONTRAST

Pause at line 166. In what ways are Elena and Eugene alike?

_____

_____

_____

_____

HISTORICAL CONTEXT

Re-read lines 167–169. Circle the tragic event that occurs.

FLUENCY

Read the boxed passage aloud until you can pronounce all the words without stumbling. Then, read the passage again, this time focusing on its meaning.

INFER

Re-read lines 176–181. Underline details that describe Mr. DePalma's reaction to the president's death. Why do you think the students react to him the way they do?

_____

_____

_____

_____

_____

_____

_____

VOCABULARY

elation (ē·lā′shən) *n.*: great joy.

INFER

Re-read lines 214–217. Why does Elena feel a conflict?

_____

_____

_____

_____

_____

_____

_____

_____

_____

_____

_____

"Listen," he repeated, "something awful has happened." A strange gurgling came from his throat, and he turned around and spat on the cement behind him.

"Gross," someone said, and there was a lot of laughter.

190 "The president is dead, you idiots. I should have known that wouldn't mean anything to a bunch of losers like you kids. Go home." He was shrieking now. No one moved for a minute or two, but then a big girl let out a "Yeah!" and ran to get her books piled up with the others against the brick wall of the school building. The others followed in a mad scramble to get to their things before somebody caught on. It was still an hour to the dismissal bell.

A little scared, I headed for El Building. There was an eerie feeling on the streets. I looked into Mario's drugstore, a favorite 200 hangout for the high school crowd, but there were only a couple of old Jewish men at the soda bar talking with the short-order cook in tones that sounded almost angry, but they were keeping their voices low. Even the traffic on one of the busiest intersections in Paterson—Straight Street and Park Avenue—seemed to be moving slower. There were no horns blasting that day. At El Building, the usual little group of unemployed men was not hanging out on the front stoop making it difficult for women to enter the front door. No music spilled out from open doors in the hallway. When I walked into our apartment, I found my 210 mother sitting in front of the grainy picture of the television set.

She looked up at me with a tear-streaked face and just said: "Dios mío,"[6] turning back to the set as if it were pulling at her eyes. I went into my room.

Though I wanted to feel the right thing about President Kennedy's death, I could not fight the feeling of **elation** that stirred in my chest. Today was the day I was to visit Eugene in his house. He had asked me to come over after school to study for an American history test with him. We had also planned to walk to the public library together. I looked down into his yard.

---

6. dios mío (dē′ōs mē′ō): Spanish for "Oh, my God."

President John F. Kennedy

220   The oak tree was bare of leaves and the ground looked gray with
ice. The light through the large kitchen window of his house
told me that El Building blocked the sun to such an extent that
they had to turn lights on in the middle of the day. I felt
ashamed about it. But the white kitchen table with the lamp
hanging just above it looked cozy and inviting. I would soon sit
there, across from Eugene, and I would tell him about my perch
just above his house. Maybe I should.

     In the next thirty minutes I changed clothes, put on a little
pink lipstick, and got my books together. Then I went in to tell

230   my mother that I was going to a friend's house to study. I did
not expect her reaction.

     "You are going out *today?*" The way she said "today" sound-
ed as if a storm warning had been issued. It was said in utter dis-
belief. Before I could answer, she came toward me and held my
elbows as I clutched my books.

IDENTIFY CAUSE & EFFECT

Pause at line 237. Elena's mother feels that Elena is not acting the way she should. Underline how she thinks Elena should behave in response to President Kennedy's death.

VOCABULARY

distraught (di·strôt′) *adj.:* deeply troubled, as with worry or grief.

dilapidated (də·lap′ə·dāt′id) *adj.:* in poor condition; shabby and neglected.

BIOGRAPHICAL CONTEXT

Pause at line 260. Like Elena, the author's first language was Spanish. How does Cofer's use of her native language add to the story?

_____
_____
_____
_____
_____
_____
_____
_____
_____
_____
_____

"Hija,[7] the president has been killed. We must show respect. He was a great man. Come to church with me tonight."

She tried to embrace me, but my books were in the way. My first impulse was to comfort her, she seemed so **distraught,** but I 240 had to meet Eugene in fifteen minutes.

"I have a test to study for, Mama. I will be home by eight."

"You are forgetting who you are, Niña.[8] I have seen you staring down at that boy's house. You are heading for humiliation and pain." My mother said this in Spanish and in a resigned tone that surprised me, as if she had no intention of stopping me from "heading for humiliation and pain." I started for the door. She sat in front of the TV holding a white handkerchief to her face.

I walked out to the street and around the chain-link fence 250 that separated El Building from Eugene's house. The yard was neatly edged around the little walk that led to the door. It always amazed me how Paterson, the inner core of the city, had no apparent logic to its architecture. Small, neat single residences like this one could be found right next to huge, **dilapidated** apartment buildings like El Building. My guess was that the little houses had been there first, then the immigrants had come in droves, and the monstrosities had been raised for them—the Italians, the Irish, the Jews, and now us, the Puerto Ricans and the blacks. The door was painted a deep green: verde, the color 260 of hope. I had heard my mother say it: verde-esperanza.

I knocked softly. A few suspenseful moments later the door opened just a crack. The red, swollen face of a woman appeared. She had a halo of red hair floating over a delicate ivory face— the face of a doll—with freckles on the nose. Her smudged eye makeup made her look unreal to me, like a mannequin[9] seen through a warped store window.

"What do you want?" Her voice was tiny and sweet sounding, like a little girl's, but her tone was not friendly.

---

7. **hija** (ē′hä) *n.:* Spanish for "daughter."
8. **niña** (nē′nyä) *n.:* Spanish for "girl."
9. **mannequin** (man′ə·kin) *n.:* life-size model of a person.

"I'm Eugene's friend. He asked me over. To study." I thrust
out my books, a silly gesture that embarrassed me almost immediately.

"You live there?" She pointed up to El Building, which
looked particularly ugly, like a gray prison, with its many dirty
windows and rusty fire escapes. The woman had stepped
halfway out and I could see that she wore a white nurse's uniform with "St. Joseph's Hospital" on the name tag.

"Yes. I do."

She looked intently at me for a couple of heartbeats, then
said as if to herself, "I don't know how you people do it." Then
directly to me: "Listen. Honey. Eugene doesn't want to study
with you. He is a smart boy. Doesn't need help. You understand
me. I am truly sorry if he told you you could come over. He cannot study with you. It's nothing personal. You understand? We
won't be in this place much longer, no need for him to get close
to people—it'll just make it harder for him later. Run back home
now."

I couldn't move. I just stood there in shock at hearing these
things said to me in such a honey-drenched voice. I had never
heard an accent like hers, except for Eugene's softer version. It
was as if she were singing me a little song.

"What's wrong? Didn't you hear what I said?" She seemed
very angry, and I finally snapped out of my trance. I turned
away from the green door and heard her close it gently.

Our apartment was empty when I got home. My mother
was in someone else's kitchen, seeking the **solace** she needed.
Father would come in from his late shift at midnight. I would
hear them talking softly in the kitchen for hours that night. They
would not discuss their dreams for the future, or life in Puerto
Rico, as they often did; that night they would talk sadly about
the young widow and her two children, as if they were family.
For the next few days, we would observe luto in our apartment;
that is, we would practice restraint and silence—no loud music

270

280

290

300

INFER

Re-read lines 272–279. Circle
the words Eugene's mother
says that reveal her attitude
toward Elena's people. Why
does El Building look particularly ugly to Elena right
now?

_____

_____

_____

SUMMARIZE

Pause at line 286. Summarize
what happens in this scene
between Elena and Eugene's
mother.

_____

_____

_____

_____

_____

_____

_____

_____

_____

_____

VOCABULARY

solace (säl'is) n.: comfort;
easing of grief.

Pause at line 313. While the
nation grieves for a slain
president, Elena must deal
with another kind of grief.
What bitter lesson has Elena
learned?

_____

_____

_____

_____

_____

_____

_____

_____

BIOGRAPHICAL
APPROACH

Why do you think Cofer
chose to tell this story?

_____

_____

_____

_____

_____

_____

_____

_____

or laughter. Some of the women of El Building would wear
black for weeks.

That night, I lay in my bed trying to feel the right thing for
our dead president. But the tears that came up from a deep
source inside me were strictly for me. When my mother came to
the door, I pretended to be sleeping. Sometime during the night,
I saw from my bed the streetlight come on. It had a pink halo

310   around it. I went to my window and pressed my face to the cool
glass. Looking up at the light, I could see the white snow falling
like a lace veil over its face. I did not look down to see it turning
gray as it touched the ground below.

American History

Historical/Biographical Analysis Chart Writers' experiences and cultural backgrounds are sometimes reflected in their stories. Complete the Historical/Biographical Analysis Chart below to increase your understanding and appreciation of "American History."

When and where is the story set?
What is the writer's background?
What story details reflect the writer's background?
What issues of the writer's time are reflected in the work?

Standards Review

 **American History**

Complete the sample test item below. Then, check your answer, and read the explanation that appears in the right-hand column.

Sample Test Item	Explanation of the Correct Answer
In this story, Elena's father has dreams of — A becoming president of the United States B settling in the suburbs C going to college D living in a small single-family house in Paterson	The correct answer is *B*. There is no mention in the story of Elena's father wanting to be president (*A*). It is Elena who wants to go to college, not her father (*C*). We're not told anything about a single-family house in Paterson (*D*), but we know from the story that Elena's father wants to move to the suburbs.

Reading Standard 3.7 (Grade 8 Review) Analyze a work of literature, showing how it reflects the heritage, traditions, attitudes and beliefs of its author. (Biographical approach)

Reading Standard 3.12 Analyze the way in which a work of literature is related to the themes and issues of its historical period. (Historical approach)

DIRECTIONS: Circle the letter of the correct response.

1. Elena's treatment by the girls at school indicates that the town of Paterson is affected by —

   A violence

   B racism

   C poverty

   D unemployment

2. Which character is probably based on the story's author?

   F Mr. DePalma

   G Elena

   H Elena's mother

   J Eugene's mother

3. Which of the following does *not* describe how the neighborhood reacted to the assassination of the president?

   A There was an eerie feeling on the streets.

   B Voices were kept low, but sounded almost angry.

   C Traffic seemed to move slower.

   D A group of unemployed men gathered outside El Building.

4. Why does Elena feel happy in the midst of a great tragedy?

   F She is no longer teased at school.

   G She is going to visit Eugene.

   H She has gotten straight A's.

   J She is allowed to go to church.

Standards Review

TestPractice **American History**

Analogies: Word Pairs

DIRECTIONS: Circle the letter of the word pair that best completes each analogy.

1. FASCINATED : INTERESTED ::
   - **A** light : dark
   - **B** pick : shovel
   - **C** furious : mad
   - **D** fast : slow

2. YOLK: EGG ::
   - **F** pupil : eyeball
   - **G** sun : moon
   - **H** car: truck
   - **J** run : jump

3. RAKE : LEAVES ::
   - **A** liquid : solid
   - **B** bright : dull
   - **C** vacuum : dirt
   - **D** wet : wild

4. HAPPY : ELATED ::
   - **F** red : orange
   - **G** smart : brilliant
   - **H** old : young
   - **J** meek : sassy

Reading Standard 1.1 Identify and use the literal and figurative meanings of words and understand word derivations.

Vocabulary in Context

DIRECTIONS: Complete the paragraph by writing words from the box in the correct blanks. Not all words from the box will be used.

Word Box

- **literally**
- **discreet**
- **linger**
- **infatuated**
- **vigilant**
- **enthralled**
- **elation**
- **distraught**
- **dilapidated**
- **solace**

Carla was (1)_____ when she learned that the ancient, creaky building she loved would have to be torn down because it was so (2)_____. Often, when she had the time, she would (3)_____ outside the old house and imagine the lives of the people who'd lived there. Even though she could not (4)_____ see them, she could well imagine them going about their business. Carla was (5)_____, however, and kept her secret imaginings to herself.

Before You Go On . . .
Check your Standards Mastery at the back of this book.

The House Guest by Paul Darcy Boles

BEFORE YOU READ

In this story, a young girl from war-torn Northern Ireland spends six weeks with an American family. Although nine-year-old Bridgie is here to learn what America is like, *she* ends up being the teacher. Through Bridgie, the family learns that the world doesn't stop at their doorstep—and that everyone needs a home.

LITERARY FOCUS: HISTORICAL CONTEXT

- The **historical period** is the time and place a story is set. "The House Guest" is set during the 1970s, when Northern Ireland was being torn apart by conflict between Protestants and Catholics. Millions of Americans watched the horrible images on television, but many remained uncertain what the violence was all about.
- Given the long and bloody history of the conflict in Northern Ireland, it's easy for one little girl to get lost in the shuffle. As you read "The House Guest," notice how Bridgie's story reflects an important **theme,** or insight into life: People everywhere need a safe and secure home.

READING SKILLS: MAKING INFERENCES

An **inference** is a type of educated guess. You use details in a selection as well as your own experience to guess about something you don't know for sure. For example, in the following passage from "The House Guest," the American narrator describes Bridgie's behavior at the dinner table:

> She always ate fast and never left anything on the plate. . . .
> I noticed she never asked for second helpings, either, but
> she'd take them when they were handed to her, even if
> she looked kind of amazed about getting them.

The narrator of the story doesn't tell you much about Bridgie's life in Northern Ireland, but you can make certain inferences based on what you know. For instance, you can infer that Bridgie has known hunger in her life—"she always ate fast and never left anything on the plate"—and she is amazed when she's offered second helpings.

Make inferences as you read "The House Guest." To make an inference:
- Look for details in the selection that reveal a character's thoughts, actions, or situation.
- Consider what you know about life.
- Make an educated guess about the character and why he or she acts or thinks a certain way.

Reading Standard 1.1 Identify and use the literal and figurative meanings of words and understand word derivations.

Reading Standard 3.12 Analyze the way in which a work of literature is related to the themes and issues of its historical period. (Historical approach)

Part 1 Chapter 9: Biographical and Historical Approach

266

SHORT STORY

PREVIEW SELECTION VOCABULARY

The following words appear in "The House Guest." Get to know these words before you begin reading.

statistics (stə·tis′tiks) *n.*: a collection of data, usually numbers, that provide detailed information on a particular subject.

*The **statistics** gave the height and weight of each newborn child.*

mammoth (mam′əth) *adj.*: very big; huge.

*The **mammoth** new parking lot will take up two city blocks.*

boulevard (bool′ə·värd′) *n.*: a broad street or avenue, often lined with trees and grass plots, and so on.

*Our house was easy to find because it was just off the **boulevard.***

mutual (myoo′choo·əl) *adj.*: shared; in common.

*Because both groups had something to gain, they had a **mutual** stake in the election results.*

DIALECT

Dialect is a way of speaking that is characteristic of a particular region or group of people. In "The House Guest," the writer uses dialect to re-create the sound and feel of the way Bridgie, a young Irish girl, speaks. Watch for these characteristics of Bridgie's dialect as you read.

Some of Bridgie's words come out in reversed order. For example, "I've a drink taken" means "I've taken a drink." Sometimes individual words and expressions can be unfamiliar:

Ut gets scrooged up, laborin' so over the bench the many hours.

Now read the sentence as if it were written in standard English:

I get very tense, laboring for so long at the workbench.

Which version gives you a better sense of Bridgie? Can you understand why the writer chose to write Bridgie's words in dialect?

As you read "The House Guest," try to "hear" Bridgie's dialogue, either in your head or by reading it aloud. Notice how the author uses dialect to make the character of Bridgie come alive.

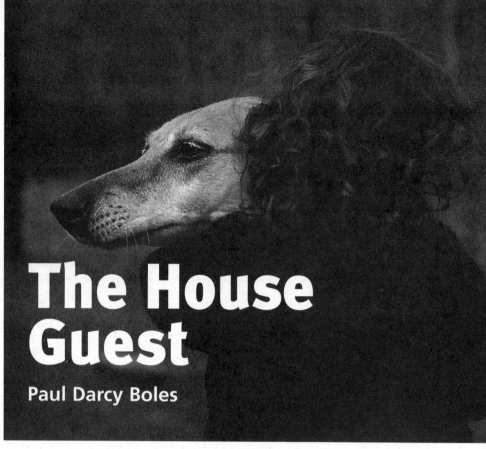

The House Guest

Paul Darcy Boles

I'm writing this at the downstairs desk where I do homework or just fool around. It's the same desk Bridgie used to come up to and stand behind sometimes. After a second or so, I would feel her standing there. Then I would turn around, making it slow because she's a kid you don't want to scare. She has big dark blue eyes, red hair about the color of the sun before it's really up. She doesn't have much of a chin; her cheekbones are high and like smooth little rocks under the clear skin. She's no beauty. I mean, she's just what she is.

10   When I turned around and she was there as I'd thought, I would say, "Can I help you, Bridgie?" She would shake her head; she'd just wanted to see if *I* was all right. And when she'd made sure I was, she would just turn around and walk off. My mother and father told me she did the same thing with them: stood and looked at them for a couple of seconds, then walked off . . . satisfied they were still themselves and handy.

She was only with us for six short weeks. It was one of these red-tape deals through the United States government; you signed up to keep a kid from Northern Ireland in your home as
20   a guest. The idea was to show the kids what America was like, as

if anybody could do that even in six years. Anyhow, I was all for it; my brother is an intern and he's working in Rome for a year, and I never had a sister.

The night Bridgie first came, after my parents brought her from the city to our town, she didn't talk much at all. I don't mean she ducked her head or looked awkward or fiddled with her feet or hid behind the furniture. It was just that she clammed up.

She had a small green bag with some extra clothes in it and an old doll that had been whacked around quite a bit. That was
30 the whole works, except for the clothes she wore. Next day, my mother took her to a couple of shops in town and bought her some new stuff. She still wasn't talking a lot, only pleases and thank you's, and when my mother took the new clothes out of the boxes to hang them up, Bridgie touched them, very politely, as if they belonged to somebody else and she shouldn't make any fuss. She was nine years old.

At first it kept on being kind of eggshelly around her. You see, we weren't supposed to ask her anything heavy about how things were in the place she'd come from. She'd been born in
40 Belfast, grew up there. She had four brothers and two sisters. She was next to the oldest. Her mother had died a year and a half before and her father took care of the family the best he could.

We got all that from the bunch of **statistics** that came before we even saw her. The people running this show wanted the kids to "fit easily into the American environment," without being pestered. I guess that was a noble idea, but it left an awful lot you couldn't say or ask.

You can hear a good deal of traffic from our dining room, not anything thunderous, but backfires and people pretending
50 they're A.J. Foyt when they zoom down the street. And a couple of times at dinner when this happened, you could see Bridgie stiffen up. She'd get quiet as a rabbit, and it wasn't even that so much as it was the way she looked out of the corners of her eyes. As if she were searching for a neat, dark place to hide in.

It didn't wreck her appetite, though. I don't mean she was born a pig, I just mean she always ate fast and never left anything on the plate. Oh, sure, my mother is a decent cook, but this was a different thing. I noticed she never asked for second helpings, either, but she'd take them when they were handed to
60 her, even if she looked kind of amazed about getting them.

It was not until the third day she was with us that she really started to open up a little. We were all sitting around yakking after the evening's parade of news on TV. There had been a clip of a building, or what was left of it, that had been bombed in Dublin. The commentator had said, in that level voice they use for good news, terrible news, and in between, that the trouble was moving out of Belfast, that it wasn't "contained" any more. Bridgie had been sitting straight as six o'clock, hands in her lap, and suddenly she said, "My da was in Dublin the once."

70 There was a good-sized stop in the talk; then my mother asked, "Did he go on a holiday?"

She gave her head a small shake. She wore her hair in two braids wound tight around her head like pale silk ropes. "Nah, ma'am. He went there in a van to help his mate he worked with down at the docks. His mate was movin' to Dublin. When my da come back he brought us a dog."

"What kind?" I asked. "What'd he look like?"

Her eyes went a pretty fair distance away. "Ah, I was a kid then, I hardly remember ut." She looked around blinking, her
80 eyes that same way, as if she were looking into the fireplace where the fire was jumping around in some pine logs and trying to see backward. Then she said, "But soft he was, with fine ears that stuck up when he was happy." She turned back from the fire and her shoulders went up in little wings, shrugging. "He come up missin' inside the week though. My ma never took to him, him makin' messes and all. But he couldn't o' helped it, so young."

WORD STUDY

In lines 68–76, Bridgie suddenly starts talking about her da. *Da* is a common word in Ireland. What do you think it means?

INFER

Pause at line 87. Circle the passage that suggests Bridgie's affection for the dog. What happened to him?

That night, after Bridgie had been tucked in bed by my mother in the room next to my parents', I asked my mother whether we could adopt Bridgie or something. My mother said that wasn't possible, she'd already asked about it. Bridgie's family needed her too much, for one thing. There were a lot of those big, iron reasons. After my mother explained them, we just sat there thinking about her. I kept wishing it was the kind of world where I happened to be President, or anyhow head of the State Department or something, and could cut through some rules.

The next day was Saturday. My mother took Bridgie into the city for lunch and a flick and some sightseeing. The flick was something made for kids, very ha-ha, and my mother said that all through it, Bridgie sat without moving and not laughing either, with the buttered-popcorn-and-soft-drink bunch hollering around them.

She liked the Carl Akeley elephants and the stuffed-looking Eskimo families in the Field Museum, but the thing she liked best was a bunch of puppies in a pet-shop window. She had to be just about dragged away. "But we can't get her a dog; it would be too cruel when she had to give it up," my mother said. "She couldn't take it back to Ireland . . ."

After that, my mother took her to one of the **mammoth** toy stores. She walked her through the doll section, but Bridgie wasn't hot about dolls. "I've got the one already," she said. "Ut's good enough."

Finally they got to the crafts part of the store, and there Bridgie finally found something she was really warm for. It was a big leatherworking set with a lot of colored chunks of leather in red, blue, green, and yellow, and the knives and tooling instruments and all the rest. It was about the most advanced leatherworking set I'd ever seen, and I asked Bridgie if she'd like me to help her get started with it.

"Nah," she said, "I'm quick at the readin' and I can soak in the directions. Don't put yourself out for me, Mitch."

INFER

Re-read lines 97–102. Why doesn't Bridgie laugh during the movie, as the other kids do?

_____

_____

_____

_____

_____

_____

_____

_____

_____

VOCABULARY

mammoth (mam'əth) adj.: very big; huge.

IDENTIFY

Pause at line 119. What did Bridgie finally find at the store that she really wanted?

_____

_____

_____

_____

_____

_____

_____

I wanted to put myself out for her all right, though, so a few nights after that I talked her into going ice-skating with me down at the town lake. She didn't exactly skate when we got there, but I pushed her around on the skates I rented for her. After a while it started to snow, and going home I carried Bridgie on my back and she carried my skates. I pranced like a horse in the snow and once I heard her laugh.

But on the porch back home, when I was brushing snow off
130 her shoulders, she said, "I shouldn't 'a gone. I've missed out a whole night o' my leatherin'."

"That's supposed to be fun, too," I said. "Like skating. How're you coming with it?"

"I'm learnin," she said. "It went slow at the first. Them directions was set down by a blitherin' lump. But now I'm swarmin' around it." Then she said, fast, "Please, Mitch, I'd like a place to work outside the fine room where I do my sleepin'."

I'd happened to look in that room and see her working, chewing her tongue and frowning and fierce. She'd been so into
140 it she hadn't even seen me. Now she said, "It's not the need o' elbow room, there's plenty o' that. It's I'm afraid o' carvin' up the pretty floor. There's the workshop out in your garage, the one

next to where ya keep the ottomobiles. It's even got the heater, if ya could spare the oil for that."

I swept out the workroom and got the heater jets open and working the next morning before I went to school. It was a place I'd spent a whole lot of my own time in as a young child, working like a fiend on model airplanes and boats. When I got home that afternoon, I found she'd spent most of the day out there; I

150 walked out of the back door and went to the workroom window, but she wasn't inside. Then she came around the corner of the garage from the lane in back of it. Her hair was mussed and she looked like she'd been doing a hundred-yard dash. "Ah, I had to take me a walk," she said. "Ut gets scrooged up, laborin' so over the bench the many hours."

I started into the workroom to turn off the lights, but she ran ahead of me. "Here, I'll do ut." She flipped them off. I could see she didn't want me to see what she was making. She shut the door. On the way back to the house she said, looking at the

160 ground, "Ya won't peach on me? Ya won't tell? Sometimes I just like swingin' around the neighborhood. I won't get lost and shame ya."

We were almost at the back-porch steps. She said, "It's fine, walkin' where ya please. Not havin' to stay in the District."

"District?" I said.

"Ah, that's the boundaries. You don't go past 'em unless you're a fool bent on destruction. The District is where you and your people stay inside of."

I'd never even started to think how it would be living inside

170 a few blocks and not stepping over a line. I did then.

She was out in the workroom the next day after breakfast; my mother told me she came in for lunch and then swept right out again. She did the same thing after dinner, till I went out and called her in because it was her bedtime. My mother said she was a little worried about all this hang-up with leathercraft, but my father said, "Maybe privacy is the rarest thing we can give her," and my mother gave in to that. I didn't tell them about

INFER

Peach on me (line 160) means "tell on me." Why do you think Bridgie asks Mitch not to tell on her?

_____

_____

_____

_____

_____

_____

_____

_____

_____

HISTORICAL CONTEXT

In lines 163–168, underline Bridgie's explanation of what a District is. What conclusions can you draw about life in Belfast?

_____

_____

_____

_____

_____

_____

_____

Circle the reason Mitch waits until 10:30 to bring Bridgie in from the workroom (lines 185–187). What do his actions suggest about Mitch's life?

_____

_____

_____

_____

_____

_____

_____

boulevard (bool'ə·värd') *n.:* a broad street or avenue, often lined with trees and grass plots, and so on.

What is Bridgie doing in lines 205–212? Circle the words she says to the stray dog.

_____

_____

_____

_____

_____

_____

_____

the walks around the neighborhood; Bridgie could take care of Bridgie, all right.

180   A couple of days before it was time for her to go back—something we weren't mentioning, any of us—my mother and father sailed off in the evening to visit some town friends. Then about nine-thirty my mother called to tell me they were going to stay longer than they'd planned, and to be sure to get Bridgie in from the workroom by around ten. After that, though, the phone rang again; it was some mad, dashing girl I'd been interested in for what seemed a hundred years. It wasn't till we'd finally said good night that I sat up and noticed it was ten-thirty.

I bolted out in the night, down the back-porch steps, and
190 yelled for Bridgie. There wasn't any answer; the whole night seemed quiet as a piece of white steel. I crunched through the snow that had fallen the day before, and looked in at the workroom window. The bench light was off.

A second later, I saw her footprints, leading back to the lane.

Halfway down the lane, though, the footprints started to get mixed up with tire tracks and were harder to make out. But that was all right because by then I could see Bridgie herself. She was easy to spot, down at the end of the lane where the
200 **boulevard** started and not far from the streetlight, kneeling down beside a ribby old black-and-tan dog. The dog looked as though it might have had Airedale in it, along with four or five other breeds; on its hind legs it would have been about as tall as Bridgie was.

She didn't turn around, maybe didn't hear me, when I came up closer. She was fitting a new collar around the dog's neck. It was acting pretty patient; she talked to it in a kind of low crooning-scolding way. "Hold your thrapple up," she was saying. "You'll be proud and solid as the Rock of Cashel now,
210 and don't be tryin' to scrape ut off or lose ut. Ut's your ticket to some fine homes. They'll feed ya up. They'll think ya been a pet, they'll b'lieve you're valuable . . ."

IDENTIFY

In lines 220–221, underline the words Bridgie says to explain what she's doing.

INFER

Pause at line 222. Why do you think Bridgie put so much effort into making the dog collars beautiful?

About that time, she saw me. She gave the green leather collar another pat, just the same, before she stood up. It was tooled with a lot of careful flowers, and I recognized one of the brass buckles from the giant leatherworking set.

"Well, you've caught me out," she said. "That was the last of the leather, so ut's just as well. I fitted out an even dozen creatures. It was hard findin' 'em all, some I had to folla for blocks.
220 But none had the collars before, and now they have. It makes their chances o' havin' a home much grander. You're not angered?"

HISTORICAL CONTEXT

Now that Bridgie has gone home, Mitch becomes more interested in the conflict in Ireland. What does Mitch reveal about the situation in Belfast (lines 240–241)?

_____

_____

_____

_____

INTERPRET

What does Mitch mean when he says "Bridgie's District is the world" (line 246)? What **theme** is suggested in these final words?

_____

_____

_____

_____

_____

_____

_____

_____

_____

_____

_____

_____

I didn't say anything. I just stuck a hand down to her and she took it. We went back along the lane. She said, "The collar's a kind o' doorkey. Ya'd be faster to take in a dog with a collar, wouldn't ya, now?" I still didn't say anything and she looked up at me. "There's no hard feelin's, for the immense cost o' the leatherin' outfit?"

I said, "It's okay, Bridgie."

230   Then I lifted her up (for nine she doesn't weigh a lot) and carried her home.

Before she went up to bed she said, "You're glad o' me? You'll ask me back some day when ut's allowed by our **mutual** governments?"

"Sure," I said. I kissed her on the forehead. She grinned quickly and broadly, and said, "Yah! Mush!" then backed away and skipped off and upstairs.

I'm writing this at the desk Bridgie used to come up to and stand behind while she looked at me to make sure I was still

240   here. I'm still here. Tonight on the news there were some cut-ins from Belfast: bombings and shootings. A while ago I heard a dog outside in the dark howling a little, then going away. I don't know if it had a collar on or not. I turned around when I heard it, but Bridgie wasn't there, of course. She's back home in her District, but maybe that's not exactly true either . . . because I think Bridgie's District is the world.

The House Guest

Historical Context Chart Use the chart below to show how the **historical context** of "The House Guest" is reflected in the story details. In the right-hand column, list details from the story that reflect the historical details described in the left-hand column.

Historical Details	Details from Story
As a result of the conflict in Northern Ireland, many people have died or been wounded. Many children have experienced the loss of a parent.	
The sound of gunfire, bombs, and explosives is a fact of life in Northern Ireland.	
The economy of Northern Ireland has suffered because of the conflict. Many people experience hunger.	

 **The House Guest**

Complete the sample test item below. Then, check your answer, and read the explanation that appears at right.

Sample Test Item	Explanation of the Correct Answer
To familiarize yourself with the **historical context** of "The House Guest," you might want to read about — **A** the dialects of modern-day Ireland **B** the history of Protestantism in Europe **C** suburban life in the United States in the 1900s **D** the history of the conflict in Northern Ireland	You can arrive at the correct answer, *D,* by narrowing the field. The question asks you to choose the kind of historical information that would most help you to understand the story. Choice *A* has nothing to do with the historical period. *B* is concerned with history, but its scope is too broad. *C* has nothing to do with Ireland.

DIRECTIONS: Circle the letter of each correct response.

1. Mitch begins to understand Bridgie's situation when she tells him about —

  A her old doll

  B the dog her *da* gave her

  C the District

  D her leatherwork

2. When Bridgie flinches at sudden, loud noises, it is probably because they remind her of —

  F a dog's barking

  G gunfire and explosions

  H thunder and lightning

  J a movie she hadn't liked

3. Which of the following is probably *not* a result of Bridgie's background?

  A her few belongings

  B her huge appetite

  C her adult behavior

  D her enjoyment of ice-skating

4. Which of the following *best* states the **theme** of the story?

  F War is unavoidable.

  G People need safety and security in a violent world.

  H The Irish are stronger than other people.

  J Having a pet is essential in times of war.

Reading Standard 3.12 Analyze the way in which a work of literature is related to the themes and issues of its historical period. (Historical approach)

Standards Review

 **The House Guest**

Dialect

DIRECTIONS: Circle the best "translation" of the passage in dialect.

1. *. . . and don't be tryin' to scrape ut off or lose ut.*

   A . . . and don't scrape it or you'll loosen it.

   B . . . and don't scrape it off or you'll lose us.

   C . . . and don't try to scrape it off or lose it.

   D . . . and don't scrape yourself trying to lose it.

2. *My da was in Dublin the once.*

   F My dad was in Dublin once.

   G My dad was first in Dublin.

   H One time in Dublin, my dad was there.

   J My dad is from Dublin.

3. *Them directions was set down by a blitherin' lump.*

   A You were blathering so much I couldn't get the directions.

   B They sat down near a babbling brook.

   C Those directions were written by an idiot.

   D The lumpy man wrote down the directions.

Reading Standard 1.1 Identify and use the literal and figurative meanings of words and understand word derivations.

Vocabulary in Context

DIRECTIONS: Write the words from the box in the correct blanks.

Word Box
statistics
mammoth
boulevard
mutual

Fred sat in the middle of a (1)_____, towering heap of books. The (2)_____ he was studying began to look less like columns of numbers than tiny flecks of dirt. Fred sighed. If he were a rock star, he thought, maybe Edie would like him more. He and Edie had a (3)_____ love of music, but this shared interest was not enough. The last time Fred had seen Edie, she was in a cab, heading down the broad (4)_____ on the way to the airport.

Before You Go On . . .

Check your Standards Mastery at the back of this book.

Epic and Myth

Academic Vocabulary for Chapter 10

These are the terms you should know
as you read and analyze the selections in this chapter.

Epic A long narrative poem that tells about the adventures of a great **hero.** Epics embody the values of the people who tell them.

Characters The people, animals, or monsters who take part in the action of a story. The **main character** of an epic is the hero (though in some epics, the hero's enemies are just as important). Many characters in epics are **subordinate characters;** they play lesser roles.

Conflict A struggle between opposing forces. An **external conflict** takes place between one character and another character, between one character and a force of nature, or between one character and society as a whole. An **internal conflict** takes place within a character's own mind or heart. In an internal conflict, a character might struggle with paralyzing fear or a need for revenge.

● ● ●

Myths Traditional stories, rooted in a particular culture, that usually explain a belief, a ritual, or a mysterious natural phenomenon. Most myths grew out of religious rituals.

Tall tale A humorous kind of folk tale that uses a great deal of exaggeration and is not meant to be taken very seriously.

Archetype Old patterns, characters, or images that appear over and over in works of literature. Archetypes can be plots (the quest for something of value), characters (the innocent hero), places (the dragon's lair), or things (the magical gold ring).

● ● ●

Homeric or heroic simile An extended simile with elaborate descriptive details that continues over a number of lines.

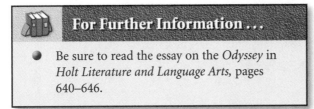

For Further Information . . .

● Be sure to read the essay on the *Odyssey* in *Holt Literature and Language Arts,* pages 640–646.

Reading Standard 1.3
Identify Greek, Roman, and Norse mythology and use the knowledge to understand the origin and meaning of new words.

Reading Standard 1.3 (Grade 8 Review)
Use word meanings within the appropriate context and show ability to verify those meanings by definition, restatement, example, comparison, and contrast.

Reading Standard 3.1 (Grade 8 Review)
Determine and articulate the relationship between the purposes and characteristics of different forms of poetry.

Reading Standard 3.3
Analyze interactions between main and subordinate characters in a literary text and explain the way those interactions affect the plot.

Reading Standard 3.12
Analyze the way in which a work of literature is related to the themes and issues of its historical period. (Historical approach)

"The Cyclops" from the *Odyssey* by Homer

In ancient Greece, heroes in epic poems like the *Odyssey* represented the highest values of Greek civilization. In Homer's day, heroes were thought of as a special class of men, somewhere between the gods and ordinary human beings. As you read "The Cyclops," see how Odysseus uses his special qualities to save himself and his men from becoming a monster's meal.

LITERARY FOCUS: HEROES AT LARGE

Epics are long narrative poems that tell of the great deeds of a hero. In an epic, the **main character** is the hero. (In many epics the hero's enemy is also a major character.) **Heroes** usually represent qualities that their society admires. Some people today, for example, see sports stars, popular singers, great scientists, or firefighters as their heroes. In epics told long ago, the heroes are often superhuman warriors, who set off on journeys to win something of great value for themselves and for their people.

The **conflicts,** or struggles between opposing forces, in an epic are usually **external,** as the heroes battle armies, monsters, or the forces of nature. Epic heroes can also face **internal conflicts**—caused by fear, doubt, weakness, and so on.

* First, read "The Cyclops" for enjoyment. Then, consider what the adventure reveals about the values of the ancient Greeks.

READING SKILLS: MONITOR YOUR COMPREHENSION

Good readers pause occasionally to make sure they understand what they have read. When you read a long, action-filled poem such as this one, it is important to stay on top of events—to understand what is happening. Pause during your reading to ask yourself the following questions:

* What has happened so far?
* What has caused those events?
* What are the most important events in this episode?
* When do the events take place?
* What might happen next?

Reading Standard 1.3
Identify Greek, Roman, and Norse mythology and use the knowledge to understand the origin and meaning of new words (e.g., the word *narcissistic* drawn from the myth of Narcissus and Echo).

Reading Standard 3.1 (Grade 8 Review)
Determine and articulate the relationship between the purposes and characteristics of different forms of poetry (e.g., epic).

Reading Standard 3.3
Analyze interactions between main and subordinate characters in a literary text (e.g., internal and external conflicts, motivations, relationships, influences) and explain the way those interactions affect the plot.

EPIC POEM

VOCABULARY DEVELOPMENT

PREVIEW SELECTION VOCABULARY

The following words appear in "The Cyclops." Become familiar with them before you begin reading.

ravage (rav′ij) *v.:* destroy violently; ruin.

The Cyclops planned to **ravage** *Odysseus and his men by eating them.*

profusion (prō·fyōō′zhən) *n.:* large supply; abundance.

With such a large flock of sheep, the Cyclops had a **profusion** *of milk, cheese, and wool.*

adversary (ad′vər·ser′ē) *n.:* enemy; opponent.

Odysseus had to find a way to defeat his **adversary,** *the Cyclops.*

WORDS FROM GREEK AND ROMAN MYTHS

Many words we use in English today come from Greek and Roman myths. For example, a journey or quest is often called an *odyssey,* named for the *Odyssey,* the epic poem from which "The Cyclops" is taken. Other words from "The Cyclops" that have been handed down are *ambrosia,* meaning "food of the gods," and *nectar,* meaning "drink of the gods." Look at the chart below to learn of other words handed down from Greek and Roman myths.

Names from Greek and Roman Myths	English Words
Ceres, Roman goddess of agriculture and fertility	cereal
Mount Olympus, legendary home of gods and goddesses	Olympics
Tantalus, character from Greek myth whose food and drink were kept just out of his reach, as punishment	tantalize
Titans, race of giant Greek gods who came before the Olympians	titanic
Vulcan, Roman god of fire and metalworkers	volcano

The Cyclops   283

Notes

THE CYCLOPS

from the **Odyssey**

Homer

translated by Robert Fitzgerald

Rijksmuseum Kroller-Muller, Otterlo, the Netherlands.

The Cyclops (detail) (late 19th or early 20th century) by Odilon Redon.

The Odyssey *is the story of the attempt of a Greek soldier, Odysseus, to return to his home following the Trojan War. An epic, the* Odyssey *is composed of many different stories, or episodes, in which the hero, Odysseus, faces all sorts of challenges.*

In this adventure, Odysseus describes his encounter with the Cyclops, Polyphemus (päl′i·fē′məs), Poseidon's one-eyed monster son. Polyphemus may represent the brute forces that any hero must overcome before he can reach home. To survive, Odysseus must rely on the special intelligence associated with his name. Odysseus is the cleverest of the Greek heroes because he is guided by the goddess of wisdom, Athena.

It is Odysseus's famed curiosity that leads him to the Cyclops's cave and that makes him insist on waiting for the barbaric giant.

Odysseus is speaking to the court of King Alcinous (al·sin′ō·əs).

From *The Odyssey* by Homer, translated by Robert Fitzgerald. Copyright © 1961, 1963 by Robert Fitzgerald; copyright renewed © 1989 by Benedict R. C. Fitzgerald. Reprinted by permission of **Farrar, Straus & Giroux, LLC.**

"We lit a fire, burnt an offering,
and took some cheese to eat; then sat in silence
around the embers, waiting. When he came
he had a load of dry boughs on his shoulder
5 to stoke his fire at suppertime. He dumped it
with a great crash into that hollow cave,
and we all scattered fast to the far wall.
Then over the broad cavern floor he ushered
the ewes he meant to milk. He left his rams
10 and he-goats in the yard outside, and swung
high overhead a slab of solid rock
to close the cave. Two dozen four-wheeled wagons,
with heaving wagon teams, could not have stirred
the tonnage of that rock from where he wedged it
15 over the doorsill. Next he took his seat
and milked his bleating ewes. A practiced job
he made of it, giving each ewe her suckling;
thickened his milk, then, into curds and whey,
sieved out the curds to drip in withy baskets,[1]
20 and poured the whey to stand in bowls
cooling until he drank it for his supper.
When all these chores were done, he poked the fire,
heaping on brushwood. In the glare he saw us.

'Strangers,' he said, 'who are you? And where from?
25 What brings you here by seaways—a fair traffic?
Or are you wandering rogues, who cast your lives
like dice, and **ravage** other folk by sea?'

We felt a pressure on our hearts, in dread
of that deep rumble and that mighty man.
30 But all the same I spoke up in reply:

'We are from Troy, Achaeans, blown off course
by shifting gales on the Great South Sea;

---

1. **withy baskets:** baskets made from willow twigs.

INFER

Pause at line 3. Odysseus and his men are in the cave of the Cyclops, Polyphemus. To whom do the men burn an offering?

_____

_____

_____

_____

MONITOR YOUR COMPREHENSION

Who is the "he" in line 3?

_____

_____

_____

_____

INTERPRET

Re-read lines 5–23, and pay attention to the Cyclops's actions. What qualities does he have?

_____

_____

_____

_____

VOCABULARY

ravage (rav'ij) v.: destroy violently; ruin.

homeward bound, but taking routes and ways
uncommon; so the will of Zeus would have it.

35 We served under Agamemnon, son of Atreus[2]—
the whole world knows what city
he laid waste, what armies he destroyed.
It was our luck to come here; here we stand,
beholden for your help, or any gifts

40 you give—as custom is to honor strangers.
We would entreat you, great Sir, have a care
for the gods' courtesy; Zeus will avenge
the unoffending guest.'

He answered this
from his brute chest, unmoved:

'You are a ninny,

45 or else you come from the other end of nowhere,
telling me, mind the gods! We Cyclopes
care not a whistle for your thundering Zeus
or all the gods in bliss; we have more force by far.
I would not let you go for fear of Zeus—

50 you or your friends—unless I had a whim to.
Tell me, where was it, now, you left your ship—
around the point, or down the shore, I wonder?'

He thought he'd find out, but I saw through this,
and answered with a ready lie:

'My ship?

55 Poseidon Lord, who sets the earth atremble,
broke it up on the rocks at your land's end.
A wind from seaward served him, drove us there.
We are survivors, these good men and I.'

Neither reply nor pity came from him,

60 but in one stride he clutched at my companions

---

2. **Agamemnon** (ag'ə·mem'nän'); **Atreus** (ā'trē·əs).

IDENTIFY

Hospitality to strangers was extremely important to the ancient Greeks. Re-read lines 38–43, and underline the words that tell what will happen if the Cyclops does not treat the Greeks well.

MONITOR YOUR COMPREHENSION

Pause at line 50. Does the Cyclops respect Zeus, as Odysseus does? Explain.

INFER

Pause at line 58. Why do you think Odysseus lies about his ship?

WORD STUDY

Underline the two gruesome **Homeric similes**—extended comparisons using *like* or *as*—in lines 59–65.

and caught two in his hands like squirming puppies
to beat their brains out, spattering the floor.
Then he dismembered them and made his meal,
gaping and crunching like a mountain lion—
65   everything: innards, flesh, and marrow bones.
We cried aloud, lifting our hands to Zeus,
powerless, looking on at this, appalled;
but Cyclops went on filling up his belly
with manflesh and great gulps of whey,
70   then lay down like a mast among his sheep.
My heart beat high now at the chance of action,
and drawing the sharp sword from my hip I went
along his flank to stab him where the midriff
holds the liver. I had touched the spot
75   when sudden fear stayed me: if I killed him
we perished there as well, for we could never
move his ponderous doorway slab aside.
So we were left to groan and wait for morning.

When the young Dawn with fingertips of rose
80   lit up the world, the Cyclops built a fire
and milked his handsome ewes, all in due order,
putting the sucklings to the mothers. Then,
his chores being all dispatched, he caught
another brace³ of men to make his breakfast,
85   and whisked away his great door slab
to let his sheep go through—but he, behind,
reset the stone as one would cap a quiver.⁴
There was a din of whistling as the Cyclops
rounded his flock to higher ground, then stillness.
90   And now I pondered how to hurt him worst,
if but Athena granted what I prayed for.
Here are the means I thought would serve my turn:

---

3. **brace** (brās) *n.*: pair.
4. **quiver** (kwiv′ər) *n.*: case for arrows.

How does Odysseus show both his bravery and his intelligence in lines 71–78?

_____

_____

_____

_____

_____

_____

WORD STUDY

Line 79 contains a famous **epithet**—a group of words used repeatedly to describe a character. How is Dawn described in this epithet?

_____

_____

_____

MONITOR YOUR COMPREHENSION

Pause at line 87. What prevents Odysseus and his men from escaping when the Cyclops leaves?

_____

_____

_____

_____

IDENTIFY

Pause at line 105. What do Odysseus and his men do with the olive tree they find in the Cyclops's cave?

_____

_____

_____

_____

VOCABULARY

profusion (prō·fyoo′zhən) n.: large supply; abundance.

CLARIFY

Pause at line 111. Apparently, it was the custom among the ancient Greeks for men to toss coins, dice, or something else for the honor of participating in a dangerous task. Why is Odysseus happy with the outcome?

_____

_____

_____

_____

_____

_____

_____

_____

a club, or staff, lay there along the fold—
an olive tree, felled green and left to season
95 for Cyclops' hand. And it was like a mast
a lugger[5] of twenty oars, broad in the beam—
a deep-seagoing craft—might carry:
so long, so big around, it seemed. Now I
chopped out a six-foot section of this pole
100 and set it down before my men, who scraped it;
and when they had it smooth, I hewed again
to make a stake with pointed end. I held this
in the fire's heart and turned it, toughening it,
then hid it, well back in the cavern, under
105 one of the dung piles in **profusion** there.
Now came the time to toss for it: who ventured
along with me? Whose hand could bear to thrust
and grind that spike in Cyclops' eye, when mild
sleep had mastered him? As luck would have it,
110 the men I would have chosen won the toss—
four strong men, and I made five as captain.

At evening came the shepherd with his flock,
his woolly flock. The rams as well, this time,
entered the cave: by some sheepherding whim—
115 or a god's bidding—none were left outside.
He hefted his great boulder into place
and sat him down to milk the bleating ewes
in proper order, put the lambs to suck,
and swiftly ran through all his evening chores.
120 Then he caught two more men and feasted on them.
My moment was at hand, and I went forward
holding an ivy bowl of my dark drink,
looking up, saying:

---

5. **lugger** (lug′ər) n.: type of sailboat.

Odysseus handing the drink to Polyphemus. Relief on a Grecian marble sarcophagus (1st century A.D.).

Museo Archeologico Nazionale, Naples, Italy.

             'Cyclops, try some wine.

Here's liquor to wash down your scraps of men.

125   Taste it, and see the kind of drink we carried

under our planks. I meant it for an offering

if you would help us home. But you are mad,

unbearable, a bloody monster! After this,

will any other traveler come to see you?'

130   He seized and drained the bowl, and it went down

so fiery and smooth he called for more:

             'Give me another, thank you kindly. Tell me,

how are you called? I'll make a gift will please you.

Even Cyclopes know the wine grapes grow

135   out of grassland and loam in heaven's rain,

but here's a bit of nectar and ambrosia!'

Three bowls I brought him, and he poured them down.

I saw the fuddle and flush come over him,

then I sang out in cordial tones:

PREDICT

Pause at line 126. Why do you think Odysseus offers the Cyclops wine?

WORD STUDY

Underline the **alliteration**—repetition of consonant sounds in words close together—in line 138. Here *fuddle* means "drunkenness."

IDENTIFY

Pause at line 143. Odysseus doesn't tell the Cyclops his real name. Underline the name he uses. What word does the name sound like?

_____

_____

MONITOR YOUR COMPREHENSION

What happens in lines 146–167?

_____

_____

_____

_____

_____

_____

_____

_____

_____

_____

WORD STUDY

Underline the **extended similes** in lines 160–163 and 166–171, which use gruesome comparisons to help you see how the eye is gouged out.

'Cyclops,

140　you ask my honorable name? Remember
　　the gift you promised me, and I shall tell you.
　　My name is Nohbdy: mother, father, and friends,
　　everyone calls me Nohbdy.'

　　　　　　　　And he said:
　　'Nohbdy's my meat, then, after I eat his friends.
145　Others come first. There's a noble gift, now.'

　　Even as he spoke, he reeled and tumbled backward,
　　his great head lolling to one side; and sleep
　　took him like any creature. Drunk, hiccuping,
　　he dribbled streams of liquor and bits of men.

150　Now, by the gods, I drove my big hand spike
　　deep in the embers, charring it again,
　　and cheered my men along with battle talk
　　to keep their courage up: no quitting now.
　　The pike of olive, green though it had been,
155　reddened and glowed as if about to catch.
　　I drew it from the coals and my four fellows
　　gave me a hand, lugging it near the Cyclops
　　as more than natural force nerved them; straight
　　forward they sprinted, lifted it, and rammed it
160　deep in his crater eye, and I leaned on it
　　turning it as a shipwright turns a drill
　　in planking, having men below to swing
　　the two-handled strap that spins it in the groove.
　　So with our brand we bored that great eye socket
165　while blood ran out around the red-hot bar.
　　Eyelid and lash were seared; the pierced ball
　　hissed broiling, and the roots popped.

In a smithy[6]
one sees a white-hot axhead or an adze[7]
plunged and wrung in a cold tub, screeching steam—
170 the way they make soft iron hale and hard—
just so that eyeball hissed around the spike.
The Cyclops bellowed and the rock roared round him,
and we fell back in fear. Clawing his face
he tugged the bloody spike out of his eye,
175 threw it away, and his wild hands went groping;
then he set up a howl for Cyclopes
who lived in caves on windy peaks nearby.
Some heard him; and they came by divers[8] ways
to clump around outside and call:
'What ails you,
180 Polyphemus? Why do you cry so sore
in the starry night? You will not let us sleep.
Sure no man's driving off your flock? No man
has tricked you, ruined you?'

Out of the cave
the mammoth Polyphemus roared in answer:

185 'Nohbdy, Nohbdy's tricked me. Nohbdy's ruined me!'

To this rough shout they made a sage[9] reply:

'Ah well, if nobody has played you foul
there in your lonely bed, we are no use in pain
given by great Zeus. Let it be your father,
190 Poseidon Lord, to whom you pray.'

So saying
they trailed away. And I was filled with laughter
to see how like a charm the name deceived them.

---

6. **smithy** (smith′ē) *n.*: blacksmith's shop, where iron tools are made.
7. **adze** (adz) *n.*: axlike tool with a long, curved blade.
8. **divers** (dī′vərz) *adj.*: diverse; various.
9. **sage** (sāj) *adj.*: wise.

FLUENCY

Read the boxed passage aloud twice. On your first reading, pause at the end of a line if it ends in punctuation. Read on when the line does not end with a comma, dash, semicolon, colon, or period. On your second reading, focus on reading with expression.

MONITOR YOUR COMPREHENSION

Re-read lines 178–191. What happens when Polyphemus's fellow Cyclopes come to his aid?

_____

_____

_____

_____

_____

_____

_____

_____

_____

_____

_____

_____

_____

_____

Odysseus escaping the cave of Polyphemus under the belly of the ram. Detail from a krater, a vessel for holding wine (c. 510 B.C.).

Badisches Landesmuseum, Karlsruhe, Germany.

HERO

Pause at line 202. What **character trait** helps Odysseus defeat the Cyclops?

Now Cyclops, wheezing as the pain came on him,

fumbled to wrench away the great doorstone

195   and squatted in the breach with arms thrown wide

for any silly beast or man who bolted—

hoping somehow I might be such a fool.

But I kept thinking how to win the game:

death sat there huge; how could we slip away?

200   I drew on all my wits, and ran through tactics,

reasoning as a man will for dear life,

until a trick came—and it pleased me well.

The Cyclops' rams were handsome, fat, with heavy

fleeces, a dark violet.

                Three abreast

205   I tied them silently together, twining

cords of willow from the ogre's bed;

then slung a man under each middle one

to ride there safely, shielded left and right.

So three sheep could convey each man. I took

210   the woolliest ram, the choicest of the flock,

and hung myself under his kinky belly,

pulled up tight, with fingers twisted deep

in sheepskin ringlets for an iron grip.

So, breathing hard, we waited until morning.

215   When Dawn spread out her fingertips of rose

the rams began to stir, moving for pasture,

and peals of bleating echoed round the pens

where dams with udders full called for a milking.

Blinded, and sick with pain from his head wound,

220   the master stroked each ram, then let it pass,

but my men riding on the pectoral fleece[10]

the giant's blind hands blundering never found.

Last of them all my ram, the leader, came,

weighted by wool and me with my meditations.

225   The Cyclops patted him, and then he said:

'Sweet cousin ram, why lag behind the rest

in the night cave? You never linger so,

but graze before them all, and go afar

to crop sweet grass, and take your stately way

230   leading along the streams, until at evening

you run to be the first one in the fold.

Why, now, so far behind? Can you be grieving

over your Master's eye? That carrion rogue[11]

and his accurst companions burnt it out

235   when he had conquered all my wits with wine.

Nohbdy will not get out alive, I swear.

Oh, had you brain and voice to tell

where he may be now, dodging all my fury!

Bashed by this hand and bashed on this rock wall

240   his brains would strew the floor, and I should have

rest from the outrage Nohbdy worked upon me.'

---

10. **pectoral fleece:** wool on an animal's chest.
11. **carrion rogue:** rotten scoundrel. *Carrion* is decaying flesh.

MONITOR YOUR COMPREHENSION

Pause at line 214. What is Odysseus's plan to save himself and his men?

COMPARE & CONTRAST

Re-read lines 226–232. How is the Cyclops's treatment of his ram different from his treatment of the Greeks?

MONITOR YOUR COMPREHENSION

What is happening in lines 242–255?

_____

_____

_____

_____

_____

_____

_____

VOCABULARY

adversary (ad′vər·ser′ē) *n.:* enemy; opponent.

MONITOR YOUR COMPREHENSION

Pause at line 271. What happens when Odysseus taunts the Cyclops?

_____

_____

_____

_____

_____

_____

_____

_____

He sent us into the open, then. Close by,
I dropped and rolled clear of the ram's belly,
going this way and that to untie the men.

245   With many glances back, we rounded up
his fat, stiff-legged sheep to take aboard,
and drove them down to where the good ship lay.
We saw, as we came near, our fellows' faces
shining; then we saw them turn to grief

250   tallying those who had not fled from death.
I hushed them, jerking head and eyebrows up,
and in a low voice told them: 'Load this herd;
move fast, and put the ship's head toward the breakers.'
They all pitched in at loading, then embarked

255   and struck their oars into the sea. Far out,
as far offshore as shouted words would carry,
I sent a few back to the **adversary**:

'O Cyclops! Would you feast on my companions?
Puny, am I, in a Caveman's hands?

260   How do you like the beating that we gave you,
you damned cannibal? Eater of guests
under your roof! Zeus and the gods have paid you!'

The blind thing in his doubled fury broke
a hilltop in his hands and heaved it after us.

265   Ahead of our black prow it struck and sank
whelmed in a spuming geyser, a giant wave
that washed the ship stern foremost back to shore.
I got the longest boathook out and stood
fending us off, with furious nods to all

270   to put their backs into a racing stroke—
row, row or perish. So the long oars bent
kicking the foam sternward, making head
until we drew away, and twice as far.
Now when I cupped my hands I heard the crew

275   in low voices protesting:

'Godsake, Captain!
Why bait the beast again? Let him alone!'

'That tidal wave he made on the first throw
all but beached us.'

                              'All but stove us in!'
'Give him our bearing with your trumpeting,
280   he'll get the range and lob[12] a boulder.'

                              'Aye
He'll smash our timbers and our heads together!'

I would not heed them in my glorying spirit,
but let my anger flare and yelled:

                              'Cyclops,
if ever mortal man inquire
285   how you were put to shame and blinded, tell him
Odysseus, raider of cities, took your eye:
Laertes' son, whose home's on Ithaca!'

At this he gave a mighty sob and rumbled:

'Now comes the weird[13] upon me, spoken of old.
290   A wizard, grand and wondrous, lived here—Telemus,[14]
a son of Eurymus;[15] great length of days
he had in wizardry among the Cyclopes,
and these things he foretold for time to come:
my great eye lost, and at Odysseus' hands.
295   Always I had in mind some giant, armed
in giant force, would come against me here.
But this, but you—small, pitiful, and twiggy—
you put me down with wine, you blinded me.

---

12. **lob** (läb) *v.*: toss.
13. **weird** (wird) *n.*: fate.
14. **Telemus** (tel'ə·məs).
15. **Eurymus** (yoo'rē·məs).

MONITOR YOUR COMPREHENSION

Pause at line 308. The Cyclops has asked Odysseus to come back and says he'll treat him well. Underline Odysseus's reply. Then, read on and underline the Cyclops's curse on Odysseus and his men.

MONITOR YOUR COMPREHENSION

Review the Cyclops's curse. What might happen next?

_____
_____
_____
_____
_____
_____
_____
_____
_____
_____
_____
_____
_____
_____
_____
_____
_____
_____

Come back, Odysseus, and I'll treat you well,
300 praying the god of earthquake to befriend you—
his son I am, for he by his avowal
fathered me, and, if he will, he may
heal me of this black wound—he and no other
of all the happy gods or mortal men.'

305 Few words I shouted in reply to him:

'If I could take your life I would and take
your time away, and hurl you down to hell!
The god of earthquake could not heal you there!'

At this he stretched his hands out in his darkness
310 toward the sky of stars, and prayed Poseidon:

'O hear me, lord, blue girdler of the islands,
if I am thine indeed, and thou art father:
grant that Odysseus, raider of cities, never
see his home: Laertes' son, I mean,
315 who kept his hall on Ithaca. Should destiny
intend that he shall see his roof again
among his family in his fatherland,
far be that day, and dark the years between.
Let him lose all companions, and return
320 under strange sail to bitter days at home.' . . ."

The Cyclops

Hero Chart What makes a hero? Listed in the left column of the chart below are some heroic traits. Give examples from "The Cyclops" to show whether or not Odysseus displays these traits. At the bottom of the chart is a row for weaknesses. If you find weaknesses in Odysseus, cite details from the story to support your opinion.

Key Traits of a Hero	Details from "The Cyclops"
Intelligence and resourcefulness	
Strength	
Bravery and loyalty	
Weaknesses	

Standards Review

 **The Cyclops**

Complete the sample test item below. The box at the right explains why three of the choices are not correct.

Sample Test Item	Explanation of the Correct Answer
The *best* description of an **epic poem** is a — A poem that tells a story B lyric poem that reveals emotions C wildly exaggerated, humorous poem D long narrative poem about the deeds of a heroic character	The correct answer is *D*; it offers the most information about what an epic poem is. *A* is incorrect; many poems, even very short ones, tell stories. Epics are not lyric poems, as *B* claims. Epics are serious, not humorous, as *C* states.

Reading Standard 3.1 (Grade 8 Review) Determine and articulate the relationship between the purposes and characteristics of different forms of poetry (e.g., epic).

Reading Standard 3.3 Analyze interactions between main and subordinate characters in a literary text (e.g., internal and external conflicts, motivations, relationships, influences) and explain the way those interactions affect the plot.

DIRECTIONS: Circle the letter of each correct answer.

1. When he first speaks to the Cyclops, Odysseus warns him that —

    A the Greeks will kill him

    B the Greeks want his land

    C Zeus will avenge the Greeks if Cyclops is not courteous

    D Zeus will kill the Cyclops if he doesn't give them money

2. The interaction between Odysseus and the Cyclops is —

    F an external conflict

    G not important to the story

    H a universal theme

    J part of the setting

3. How does the Cyclops treat the Greeks?

    A He devours some of them.

    B He opens his home to them.

    C He helps them on their way.

    D He kills all of them.

4. How does Odysseus win the battle with the Cyclops?

    F He tricks the Cyclops.

    G He kills the giant.

    H He calls on Zeus to help him.

    J He betrays his men.

Standards Review

 **The Cyclops**

Words from Myths

Myths often attempt to explain the mysteries of nature, the origins of rituals, and the relationships between gods and humans. Many words from Greek and Roman myths live on in the English language. For example, some common English words are derived from the names of Greek and Roman gods and goddesses.

DIRECTIONS: Match each Greek or Roman god's or goddess's name or home with the English word that is derived from it.

Reading Standard 1.3 Identify Greek, Roman, and Norse mythology and use the knowledge to understand the origin and meaning of new words (e.g., the word *narcissistic* drawn from the myth of Narcissus and Echo).

1. _____ Vulcan   **a.** Olympics

2. _____ Ceres   **b.** tantalize

3. _____ Mount Olympus   **c.** titanic

4. _____ Titans   **d.** cereal

5. _____ Tantalus   **e.** volcano

Vocabulary in Context

DIRECTIONS: Complete the paragraph below by writing a word from the word box to fit each numbered blank. Use each word only once.

Word Box
ravage
profusion
adversary

As the epic poem the *Odyssey* reveals, Odysseus had more than one

(1) _____. In fact, he had a (2) _____

of enemies, both monsters and men—and even gods. Some of his enemies

hated Odysseus so much they actually wanted to

(3) _____ him and his men, while others were content to

prevent him from reaching home.

 Before You Go On . . .

Check your Standards Mastery at the back of this book.

Paul Bunyan's Been There retold by Maurice Dolbier

BEFORE YOU READ

"Paul Bunyan's Been There" is a tall tale about the amazing Paul Bunyan and his role in creating America. The stories about Paul Bunyan were written to create a kind of epic hero—he is super strong and fearless—but stories about him are also comical, and they get more exaggerated the more often they are told. As you read the story, look for the qualities that make Paul Bunyan a typical American hero.

LITERARY FOCUS: TALL TALES

Myths are traditional stories, rooted in a particular culture, that usually explain a belief, a ritual, or a mysterious natural phenomenon. Myths might tell people where they came from, where they are going, or how they should live. Many societies have myths that spring from their religious beliefs or traditions.

A **tall tale,** on the other hand, is a kind of humorous folk tale. Tall tales are exaggerated, far-fetched stories that give humorous explanations for things, like how waterfalls or mountains came to be. Tall tales were never part of a people's religious beliefs.

- "Paul Bunyan's Been There" tells about the settlement of the western United States. Read the story, and then think about how Paul Bunyan is a kind of comic imitation of the epic hero. How is he typically "American"?

READING SKILLS: IDENTIFYING CAUSE AND EFFECT

When one event leads to another event, they have a **cause-and-effect relationship**. A **cause** is *why* something happens. An **effect** is *what happens* as a result. For example, a tornado strikes a farm, and the barn is blown away. The cause is the tornado; the missing barn is the effect. The cause always happens before the effect.

Writers often signal cause-and-effect relationships with words such as *because, consequently, for, if, then, so, thus, since,* and *therefore.* To find cause-and-effect relationships:

- Look for signal words that show cause and effect.
- To find the effect, ask yourself *what* has happened. You may find multiple effects.
- To find the cause, ask yourself *why* it happened. You may find multiple causes.

Reading Standard 1.3 (Grade 8 Review) Use word meanings within the appropriate context and show ability to verify those meanings by definition, restatement, example, comparison, and contrast.

Reading Standard 3.12 Analyze the way in which a work of literature is related to the themes and issues of its historical period. (Historical approach)

VOCABULARY DEVELOPMENT

USING CONTEXT CLUES

Stories like "Paul Bunyan's Been There" often contain words and expressions particular to a region or time period. When you come across an unfamiliar word in your reading, you should use **context clues**—surrounding words and phrases—to figure out its meaning.

Common types of context clues include *definitions, contrasts, synonyms,* and *examples.* In the passages below, the context clues for the boldface words are underlined.

DEFINITION: You might find a definition right in the sentence or paragraph. It may come before or after the unfamiliar word. For example:

The men got almighty tired of **sourdough.** *That's a kind of fermented dough that rises like yeast.*

CONTRAST: A contrast clue will usually be set off with a word or phrase such as *unlike, not, instead of, in contrast to, contrary to.* For example:

The cold was mighty **intense,** *not gentle.*

SYNONYM: Sometimes you can find a synonym nearby for the word you are trying to define. For example:

The loggers sat around the campfire telling **yarns.** *These stories helped them to pass the time.*

As you read "Paul Bunyan's Been There," look for context clues that might help you define unfamiliar words. If you are not sure you have defined a word correctly, use a dictionary to check its meaning.

Paul Bunyan's Been There

retold by Maurice Dolbier

Wherever you go in this big country, you're likely to find somebody who'll tell you that Paul Bunyan's been there. Been there and done things. Like digging the Great Lakes so that Babe would have watering troughs that wouldn't run dry, or digging a canal that turned out to be the Mississippi River.

You'll hear that the dirt he threw off to the right became the Rocky Mountains, and the dirt he threw off to the left became the Appalachians.

You'll hear that Kansas used to be full of mountains before
10 Paul Bunyan came. He turned it upside-down. Now it's flat as a pancake because all its mountain peaks are inside the ground, pointing to the center of the earth.

You'll hear that Paul got so sad at what he saw going on in New York City that he fell to crying, and his tears started the Hudson River.

Western deserts or Southern swamps, Eastern shores or Northern forests, Paul is said to have been there and done things. And if by chance you can't find any stories about his having been in your neck of the woods, fix some up. Everybody else has.

Right now, let's stick to the Northern forests, because we know for sure that Paul was there. Paul and his men and the Blue Ox. They logged all through Michigan and Minnesota and the Dakotas, North and South, and they were always pushing westward to where the redwoods waited.

Maybe you'd like to know what life was like in those lumber camps of Paul Bunyan?

Well, the day started when the owls in the woods thought it was still night. The Little Chore Boy would blow his horn, and the men would tumble out of their beds for chow.

There were always flapjacks for breakfast. These were made on a big round griddle about two city blocks wide. Before the batter was poured on, five men used to skate up and down and around it with slabs of bacon tied on their feet. It'd take an ordinary man a week to eat one of the flapjacks that came off that griddle. Paul used to eat five or six every morning.

After breakfast came the work. The loggers tramped off to the woods. One crowd cleared the paths, another cut down the trees, another cut them up into logs, another piled them on carts or sledges. Then Babe the Blue Ox hauled the carts down to the water.

Soon after sunset, the men would all be back at the camp for supper. That was either baked beans or pea soup. Sometimes the cooks would surprise them, and serve pea soup or baked beans.

Sourdough Sam never liked to work very hard. One time he just dumped some split peas in the lake and then boiled the lake water and served it.

Matter of fact, Sam didn't stay with Paul Bunyan long. The men didn't mind that he was lazy, but they got almighty tired of sourdough. That's a kind of fermented dough that rises like yeast, and Sam used it in all his recipes. He put it in the coffee

WORD STUDY

In lines 31–36, underline the **context clues** that tell you that *flapjacks* is another word for *pancakes*.

IDENTIFY

Pause at line 48. List at least three exaggerations you've found in the tale so far.

**IDENTIFY
CAUSE & EFFECT**

Pause at line 55. What
caused Little Chore Boy to
rise into the air?

_____

_____

_____

_____

_____

_____

IDENTIFY

Exaggeration is a key compo-
nent of tall tales. Underline
examples of exaggeration in
lines 71–79.

**IDENTIFY
CAUSE & EFFECT**

Pause at line 85. Why were
the clouds "slipping and
slopping around in the
mud"?

_____

_____

_____

_____

_____

_____

_____

_____

_____

_____

one morning. The Little Chore Boy drank a cup, and then started to rise into the air and float across the lake. They had to lasso
him and pull him down.

After supper, they'd sit around and talk and sing and tell
yarns so whopping that you'd never believe them.

Then, about nine o'clock, they turned in.

Of course, it wasn't all work at Paul's camp. The men

60 would hunt and fish, and sometimes they'd have logrolling con-
tests. That's when you stand on a log in the middle of the water
and start the log rolling under you, trying to keep your balance
as long as you can. Joe Murfraw used to win, mostly. Paul
Bunyan himself never took part, except to demonstrate, because
nobody could beat him anyway. He used to get the logs rolling
so fast under foot that they set up a foam solid enough for him
to walk to the shore on.

These are the things that went on fairly regularly, but I
couldn't tell you what a typical day at Paul's camp was like. No

70 day was typical. They were all special, and so was the weather.

There were fogs so thick that you could cut houses out of
them, the way they do with snow and ice in the far north.

There were winds that blew up and down and in every
direction at once.

There were thaws so quick that when the snow melted it
just stayed there in big drifts of water for a week.

There was one time when all four seasons hit at once, and
the whole camp came down with frostbite, sunstroke and spring
fever.

80 There was another time when the rain didn't come from
the skies at all. It came up from China, away underneath the
world. Up from the ground it came, first in a drizzle and then in
a pour, and it went straight up into the air. It got the sky so wet
that the clouds were slipping and slopping around in the mud
for a month.

But most of the stories you hear are about the winters that Paul Bunyan's loggers had to put up with. No one ever had winters like them before or since.

The cold was mighty intense. It went down to 70 degrees
90   below zero, and each degree was 16 inches long. The men couldn't blow out the candles at night, because the flames were frozen, so they had to crack the flames off and toss them outdoors. (When the warm weather came, the flames melted and started quite a forest fire.)

It was so cold that the words froze in mid-air right after they'd come out of people's mouths, and all the next summer nobody had to talk. They had a winter's supply of conversation on hand.

The cold wasn't the only thing that was peculiar.
100   Sometimes the snow was too. One winter it came down in big blue flakes, and Johnny Inkslinger used the icicles to write down the figures in his books. That's how he got the idea for inventing fountain pens. And the men used to have snowball fights until they were blue in the face.

FLUENCY

Read the boxed passage aloud twice. On your second reading, emphasize the humorous and exaggerated details.

IDENTIFY CAUSE & EFFECT

Re-read lines 99–104. Underline three effects of the winter's blue snowfall.

Notes _____

_____

_____

_____

_____

_____

IDENTIFY

According to lines 105–107, what two forces of nature did Paul have to deal with?

_____

_____

IDENTIFY
CAUSE & EFFECT

Pause at line 129. What happens when Paul Bunyan brings in monster bumblebees to guard the camp?

_____

_____

_____

_____

_____

INTERPRET

Review the tall tale. Find an episode that shows that Paul is super strong. Find another that shows he is clever. Describe the episodes below.

_____

_____

_____

_____

_____

_____

_____

_____

Yes, the weather did all it could to upset Paul Bunyan's operations. And when the weather gave up, the mosquitoes tried.

One spring day, the men were working in a swamp, near a lake in northern Michigan, when they heard a droning noise.
110 They looked up to see the whole stretch of western horizon black with flying creatures heading right toward them. The men didn't stop to inquire. They dropped their tools and went hot-foot back to the camp and locked themselves up in the bunkhouse.

Pretty soon they heard a terrible racket overhead, and then long things like sword blades began piercing through the tin roof. Paul Bunyan grabbed a sledgehammer and began pounding those stingers flat, so the mosquitoes couldn't get out. The rest of the mosquito army saw that it was no use and flew away.

120 Paul figured they'd be back with some new ideas, and he'd better have a new idea, too, just in case. So he sent Swede Charlie on a trip down into Indiana. He'd heard they had a special kind of monster bumblebee there. Charlie brought some of these back, and Paul trained them to fly in a protective circle around the camp. He thought that the next time the mosquitoes came they'd have a surprise. They did, and he did too. The bumblebees and the mosquitoes liked each other so much that they married and had children, and the children grew up with stingers in back and in front.

130 You won't hear anyone say that Paul Bunyan was ever stumped by any problem that came up. I won't say, either. But that section of timberland up in Michigan was the only place that Bunyan's men moved away from while there were still trees to be cut. I suppose they got a better offer.

Paul Bunyan's Been There

Cause-and-Effect Chart "Paul Bunyan's Been There" tells—in a very exaggerated way—about how some of the natural features of the United States came to be. It also tells about logging in the American northwest as the territory was being settled. The selection contains a series of causes and effects, describing in a comic way Paul's actions and why he took them. Some of those causes and effects are filled in on the chart below. Complete the chart by filling in the rest.

Cause → Why something happens	Effect What happens as a result
1. Babe, the Blue Ox, is thirsty.	
2.	He creates the Mississippi River.
3. Paul throws dirt to the right.	
4. Paul throws dirt to the left.	
5.	Kansas becomes flat.
6. Paul feels sad about New York City.	
7. Winters are cold.	
8.	The fountain pen is invented.
9. Mosquitoes attack.	
10. Bumblebees like the mosquitoes.	

Standards Review

LITERATURE

 **Paul Bunyan's Been There**

Complete the sample test item below. Then, read the explanation at right.

Sample Test Item	Explanation of the Correct Answer
Paul Bunyan is credited with all of the following deeds *except* — **A** flattening Kansas **B** digging the Great Lakes **C** building New York City **D** creating the Mississippi River	The correct answer is *C*. New York City already exists when Paul goes there. *A*, *B*, and *D* are all among Paul's deeds.

DIRECTIONS: Circle the letter of each correct answer.

1. As a typical American hero, Paul Bunyan is all of the following except —

   A a strong man

   B a hardworking laborer

   C a resourceful leader

   D a noble warrior

2. Paul Bunyan's job as a logger indicates that Americans value —

   F good manners

   G hard work

   H great wealth

   J military expertise

3. Which of the following statements contains **exaggeration**?

   A Paul eats more in a day than a regular man can eat in a week.

   B Paul can withstand very cold temperatures.

   C Paul is good at hunting, fishing, and log rolling.

   D Paul sends Swede Charlie on a trip to Indiana.

4. Heroes in old myths and legends have to face monsters. What "monsters" does Paul face?

   F giant mosquitoes

   G a blue ox

   H evil wizards

   J fire-breathing dragons

Reading Standard 3.12
Analyze the way in which a work of literature is related to the themes and issues of its historical period. (Historical approach)

Standards Review

TestPractice **Paul Bunyan's Been There**

Context Clues

DIRECTIONS: Use context clues to help you figure out the meaning of the boldface word. Circle the letter of the correct answer.

1. "Like digging the Great Lakes so that Babe would have watering **troughs** that wouldn't run dry . . ."

   A containers for water

   B steam shovels

   C tough love

   D swimming pools

2. "The men would tumble out of their beds for **chow**. There were always flapjacks for breakfast."

   F work

   G food

   H goodbye

   J dinner

3. "They'd sit around and talk and sing and tell yarns so **whopping** that you'd never believe them."

   A noisy

   B soft

   C tangled

   D exaggerated

4. "There were **thaws** so quick that when the snow melted it just stayed there in big drifts of water for a week."

   F freezing temperatures

   G puddles

   H spells of warm weather

   J snowdrifts

5. "The men didn't stop to inquire. They dropped their tools and went **hotfoot** back to the camp."

   A as fast as possible

   B injured

   C two by two

   D skipping

6. "Pretty soon they heard a terrible **racket** overhead, and then long things like sword blades began piercing through the tin roof."

   F scam

   G sting

   H noise

   J paddle

Reading Standard 1.3 (Grade 8 Review) Use word meanings within the appropriate context and show ability to verify those meanings by definition, restatement, example, comparison, or contrast.

Drama

Academic Vocabulary for Chapter 11

These are the terms you should know as you read and analyze the plays in this chapter.

———

Play A story acted out live, using dialogue and action.

Tragedy A play that presents serious and important actions and ends unhappily for the main character.

Tragic hero An admirable figure who has a personal failing that leads to his or her downfall.

Tragic flaw A failing that leads a character to make choices that result in tragedy.

Comedy A play that ends happily, in which the main character gets what he or she wants.

● ● ●

Dialogue Conversations between characters in a play.

Monologue A long speech made by one character to one or more other characters onstage.

Soliloquy A speech made by a character who is alone onstage, speaking to himself or herself or to the audience.

Aside A short speech, delivered to the audience or to another character, that others onstage are not supposed to hear.

● ● ●

Stage directions Descriptions of how characters move onstage and how they speak their lines.

Props The portable items (properties) that actors carry or handle onstage.

Reading Standard 1.2 (Grade 8 Review) Understand the most important points in the history of English language and use common word origins to determine the historical influence on English word meanings.

Reading Standard 1.3 Identify Greek, Roman, and Norse mythology and use the knowledge to understand the origin and meaning of new words (e.g., the word *narcissistic* drawn from the myth of Narcissus and Echo).

Reading Standard 3.1 Articulate the relationship between the expressed purposes and characteristics of different forms of dramatic literature (e.g., comedy, tragedy, drama, dramatic monologue).

Reading Standard 3.10 Identify and describe the function of dialogue, scene designs, soliloquies, asides, and character foils in dramatic literature.

For Further Information …

Be sure to read these essays in *Holt Literature and Language Arts*:

● **Drama: Forms and Stagecraft**, pages 752–754.

● **How to Read Shakespeare**, pages 781–782.

The Tragedy of Romeo and Juliet,
Act II, Scene 2
by William Shakespeare

Reading Standard 1.2 (Grade 8 Review)
Understand the most important points in the history of English language and use common word origins to determine the historical influence on English word meanings.

Reading Standard 3.1
Articulate the relationship between the expressed purposes and characteristics of different forms of dramatic literature (e.g., comedy, tragedy, drama, dramatic monologue).

Reading Standard 3.10
Identify and describe the function of dialogue, scene designs, soliloquies, asides, and character foils in dramatic literature.

BEFORE YOU READ

Romeo and Juliet are one of the most famous couples in all of literature. In telling the story of these young lovers, William Shakespeare used his dramatic skills to bring to life a tale filled with action, passion, humor, and tragedy. Romeo and Juliet are teenagers, like you. Do you think that their story could take place today?

LITERARY FOCUS: TRAGEDY

A tragedy tells about serious and important actions that end unhappily. In fact, tragedies often end in death. *Romeo and Juliet* is a tragedy about two teenagers who fall in love. As you read this scene at the balcony, look for hints that foreshadow what will happen to their love.

READING SKILLS: PARAPHRASING

When you paraphrase a text, you restate it using your own words. Note that a paraphrase differs from a summary. A paraphrase is a detail-by-detail retelling; a summary is a condensed form of the original text—made up of only the main details. Here is a checklist for paraphrasing:

- Have you replaced difficult words with simpler words?
- Have you restated figures of speech (similes and metaphors) in your own words? Have you clarified what is being compared with what?
- Have you restructured sentences so that they are clearer? For example, if a sentence says "Bury me not on the lone prairie," you might paraphrase it to read "Don't bury me on the lonely prairie."
- Does your paraphrase include all the details in the original text?

VOCABULARY DEVELOPMENT

WORD ORIGINS: ARCHAIC WORDS

Shakespeare wrote this play around four hundred years ago, so it's only natural that a great many of the words he uses have either disappeared from the English language or taken on new meanings. Words that have dropped out of common use are called **archaic** (är·kā′ik) words. Footnotes will help you with the meanings of these outdated words and expressions.

Below are some of the archaic words you will encounter as you read *The Tragedy of Romeo and Juliet.*

'a: he.

a': on.

alike: both.

an' or **and:** if.

anon: soon; right away; coming.

but: if; except; only.

counsel: private thoughts.

frank: generous.

Good-den or **go-den** or **God-den:** Good evening (said in the late afternoon).

hap or **happy:** luck; lucky.

humor: mood; moisture.

Jack: common fellow; ordinary guy.

maid: unmarried girl.

mark: listen to.

Marry: mild oath shortened from "by the Virgin Mary."

nice: trivial; foolish.

owes: owns.

shrift: forgiveness for sins that have been confessed to a priest. After confessional, a person was said to be **shriven.**

soft: quiet; hush; slow up.

stay: wait.

still: always.

strange: aloof or cold.

wherefore: why.

withal: with that; with.

wot: know.

THE TRAGEDY OF ROMEO AND JULIET
ACT II, SCENE 2

William Shakespeare

The Tragedy of Romeo and Juliet takes place long ago in Verona, Italy. Two families, the Montagues and the Capulets, are sworn enemies. Even their servants fight when they meet in the street. When we first meet Romeo, who is a Montague, he is pining for a girl named Rosaline, who does not return his affections. To distract Romeo, his friends Mercutio and Benvolio take him to a party at the home of the Capulets. It's a masquerade, so the boys wear masks. There, Romeo and Juliet, who is a Capulet, fall in love at first sight. Only after they talk and share their first kiss do they discover they have fallen in love with an enemy. Following the party, Romeo makes his way to Juliet's house, where he hides in the orchard, hoping to catch a glimpse of his new love. His friends have just left him. They have been teasing him for being in love—but they think he still loves Rosaline.

Scene 2. *Capulet's orchard.*

Romeo (*coming forward*).

  He jests at scars that never felt a wound.

  [*Enter* JULIET *at a window.*]

  But soft! What light through yonder window breaks?
  It is the East, and Juliet is the sun!

PARAPHRASE

Paraphrase line 1. What is Romeo saying to Benvolio, who has just left the scene?

_____
_____
_____
_____
_____
_____
_____
_____
_____
_____
_____
_____
_____
_____
_____
_____
_____
_____

Arise, fair sun, and kill the envious moon,

5   Who is already sick and pale with grief

That thou her maid[1] art far more fair than she.

Be not her maid, since she is envious.

Her vestal livery[2] is but sick and green,[3]

And none but fools do wear it. Cast it off.

10   It is my lady! O, it is my love!

O, that she knew she were!

She speaks, yet she says nothing. What of that?

Her eye discourses;[4] I will answer it.

I am too bold; 'tis not to me she speaks.

15   Two of the fairest stars in all the heaven,

Having some business, do entreat her eyes

To twinkle in their spheres till they return.

What if her eyes were there, they in her head?

The brightness of her cheek would shame those stars

20   As daylight doth a lamp; her eyes in heaven

Would through the airy region stream so bright

That birds would sing and think it were not night.

See how she leans her cheek upon her hand!

O, that I were a glove upon that hand,

That I might touch that cheek!

Juliet.   Ay me!

25   **Romeo.**   She speaks.

O, speak again, bright angel, for thou art

As glorious to this night, being o'er my head,

As is a wingèd messenger of heaven

Unto the white-upturnèd wond'ring eyes

30   Of mortals that fall back to gaze on him

When he bestrides the lazy puffing clouds

---

1. **thou her maid:** Juliet, whom Romeo sees as the servant of the virgin goddess of the moon, Diana in Roman mythology.
2. **vestal livery:** maidenly clothing.
3. **sick and green:** Unmarried girls supposedly had "greensickness," or anemia.
4. **discourses:** speaks.

INTERPRET

Re-read lines 2–6. What does Romeo compare Juliet to? Why is the moon envious?

_____

_____

_____

_____

_____

_____

_____

_____

_____

_____

_____

_____

_____

_____

_____

_____

_____

_____

_____

_____

CLARIFY

Re-read lines 10–23. Underline all the lines in which Romeo compares Juliet's eyes to stars.

An **aside** is a remark that other characters onstage are not supposed to hear. Whom is Romeo speaking to in line 37? Who is not supposed to hear him?

_____

_____

_____

_____

PARAPHRASE

Underline lines 43–44, which are often quoted. Restate Juliet's lines in your own words.

_____

_____

_____

_____

_____

_____

_____

CONNECT

Romeo finally speaks to Juliet in lines 49–51, but Juliet has to ask who he is (lines 52–53). Why can't she see him?

_____

_____

_____

_____

And sails upon the bosom of the air.

Juliet.

    O Romeo, Romeo! Wherefore[5] art thou Romeo?

    Deny thy father and refuse thy name;

35   Or, if thou wilt not, be but sworn my love,

    And I'll no longer be a Capulet.

Romeo (*aside*).

    Shall I hear more, or shall I speak at this?

Juliet.

    'Tis but thy name that is my enemy.

    Thou art thyself, though not[6] a Montague.

40   What's Montague? It is nor hand, nor foot,

    Nor arm, nor face. O, be some other name

    Belonging to a man.

    What's in a name? That which we call a rose

    By any other word would smell as sweet.

45   So Romeo would, were he not Romeo called,

    Retain that dear perfection which he owes[7]

    Without that title. Romeo, doff thy name;

    And for thy name, which is no part of thee,

    Take all myself.

Romeo.   I take thee at thy word.

50   Call me but love, and I'll be new baptized;

    Henceforth I never will be Romeo.

Juliet.

    What man art thou, that, thus bescreened in night,

    So stumblest on my counsel?[8]

Romeo.   By a name

    I know not how to tell thee who I am.

55   My name, dear saint, is hateful to myself

    Because it is an enemy to thee.

    Had I it written, I would tear the word.

---

5. **Wherefore:** why. In other words, "Why is your name Romeo?" (It is the name of her enemy.)

6. **though not:** even if you were not.

7. **owes:** owns.

8. **counsel:** private thoughts.

Juliet.

My ears have yet not drunk a hundred words

Of thy tongue's uttering, yet I know the sound.

60   Art thou not Romeo, and a Montague?

Romeo.

Neither, fair maid, if either thee dislike.

Juliet.

How camest thou hither, tell me, and wherefore?

The orchard walls are high and hard to climb,

And the place death, considering who thou art,

65   If any of my kinsmen find thee here.

Romeo.

With love's light wings did I o'erperch[9] these walls;

For stony limits cannot hold love out,

And what love can do, that dares love attempt.

Therefore thy kinsmen are no stop to me.

Juliet.

70   If they do see thee, they will murder thee.

Romeo.

Alack, there lies more peril in thine eye

Than twenty of their swords! Look thou but sweet,

And I am proof[10] against their enmity.

Juliet.

I would not for the world they saw thee here.

Romeo.

75   I have night's cloak to hide me from their eyes;

And but[11] thou love me, let them find me here.

My life were better ended by their hate

Than death proroguèd,[12] wanting of thy love.

Juliet.

By whose direction found'st thou out this place?

---

9. **o'erperch:** fly over.
10. **proof:** armored.
11. **but:** if only.
12. **proroguèd:** postponed.

PARAPHRASE

Paraphrase lines 58–59. What does Juliet mean?

_____

_____

_____

_____

_____

_____

_____

CLARIFY

What is Juliet's concern in lines 62–70?

_____

_____

_____

_____

_____

_____

_____

_____

_____

_____

_____

_____

Romeo.

80   By Love, that first did prompt me to inquire.

        He lent me counsel, and I lent him eyes.

        I am no pilot; yet, wert thou as far

        As that vast shore washed with the farthest sea,

        I should adventure for such merchandise.

Juliet.

85   Thou knowest the mask of night is on my face;

        Else would a maiden blush bepaint my cheek

        For that which thou hast heard me speak tonight.

        Fain would I dwell on form—fain, fain deny

        What I have spoke; but farewell compliment.[13]

90   Dost thou love me? I know thou wilt say "Ay";

        And I will take thy word. Yet, if thou swear'st,

        Thou mayst prove false. At lovers' perjuries,

        They say Jove laughs. O gentle Romeo,

        If thou dost love, pronounce it faithfully.

95   Or if thou think'st I am too quickly won,

        I'll frown and be perverse and say thee nay,

        So thou wilt woo; but else, not for the world.

        In truth, fair Montague, I am too fond,[14]

        And therefore thou mayst think my havior[15] light;

100   But trust me, gentleman, I'll prove more true

        Than those that have more cunning to be strange.[16]

        I should have been more strange, I must confess,

        But that thou overheard'st, ere I was ware,

        My truelove passion. Therefore pardon me,

105   And not impute this yielding to light love,

        Which the dark night hath so discoverèd.[17]

---

13. **compliment:** good manners.
14. **fond:** affectionate; tender.
15. **havior:** behavior.
16. **strange:** aloof or cold.
17. **discoverèd:** revealed.

WORD STUDY

Fain (fān), in line 88, is stated three times. It means "gladly."

FLUENCY

Read the boxed monologue aloud twice. Before you read it the first time, circle all the punctuation marks you find in the speech: periods, commas, semicolons, dash, question mark. You have to pause at these marks of punctuation. If a line does not end with a punctuation mark, read right on to the next line. In your second reading, try to use your voice to indicate where Juliet switches from embarrassment, to frankness, to pleading, to anxiety, and to doubt.

Romeo.

     Lady, by yonder blessèd moon I vow,

     That tips with silver all these fruit-tree tops—

Juliet.

     O, swear not by the moon, the inconstant moon,

110   That monthly changes in her circle orb,

     Lest that thy love prove likewise variable.

Romeo.

     What shall I swear by?

Juliet.   Do not swear at all;

     Or if thou wilt, swear by thy gracious self,

     Which is the god of my idolatry,

     And I'll believe thee.

INTERPRET

Re-read lines 109–111. Why is Juliet afraid of having Romeo swear by the moon?

115 **Romeo.**   If my heart's dear love—
Juliet.

    Well, do not swear. Although I joy in thee,

    I have no joy of this contract tonight.

    It is too rash, too unadvised, too sudden;

    Too like the lightning, which doth cease to be

120 Ere one can say it lightens. Sweet, good night!

    This bud of love, by summer's ripening breath,

    May prove a beauteous flower when next we meet.

    Good night, good night! As sweet repose and rest

    Come to thy heart as that within my breast!

Romeo.

125 O, wilt thou leave me so unsatisfied?
Juliet.

    What satisfaction canst thou have tonight?
Romeo.

    The exchange of thy love's faithful vow for mine.
Juliet.

    I gave thee mine before thou didst request it;

    And yet I would it were to give again.
Romeo.

130 Wouldst thou withdraw it? For what purpose, love?
Juliet.

    But to be frank[18] and give it thee again.

    And yet I wish but for the thing I have.

    My bounty[19] is as boundless as the sea,

    My love as deep; the more I give to thee,

135 The more I have, for both are infinite.

    I hear some noise within. Dear love, adieu!

    [NURSE *calls within.*]

    Anon, good nurse! Sweet Montague, be true.

    Stay but a little, I will come again.   [*Exit.*]

---

18. **frank:** generous.
19. **bounty:** capacity for giving.

Romeo.

    O blessèd, blessèd night! I am afeard,

140   Being in night, all this is but a dream,

    Too flattering-sweet to be substantial.

    [*Enter* JULIET *again.*]

Juliet.

    Three words, dear Romeo, and good night indeed.

    If that thy bent[20] of love be honorable,

    Thy purpose marriage, send me word tomorrow,

145   By one that I'll procure to come to thee,

    Where and what time thou wilt perform the rite;

    And all my fortunes at thy foot I'll lay

    And follow thee my lord throughout the world.

Nurse (*within*). Madam!

Juliet.

150   I come anon.—But if thou meanest not well,

    I do beseech thee—

Nurse (*within*). Madam!

Juliet.   By and by I come.—

    To cease thy strife[21] and leave me to my grief.

    Tomorrow will I send.

Romeo.   So thrive my soul—

Juliet.

155   A thousand times good night!   [*Exit.*]

Romeo.

    A thousand times the worse, to want thy light!

    Love goes toward love as schoolboys from their books;

    But love from love, toward school with heavy looks.

    [*Enter* JULIET *again.*]

---

20. **bent:** intention.
21. **strife:** efforts to win her.

INTERPRET

What is Romeo afraid of in lines 139–141?

IDENTIFY

In lines 142–148, Juliet returns with a plan. Underline her proposal to Romeo.

PARAPHRASE

Underline Romeo's comment in lines 157–158. Paraphrase what he says about leaving Juliet.

PARAPHRASE

Restate lines 166–167 in your own words.

_____

_____

_____

_____

_____

_____

_____

_____

INTERPRET

What does Juliet mean by the statement "'Tis twenty years till then" (line 170)?

_____

_____

_____

_____

_____

_____

_____

_____

_____

Juliet.

> Hist! Romeo, hist! O for a falc'ner's voice

160

> To lure this tassel gentle²² back again!
>
> Bondage is hoarse²³ and may not speak aloud,
>
> Else would I tear the cave where Echo²⁴ lies
>
> And make her airy tongue more hoarse than mine
>
> With repetition of "My Romeo!"

Romeo.

165

> It is my soul that calls upon my name.
>
> How silver-sweet sound lovers' tongues by night,
>
> Like softest music to attending ears!

Juliet.

> Romeo!

Romeo.   My sweet?

Juliet.   What o'clock tomorrow

> Shall I send to thee?

Romeo.   By the hour of nine.

Juliet.

170

> I will not fail. 'Tis twenty years till then.
>
> I have forgot why I did call thee back.

Romeo.

> Let me stand here till thou remember it.

Juliet.

> I shall forget, to have thee still stand there,
>
> Rememb'ring how I love thy company.

Romeo.

175

> And I'll still stay, to have thee still forget,
>
> Forgetting any other home but this.

Juliet.

> 'Tis almost morning. I would have thee gone—

---

22. **tassel gentle:** male falcon.
23. **Bondage is hoarse:** Juliet is in "bondage" to her parents and must whisper.
24. **Echo:** In Greek mythology, a girl who could only repeat others' final words.

And yet no farther than a wanton's[25] bird,

That lets it hop a little from his hand,

180   Like a poor prisoner in his twisted gyves,[26]

And with a silken thread plucks it back again,

So loving-jealous of his liberty.

Romeo.

I would I were thy bird.

Juliet.   Sweet, so would I.

Yet I should kill thee with much cherishing.

185   Good night, good night! Parting is such sweet sorrow

That I shall say good night till it be morrow.   [*Exit.*]

Romeo.

Sleep dwell upon thine eyes, peace in thy breast!

Would I were sleep and peace, so sweet to rest!

Hence will I to my ghostly friar's[27] close cell,

190   His help to crave and my dear hap[28] to tell.   [*Exit.*]

25. **wanton's:** careless child's.
26. **gyves** (jīvz): chains, like the threads that hold the bird captive.
27. **ghostly friar's:** spiritual father's.
28. **hap:** luck.

INTERPRET

What does Juliet compare Romeo to? Underline the comparison in lines 178–182.

_____

_____

INTERPRET

What does line 184 mean, and what could it **foreshadow**?

_____

_____

_____

_____

WORD STUDY

An **oxymoron** is an expression that combines terms that seem contradictory. Underline the oxymoron in line 185. How does Juliet feel about parting?

_____

_____

_____

IDENTIFY

Romeo speaks the last four lines of this scene alone on-stage. What is he about to do?

_____

_____

_____

The Tragedy of Romeo and Juliet, Act II, Scene 2

Elements Chart The characters in *The Tragedy of Romeo and Juliet* speak in **dialogue, monologues, soliloquies,** and **asides.** They use **metaphors** and other figures of speech. Fill in the chart by identifying passages from the selection that contain these elements. Identify who is speaking, describe the passage, and include the line numbers.

Elements	Example from Play
Dialogue	
Monologue	
Soliloquy	
Aside	
Metaphor or other figure of speech	

Standards Review

LITERATURE

Test Practice

The Tragedy of Romeo and Juliet, Act II, Scene 2

Complete the sample test item below. Then, check your answer, and read the explanation that appears in the right-hand column.

Sample Test Item	Explanation of the Correct Answer
Juliet says "My bounty is as boundless as the sea, / My love as deep." In these lines she is comparing — A her love for Romeo to the depth of the sea B her father's fortune to the vast sea C Romeo's love to the wild sea D the depth of her love to her riches	The correct answer is *A*. *B* is not correct because her father is not mentioned. *C* is not correct because she says it is "my" bounty. *D* is not correct because riches are not mentioned at all.

DIRECTIONS: Circle the letter of the best response.

1. In lines 2–25, Romeo speaks in —

   A a dialogue

   B a monologue

   C an aside

   D a soliloquy

2. Romeo says: "But soft! What light through yonder window breaks? / It is the East, and Juliet is the sun!" What comparison is he making?

   F He is comparing Juliet to the sun.

   G He is comparing himself to the East wind.

   H He is comparing a broken window to the sun.

   J He is comparing the East to Juliet.

3. In lines 26–32, Romeo compares —

   A Juliet to an angel

   B himself to a cloud

   C an angel to messengers of heaven

   D mortals to angels

4. Which is the best **paraphrase** of Juliet's question "Wherefore art thou Romeo?" (line 33)

   F Where are you, Romeo?

   G Why are you called Romeo?

   H Where are you hiding, Romeo?

   J Why did you do this, Romeo?

Reading Standard 3.1 Articulate the relationship between the expressed purposes and characteristics of different forms of dramatic literature (e.g., comedy, tragedy, drama, dramatic monologue).

Reading Standard 3.10 Identify and describe the function of dialogue, scene designs, soliloquies, asides, and character foils in dramatic literature.

Standards Review

TestPractice ## The Tragedy of Romeo and Juliet, Act II, Scene 2

Academic Vocabulary

Reading Standard 1.2 (Grade 8 Review) Understand the most important points in the history of English language and use common word origins to determine the historical influence on English word meanings.

DIRECTIONS: Match each term with its definition by writing the correct letter on the lines provided.

_____ **1.** tragedy

a. a long speech made by one character to one or more other characters onstage

_____ **2.** comedy

b. a play that ends happily, in which the main character gets what he or she wants

_____ **3.** monologue

c. a play that presents serious and important actions and ends unhappily for the main character

_____ **4.** soliloquy

d. a speech made by a character who is alone onstage, speaking to himself or herself or to the audience

Archaic Words in Context

DIRECTIONS: Have some fun. Try speaking like someone from Shakespeare's time. Complete the paragraph below by writing the correct archaic word from the word box in each numbered blank.

Word Box

maid

nice

Jack

hap

stay

"(1)_____!" shouted I, running like Mercury after the school bus. It was my good (2) _____ that the driver was a regular (3) _____ and stopped the bus so that I might board. Would but that I were never so (4) _____ that I would sleep past my clock's alarm! Perhaps I am not so luckless a fool, thought I, when there, the only seat remaining, 'twas next to Julie, the fairest (5) _____ in the ninth grade!

Before You Go On...

Check your Standards Mastery at the back of this book.

Pyramus and Thisby

from **A Midsummer Night's Dream**   by William Shakespeare

BEFORE YOU READ

You are about to read the "Pyramus and Thisby" scene from Shakespeare's comedy *A Midsummer Night's Dream*. In this scene a group of working men present a play to celebrate a duke's wedding. This play-within-a-play echoes the story of Romeo and Juliet, but here the lovers' story becomes a comedy. As you read, watch for the ways in which the actors mangle the tragic story of Pyramus and his beloved Thisby. Notice how the noble audience makes sarcastic remarks about the amateur acting.

LITERARY FOCUS: COMEDY

A **comedy** is a play that ends happily. Most comedies make us laugh. "Pyramus and Thisby" is supposed to be a tragedy, but amateur acting turns it into a **farce**, or comedy with ridiculous situations and comical physical actions.

Comedies, like most plays, contain key elements, including **dialogue** (conversation between characters), **monologues** (long speeches delivered to one or more characters), **soliloquies** (long speeches delivered by a character alone onstage), and **stage directions** (notes to actors on when to enter and exit, and so on).

Commoners play the parts in "Pyramus and Thisby." Their audience is a duke, Theseus; his bride, Hippolyta; and their friends.

READING SKILLS: RECOGNIZING HUMOR

The essence of humor is surprise. Not every surprise is funny, but nothing is funny without being surprising. We laugh at surprising situations, surprising actions, and surprising word choices. Look for these elements of humor as you read:

- **Comical physical actions,** including silly actions like slipping on a banana peel or hitting the wrong person in the face with a pie
- **Disguises,** including men playing women's parts and women playing men's parts
- **Parodies,** or mockeries, of other works of literature
- **Puns,** or plays on two possible meanings of words
- **Exaggeration,** or overstatement, talking about something and making it more important than it really is or acting in an exaggerated way (overdoing it)
- **Understatement,** or making something less significant than it really is

Reading Standard 1.3 Identify Greek, Roman, and Norse mythology and use the knowledge to understand the origin and meaning of new words (e.g., the word *narcissistic* drawn from the myth of Narcissus and Echo).

Reading Standard 3.1 Articulate the relationship between the expressed purposes and characteristics of different forms of dramatic literature (e.g., comedy, tragedy, drama, dramatic monologue).

VOCABULARY DEVELOPMENT

WORD ORIGINS: GREEK AND ROMAN MYTHOLOGY

Shakespeare's version of "Pyramus and Thisby" in *A Midsummer Night's Dream* is based on a story by an ancient Roman writer named Ovid. Many of Ovid's stories are based on Greek and Roman folk tales and myths. The names of some of Shakespeare's characters are also based on Greek and Roman myths. For instance, in *Romeo and Juliet,* Romeo's friend Mercutio is named after the Roman god Mercury.

Numerous words that appear in Shakespeare and in our own daily language have mythological origins. These include:

mercurial *adj.:* Mercury, the Roman god who served as messenger to the other gods, was known for his speed. His name was given to a planet and an element. The word *mercurial* means "quick; changeable."

narcissistic *adj.:* Narcissus, a character in Greek myth, fell in love with his own reflection. Today *narcissistic* means "in love with oneself."

furious *adj.:* The *Furies* are female spirits in Greek mythology who torment people who commit unavenged crimes. *Furious* has come to mean "very angry."

echo *n.:* Echo, a Greek nymph, pined away from unreturned love for Narcissus until only her voice was left. Today *echo* means "the repetition of a sound or word."

jovial *adj.:* Jove, or Jupiter, the chief Roman god, was considered the source of happiness and joy. Today *jovial* means "good humored or merry."

panic *n.:* Pan, a Greek god of fields, forests, and wild animals, was known for causing mischief. *Panic* has come to mean "sudden fear" (as if caused by the actions of Pan).

Depiction of Thisby and Pyramus, located at the House of Dionysos, Paphos, Cyprus. Mosaic.

Pyramus and Thisby

from **A Midsummer Night's Dream**

William Shakespeare

Notes

CHARACTERS

Peter Quince, a carpenter, the director of the play, who also
   delivers the Prologue

Nick Bottom, a weaver, who takes the part of the lover Pyramus

Francis Flute, a bellows-mender, who takes the part of Thisby

Robin Starveling, a tailor, who represents Moonshine

Tom Snout, a tinker, who plays the Wall

Snug, a joiner, or cabinet-maker, who plays the Lion

Theseus, Duke of Athens

Hippolyta, queen of the Amazons and bride of Theseus

Lysander, a young gentleman of the court

Demetrius, a young gentleman of the court

IDENTIFY

Which actor is speaking the lines of the prologue? How can you tell?

_____

_____

_____

RECOGNIZE HUMOR

When Theseus remarks that the actor speaking the prologue does not "stand upon points," (line 11), he means the actor does not pay attention to punctuation. He pauses in the wrong places, so his speech makes no sense. Read the prologue aloud to show how silly it sounds.

CLARIFY

Pause at line 18. What does the noble audience think of the performance so far?

_____

_____

_____

CLARIFY

Re-read lines 23–26. Why is the wall a problem for the lovers, Pyramus and Thisby?

_____

_____

_____

[*Enter the* PROLOGUE (QUINCE)].

Prologue. If we offend, it is with our good will.
    That you should think, we come not to offend,
But with good will. To show our simple skill,
    That is the true beginning of our end.
5 Consider, then, we come but in despite.[1]
    We do not come, as minding to content you,
Our true intent is. All for your delight,
    We are not here. That you should here repent you,
The actors are at hand; and, by their show,
10 You shall know all, that you are like to know.

Theseus. This fellow doth not stand upon points.[2]

Lysander. He hath rid his prologue like a rough colt;
    he knows not the stop. A good moral, my lord:
    it is not enough to speak, but to speak true.

15 **Hippolyta.** Indeed he hath played on this prologue like a child
    on a recorder, a sound, but not in government.[3]

Theseus. His speech was like a tangled chain; nothing impaired,
    but all disordered. Who is next?

[*Enter* PYRAMUS *and* THISBY *and* WALL *and*
MOONSHINE *and* LION [*as in dumbshow*].]

Prologue. Gentles, perchance you wonder at this show;
20   But wonder on, till truth make all things plain.
This man is Pyramus, if you would know;
    This beauteous lady Thisby is certain.
This man, with lime and roughcast, doth present
    Wall, that vile Wall which did these lovers sunder;
25 And through Wall's chink, poor souls, they are content
    To whisper. At the which let no man wonder.
This man, with lantern, dog, and bush of thorn,
    Presenteth Moonshine; for, if you will know,
By moonshine did these lovers think no scorn

---

1. **despite:** ill will.
2. **stand upon points:** pay attention to punctuation marks.
3. **not in government:** undisciplined.

30   To meet at Ninus' tomb, there, there to woo.

This grisly beast, which Lion hight[4] by name,

The trusty Thisby, coming first by night,

Did scare away, or rather did affright;

And, as she fled, her mantle she did fall,

35   Which Lion vile with bloody mouth did stain.

Anon come Pyramus, sweet youth and tall,

And finds his trusty Thisby's mantle slain:

Whereat, with blade, with bloody blameful blade,

He bravely broached[5] his boiling bloody breast;

40   And Thisby, tarrying in mulberry shade,

His dagger drew, and died. For all the rest,

Let Lion, Moonshine, Wall, and lovers twain

At large[6] discourse, while here they do remain.

Theseus. I wonder if the lion be to speak.

45   **Demetrius.** No wonder, my lord. One lion may, when many

asses do.

[*Exit* LION, THISBY *and* MOONSHINE.]

Wall. In this same interlude it doth befall

That I, one Snout by name, present a wall;

And such a wall, as I would have you think,

50   That had in it a crannied hole or chink,

Through which the lovers, Pyramus and Thisby,

Did whisper often very secretly.

This loam, this roughcast, and this stone, doth show

That I am that same wall; the truth is so;

55   And this the cranny is, right and sinister,[7]

Through which the fearful lovers are to whisper.

Theseus. Would you desire lime and hair to speak better?

Demetrius. It is the wittiest partition[8] that ever I heard

discourse, my lord.

60   **Theseus.** Pyramus draws near the wall. Silence!

---

4. **hight:** is called
5. **broached:** stabbed.
6. **at large:** at length.
7. **sinister:** left.
8. **partition:** wall.

IDENTIFY

The prologue introduces the characters in the play. Re-read lines 21–31, and circle the characters' names.

RECOGNIZE HUMOR

Read aloud lines 38–39. The writers of the play are using **alliteration** (repetition of consonant sounds) to sound poetic. What is the effect of the alliteration? Why?

_____

_____

_____

IDENTIFY

Pause at line 39. What has happened to Pyramus, and why?

_____

_____

_____

RECOGNIZE HUMOR

Pause at line 59. What is funny or surprising about the Wall?

_____

_____

Underline the **repetition** in
lines 61–68. What effect does
this repetition have?

_____

_____

_____

_____

_____

Pause at line 72. A **farce** is a
type of comedy with ridiculous situations and comical
physical action. What is comical in this scene between
Pyramus and the Wall?

_____

_____

_____

_____

_____

Pause at line 78. What does
Pyramus do that an actor
should not do?

_____

_____

_____

_____

Pyramus. O grim-looked night! O night with hue so black!

  O night, which ever art when day is not!

 O night, O night! Alack, alack, alack,

  I fear my Thisby's promise is forgot!

65 And thou, O wall, O sweet, O lovely wall,

 That stand'st between her father's ground and mine!

 Thou wall, O wall, O sweet and lovely wall,

  Show me thy chink, to blink through with mine

   eyne!

[WALL *holds up his fingers.*]

 Thanks, courteous wall. Jove shield thee well for this!

70   But what see I? No Thisby do I see.

 O wicked wall, through whom I see no bliss!

  Cursed be thy stones for thus deceiving me!

Theseus. The wall, methinks, being sensible,[9] should

 curse again.

75 **Pyramus.** No, in truth, sir, he should not. "Deceiving me" is

 Thisby's cue. She is to enter now, and I am to spy her

 through the wall. You shall see it will fall pat as I told you.

 Yonder she comes.

[*Enter* THISBY]

Thisby. O wall, full often hast thou heard my moans,

80   For parting my fair Pyramus and me!

 My cherry lips have often kissed thy stones,

  Thy stones with lime and hair knit up in thee.

Pyramus. I see a voice: now will I to the chink,

 To spy an I can hear my Thisby's face.

85 Thisby!

Thisby. My love thou art, my love I think.

Pyramus. Think what thou wilt, I am thy lover's grace,

 And, like Limander,[10] am I trusty still.

---

9. being sensible: conscious.

10. Limander: instead of *Leander,* a legendary Greek lover.

Thisby. And I like Helen,[11] till the Fates[12] me kill.

90 **Pyramus.** Not Shafalus to Procrus[13] was so true.

Thisby. As Shafalus to Procrus, I to you.

Pyramus. O kiss me through the hole of this vile wall!

Thisby. I kiss the wall's hole, not your lips at all.

Pyramus. Wilt thou at Ninny's tomb meet me straightway?

95 **Thisby.** 'Tide life, 'tide death,[14] I come without delay.

[*Exeunt* PYRAMUS *and* THISBY.]

Wall. Thus have I, Wall, my part dischargèd so;

And, being done, thus wall away doth go. [*Exit.*]

Theseus. Now is the moon used between the two neighbors.

Demetrius. No remedy, my lord, when walls are so willful to

100 hear without warning.

Hippolyta. This is the silliest stuff that ever I heard.

Theseus. The best in this kind are but shadows; and the worst are

no worse, if imagination amend them.

Hippolyta. It must be your imagination then, and not theirs.

105 **Theseus.** If we imagine no worse of them than they of them-

selves, they may pass for excellent men. Here come two

noble beasts in, a man and a lion.

[*Enter* LION *and* MOONSHINE.]

Lion. You, ladies, you, whose gentle hearts do fear

The smallest monstrous mouse that creeps on floor,

110 May now perchance both quake and tremble here,

When lion rough in wildest rage doth roar.

Then know that I, as Snug the joiner, am

A lion fell,[15] nor else no lion's dam;

---

11. **Helen:** instead of *Hero,* Leander's true love. Helen was in another legend.
12. **Fates:** in Greek mythology, the three goddesses who controlled the future. The word *fate* means "destiny."
13. **Shafalus to Procrus:** Cephalus and Procris are meant, who are legendary lovers.
14. **'tide:** betide; happen.
15. **fell:** fierce.

RECOGNIZE HUMOR

Re-read lines 83–84. What two words does the actor playing Pyramus mix up?

_____

_____

COMPARE & CONTRAST

Re-read lines 101–107. How do Hippolyta's and Theseus's assessments of the play differ?

_____
_____
_____
_____
_____
_____
_____
_____
_____
_____

CLARIFY

Earlier in the play, the performers had discussed how to present a lion without frightening the ladies in the audience. In lines 108–113, underline the name of the actor who plays Lion.

CLARIFY

Pause at line 133. What do the nobles find ridiculous about Moonshine?

_____

_____

_____

_____

RECOGNIZE HUMOR

Re-read lines 141–143. At this point, what does the actor playing Moonshine do?

_____

_____

_____

_____

_____

_____

_____

_____

For, if I should as lion come in strife

115   Into this place, 'twere pity on my life.[16]

Theseus. A very gentle beast, and of a good conscience.

Demetrius. The very best at a beast, my lord, that e'er I saw.

Lysander. This lion is a very fox for his valor.

Theseus. True; and a goose for his discretion.

120 **Demetrius.** Not so, my lord; for his valor cannot carry his discretion, and the fox carries the goose.

Theseus. His discretion, I am sure, cannot carry his valor; for the goose carries not the fox. It is well. Leave it to his discretion, and let us listen to the moon.

125 **Moonshine.** This lanthorn[17] doth the hornèd moon present—

Demetrius. He should have worn the horns on his head.

Theseus. He is no crescent, and his horns are invisible within the circumference.

Moonshine. This lanthorn doth the hornèd moon present;

130   Myself the man i' th' moon do seem to be.

Theseus. This is the greatest error of all the rest. The man should be put into the lanthorn. How is it else the man i' th' moon?

Demetrius. He dares not come there for the candle; for, you see,

135   it is already in snuff.[18]

Hippolyta. I am aweary of this moon. Would he would change!

Theseus. It appears, by his small light of discretion, that he is in the wane; but yet, in courtesy, in all reason, we must stay the time.

140 **Lysander.** Proceed, Moon.

Moonshine. All that I have to say is to tell you that the lanthorn is the moon; I, the man i' th' moon; this thorn bush, my thorn bush; and this dog, my dog.

Demetrius. Why, all these should be in the lanthorn; for all

145   these are in the moon. But, silence! Here comes Thisby.

---

16. **'twere pity on my life:** I should be hanged for it.
17. **lanthorn:** lantern.
18. **in snuff:** in need of snuffing, or putting out.

[*Enter* THISBY.]

Thisby. This is old Ninny's tomb. Where is my love?

Lion. Oh—

[*The* LION *roars.* THISBY *runs off.*]

Demetrius. Well roared, Lion.

Theseus. Well run, Thisby.

150   **Hippolyta.** Well shone, Moon. Truly, the moon shines with

      a good grace.

              [*The* LION *shakes* THISBY'S *mantle, and exit.*]

Theseus. Well moused,[19] Lion.

Demetrius. And then came Pyramus.

Lysander. And so the lion vanished.

[*Enter* PYRAMUS.]

155   **Pyramus.** Sweet Moon, I thank thee for thy sunny beams;

      I thank thee, Moon, for shining now so bright;

      For, by thy gracious, golden, glittering gleams,

        I trust to take of truest Thisby sight.

          But stay, O spite!

160   But mark, poor knight,

      What dreadful dole[20] is here!

          Eyes, do you see?

          How can it be?

      O dainty duck! O dear!

165   Thy mantle good,

      What, stained with blood!

      Approach, ye Furies fell![21]

        O Fates, come, come,

        Cut thread and thrum;[22]

170   Quail, crush, conclude, and quell![23]

---

19. **moused:** shaken, as if by a cat that has caught a mouse.
20. **dole:** sorrow.
21. **Furies fell:** In Greek mythology, the Furies are female spirits who avenged unpunished crimes.
22. **thrum:** the very end of the thread.
23. **quell:** slay; kill.

RECOGNIZE HUMOR

Pause at line 149. Comedy often has people in disguise, or has men play women and women play men. Thisby is played by a man. What does "she" do here?

_____

_____

_____

_____

_____

_____

_____

_____

_____

_____

_____

_____

_____

_____

RECOGNIZE HUMOR

These amateur actors think that *more* alliteration is better. Underline examples of **alliteration** in Pyramus's speech (lines 155–170). Say the speech aloud to hear its comical sounds.

FLUENCY

Read Pyramus's final speech (lines 174–189) aloud at least twice. Skip the stage directions in brackets. Use a lot of exaggeration, and have a good time hamming it up, as Pyramus most certainly does.

IDENTIFY

In lines 194–195, what problem with the staging does Hippolyta observe?

_____

_____

_____

_____

_____

_____

_____

_____

_____

_____

_____

_____

_____

_____

_____

_____

_____

_____

_____

Theseus. This passion, and the death of a dear friend, would go near to make a man look sad.

Hippolyta. Beshrew my heart, but I pity the man.

Pyramus. O wherefore, Nature, didst thou lions frame?
175   Since lion vile hath here deflow'red my dear:
Which is—no, no—which was the fairest dame
    That lived, that loved, that liked, that looked with cheer.
      Come, tears, confound;[24]
      Out, sword, and wound
180   The pap of Pyramus;
      Ay, that left pap,[25]
      Where heart doth hop.   *[Stabs himself.]*
    Thus die I, thus, thus, thus.
      Now am I dead,
185   Now am I fled;
    My soul is in the sky.
      Tongue, lose thy light;
      Moon, take thy flight.

          [Exit MOONSHINE.*]*

    Now die, die, die, die, die.   *[Dies.]*

190 **Demetrius.** No die, but an ace, for him; for he is but one.

Lysander. Less than an ace, man; for he is dead, he is nothing.

Theseus. With the help of a surgeon he might yet recover, and yet prove an ass.

Hippolyta. How chance Moonshine is gone before Thisby comes
195   back and finds her lover?

Theseus. She will find him by starlight. Here she comes; and her passion ends the play.

[Enter THISBY.*]*

Hippolyta. Methinks she should not use a long one for such a Pyramus. I hope she will be brief.

---

24. **confound:** destroy.
25. **pap:** breast.

Demetrius. A mote will turn the balance, which Pyramus, which
        Thisby, is the better; he for a man, God warr'nt us; she for a
        woman, God bless us!

Lysander. She hath spied him already with those sweet eyes.

Demetrius. And thus she means, videlicet.²⁶

Thisby. Asleep, my love?

        What, dead, my dove?

    O Pyramus, arise!

        Speak, speak. Quite dumb?

        Dead, dead? A tomb

Must cover thy sweet eyes.

        These lily lips,

        This cherry nose,

These yellow cowslip cheeks,

        Are gone, are gone.

        Lovers, make moan.

His eyes were green as leeks.

        O Sisters Three,²⁷

        Come, come to me,

With hands as pale as milk;

        Lay them in gore,

        Since you have shore²⁸

With shears his thread of silk.

        Tongue, not a word.

        Come, trusty sword,

Come, blade, my breast imbrue!²⁹

[*Stabs herself.*]

        And farewell, friends.

        Thus Thisby ends.

      Adieu, adieu, adieu.

                           [*Dies.*]

Line numbers: 200, 205, 210, 215, 220, 225

DRAW CONCLUSIONS

Re-read lines 196–204. What do you think Thisby is doing while the audience is making its sarcastic comments?

_____

_____

_____

_____

RECOGNIZE HUMOR

There are many humorous parts to Thisby's overwritten speech in lines 205–228. Underline and describe one of the comic parts.

_____

_____

_____

_____

_____

_____

_____

_____

_____

_____

_____

_____

---

26. **videlicet:** Latin for "that is" or "namely."
27. **Sisters Three:** the Fates.
28. **shore:** cut.
29. **imbrue:** drench with blood.

IDENTIFY

Bottom is the name of the
character who plays Pyramus.
What does he do in lines
231–234?

_____

_____

_____

_____

_____

IDENTIFY

What does Theseus think of
the playwright's skill (lines
235–241)?

_____

_____

_____

_____

_____

_____

_____

_____

_____

_____

_____

_____

_____

_____

French comb with the story of Pyramus and Thisby.

Theseus. Moonshine and Lion are left to bury the dead.

230   **Demetrius.** Ay, and Wall too.

Bottom. [*Starting up*] No, I assure you; the wall is down that
    parted their fathers. Will it please you to see the epilogue,
    or to hear a Bergomask dance between the two of our
    company?

235   **Theseus.** No epilogue, I pray you; for your play needs no excuse.
    Never excuse, for when the players are all dead, there need
    none to be blamed. Marry, if he that writ it had played
    Pyramus and hanged himself in Thisby's garter, it would
    have been a fine tragedy: and so it is, truly; and very
240   notably discharged. But, come, your Bergomask. Let your
    epilogue alone.   [*A dance*]

    The iron tongue of midnight hath told twelve.
    Lovers, to bed; 'tis almost fairy time.
    I fear we shall outsleep the coming morn,
245   As much as we this night have overwatched.
    This palpable-gross[30] play hath well beguiled
    The heavy gait of night. Sweet friends, to bed.
    A fortnight hold we this solemnity,
    In nightly revels and new jollity.   [*Exeunt.*]

---

30. **palpable-gross:** obviously strange.

Pyramus and Thisby

Humor Chart Most comedies are funny; though the characters in a comedy take their problems very seriously, the audience is meant to laugh at them. The chart below lists some elements of humor. Fill in the right-hand column with examples of each element from "Pyramus and Thisby." Be sure to include the line numbers for your examples.

Element of Humor	Example from "Pyramus and Thisby"
Comic actions	
Comic misuse of language	
Parody, or ridicule of writing styles	
Comic alliteration	
Comic disguises or costumes	

Standards Review

 **Pyramus and Thisby**

Complete the sample test item below. Then, check your answer, and read the explanation that appears in the right-hand column.

Sample Test Item	Explanation of the Correct Answer
"Pyramus and Thisby" is a **farce** because it has — **A** ridiculous situations **B** animal characters **C** young lovers **D** common people as characters	*A* is the correct answer, because all farces feature ridiculous situations. A farce does not need animal characters, *B*, young lovers, *C*, or common people, *D*.

DIRECTIONS: Circle the letter of each correct response.

1. The play-within-a-play is about —

   A Theseus and his upcoming wedding

   B a group of workmen

   C Pyramus and his beloved Thisby

   D Lysander and Demetrius and their loves

2. Which of the following lines is a **parody** of the literary element **alliteration**?

   F "This fellow doth not stand upon points."

   G "His speech was like a tangled chain. . . ."

   H "It is not enough to speak, but to speak true."

   J "He bravely broached his boiling bloody breast."

3. In which of the following lines does the speaker use a **pun**, a comical play on a word with two meanings?

   A "I wonder if the lion be to speak."

   B "One lion may [speak], when many asses do."

   C "Would you desire lime and hair to speak better?"

   D "It is the wittiest partition that ever I heard discourse, my lord."

4. Which of the following scenes uses **comic exaggeration** to make fun of tragic death scenes?

   F Pyramus's speech beginning "Thus die I, thus, thus, thus" (line 183)

   G Theseus's last monologue, at the play's end

   H The Prologue's speech (lines 1–10)

   J Lion's speech to the ladies (lines 108–115)

Reading Standard 3.1
Articulate the relationship between the expressed purposes and the characteristics of different forms of dramatic literature (e.g., comedy, tragedy, drama, dramatic monologue).

Standards Review

 **Pyramus and Thisby**

Word Origins: Greek and Roman Mythology

DIRECTIONS: Match each word on the left with its origin. Write the correct letter on the line.

_____ **1.** mercurial   **a.** The Furies

_____ **2.** jovial   **b.** Narcissus

_____ **3.** furious   **c.** Pan

_____ **4.** narcissistic   **d.** Jove

_____ **5.** panic   **e.** Mercury

Reading Standard 1.3 Identify Greek, Roman, and Norse mythology and use the knowledge to understand the origin and meaning of new words (e.g., the word *narcissistic* drawn from the myth of Narcissus and Echo).

Vocabulary in Context

DIRECTIONS: Complete the paragraph below by writing the correct word from the word box in each numbered blank. Use each word only once.

Word Box

jovial

narcissistic

echo

mercurial

furious

panic

The (1) _____ actor could not stop admiring his face in the dressing room mirror. "Ten more minutes, Mr. Tayback!" the jolly and (2) _____ stage manager called outside the door. "Ten more minutes!" The moody and (3) _____ actor quickly shot back, "Is there an (4) _____ in here?" "What's the problem?" the stage manager asked, opening the dressing room door. "Begone!" screamed the (5) _____ actor, throwing his Romeo wig at the door. Telling himself not to (6) _____, the stage manager tried to calm his sudden fear that the show would be a disaster.

Before You Go On . . .

Check your Standards Mastery at the back of this book.

Part Two

Reading Comprehension

Informational Materials

Academic Vocabulary

These are the terms you should know
as you read and analyze these selections.

———————

Source A person, book, or document that provides information on a topic.

Elaboration The addition of ideas to support the ideas already presented in a work.

Synthesis The merging of information gathered from more than one source.

Argument A series of statements designed to convince the reader to accept a claim, or opinion.

Claim An opinion on a topic or issue, which is often stated as a generalization, or broad statement that covers many situations.

Evidence Support for an idea. Evidence includes facts, statistics, examples, anecdotes (brief stories about real people), and quotations.

Credibility The believability of an argument or statement.

For Further Information ...

Be sure to read about the following in *Holt Literature and Language Arts*:

- **Generating research questions**, pages 26, 43.
- **Primary and secondary sources**, pages 96, 578–579.
- **Synthesizing sources**, pages 183, 231, 374, 918.
- **Evaluating arguments**, pages 308–309, 516–517, 718.

Reading Standard 2.3 Generate relevant questions about readings on issues that can be researched.

Reading Standard 2.4 Synthesize the content from several sources or works by a single author dealing with a single issue; paraphrase the ideas and connect them to other sources and related topics to demonstrate comprehension.

Reading Standard 2.5 Extend ideas presented in primary or secondary sources through original analysis, evaluation, and elaboration.

Reading Standard 2.8 Evaluate the credibility of an author's argument or defense of a claim by critiquing the relationship between generalizations and evidence, the comprehensiveness of evidence, and the way in which the author's intent affects the structure and tone of the text (e.g., in professional journals, editorials, political speeches, primary source material).

The Great American Art Heist by Robert Byrd

BEFORE YOU READ

In this article, you'll read about a famous unsolved mystery— "the biggest art heist ever." (A *heist* [hīst] is a BIG robbery.) After you absorb all the details about the crime and the suspects, think of the questions *you'd* like answered.

INFORMATIONAL FOCUS: HOW TO GENERATE RESEARCH QUESTIONS

Research involves answering questions. To develop good questions for research based on informational materials:

- Start by filling in a KWL chart like the one below.
- Ask the **5W-How?** questions rather than yes-or-no questions. Who was involved? What happened? When and where did it happen? Why and how did it happen?
- Ask specific questions that can be answered within the scope of your research. You could answer the question: How did the museum begin its collection? It would be difficult, however, to answer the question: What is great art?

READING SKILLS: MAKE A KWL CHART

Get ready to read about this true-life crime by filling in the first two columns of the KWL chart below. In the first column, list what you know about museums and their security systems. In the second column, list some of the questions about this theft you would like answered. Then, after you read the article, fill out the last column. Some of the items in the first two columns have been filled in for you.

Museums and the Art World

What I Already KNOW	What I WANT to Find Out	What I LEARNED
	How did the thieves get into the museum?	
Museums have security systems.		
	What did they steal?	

The Great American Art Heist

Robert Byrd

*It was the biggest art theft ever—thirteen items worth
more than $200 million swiped from the Gardner
Museum in Boston. It happened in 1990, and 10 years
later, none of the plunder has been recovered and no
one has been arrested. Instead there's just a bewildering
trail of false leads and dead ends.*

Shortly after 1:00 A.M. on the night of March 18, 1990, two men
dressed as Boston cops rang the bell at the small side door of the
museum. They asked the young security guard to let them in
10 because there was a "disturbance in the neighborhood."
Once inside, the thieves quickly handcuffed the guard and his
partner, herded them into the basement, and duct-taped them
to the pipes.

The two imposters, who were wearing false mustaches as well
as false uniforms, then disabled the security system to prevent the
alarms on individual paintings from going off and removed the
videotapes in the cameras that were triggered whenever someone
went into a room. For the next hour and twenty-one minutes they
plundered the premises, while motion detectors fed information
20 about their movements to a central computer.

They took Vermeer's *The Concert,* one of only 32 known
paintings by this artist. They took two paintings by Rembrandt,
including *Storm on the Sea of Galilee,* his only seascape, and
A Lady and Gentleman in Black. Perhaps because they were
frustrated by the special bolts that held these paintings on the
wall, they slashed them from their frames, leaving a trail of

Pause at line 20. What
questions do you have about
the information so far? Think
of at least two.

_____

_____

_____

_____

_____

_____

IDENTIFY

How is the Gardner different from most museums? Circle the differences (lines 38–42).

Isabella Stewart Gardner Museum, Boston, Massachusetts, USA/Bridgeman Art Library.

Isabella Stewart Gardner (1888) by John Singer Sargent. Oil on canvas.

DRAW CONCLUSIONS

Pause at line 54. What question does the information in the paragraph help clear up?

350-year-old paint chips and varnish. They took a self-portrait by Rembrandt the size of a postage stamp, an oil painting by Manet, drawings by Degas, a 3000-year-old Chinese beaker,
30 and the bronze eagle from a Napoleonic flagstaff.

The theft shocked Boston, where the Gardner is a beloved institution. The museum is an imitation Venetian palace built by the eccentric Boston socialite Isabella Stewart Gardner at the turn of the century. Three floors of galleries open onto a central glass-roofed court filled with flowers where concerts are often held. One visitor said, "This museum is my oasis—fresh water when I need it."

The Gardner is what is called a house museum. Mrs. Gardner lived on the fourth floor until her death in 1924, and her will
40 required that the museum's director always live there. Her will also demanded that nothing in the museum be rearranged or replaced after her death. The art is displayed in rooms set up exactly as they were when Mrs. Gardner died, down to a vase of violets on a table laid out as if for tea.

It wasn't clear to anyone why the thieves took some paintings and left others. They took the valuable Vermeer and the Rembrandts, but they left behind masterpieces such as Titian's *The Rape of Europa,* which the Dutch master Rubens called "the greatest painting in the world." The Degas pictures weren't
50 considered that valuable, and nobody could figure out why the thieves took the bronze eagle. One investigator said, "It suggests they might have been under orders to steal the Vermeer and the Rembrandts and freelanced the rest." Another simply said, "We don't understand the shopping list."

Many people thought the thieves must have had a buyer before they went in. Otherwise, how could they get rid of the booty? The artworks would be extremely difficult to sell because they are so well known. As an FBI spokesman put it, "What does a thief do with a Vermeer? You don't just roll it up and walk into
60 a gallery and say, 'Can I have $30 million for this?'"

An FBI supervisor said that in his opinion the thieves hoped to "ransom back" the paintings to the museum. "Then, when it was printed the day after the robbery that these paintings were not insured, these people didn't know what to do with them."

For years the FBI tracked down hundreds of leads only to have them all turn into dead ends. Two American teachers who had gone to dine at the mansion of an eccentric Japanese artist and collector thought they saw *Storm on the Sea of Galilee* in his crimson ballroom. But when the FBI and Japanese police

70 arrived, the collector offered them fruit and expressed surprise that there was such a fuss over a copy he had owned for 40 years.

But then, seven years after the heist, an ex-con named Billy Youngworth III, who had just been arrested on other charges, claimed he knew where the paintings were hidden. He and his associate Myles Connor would arrange the return of the paintings in exchange for immunity from prosecution, the $5 million reward the museum was offering for the paintings, and Connor's release from prison.

Myles J. Connor, Jr., a

80 legendary art thief, couldn't have robbed the Gardner because he was in prison at the time. But he might have masterminded the heist from prison. And he had used stolen art-work—including a Rembrandt—to bargain his way out of prison

90 before. When he was asked what Connor knew about the Gardner heist, his lawyer said, "Myles has never indicated to me that

Known as "Mrs. Jack," Isabella enjoyed shocking Boston's stuffy upper class by walking a circus lion and hanging out with heavyweight champ John L. Sullivan.

IDENTIFY

Explain the FBI supervisor's theory of the thieves' motive (lines 61–64). Underline the reason the plan didn't work.

_____

_____

_____

WORD STUDY

Circle the word *leads* in line 65. What part of speech is it? How do you think it is pronounced? What does it mean in this **context**?

_____

_____

_____

_____

_____

_____

_____

_____

_____

_____

TEXT STRUCTURE

Some information in this article is provided through **captions**. Circle details in this caption that show that Mrs. Gardner was unusual.

GENERATE
QUESTIONS

Pause at line 107. Think
about the information you
have learned so far. Go back
and underline details you
have questions about.

IDENTIFY

Pause at line 113. Circle the
items Youngworth gave to
the *Herald*. Then, underline
the FBI analysis of those
items.

INFER

What inference can you
make about Isabella Gardner
from the information in the
caption?

he knows who was responsible for that theft or where the artwork is, but if they would release him from prison, he would
probably find it for them. The man has contacts you wouldn't
believe."

100   The FBI said they wouldn't negotiate until they had "con-
crete evidence" that Youngworth and Connor could deliver the
paintings. So in one of the weirder episodes in American jour-
nalism, Youngworth arranged to have Tom Mashberg, a *Boston
Herald* reporter who had been writing about the case, taken to
the stash. Mashberg was driven in the dead of night to a seedy
warehouse outside of Boston. By flashlight he was shown a
painting he says looked like *Storm on the Sea of Galilee*. He
claims that Rembrandt's signature was on the ship's rudder.

A short time later, Youngworth gave the *Herald* photographs of the Rembrandts and a small bottle of paint chips said
110   to be from *Storm on the Sea of Galilee*. But the FBI and the
Gardner Museum, which compared the paint chips with the
paint chips left behind in the heist, concluded "both the photographs and paint chips are not what they purport to be."

El Jaleo (1882) by John Singer Sargent. Oil on canvas.

*Isabella Gardner borrowed this painting from its owner and then
conveniently "forgot" to return it. "More than three-quarters of what you
see in museums was looted or stolen," says Myles Connor.*

Isabella Stewart Gardner Museum, Boston, Massachusetts, USA/Bridgeman Art Library.

The Concert (c.1658-60) by Jan Vermeer. Oil on canvas. Stolen.

At that point the talks broke down. Youngworth and Connor still wanted to deal, but as a source familiar with the case put it, "It's absurd. They're just trying to keep their names in the paper." Connor had said he couldn't return the paintings unless he was released from prison because he needed to "access certain information." He was released in June of this year but

120 nothing further has been heard from him.

"I've never seen anything quite like a case like this," one investigator said. "Every time we think we know what we're dealing with, things change and we're back to square one." Because Isabella's will prevents any changes at the Gardner, small cards have been posted where the paintings once hung. They read "Stolen on March 18, 1990."

GENERATE QUESTIONS

Pause at line 120. If you had the opportunity to question Youngworth and Connor, what would you ask?

_____

_____

_____

_____

FLUENCY

Read the boxed passage aloud as though you were a newscaster reporting the event. Strive for a rapid yet smooth delivery.

PREDICT

Do you think this mystery will ever be solved? Why or why not?

_____

_____

_____

_____

_____

_____

_____

_____

The Great American Art Heist

5 W-How?   Good research starts with good questions. Imagine you are investigating the art heist at the Gardner Museum. Think about the information you learned from the article. Then, using the investigation guide below, frame questions to shape your investigation.

A good way to frame questions is to ask **5 W-How?** questions. These questions ask *Who? What? When? Where? Why?* and *How?* Remember: You can ask more than one of each type of question. Some sample questions are filled in.

Investigation Guide	
Who?	Who were the guards on duty?
What?	What was stolen?
When?	
Where?	
Why?	
How?	

Standards Review

 **The Great American Art Heist**

Complete the sample test item below by circling the correct answer.
Then, read the explanation to the right.

Sample Test Item	Explanation of the Correct Answer
What is the topic of "The Great American Art Heist"? A the biggest art thefts ever B the art collector Isabella Gardner C preventing art heists D the art theft at the Gardner Museum	*D* is the correct answer. *A* is not correct because the article mentions no other major art thefts. *B* is not correct because Gardner is discussed but is not the focus. *C* is not correct because the article doesn't discuss in detail the prevention of art thefts.

DIRECTIONS: Circle the letter of each correct response.

1. Who was Isabella Gardner?

   A a famous painter

   B a suspected art thief

   C founder of an art museum

   D a police investigator

2. You learn that the burglars disabled the security system. Which of the following is a **relevant question** to ask?

   F How did the burglars know so much about the security system?

   G Where did they get their disguises?

   H Why did Vermeer produce only 32 paintings?

   J Why did the burglars leave a trail of paint chips behind?

3. Which of the following theories best explains why the thieves took some paintings and not others?

   A Dutch artist Rubens is now unpopular.

   B The museum's director lived above the museum.

   C The museum's layout is confusing.

   D An art collector wanted specific paintings.

4. According to one FBI supervisor, what one important question did the thieves forget to ask?

   F How much were the paintings worth?

   G Were the paintings insured?

   H Who is Billy Youngworth III?

   J Where did each painting hang?

Reading Standard 2.3
Generate relevant questions about readings on issues that can be researched.

Standards Review

 **The Great American Art Heist**

Multiple-Meaning Words

DIRECTIONS: Circle the answer in which the underlined word is used in the same way it is used in the passage from "The Great American Art Heist."

1. "The two imposters . . . then <u>disabled</u> the security system to prevent the alarms on individual paintings from going off. . . ."

   A The federal government has passed laws to protect the <u>disabled</u>.

   B The peasant became <u>disabled</u> when he stepped on a land mine.

   C The hacker <u>disabled</u> the computer system for the entire office.

   D The <u>disabled</u> athlete was unable to complete the Boston Marathon.

2. "They were frustrated by the special <u>bolts</u> that held these paintings on the wall. . . ."

   F The dogs howled as <u>bolts</u> of lightning flashed across the sky.

   G Sturdy <u>bolts</u> prevented the gate from opening in the wind.

   H The <u>bolts</u> of velvet came in fourteen different colors.

   J Jim <u>bolts</u> his lunch so he has time to play with friends.

3. "An ex-con named Billy Youngworth III, who had just been <u>arrested</u> on other charges. . . ."

   A Penicillin has <u>arrested</u> the spread of many diseases.

   B Her attention was <u>arrested</u> by the beautiful roses.

   C The blizzard <u>arrested</u> their passage over the mountain.

   D The police finally <u>arrested</u> the escaped convict.

4. "'They're just trying to keep their names in the <u>paper</u>.'"

   F The party hats were made of <u>paper</u>.

   G The sweater was so old it was <u>paper</u>-thin.

   H We get the <u>paper</u> delivered each day.

   J They decided to <u>paper</u> the neighborhood with fliers.

Reading Standard 1.1
Identify and use the literal and figurative meanings of words and understand word derivations.

 Before You Go On . . .

Check your Standards Mastery at the back of this book.

A Hill Reveals Its Secrets / D. H. Lawrence at Tarquinia / Protecting the Past

In these three articles, you'll read about the Etruscan (i·trus'kən) tombs of Tarquinia (tär·kwin'ē·ə), Italy, one of the most famous and ancient cemeteries in the world.

INFORMATIONAL FOCUS: MAGAZINE ARTICLES

Magazine articles are meant to teach as well as entertain. They deliver factual information about a topic, such as dates, quotations, and statistics. Articles also aim to engage the reader in the subject matter through photographs, illustrations, text features, and catchy graphics.

The three informational articles you're about to read are all on the same topic: the remarkable tombs of Tarquinia. As you read, look for—

- the **main idea** of each piece
- **details** that support the main idea
- **design features** like eye-catching type treatments, heads, and features
- **art and visuals** like photographs, charts, and illustrations

READING SKILLS: SYNTHESIZING SOURCES

When you **synthesize,** you pull together information on a topic from a variety of sources. Synthesizing, or connecting, the information helps you deepen your understanding of the subject. Here are guidelines for synthesizing sources:

- **Find the main ideas** and **supporting evidence,** such as facts, statistics, examples, anecdotes (brief stories about real people), or quotations.
- **Compare and contrast** the information in your sources. If any information is conflicting, do additional research to clear up the matter.
- **Connect to other sources.** Connect ideas to related topics and to other articles you've read. To make connections to other sources, gather together main ideas and supporting details in a chart like the one below. Then, use what you've learned to come to a **conclusion** about the topic.

Source 1	Source 2	Source 3
Main Ideas	**Main Ideas**	**Main Ideas**
Details	**Details**	**Details**
Synthesis, or Connecting Ideas		

Reading Standard 1.1 Identify and use the literal and figurative meanings of words and understand word derivations.

Reading Standard 2.4 Synthesize the content from several sources or works by a single author dealing with a single issue; paraphrase the ideas and connect them to other sources and related topics to demonstrate comprehension.

DRAW CONCLUSIONS

What is the purpose of the statement that appears below the article's title?

_____

_____

_____

_____

_____

IDENTIFY

Pause at line 7. What is the **main idea** of the first paragraph?

_____

_____

_____

_____

_____

WORD STUDY

Re-read lines 8–14. What do you think *decipher* (dē·sī′fər) means?

_____

_____

_____

_____

A Hill Reveals Its Secrets

R. Anthony Kugler

Not far from Rome, tombs long hidden from view tell of an advanced civilization that influenced even that of the mighty Romans.

On a hill called Monterozzi, just east of the little town of Tarquinia and an hour or so north of Rome, lies one of the most famous cemeteries in the world. It is perhaps more accurate to call it a necropolis (Greek for "city of the dead"), since what marks the site of Tarquinia are not the orderly rows of headstones we associate with cemeteries, but rather remarkable painted tombs carved out of rock as houses for the afterlife.

The builders of the tombs were a people called the Etruscans, and their influence over central Italy in the days
10 before the Romans was strong. We still know relatively little about them. Their language is difficult to decipher; their religious practices mysterious; and their origins unclear. Much of what we do know comes from their tomb paintings, at places such as Veii, Vulci, and Caere, but above all at Tarquinia.

Tombs for the Rich

Most of the paintings at Tarquinia were made within a span of roughly 350 years, from around 600 B.C. to around 250 B.C. Because no other Etruscan site offers such a long, unbroken series of paintings, archaeologists rely on Tarquinia for evidence

20 of shifting artistic styles and tastes. Many of the paintings depict celebrations, with large banquets, dancing, horse races, boxing matches, and other athletic events. Whether these were meant to represent the events of the funeral (many ancient peoples held funeral games at the death of an important individual), life in the afterworld, or simply some of the dead person's favorite activities is not always easy to tell. What is clear is that the kind of life these scenes depict was only for the wealthiest and most powerful Etruscans. Poor Etruscans did not leave painted tombs behind, and what they thought about life and death is a question

30 that remains to be answered.

The Romans borrowed many features of the Etruscan culture, particularly in the area of religion. Yet, even to them, the great painted tombs of Tarquinia were strange and mysterious—and even a little frightening. With the exception of the occasional grave robber or brave curiosity seeker, most people probably stayed away from the tombs, just as many people today avoid cemeteries. It was not until 1489, at the dawn of the period in history known as the Renaissance, when people throughout Europe were filled with a desire for new knowledge, that an

40 organized excavation of the tombs took place.

Answers in a Sketchbook

Since that time, thousands of people have made their way through the tombs, although not always gently. Early visitors, in particular, were not always careful to leave the tombs just as they had found them. Nevertheless, we have reason to be grateful to several early visitors, for their notes and sketchbooks often provide information no longer obtainable from the tombs themselves.

IDENTIFY

Locate and circle factual details in lines 16–17.

CLARIFY

Re-read lines 20–26. What two theories do researchers have about the purpose of the tomb paintings?

_____
_____
_____
_____
_____
_____
_____
_____
_____
_____
_____
_____

IDENTIFY

Underline the details in lines 26–30 that support the conclusion that the tombs of Tarquinia were only for the richest and most powerful Etruscans.

IDENTIFY CAUSE & EFFECT

Pause at line 40. Locate and underline what the writer says caused the organized excavation of the tombs.

IDENTIFY

Pause at line 55. Why are Byres's drawings from the 1780s so helpful to restorers today?

_____

_____

_____

_____

_____

IDENTIFY

Re-read the boxed feature above the photograph of the sculpture. What "stunned" researchers in the 1950s?

_____

_____

_____

INTERPRET

Photographs can provide information. What do you learn from the photo of this sculpture?

_____

_____

_____

_____

_____

_____

_____

_____

_____

50   For example, in the 1780s, an English traveler named James Byres sketched several tombs that have since disappeared, utterly destroyed by water or neglect. Byres's drawings are equally helpful for the tombs that remain, as all have suffered considerably since his time. Faced with the difficult task of redrawing a damaged figure or strengthening a faded line, restorers at Tarquinia often refer to Byres's sketches to make sure their work reflects the intent of the original artist.

DIG DATA:

The ancient hill still holds a number of surprises. In the 1950s, researchers were stunned when new surveying methods revealed thousands of tombs hidden on a hillside they thought they knew well. The continuing discovery of more advanced techniques brings new hope to restorers and archaeologists, both of whom share a single goal: to bring to light the magnificence of ancient Tarquinia.

60

D. H. Lawrence at Tarquinia

R. Anthony Kugler

The lamp begins to shine and smell, then to shine without smelling: the guide opens the iron gate, and we descend the steep steps down into the tomb. It seems a dark little hole underground: a dark little hole, after the sun of the upper world. But the guide's lamp begins to flare up, and we find ourselves in a little chamber in the rock…

With these words, published in 1932 in a book called *Etruscan Places*, the English writer D. H. Lawrence describes his first visit to a tomb at Tarquinia. The book is a wonderfully

10   detailed description of the Italian countryside and of the Etruscan sites Lawrence visited. However, the way he visited those sites, especially the tombs, seems terribly outdated today.

For Lawrence, as for many travelers of his time, visiting an archaeological site was a personal adventure, one for which you hired a private guide, packed a picnic lunch, and walked where you pleased. Pleasant as this may sound, Lawrence's approach is no longer practical today. If the tombs at Tarquinia are to be saved from the damage that Lawrence himself saw

20   and lamented, visitors must obey all the rules—that means visiting only with an official guide, taking no photographs, and respecting the antiquity and fragility of the ruins.

Read Lawrence's book, by all means, but please

30   don't use it as a guidebook to visiting Tarquinia.

Adriatic Sea

Tarquinia

Rome

ITALY

Mediterranean Sea

IDENTIFY

Pause at line 9. Underline the source for the quote at the beginning of this article.

IDENTIFY

What is the **main idea** of this article?

_____

_____

_____

_____

_____

SYNTHESIZE SOURCES

How is the focus of "A Hill Reveals Its Secrets" similar to and different from the focus of "D. H. Lawrence at Tarquinia"?

_____

_____

_____

_____

_____

_____

_____

_____

_____

IDENTIFY

Pause at line 14. What is the **main idea** presented in the first paragraph?

_____

_____

_____

_____

_____

_____

_____

_____

_____

_____

_____

_____

_____

PROTECTING THE PAST

R. Anthony Kugler

Ancient tomb artists did not paint with future visitors in mind. Today's conservators, on the other hand, must keep both the ancients and visitors in mind.

Have you ever been in an old, dark, unfinished basement, with damp walls of rough stone? Imagine how difficult it would be to preserve a priceless piece of ancient art—a marble statue, perhaps—in such conditions. Dirt, dust, and mildew would all be major concerns. Now imagine the same scene, but the artwork is not a statue but a painting created on those same wet
10   walls with the lightest, most delicate paints. Preservation would seem an almost impossible task. Yet, Italian experts and others working to save the irreplaceable Etruscan tomb paintings found at Tarquinia and other sites in the countryside north of Rome face similar situations every day.

OPENING A TOMB—WHAT'S THE HARM?

Dirt, dust, and mildew, however, are not the only concerns. There are other, man-made threats as well. These are far more serious, especially since their damage occurs more quickly than that caused by water and dirt. Air pollution from cars and power

20 plants, for example, attacks the plaster applied to the tomb walls before painting and causes it to crumble. The greatest danger to tomb paintings, however, may come from their admirers.

For example, when tourists anxious for a glimpse of the Etruscan "Tomb of Hunting and Fishing" enter the small room, their breath and body heat quickly change the climate inside. Such rapid temperature changes cause the paint to separate from the plaster. Just minutes later, as these same tourists head to the next tomb, a few more flakes of ancient paint fall to the floor. Thus, the fame of Etruscan paintings has become their

30 worst enemy.

STAY OR LEAVE?

Restorers take special care to alter as little as possible the artwork and its surroundings. If a painting can be left in the tomb with a simple chemical coating to protect it, that is almost always the preferred method. In many cases, however, the damage has already gone too far, and the painting must be removed to a museum.

Removing a thin sliver of painted plaster from an ancient tomb is a delicate and dangerous job. One method, called *strappo*,

40 involves gluing a thick sheet of canvas to the front of the painting and then pulling it off slowly and carefully. As the canvas is removed, it brings with it the topmost layer of paint and plaster, revealing the image in reverse. Strappo is not a perfect method, but in skilled hands, it has saved hundreds of Etruscan paintings from the decay that increasingly threatens them.

IDENTIFY

Re-read lines 15–30. Underline the factors that contribute to the decay of the tombs. Circle the detail that supports the conclusion that "the greatest danger to tomb paintings, however, may come from their admirers."

IDENTIFY CAUSE & EFFECT

Re-read lines 32–37. Why must the tomb paintings sometimes be removed to museums? Underline the reason.

PARAPHRASE

Paraphrase how the *strappo* method works (lines 38–45).

_____
_____
_____
_____
_____
_____
_____
_____
_____
_____
_____
_____

A Hill Reveals Its Secrets / D. H. Lawrence at Tarquinia / Protecting the Past

Synthesizing Sources In the chart below, list the main ideas and supporting details from the three articles you have just read. In the lines below the chart, **synthesize** the information from all three sources into one overall **conclusion**.

Source	Main Idea	Supporting Evidence
"A Hill Reveals Its Secrets"		
"D. H. Lawrence at Tarquinia"		
"Protecting the Past"		

Synthesis:

_____

_____

_____

Standards Review

TestPractice

A Hill Reveals Its Secrets / D. H. Lawrence at Tarquinia / Protecting the Past

Complete the sample test item below by circling the correct answer. Then, read the explanation to the right.

Sample Test Item	Explanation of the Correct Answer
The three articles all agree that the tombs of Tarquinia are— **A** best preserved using the *strappo* technique **B** famous because of D.H. Lawrence. **C** where poor Etruscans buried their dead **D** decaying and need to be preserved	*D* is the correct answer. Only "Protecting the Past" mentions the *strappo* technique, so *A* is incorrect. *B* is incorrect because the tombs were famous well before Lawrence's visit. *C* is not correct because "A Hill Reveals Its Secrets" states that only the rich were entombed at Tarquinia.

DIRECTIONS: Circle the letter of the correct answer for each item below.

1. What do you learn about the Etruscans in "A Hill Reveals Its Secrets"?

    A The wealthy were buried in painted rock-carved tombs.

    B They were better than Greeks at tomb building.

    C Much is known about their lives.

    D They preserved their tombs using *strappo*.

2. "D. H. Lawrence at Tarquinia" differs from the other two articles in that it describes the—

    F *strappo* technique

    G visit of a famous author

    H origins of the tombs

    J destruction of the tombs

3. Which article(s) might you cite in a research report on techniques for removing paintings from plaster?

    A "A Hill Reveals Its Secrets"

    B "D. H. Lawrence at Tarquinia"

    C "Protecting the Past"

    D all three articles

4. Which is the best **synthesis** of the ideas in the three articles?

    F We don't know much about the ancient Etruscans.

    G It is important to preserve the tombs at Tarquinia.

    H Tombs are easily destroyed.

    J Famous writers should stop destroying tombs.

Reading Standard 2.4 Synthesize the content from several sources or works by a single author dealing with a single issue; paraphrase the ideas and connect them to other sources and related topics to demonstrate comprehension.

Standards Review

A Hill Reveals Its Secrets / D. H. Lawrence at Tarquinia / Protecting the Past

Word Origins

Many English words contain parts, or **roots**, that come from ancient Greek and Latin. For example, the word *necropolis* is made up of two Greek root words—*nekros,* meaning "dead body," and *polis,* meaning "city." So *necropolis* literally means "city of the dead," in other words, a cemetery. Knowing what a root word means can help you figure out the meaning of other words that come from the same or similar roots.

Below are some Greek and Latin roots or root words and their definitions.

akro	Greek, meaning "at the top"
polis	Greek, meaning "city"
manus	Latin, meaning "hand"
fin	Latin, meaning "end"
port	Latin, meaning "carry"

DIRECTIONS: Using the list above, circle the letter of the correct definition for each word.

1. **acropolis**

   A   waterway

   B   high city

   C   police force

   D   mountainside

2. **finale**

   F   fishing

   G   fortunate

   H   ending

   J   complication

3. **portable**

   A   transparent

   B   troublesome

   C   capable

   D   carryable

4. **manuscript**

   F   handwriting

   G   parchment

   H   directions

   J   briefcase

Reading Standard 1.1
Identify and use the literal and figurative meanings of words and understand word derivations.

Before You Go On ...

Check your Standards Mastery at the back of this book.

What we know about dinosaurs comes largely from the fossil remains unearthed millions of years after the last dinosaur died. In the first article that follows, you'll learn of the best T. Rex specimen found to date and why that discovery is so remarkable. Then, in the second article, you'll learn about the challenges faced by scientists who work with plant and animal fossils.

INFORMATIONAL FOCUS: SCIENTIFIC WRITING

Articles about science mainly focus on explaining new developments, new discoveries, new research strategies, and so on. Scientific writing is based on **facts**—information that can be proved correct. Science articles usually zero in on a single topic; for example, space rocks, whale migration patterns, or volcanic activity in Mexico. The writers then explore several aspects of the topic and give supporting details that help explain those aspects.

Most science articles contain the following:
- Statistics, data, or other provable facts
- Specialized vocabulary related to science
- Visual aids, such as illustrations, charts, graphs, or photographs
- Captions that explain the visual aids

READING SKILLS: IDENTIFY AND ELABORATE ON MAIN IDEAS

The articles you are about to read contain information on fossils. To get the most out of the texts, pause occasionally as you read to **identify the main idea of a passage**—the main message or insight the author is trying to convey.

To identify a **main idea**—
- Pause at the end of each paragraph or section.
- Look for key statements that express the writer's opinion.
- Decide what is the main idea and what are supporting details.
- State the main idea in your own words.

Once you identify a main idea, **elaborate** on it. To elaborate on an idea—
- Connect the main idea to your own prior knowledge.
- Formulate questions you may still have.
- Do further research, or develop your own opinions about the subject.

Reading Standard 1.3 (Grade 8 Review) Use word meanings within the appropriate context and show ability to verify those meanings by definition, restatement, example, comparison, or contrast.

Reading Standard 2.5 Extend ideas presented in primary or secondary sources through original analysis, evaluation, and elaboration.

PREDICT

Read the title of the article. What do you think the article will be about?

_____

_____

_____

_____

IDENTIFY & ELABORATE

Re-read lines 6–14. This passage is about Tyrannosaurus Rex dinosaurs. What do you already know about dinosaurs and the Tyrannosaurus Rex?

_____

_____

_____

_____

WORD STUDY

Vertebrae (vʉr′tə·brā), in line 19, is a scientific term for "backbones."

IDENTIFY

Read on to line 25. What did Susan Hendrickson find?

_____

_____

_____

_____

_____

You Too Could Find a Dinosaur

John Shepler

Something was bothering Susan Hendrickson that misty morning of August 12, 1990. She sensed that something, perhaps someone, important was waiting for her on the barren cliff face three miles from camp. So, she passed on a trip to town and headed off on a prospecting walk with her dog, Gypsy.

Susan is a fossil collector. Her job is to find and recover the bones of ancient animals or impressions of shells and ferns cast in fine detail within the rocks of north-central South Dakota. Her colleagues at the Black Hills Institute of Geological Research
10 then prepare and sell the fossil specimens to museums, professional researchers and collectors around the world. There's always an element of thrill in each find, no matter how small. But there's also the possibility of finding something big, perhaps as big and rare as a Tyrannosaurus Rex dinosaur.

Susan's hunch was right. There were bones, huge bones sticking out of that unexplored cliff face. They'd been weathering out for almost a hundred years, and some were literally dropping out of the rock and onto the ground. Most impressive was a string of vertebrae going right into the hill. Susan grabbed
20 a couple of fragments of vertebrae and carried them to the site

where her boss and president of the institute, Peter Larson, was excavating a partial Triceratops skull. When Peter looked at them, he knew immediately what they had found. The bones of carnivorous dinosaurs are unique in their sponge-like construction, and these were certainly the dorsal vertebrae of T. Rex.

Tyrannosaurus Rex is famous as the giant flesh-ripping "thunder lizard" of *Jurassic Park*. There must have been millions of them prowling the dense forests of the Late Cretaceous Period, some 70 million years ago. Yet only 25 skeletons of

30 Tyrannosaurus Rex have ever been found and only one of those by a professional research scientist. All the rest have been spotted by keen observers, enthusiasts and collectors who were in the right place at the right time to catch them as they re-emerged from the rocks and into the eroding sun and wind.

That's important, because fossils start to disintegrate almost immediately after they lose the protection of the rocks that have encased them for tens of millions of years. "Science depends on amateurs," I hear Peter Larson say, as he spoke at the opening of the new Robert Solem Wing of Burpee Museum of Natural

40 History here in Rockford, Illinois. There are simply not enough professionals to cover the territory.

Susan Hendrickson found the best Tyrannosaurus Rex specimen yet. Peter Larson quickly named it Sue, after its discoverer. Only later, when the pelvic bones had been recovered and examined, did they find that Sue was indeed a female dinosaur. That was just the beginning of what they learned. Sue clearly had broken a leg, but that is not how she died. The leg had healed during a long period of convalescence, where her survival had almost certainly depended upon the long-term care provid-

50 ed by her mate. It is likely that T. Rex, for all its infamy, was both monogamous and nurturing.

These are the little pieces of the puzzle that come from studying bones, footprints, and impressions of leaves— even the contents of dino droppings that reveal what was on the menu in

WORD STUDY

Dorsal, in line 25, is an adjective that means "relating to the back."

IDENTIFY & ELABORATE

Find the **main idea** in lines 26–34. What can you add to this idea?

_____

_____

_____

_____

_____

_____

_____

_____

IDENTIFY CAUSE & EFFECT

Underline the sentence in lines 37–41 that tells why amateur fossil hunters are important.

IDENTIFY

Re-read lines 45–51. Underline at least three things the scientists learned from Sue's pelvic bones. Circle the **conclusion** the scientists drew from their observations.

IDENTIFY

Here, the writer expresses his beliefs. What **opinion** does he convey in lines 56–58? Underline it.

IDENTIFY & ELABORATE

Underline the three types of amateur scientist the writer mentions in lines 59–65. Do you or does anyone you know have an interest in these fields? Explain.

_____

_____

IDENTIFY CAUSE & EFFECT

Pause at line 77. The writer read a book about science projects when he was ten years old. What effect did it have on his future?

_____

_____

_____

_____

INFER

What is the overall purpose of this article?

_____

_____

_____

_____

prehistoric times. As I watch the slides and listen to the enthusiasm of discovery in Peter Larson's voice, I can't help but think there is more opportunity for scientific discovery by people like ourselves than we can possibly imagine.

60 The need is there, too. Professional paleontologists can't possibly be everywhere and find everything. Amateur fossil hunters, with their boundless enthusiasm and thirst for weekend and summer adventures, will continue to find rare bones just around the next big rock. Amateur astronomers will continue to find new comets among the stars, as they peer through telescopes of their own making. Amateur radio operators have often been the first to pioneer new communications technologies such as long distance short wave radio, satellites, bouncing radio signals off the moon and meteor trails.

One of my most cherished books from childhood is *The*
70 *Scientific American Book of Projects for the Amateur Scientist* by C. L. Stong. I found it at the Museum of Science and Industry when I was 10 years old, and I pored over the chapters on digging archaeological ruins, forecasting the weather, detecting earthquakes, seeing atomic particle tracks and building computers that play games. Some of these led to science fair projects in high school and enthusiasm for a career in engineering. Part of science is learning, but a lot of it is just plain fun.

Perhaps you'll get the fossil hunting bug when you see Sue towering within the Field Museum of Natural History in
80 Chicago or just watching the preparation of the bones now underway. Perhaps you'll even have a dinosaur named after you, like Sue Hendrickson did. Perhaps you'll just enjoy collecting fossils and rocks on family outings or the beauty of the stars on a summer night. Maybe you'll embark on a learning expedition that will lead you to teach science or do research in a prestigious institution. There's so much science to go around . . . there's really more than enough for everyone.

The Dinosaurs Weren't Alone

from NOVA Online

Dinosaurs may have ruled the earth, but they were never alone on it. A colorful cast of characters, including pump-headed insects, gigantic amphibian reptiles and tiny woodland mammals, coexisted with dinosaurs throughout the Mesozoic age. Supporting this ancient ecosystem was an equally fascinating array of plants. "If we want to understand the environment dinosaurs came from and why they succeeded, we have to use all the information available to us," says Kevin Padian, professor of Integrative Biology at the University of California at Berkeley.

10   Richard Stucky of the Denver Museum of Natural History agrees. "We want to know what dinosaurs were like, how they interacted with one another and what kinds of communities they lived in. Studying the environment can give us important clues." But finding and piecing together these clues is tricky.

It is the rare living thing that becomes a fossil in death. The vast majority of organisms, whether they be plants, animals or

IDENTIFY

Pause at line 14. Like many **sources**, this article contains several viewpoints. Underline the names of the two experts quoted here.

IDENTIFY

Identify the **main idea** of the first paragraph.

_____

_____

_____

_____

_____

_____

IDENTIFY

Underline the sentence in lines 17–20 that tells what the rest of the article is about.

WORD STUDY

Underline *vertebrates* in line 22. Circle the **context clue** that tells you the meaning of this scientific word.

IDENTIFY

Pause at line 33. Identify the **main idea** of this paragraph.

_____

_____

_____

_____

_____

WORD STUDY

Underline the word *phytosaur* in line 38. Circle the **context clue** that tells you what it is.

IDENTIFY
CAUSE & EFFECT

Pause at line 50. According to Professor Padian, why did dinosaurs do "very well"?

_____

_____

_____

insects, simply decompose. But sometimes, if conditions are just right, an organism can be preserved for millions of years. Find out how some ancient organisms beat the clock—and what role

20   they may have played in the lives of the dinosaurs.

Animals

The first step towards fossilization for vertebrates, or animals with backbones, is rapid burial in sediment. One scenario might be a drowned animal that washes downstream and lodges into a riverbank, where it quickly becomes covered in sand or mud. The animal's soft parts, namely its flesh and organs, rot away, while sediments surround and protect the animal's hard parts—its bones and teeth. Over time, mineral-rich water percolates through the bones' tiny pores and, gradually, the

30   bones absorb these minerals and turn to stone. But this is only the beginning. For a fossil to survive through time, the surrounding rock must withstand the forces of erosion and tectonic activity as well.

The fossil record reveals that dinosaurs first appeared in the Triassic period, between 250 to 213 million years ago. It also reveals that the first turtle, the first salamander, and the first frog appeared in the Triassic, as did the first crocodilian reptile, the phytosaur. On land, mammals also made their debut during this period, in the form of small insect-and-seed-eating critters that

40   scurried around the forest underbrush. Knowing the vertebrate players is important, according to Kevin Padian, professor of Integrative Biology at the University of California at Berkeley, because it gives insight into how dinosaurs may have gotten their first toehold in their climb to supremacy. "It's pretty clear that the first dinosaurs weren't directly competing with other animals for food. Phytosaurs were in the water eating mainly fish and there were reptilian herbivores on land, like some of the aetosaurs. But early dinosaurs were small bipedal carnivores— meaning they had their hands free and ate meat. So they did

50   very well."

PLANTS

Figuring out the relationship between plants and dinosaurs can be revealing, but is difficult to do. The problem is not for a lack of specimens. Plant fossils easily outnumber bone fossils, and they come in many more forms. The billions and billions of tons of coal in the world are ancient plant remains, as are compressed leaves, leaf imprints, pollen grains and pieces of fossilized wood. The difficulty is that bone fossils and plant fossils are rarely found at the same site. "It has to do with the chemical

60 conditions that favor preservation of bones as opposed to those that favor the preservation of plant matter," explains Scott Wing, Curator in the Department of Paleobiology at the Smithsonian's Museum of Natural History. "Plant matter is preserved best in an acidic environment, like in a peat bog. Whereas bones, having a lot of calcium in them, are essentially demineralized by acidic conditions. If you drop a bone in a bog, it gets rubbery, loses its calcium and it's difficult for it to be preserved. Conversely, if you take a piece of plant and drop it in a nice alkaline soil where a bone would likely be preserved, the plant is going to be degrad-

70 ed, not only by the chemical conditions, but also by all organisms that live in the soil."

Despite this wrinkle, plant groups of the Mesozoic are well known. The major players were conifers, a tree similar to today's Norfolk Island Pines; cycads, a palm-like tree with leathery leaves and great big cones that still grow in some tropical areas; bennettitales, a wholly extinct group of plants that had leaves like cycads, but were more closely related to flowering plants; and ferns, which were more varied and abundant than they are today. Flowering plants, or angiosperms, first appeared near the

80 end of the Mesozoic, around 144 million years ago, and quickly took hold, constituting nine-tenths of all known plant species by the end of the period. Grass, so common today, was completely nonexistent.

IDENTIFY

Re-read lines 52–59. Underline the reason it is difficult to understand the relationship between plants and dinosaurs. Then, read on and circle the place that plant matter is best preserved. Where is bone best preserved? Circle it.

EVALUATE

Pause at line 71. How can you tell that the support for the main idea of this paragraph is valid or trustworthy?

WORD STUDY

Circle the scientific terms in lines 76 and 79. Then, underline context clues that define them.

Notes

Extrapolate (ek·strap′ə·lāt), in line 97, is a verb meaning "draw a conclusion based on facts and/or observances."

Albeit (ôl·bē′it), in line 99, comes from the Middle English *al be it* (al[though] it be). The word means "although."

Think about the information given in this article. Describe the article's purpose.

_____

_____

_____

_____

_____

_____

_____

_____

If plant fossils and dinosaur fossils tend to avoid one another, how *do* paleontologists answer questions like, "What did herbivorous dinosaurs eat?" "You use some manner of correlation," explains Peter Dodson, Professor of Anatomy in Geology, at the University of Pennsylvania. "Some of the large, important fossil deposits of the American and Canadian west

90 are geographically quite widespread. So you find bones and skeletons in one place and maybe a few miles away you find rich plant deposits. You build up a picture from all the material that's available from different geographical localities." Richard Stucky, Curator of Paleontology at the Denver Museum of Natural History, agrees. "Oftentimes you get sites with specimens above and below the time period you're looking at and you can extrapolate that a particular critter or plant lived through the period you're interested in."

Another source of information on dinosaur diets, albeit a

100 rare one, is coprolite, or fossilized dung. "Coprolites give information about what one particular individual was eating, but you don't usually know what genus or even what species was producing the coprolite unless you find it inside a dinosaur skeleton," explains Scott Wing. "In general, it's a pretty speculative endeavor. You've got your plant fossils and you've got your dinosaur fossils—and they're often not from the same places or even from the same times. We can track changes in plants through time and we can track changes in dinosaurs through time, but we don't have any very good way of establishing cause

110 and effect. So the real answer to 'What did dinosaurs eat?' is that, most of the time, we don't know."

You Too Could Find a Dinosaur / The Dinosaurs Weren't Alone

Analysis, Evaluation, and Elaboration Grid The articles "You Too Could Find a Dinosaur" and "The Dinosaurs Weren't Alone" are about prehistoric plants and dinosaurs. Fill in the chart below to help you analyze, evaluate, and elaborate on these sources. Use details from the texts.

- **Analyze:** What is the main idea of each article?

- **Evaluate:** Has the writer provided adequate evidence?

- **Elaborate:** What information could you add?

	You Too Could Find a Dinosaur	The Dinosaurs Weren't Alone
ANALYZE		
EVALUATE		
ELABORATE		

Standards Review

Test Practice

You Too Could Find a Dinosaur / The Dinosaurs Weren't Alone

Improve your test-taking skills by completing the sample test item below. Then, check your answer, and read the explanation that appears in the right-hand column.

Sample Test Item	Explanation of the Correct Answer
"You Too Could Find a Dinosaur" describes— A Susan Hendrickson's discovery B Tyrannosaurus Rex's meals C Peter Larson's background D the writer's own discoveries	The correct answer is *A*. Although the article mentions that T. Rex was a meat-eater, the article does not describe its meals (*B*). The article does not describe Peter Larson's background (*C*) or the writer's discoveries (*D*).

DIRECTIONS: Circle the letter of each correct response.

1. One **main idea** of "You Too Could Find a Dinosaur" is that —

   A nobody cares about fossils

   B many amateurs have found important fossils

   C people carelessly destroy fossils

   D amateurs should never touch fossils

2. The author's purpose in writing "You Too Could Find a Dinosaur" was probably to —

   F inform people about the importance of fossils

   G get more funding for research

   H interest amateurs in making scientific discoveries

   J persuade people to get advanced degrees in paleontology

3. "The Dinosaurs Weren't Alone" is an example of —

   A scientific writing

   B a persuasive essay

   C a humorous story

   D a political commentary

4. According to "The Dinosaurs Weren't Alone"—

   F scientists know everything that dinosaurs ate

   G all dinosaurs ate the same thing

   H plant and animal fossils can be found together

   J scientists don't really know what dinosaurs ate

Reading Standard 2.5 Extend ideas presented in primary or secondary sources through original analysis, evaluation, and elaboration.

Standards Review

 **TestPractice**

You Too Could Find a Dinosaur / The Dinosaurs Weren't Alone

Specialized Vocabulary

People engaged in a particular activity or occupation often use specialized vocabulary. This language helps people in a field like science communicate with each other, but it can be hard for people outside the field to understand. Many articles about scientific topics—especially when the information is technical—contain specialized vocabulary.

In the following sentence taken from "You Too Could Find a Dinosaur," notice the boldface word:

> Her job is to find and recover . . . **impressions** of shells and ferns cast in fine detail within the rocks of north-central South Dakota.

The context clue "cast in fine detail within the rocks" tells you that the definition of *impressions* is "indentations or prints found in rocks."

DIRECTIONS: Use context clues to figure out the meaning of specialized vocabulary. Circle the letter of the best answer.

> **Reading Standard 1.3 (Grade 8 Review)** Use word meanings within the appropriate context and show ability to verify those meanings by definition, restatement, example, comparison, or contrast.

1. The bones of **carnivorous,** or meat-eating, dinosaurs have a sponge-like construction. Carnivorous dinosaurs ate—

   A sponges   C animals

   B plants   D bones

2. The fossilized backbones, or **vertebrae,** suggest that the dinosaur walked upright on two legs. Vertebrae are bones in the—

   F spine   H head

   G feet   J chest

3. The **astronomers** were delighted that the night was clear, perfect for peering at the sky through telescopes. Astronomers study—

   A weather   C oceans

   B planets and stars   D volcanoes

4. The team of archaeologists was **excavating** a site, digging though layer after layer of rubble and rock. *Excavating* means—

   F climbing   H locating

   G burying   J uncovering

 Before You Go On . . .

Check your Standards Mastery at the back of this book.

What Caffeine Does to You by Kerry George

Like most people, you've probably read your share of advice articles. You've read about what you should and should not eat, drink, wear, and watch. Why do you forget most of these articles, while a few stick with you? It is the power of an author's argument that makes an article convincing.

INFORMATIONAL FOCUS: ARGUMENT

A **claim** is the position a writer takes on an issue. A writer creates an **argument**, a series of persuasive details, to support his or her claim. The writer of the article you are about to read thinks that too much caffeine is unhealthy. She presents a series of details, or evidence, to defend this claim.

An argument usually consists of a mixture of logical and emotional appeals: It appeals to both our hearts and our minds. Writers build **logical appeals** by presenting facts and statistics. Writers create **emotional appeals** through the use of loaded words and their **tone,** or attitude. If you find that a piece of writing relies mainly on emotional appeals, the writer is probably unable to support his or her argument with hard evidence.

Generalizations are broad statements about something or someone. Some generalizations can be supported, but others are unfair statements that reflect bias or unsound thinking.

- As you read, consider and identify the writer's argument. What is the point he or she is making?
- Distinguish between logical and emotional appeals as you evaluate the writer's evidence.
- Identify generalizations, and decide whether or not they are justified.

READING SKILLS: IDENTIFYING THE MAIN IDEA

"What Caffeine Does to You" is divided into sections. Each section contains a main idea and evidence that supports it. As you read, pause at the end of each section. Then, identify the main idea of the section, and state it in your own words.

To identify a main idea:
- Pause after each section.
- Look for key statements that express the writer's opinion.
- Identify details that support this main idea.
- State the main idea in your own words.

Reading Standard 1.1 Identify and use the literal and figurative meanings of words and understand word derivations.

Reading Standard 2.8 Evaluate the credibility of an author's argument or defense of a claim by critiquing the relationship between generalizations and evidence, the comprehensiveness of evidence, and the way in which the author's intent affects the structure and tone of the text (e.g., in professional journals, editorials, political speeches, primary source material).

WHAT CAFFEINE DOES TO YOU

Kerry George

It's 10 p.m. and you still haven't finished your homework. Your first reaction is to reach for another can of soda with caffeine. After all, you feel peppy and awake when you drink it. The problem is: Most Americans drink too much caffeine, and this can cause health problems. Although it's OK to have some caffeine, kids and teens reportedly have been drinking an average of more than 64 gallons of soda with caffeine a year.

WHAT IS CAFFEINE?

10   *Caffeine* (ka·fēn′) is a natural substance that is found in the leaves, seeds, or fruits of more than 60 kinds of plants. The four most common sources of caffeine are coffee beans, tea leaves, cacao, and kola nuts. These are used to make coffee, tea, chocolate (made from cacao), and cola drinks (made with kola nuts).

But caffeine is found in other foods, too. Because coffee is a popular flavor, it's added to foods such as ice cream, frozen yogurt, candies, cakes, cookies, and muffins. Caffeine also is added to pain relievers and some over-the-counter medicines.

With so many drinks and products containing caffeine, staying awake has never been so easy. What's the downside?
20   Some kids are paying the price for catching a caffeine buzz.

AN ADDICTIVE DRUG

Although caffeine is a natural substance, it is also the world's most popular drug. It's a drug because it affects the body's nervous system. Caffeine is a mild *stimulant* (stim′yoo·lənt), and this type of drug perks up your body and makes it react more quickly to things. Stimulants also keep you from feeling sleepy and tired.

But that's not all. Caffeine also increases the flow of blood in your veins. It may even increase the need for you to go to the bath-
30   room by making the kidneys, which produce urine, work harder. Because of this, caffeine can cause you to become *dehydrated* (dē·hī′drāt·əd), which means that your body gets weak from not

IDENTIFY

Subheads reveal the type of information contained in the passages that follow. Scan the subheads of this article. Under which subhead would you find advice on lowering your caffeine intake?

AUTHOR'S ARGUMENT

Pause at line 7. Circle the sentence that contains the **main idea.**

IDENTIFY

Re-read lines 12–17, and circle the types of food, drink, and other substances that may contain caffeine.

CLARIFY

In your own words, describe how caffeine affects the body (lines 24–27).

AUTHOR'S ARGUMENT

Logical appeals are based on facts. Underline the statements in lines 28–36 that are examples of logical appeals. How do these appeals support the author's argument?

_____

_____

_____

_____

_____

IDENTIFY CAUSE & EFFECT

Re-read lines 38–46, in which the writer presents a series of possible causes and effects. Circle each cause, and underline each effect.

AUTHOR'S ARGUMENT

A **generalization** is a broad statement. Locate the generalizations in lines 53–57, and underline them. Do you think these generalizations are too broad? What sort of facts might the writer have used to make the same point?

_____

_____

_____

_____

having enough water. On a hot day or after playing sports, you need to give your body fluids, such as water, in order to replace the water lost through sweating. Beverages containing caffeine make it harder for you to keep enough water in your body.

GETTING THE JITTERS

Usually when people first drink caffeine, they feel a burst of energy. But the effects don't last long. However, if you drink too much caffeine at one time, it can make you feel nervous or jumpy. Your hands may shake. You may feel like there's something you forgot to do. Too much caffeine before bedtime will make it hard to fall asleep. If you don't get enough sleep, you may not be able to pay attention in school the next day. Too much caffeine also can make you feel sick and anxious with stomachaches, headaches, and a racing heartbeat.

People differ greatly in how caffeine affects them. Some can drink several cups of soda with caffeine in an hour and feel no effects, while others will feel the effects of caffeine after one cup. On average, the smaller the person, the less caffeine is necessary to produce side effects. However, your caffeine sensitivity is most affected by the amount of caffeine you use.

It takes less caffeine to affect kids than it does an adult. Many kids are getting addicted to caffeine and don't even know it. This is because kids are bypassing milk in the cafeteria for cans of soda and are buying "big gulps" after school that contain huge amounts of caffeine.

If you begin to drink caffeine every day, you will usually need to drink that same amount of caffeine just to feel normal. Also, you can build up tolerance to caffeine just as you can with other drugs. This means you need more caffeine to get the same effect. And if caffeine users don't get their regular daily dose, watch out! People who are used to getting a certain amount of caffeine per day—and one day don't—may develop headaches, stomachaches, and feel sleepy or grumpy all day. These symptoms can happen within 12 to 24 hours of not having caffeine.

ARE YOU A CAFFEINE JUNKIE?

Although the effects of caffeine vary from person to person, experts agree that for most adults, drinking no more than
70   240 milligrams of caffeine per day generally doesn't cause any bad effects. But most preteens are smaller than adults. For them, 240 milligrams is too much.

It's important to limit the amount of caffeine you drink. If you really love soda, it is probably safe to drink about 100 milligrams of caffeine (that's about two cans of soda) a day without any side effects. But if you start to feel that you can't sit still, or if you can't sleep at night, stop drinking caffeine.

CUTTING OUT THE CAFFEINE

It's easy to cut the caffeine from your daily diet. Here are
80   some helpful suggestions:

- Read labels carefully. Look for the words "caffeine-free" to be sure of what you are getting. Approximately 75 percent of soft drinks consumed in the United States contain caffeine.

- In general, drink caffeine-free beverages instead of those with caffeine. Most clear sodas don't have caffeine. Other soda flavors such as orange or root beer are usually caffeine-free, but it's a good idea to check the label. Get creative with other drinks such as water, fruit juice, milk, decaffeinated iced tea, and herbal teas.

90   - If you need to cut back the amount of caffeine you drink, do so gradually to get your body accustomed to less.

- As you cut back, you may find yourself feeling tired. Your best bet is to get some exercise. If you're really tired, take a nap. Your energy levels will return to normal in a few days, after you've kicked the habit.

- Choose baked goods, ice cream, and candy that do not contain chocolate or coffee.

- Make sure you avoid caffeine before bedtime.

You can help the whole family cut down on caffeine. Ask
100 your parents and siblings to help you look for caffeine on the labels of medicines and foods.

INTERPRET

Circle the **loaded word** in the subhead in line 67. What kind of associations does the word bring to mind?

_____

_____

_____

_____

_____

_____

IDENTIFY

Pause at line 72. How much caffeine a day is "too much" for preteens? Circle the detail that tells you.

ANALYZE

Bulleted lists present information in clear, short chunks. Skim lines 81–98. What is the purpose of the list?

_____

_____

_____

_____

_____

_____

_____

What Caffeine Does to You

Argument-Evaluation Chart The writer of "What Caffeine Does to You" makes the claim that it's important to give up or limit caffeine. Evaluating an argument involves looking at the details that support the claim. To organize your ideas, complete this chart using examples from the text.

Claim	
Logical Appeals	
Emotional Appeals	
Generalizations	
Loaded Words	
My Evaluation	

Standards Review

 **TestPractice** : **What Caffeine Does to You**

Complete the sample test item below. Then, read the explanation at right.

Sample Test Item	Explanation of the Correct Answer
Which detail does *not* support the claim that caffeine is bad for you? **A** It affects the body's nervous system. **B** If you don't get your daily dose, you may feel ill or tired. **C** The body develops a tolerance for it, so you keep needing more. **D** It is found in many foods.	The correct answer is *D*. *A, B,* and *C* are factual details that strengthen the claim. *D* is also a factual statement, but it doesn't support the claim.

DIRECTIONS: Circle the letter of each correct response.

1. Which type of **text feature** does this article contain?

   A captions

   B footnotes

   C subheads

   D illustrations

2. An example of an **emotional appeal** from the article is—

   F "But caffeine is found in other foods, too."

   G "It's easy to cut the caffeine from your daily diet."

   H "As you cut back, you may find yourself feeling tired."

   J "Make sure you avoid caffeine before bedtime."

3. The **purpose** of this article is to persuade you to—

   A get enough sleep

   B choose soft drinks over coffee

   C consider cutting down on caffeine

   D get your family to read labels

4. An example of a **logical appeal** is—

   F "It's easy to cut the caffeine from your daily diet."

   G "Are you a caffeine junkie?"

   H "Caffeine is a natural substance that is found in . . . 60 kinds of plants."

   J "And if caffeine users don't get their regular daily dose, watch out!"

Reading Standard 2.8
Evaluate the credibility of an author's argument or defense of a claim by critiquing the relationship between generalizations and evidence, the comprehensiveness of evidence, and the way in which an author's intent affects the structure and tone of the text.

Standards Review

 **What Caffeine Does to You**

Mathematical Prefixes

"What Caffeine Does to You" is about the harm caffeine may do to your body. The writer of the article provides specific guidelines for limiting the amount of caffeine a person should have. Many words that convey amounts or measurements are formed with prefixes that indicate quantity. The chart below lists common prefixes you'll encounter in math and science class as well as at the grocery or computer store.

Prefix	Meaning and Origin	Example Words
deca–	ten; from Greek *deka*	decagram; decahedron
deci–	tenth; from Latin *decimus*	decimal; decimeter
centi–	hundred; from Latin *centum*	centimeter; centigram
milli–	thousandth; from Latin *mille*	milliliter; milligram
micro–	small; from Greek *mikros* or Latin *micro*	microscope; microcosm
mega–	large; from Greek *megas*	megabyte; megaphone

DIRECTIONS: Match each mathematical prefix with its definition and origin.

_____ 1. *centi–*   **a.** tenth; from Latin *decimus*

_____ 2. *mega–*   **b.** small; from Greek *mikros* or Latin *micro*

_____ 3. *deci–*   **c.** large; from Greek *megas*

_____ 4. *micro–*   **d.** thousandth; from Latin *mille*

_____ 5. *milli–*   **e.** hundred; from Latin *centum*

Reading Standard 1.1
Identify and use the literal and figurative meanings of words and understand word derivations.

Before You Go On...

Check your Standards Mastery at the back of this book.

380   Part 2   **Informational Materials**

Consumer, Workplace, and Public Documents

Academic Vocabulary

These are the terms you should know as you read
and analyze the selections that follow.

———————

Consumer documents Documents used in the selling and
buying of products. Many consumer documents, such
as warranties, protect the rights of the purchaser
and the seller. Other consumer documents include
advertisements, contracts, instruction manuals, and
product information.

Public documents Documents that inform the public.
Public documents are created by governmental,
social, religious, or news-gathering organizations.
They include safety information, government
regulations, schedules of events, explanations of
services, and newspaper items.

Workplace documents Documents used in offices,
factories, and other work sites to communicate
information. These include business letters,
contracts, instruction manuals, memorandums,
and safety information.

Technical documents Documents used to explain or
establish procedures for using technology, such as
mechanical, electronic, or digital products or
systems. Technical documents include how-to
instructions, installation instructions, and instructions on carrying out scientific procedures.

Functional documents Any documents prepared for a
specific function, such as consumer, public, workplace,
and technical documents.

For Further Information ...

● Be sure to see Chapter 12 in *Holt Literature
and Language Arts*, beginning on page 945.

Reading Standard 2.1
Analyze the structure and format of functional workplace documents, including the graphics and headers, and explain how authors use the features to achieve their purposes.

Reading Standard 2.2
Prepare a bibliography of reference materials for a report using a variety of consumer, workplace, and public documents.

Reading Standard 2.6
Demonstrate use of sophisticated learning tools by following technical directions (e.g., those found with graphic calculators and specialized software programs and in access guides to World Wide Web sites on the Internet).

Reading Standard 2.7
Critique the logic of functional documents by examining the sequence of information and procedures in anticipation of possible reader misunder-standings.

The Heimlich Maneuver

What do you do during an emergency on the job? How do you handle first aid? The following workplace document might be posted on a company bulletin board or in the medical office or placed in the server of a company's Web site. It also might appear in restaurants.

FOCUS: WORKPLACE DOCUMENT

The following document explains how to deal with one type of emergency. As with many workplace documents, it includes graphics that will help you follow the text:

- Boldface text calls out important information.
- A numbered list gives step-by-step instructions.
- A bulleted list presents specialized instructions.
- An illustration accompanies the text, demonstrating what to do.

TERMS TO KNOW

Boldface—a heavier, darker type.

Cross-reference—words, usually in parentheses, telling you to look at an illustration or at a different section of the text.

Graphics—visual materials that enhance the text, such as art, photos, drawings, and diagrams.

Figure—an illustration or diagram.

Format—the design of a document.

Header—a label or heading that begins a section of a document.

Point-by-point sequence—a sequence that states each point as a separate item, in no particular order.

Step-by-step sequence—a sequence that tells what to do first, second, third, and so on.

Reading Standard 2.1
Analyze the structure and format of functional workplace documents, including the graphics and headers, and explain how authors use the features to achieve their purposes.

The Heimlich Maneuver

Choking can be caused by food, drink, gum, or objects accidentally inhaled through the nose or mouth that block the airway to the lungs. If air is unable to reach the lungs, death may result. The Heimlich maneuver is one of the most effective ways to help a choking person. (See diagram.) *cross-reference*

1 **Make sure the victim is choking**. *bold* The victim will not be able to talk but will probably communicate through signs and actions, such as grabbing his or her throat. Get someone to call 911.

2 Stand behind the victim and put your arms around his or her abdomen.

3 Make a fist at the bottom of the victim's breastbone.

4 Push your fist upward into the victim's chest in a quick motion, putting pressure on the lungs. This will push air out of the lungs and into the windpipe, forcing the object to dislodge from the throat. *step by step*

5 Repeat the procedure. It may take many tries before you dislodge the object.

- **If the victim is pregnant or obese,** *bold* pressure should be directed to the chest instead of the abdomen.

- **If the victim is unconscious,** *bold* turn him or her onto the back. Put your hand against the victim's middle abdomen. Place your other hand on top, and push upward with a sharp thrust. Try to remove the obstruction with your fingers. If the victim stops breathing, begin artificial respiration.

- **If the victim is a child,** *bold* put the heel of your hand above the navel and well below the rib cage. Cover it with the other hand and push down with a sharp upward movement. The child should be on his or her back.

- **If the victim is a baby,** *bold* straddle the infant over your arm with its head lower than the torso. Hold the baby's jaw in your hand to support the head. Give four back blows between the shoulder blades to dislodge the foreign object.

Push upward into the chest

The Heimlich Maneuver

graphics figure

"Heimlich Maneuver" from *The Big Book of Life's Instructions,* edited by Sheree Bykofsky and Paul Fargis. Copyright © 1995 by **The Stonesong Press, Inc.** Reprinted by permission of the publisher.

PURPOSE

Read the first paragraph. Underline the sentence that explains the purpose for performing the Heimlich maneuver.

SEQUENCE

The first five steps are arranged in **step-by-step sequence.** What should you do before beginning the maneuver?

_____

_____

_____

TEXT FEATURES

What is the purpose of the illustration?

_____

_____

SEQUENCE

The bulleted steps are arranged in **point-by-point sequence.** Read these steps. Underline the special situations these steps refer to.

Standards Review

DOCUMENTS

TestPractice

The Heimlich Maneuver

Complete the sample test item below. The box at the right explains why three of these choices are not correct.

Sample Test Item	Explanation of the Correct Answer
The purpose of a **cross-reference** is to— A refer you to a different section of a document B show the different parts of an illustration C highlight important information D show the order of steps	The correct answer is A. Labels show the parts of illustrations, not cross-references, so B is incorrect. Information is highlighted by things such as color, typeface, and size, so C is incorrect. Usually numbers or letters show the order of steps, so D is incorrect.

DIRECTIONS: Circle the letter of the best response to each item.

1. The **cross-reference** to the illustration in this document appears in—

   A boldface

   B italics

   C parentheses

   D capitals

2. The first five steps of the maneuver are in **step-by-step sequence** because—

   F the steps may all be done at once

   G the steps must be done in the order listed

   H the steps can be done in any order

   J the victim may be unable to count

3. You can find important information in the bulleted list quickly because—

   A it is numbered

   B it is printed in boldface

   C it is in parentheses

   D it is underlined

4. The **graphic** in this chart is placed—

   F at the most attractive point

   G near the steps it refers to

   H at the end of the steps

   J in the middle of the steps

Tools of the Trade *from* **The Newspaper Designer's Handbook**

Almost any kind of machine, from computers to waffle makers, comes with technical directions. These instructions for operating the equipment can be very complicated. Practice in reading technical directions can be helpful. Take a look, for instance, at "Tools of the Trade." It explains how computers are used in putting a newspaper together, provides photographs of important computer accessories, and gives step-by-step instructions for formatting a disk.

FOCUS: TECHNICAL DOCUMENT

The following article is from a handbook for newspaper designers. It presents information on workplace tools—including computers—and how to use them. Look for these graphic features, which will help you find the information you need:

- Photographs of computer equipment accompany the text.
- Boldface headers and italic captions clearly identify each type of equipment and describe its function.
- Numbered lists provide step-by-step instructions for formatting a disk.

TERMS TO KNOW

Bullets—dots, diamonds, squares, or other shapes used to introduce lists in point-by-point order.

Caption—text that labels, explains, or describes an illustration, diagram, or photograph.

Figure—an illustration or diagram, often numbered.

Format—the design or layout of a document.

Graphic—any visual device used to illustrate, demonstrate, or highlight the text.

Header—a label or heading that begins a section of a document.

Point-by-point sequence—a sequence that states each point in no particular order.

Step-by-step sequence—a sequence that tells what to do first, second, third, and so on.

Reading Standard 2.6 Demonstrate use of sophisticated learning tools by following technical directions (e.g., those found with graphic calculators and specialized software programs and in access guides to World Wide Web sites on the Internet).

Read the first paragraph.
What kind of information is
given in parentheses?

*It is telling you
what it was for*

Tools of the Trade

In the old days, page designers spent a lot of time drawing boxes (to show where photos went). And drawing lines (to show where text went). And drawing *more* boxes (for graphics and sidebars and logos).

Nowadays, most designers do their drawing on computers. But those old tools of the trade are still handy: pencils (for drawing lines), rulers (for measuring lines), calculators (for estimating the sizes of those lines and boxes), and our old favorite, the proportion wheel (to calculate the dimensions of boxes as they grow larger or smaller).

The electronic newsroom has arrived, however. So if you're serious about newspapering, get comfortable with computers. They're indispensable tools that improve performance and save time when it comes to:

- **Writing and editing stories.** Most newsrooms tossed out their typewriters years ago. Today, reporters and editors use computers to type, edit, file stories, fit headlines and search databases.

- **Producing photos.** Digital photography lets you adjust the size, shape, and quality of images electronically.

- **Pagination.** At most newspapers, pages are created electronically with desktop publishing software.

- **Creating illustrations and graphics.** With a good drawing program, it's easy to create full-color artwork in any style. And even if you're not an artist, you can still buy clip art or subscribe to wire services, which provide first-class graphics you can rework, resize, or simply store in an electronic archive for later use.

Some of the computer accessories newspaper people use are shown on the opposite page.

TEXT FEATURES

What information do the **boldface bullets** and **headers** highlight?

*It takes you to
exactly what people
these days do or
use electronics
to do or achieve*

Computer Accessories

Floppy disks and CDs:
Information can be stored in a computer's internal memory drive, or it can be transported from computer to computer via portable disks. Floppy disks came first; they can hold a megabyte or two. Compact disks (CDs) are far more powerful, storing 600 megabytes of data—perfect for photos, video, and music.

Printer: *Once you design your news feature on the computer, how do you print the thing out? Many desktop publishers use laser printers like this one: high resolution devices that output near-typeset quality type and graphics.*

Scanner: *This device can capture photos or artwork electronically. It scans images like a photocopying machine, after which you can adjust their size, shape and exposure on your computer screen—avoiding the traditional darkroom altogether.*

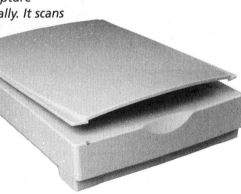

Modem: *A device that allows computers to communicate with each other and transmit data (text, images, page layouts) over telephone lines. Newer computers use their built-in modems to link users to electronic databases and information services.*

TEXT FEATURES

Scan this page. How do you know what each photograph shows you?

We usually see it everyday.

TEXT FEATURES

What kind of information is supplied in the captions to the photos?

It tells you what each item here does or how it works

It tells you that formatting might varie depending on what computer you have or how and when it is updated

Look at the numbered lists. What kind of sequence do these **technical directions** follow?

A numbered or chronological sequence, step by step

Before you can store your news story on a disk, you must format the disk, or prepare it to receive data. The following directions show how to accomplish this using a PC. Keep in mind, however, that operating systems are constantly being updated, so directions may vary slightly depending on the computer you're working on.

Formatting a Disk on a PC

If you have this type of computer, you can format a disk in two major ways.

Using DOS:

1. Turn on the computer.
2. Use the DOS commands when your screen displays the C prompt (C:\ or C:\>).
3. If Windows loads automatically when you turn on your computer, you can get back to the C prompt by double-clicking with the mouse or highlighting the arrow keys and pressing ENTER on the MS-DOS icon on the Main Windows window.
4. Insert a disk in Drive A to start formatting.

Using Format Disk Command:

1. Turn on the computer.
2. Insert a disk in Drive A.
3. Double-click on the File Manager icon, which will display the File Manager window on the screen.
4. Click and hold on Disk at the very top of the File Manager window.
5. Move the mouse's arrow down to the Format disk.
6. Release the mouse's button.
7. A Format Disk window will appear on the screen.
8. If it doesn't say Drive A, click on the arrow next to the Disk In Box.
9. Click on OK to start formatting.

 **Tools of the Trade**

Complete the sample test item below. The box at the right explains why three of these choices are not correct.

Sample Test Item	Explanation of the Correct Answer
In this article, **bullets** are used to— A introduce captions B show items in list form C refer you to the illustrations D list steps in the correct order	The correct answer is *B*. The captions are introduced by bold-face headers, so *A* is incorrect. *C* is incorrect because the bullets are not related to the illustrations. Bullets are used to show items in list form, but not in any particular order; therefore, *D* is incorrect.

DIRECTIONS: Circle the letter of the best response for each item.

1. Which **text feature** is *not* used to explain the illustrations?

   A boldface

   B italics

   C captions

   D numbers

2. Which part of the article involves **technical directions**?

   F the photos of tools of the trade

   G the section on formatting a disk

   H the list of how computers can be used

   J the captions for the illustrations

3. The technical directions are given in—

   A a bulleted list

   B a cross-reference

   C a caption

   D a numbered list

4. What **technical direction** is the same for the two methods of formatting a disk?

   F Turn on the computer.

   G Use the DOS commands.

   H Release the mouse's button.

   J Click on OK to start formatting.

Reading Standard 2.6 Demonstrate use of sophisticated learning tools by following technical directions (e.g., those found with graphic calculators and specialized software programs and in access guides to World Wide Web sites on the Internet).

Earthquake: Duck, Cover & Hold

We've all known the frustration that comes from trying to follow procedures that are poorly written. Unclear writing can lead to confusion and frustration. The following tips on earthquake preparedness are meant to be easily grasped and understood. Do they seem clear and logical to you?

FOCUS: FUNCTIONAL DOCUMENT

The following functional document explains what to do in the event of an earthquake.

- To make the information clear and accessible, a variety of text features are used, such as boldface headers; different kinds of type; bulleted lists; and checklists.
- Information is presented in the logical sequence most appropriate for understanding, such as **step-by-step** or **point-by-point sequence.**
- International **symbols** accompany the text to show clearly what to do.

TERMS TO KNOW

International symbols—symbols used in directions that can be recognized worldwide.

Logo—a graphic form of a name or phrase.

Logical sequence—a sequence that makes sense.

Chronological sequence—a sequence in time order.

Point-by-point sequence—a sequence that states each point in no particular order.

Step-by-step sequence—a sequence that tells what to do first, second, third, and so on.

Reading Standard 2.7
Critique the logic of functional documents by examining the sequence of information and procedures in anticipation of possible reader misunderstandings.

EARTHQUAKE:
Duck, Cover & Hold

No matter where you are, know how to protect yourself and your family during an earthquake. Practice taking cover as if there were an earthquake and learn the safest places in your home and work. Practice getting out of your home and check to see if the planned exits are clear and if they can become blocked in an earthquake. Practice turning off your electricity and water. Know how to turn off the gas, but do not practice this step. In the event of an earthquake, once you turn off your gas, only your utility company should turn it back on, for safety reasons.

10 ### TIPS

- When in a HIGH-RISE BUILDING, move against an interior wall if you are not near a desk or table. Protect your head and neck with your arms. Do not use the elevators.

- When OUTDOORS, move to a clear area away from trees, signs, buildings, or downed electrical wires and poles.

- When on a SIDEWALK NEAR BUILDINGS, duck into a doorway to protect yourself from falling bricks, glass, 20 plaster and other debris.

- When DRIVING, pull over to the side of the road and stop. Avoid overpasses and power lines. Stay inside your vehicle until the shaking stops.

- When in a CROWDED STORE OR OTHER PUBLIC PLACE, move away from display shelves containing objects that could fall. Do not rush for the exit.

- When in a STADIUM OR THEATER, stay in your seat, get below the level of the back seat and cover your head and neck with your arms.

From "Earthquake Preparedness Tips" from *California Governor's Office of Emergency Services* website, accessed February 12, 2002 at http://www.oes.ca.gov/CEPM2002.nsf/htmlmedia/body_directory.html. Reprinted by permission of the **California Governor's Office of Emergency Services.**

TEXT FEATURES

Locate and underline the subtitle of this article, which tells what to do during an earthquake. On page 392, circle where the information is repeated.

PURPOSE

What is the purpose of the first block of italic text?

It tells you to always be prepared for an earthquake

SEQUENCE

The bulleted tips are in a **point-by-point sequence.** What kind of information is highlighted by the words in capital, or uppercase, letters?

It tells you where you are to read this paragraph it tells you how to prepare at different locations of earthquakes

Duck

DUCK or DROP down on the floor.

Cover

Take COVER under a sturdy desk, table or other furniture. If that is not possible, seek cover against an interior wall and protect your head and neck with your arms. Avoid danger spots near windows, hanging objects, mirrors or tall furniture.

Hold

If you take cover under a sturdy piece of furniture, HOLD on to it and be prepared to move with it. Hold the position until the ground stops shaking and it is safe to move.

SEQUENCE

International symbols illustrate what to do in an earthquake. What kind of sequence do the symbols follow?

step by step
sequence

PURPOSE

Pause at line 33. Underline why it is helpful to know what causes earthquakes.

SEQUENCE

Number the paragraphs within lines 31–63. Why would it be confusing if paragraph 2 came *after* paragraph 3 instead of *before* it?

the ending of
P2 leads to P3

30 **EVER WONDER WHAT CAUSES EARTHQUAKES?**

31 P 1 It's probably not something you think about first when earthquakes are mentioned, but knowing what causes these shakers can help you understand your surroundings.

P 2 The earth is divided into three main layers—a hard outer crust, a soft middle layer and a center core. The outer crust is broken into massive, irregular pieces called "plates." These plates have been moving very slowly for billions of years, driven by energy forces deep within the earth. It is this movement that has shaped the physical features of the earth—mountains, valleys,

40 plains and plateaus. Earthquakes occur when these moving plates grind and scrape against each other.

P 3 In California, two of these plates meet: the Pacific Plate and the North American Plate. The Pacific Plate covers most of the Pacific Ocean floor and the California coastline. The North American Plate stretches across the North American continent and parts of the Atlantic Ocean. The primary boundary between them is the San Andreas fault. It is more than 650 miles long and extends 10 miles deep. Many smaller faults, such as the Hayward fault in the north and the San Jacinto fault in the

50 south, branch from the San Andreas fault. Experts suspect there are many other faults that haven't been discovered yet.

¶4 The Pacific Plate grinds northwestward past the North American Plate at a rate of about two inches per year. Parts of the San Andreas fault system adapt to this movement by a constant "creep" resulting in frequent, but moderate, earth tremors. In other areas, movement is not constant and strain can build up for hundreds of years, resulting in strong earthquakes when it's released.

¶5 Unlike other natural disasters, there is no warning for
60 earthquakes. One could hit today, tomorrow, or next week. Future earthquakes are a serious threat to Californians, who could face loss of life, injury and property damage. Consider the sizable damage caused by past quakes, shown in the box below.

SOME SIGNIFICANT CALIFORNIA EARTHQUAKES

Northridge, M6.7—January 17, 1994
57 deaths—more than 11,000 injuries—$40+ billion in damage

Landers, M7.3/**Big Bear,** M6.7—June 28, 1992
1 death—$93 million in damage

Humboldt County, M6.9—April 25, 1992
$60 million in damage

Sierra Madre, M5.8—June 28, 1991
1 death—over 30 injuries—$33.5 million in damage

Loma Prieta, M7.1—October 17, 1989
63 deaths—3,757 injuries, $5.9 billion in damage

Whittier-Narrows, M5.9—October 1, 1987
Aftershock, M5.3—October 4, 1987
8 deaths—200 injuries—$358 million in damage

Kern County, M7.7—July 21, 1952
12 deaths—18 injuries—$50 million in damage

San Francisco, M8.3—April 18, 1906
700–800 deaths—$400 million in damage

*M = Magnitude on the Richter scale.

SEQUENCE

What kind of sequence is the boxed information about earthquakes presented in?

point by point sequence

FORMAT

Pause at line 63. What does the **cross-reference** tell you?

It tells you to look at the box below

IDENTIFY

According to the boxed information, what earthquake was the worst in terms of fatalities?

700 - 800 deaths San Francisco

EMERGENCY SUPPLIES CHECKLIST

Stocking up now on emergency supplies <u>can add to your safety and comfort during and after an earthquake.</u> Store enough supplies for at least 72 hours.

ESSENTIALS

- ☐ Water – 1 gallon per person per day (a week's supply of water is preferable)
- ☐ Water purification kit
- ☐ First aid kit, freshly stocked
- ☐ First aid book
- ☐ Food
- ☐ Can opener (non-electric)
- ☐ Blankets or sleeping bags
- ☐ Portable radio, flashlight and spare batteries
- ☐ Essential medications
- ☐ Extra pair of eyeglasses
- ☐ Extra pair of house and car keys
- ☐ Fire extinguisher—A-B-C type
- ☐ Food, water and restraint (leash or carrier) for pets
- ☐ Cash and change

SANITATION SUPPLIES

- ☐ Large plastic trash bags for waste; tarps and rain ponchos
- ☐ Large trash cans
- ☐ Bar soap and liquid detergent
- ☐ Shampoo
- ☐ Toothpaste and toothbrushes
- ☐ Feminine hygiene supplies
- ☐ Toilet paper
- ☐ Household bleach

SAFETY AND COMFORT

- ☐ Sturdy shoes
- ☐ Heavy gloves for clearing debris
- ☐ Candles and matches
- ☐ Light sticks
- ☐ Change of clothing
- ☐ Knife or razor blades
- ☐ Garden hose for siphoning and firefighting
- ☐ Tent
- ☐ Communication kit: paper, pens, stamps

COOKING

- ☐ Plastic knives, forks, spoons
- ☐ Paper plates and cups
- ☐ Paper towels
- ☐ Heavy-duty aluminum foil
- ☐ Camping stove for outdoor cooking (caution: before using fire to cook, make sure there are no gas leaks; never use charcoal indoors)

Ready To Ride It Out?

Standards Review

 **Earthquake: Duck, Cover & Hold**

Complete the sample test item below. The box at the right explains why three of these choices are not correct.

Sample Test Item	Explanation of the Correct Answer
The **international symbols** within the illustrations— **A** show what to do in an earthquake **B** show how much damage earth-quakes do **C** explain what causes earthquakes **D** illustrate the different supplies you will need	The correct answer is *A*. The symbols show how to duck, cover, and hold during an earthquake. No symbols are used to illustrate earth-quake damage, (*B*), the cause of earth-quakes, (*C*), or various supplies, (*D*).

DIRECTIONS: Circle the letter of the best response to each item.

1. Which of the following is presented in a **step-by-step sequence**?

   A the list of sanitation supplies

   B the list of important earthquakes

   C the process of duck, cover, and hold

   D the tips on what to do in different places

2. "Ever Wonder What Causes Earthquakes?" explains how—

   F the movement of plates can create earthquakes

   G San Francisco was destroyed in an earthquake

   H scientists measure earthquakes

   J we know an earthquake is coming

3. "Some Significant California Earthquakes" follows—

   A a point-by-point sequence

   B a step-by-step sequence

   C a chronological order

   D no particular order

4. The "Essentials" checklist is organized by—

   F order of importance

   G chronological order

   H order of easiest to find

   J alphabetical order

Reading Standard 2.7 Critique the logic of functional documents by examining the sequence of information and procedures in anticipation of possible reader misunder-standings.

Works Cited List: Earthquake Preparedness

BEFORE YOU READ

How to prepare for an earthquake is a serious topic. To find out more about it, you might want to do some research on the Internet. If you prepare a report on your research, you'll need to include a bibliography or *Works Cited* list.

FOCUS: DOCUMENTATION

- The following *Works Cited* is a listing of Internet resources on the topic of earthquake preparedness.
- The citations are listed in alphabetical order by author and title, following the style of the Modern Language Association.
- The electronic address (URL) is listed last in each citation.
- The date the Web site was accessed comes right before the URL.

TERMS TO KNOW

Bibliography—a list of sources of information on a subject, also called *Works Cited*.

Citation—an entry in a list of sources of information on a subject.

Database—a large collection of information stored in a computer, organized so that it can be expanded, updated, and retrieved rapidly for various uses.

Source—a book, document, or person that provides information.

URL—uniform resource locator, a site's Internet address.

b1. a
2 c
c3. a
b4. a
5. a
6. a
c7. b
8. a c
c9. b
b10 a
b11. c
c12 a
a 13 b
c 14 b
b 15. a
c 16. a

17. b
18 a
b19 c
b20. a
a21. c
c22. a
c 23 a
24. a

Reading Standard 2.2
Prepare a bibliography of reference materials for a report using a variety of consumer, workplace, and public documents.

Order in Which Information Is Presented in an Internet Citation

1. Author's Last Name [,] Author's First Name and Middle Initial (if given) [,] abbreviation such as Ed (if appropriate) [.]
2. ["] Title of Work Found in Online Scholarly Project, on Database or in Periodical ["] or ["] Title of Posting to Discussion List or Forum (taken from the subject line) [.] ["] Followed by the description Online posting [.]
3. Title of Book (underlined) [.]
4. The abbreviation Ed. followed by Name of Editor (if relevant and not cited earlier, as in Ed. Susan Smith) [.]
5. Publication information for any print version of the source: City of Publication [:] Name of Publisher [,] year of publication [.]
6. Title of Scholarly Project, Database, Magazine, Professional Site, or Personal Site (underlined) [.]
7. Name of Editor of Scholarly Project or Database (if available) [.]
8. Volume number, issue number, or other identifying number of the source (if available) [.]
9. Date of electronic publication, posting, or latest update (often found at the bottom of the site's home page)[.]
10. Name of Subscription Service [,] and, if a library, Name of Library [,] Name of City [,] and Abbreviation of State in which library is located [.]
11. For a posting to a discussion list or forum, Name of List or Forum [.]
12. If sections are numbered, number range or total number of pages, paragraphs, or other sections (if information is available) [.]
13. Name of Institution or Organization Sponsoring or Associated with the Web Site [.]
14. Date on which source was accessed [.]
15. [<] Electronic address (URL) of source [>] or, if a subscription service, [<] URL of service's main page (if known) [>] and [Keyword: Keyword Assigned by Service] or [Path: sequence of topics followed to reach the page cited, as in the first topic [;] second topic [;] third topic [;] and so on, ending with the page you are citing] [.]

WORKS CITED

American National Red Cross. "Earthquake," 2001. 14 Mar. 2002. <http://www.redcross.org/services/disaster/keepsafe/readyearth.html>

California Governor's Office of Emergency Services. "Earthquake Planners." Ready to Ride It Out? Earthquake Preparedness Resources 2000. 6 Mar. 2002 <http://www.oes.ca.gov/oeshomep.nsf/21c34a7f4ddb32098825645300503679/cc054ff97a8016598825644c0003d18f?OpenDocument>

Earthquake Safety Kit. "Full Product List." Earthquake Safety Kit. 14 Mar. 2002. <http://www.earthquakesafetykit.com/mof15/Full_Product_List/full_product_list.html>

Federal Emergency Management Agency. "Fact Sheet: Earthquakes." 10 Jan. 1998. Virtual Library and Electronic Reading Room. 6 Mar. 2002. <http://www.fema.gov/library/quakef.htm>

Global Earthquake Response Center. "Office Equipment." Catalogue. Global Earthquake Response Center. 14 Mar. 2002. <http://www.earthquake.com/catalog/WebMagic_Pro?page=../main.html&cart_id=>

Los Angeles City Fire Department. "The Earthquake Preparedness Handbook," 1997. 6 Mar. 2002. <http://www.lafd.org/eqindex.htm>

Teves, Oliver. "Strong Earthquake Rocks Southern Philippines, Causing Eight Deaths, Injuring 15 People." Associated Press. San Francisco Gate. 3/6/02 3:26 PST. 6 Mar. 2002. <http://www.sfgate.com/cgibin/article.cgi?file=/news/archive/2002/03/06/international0626EST0546.DTL>

TerBush Industries. "School Emergency Student Locator Signs." Advertisement. TerBush Industries. 14 Mar. 2002. <http://www.terbushind.com/MERCHANT2/merchant.mv?Screen=PROD&Store_Code=TI&Product_Code=SESLS&Category_Code=PF>

U.S. Geological Survey. "Earthquake Hazards Program," 2 Oct. 2000. 6 Mar. 2002. <http://quake.wr.usgs.gov/prepare/>

 **Works Cited List**

Complete the sample test item below. The box at the right explains why three of these choices are not correct.

Sample Test Item	Explanation of the Correct Answer
The first piece of information listed in a **bibliographic citation** is the— A title of the work B URL C author's last name D date of access	The correct answer is C. The title is listed second, unless there is no author, so A is incorrect. The URL is listed last, so B is incorrect. The date of access is listed before the URL, so D is incorrect.

DIRECTIONS: Circle the letter of the best response for each item.

1. In a *Works Cited* list, citations are listed—

   A by URL

   B by electronic publication date

   C by the date the article was accessed

   D alphabetically by author and title

2. In a citation, the date an article was accessed goes—

   F after the title of the work

   G before the author's name

   H after the URL

   J before the URL

3. Which of the following is *most* likely to be a **workplace document**?

   A Global Earthquake Response Center. "Office Equipment." Catalogue. Global Earthquake Response Center.

   B American National Red Cross. "Earthquake," 2001.

   C TerBush Industries. "School Emergency Student Locator Signs." Advertisement. TerBush Industries.

   D Teves, Oliver. "Strong Earthquake Rocks Southern Philippines, Causing Eight Deaths, Injuring 15 People." Associated Press. San Francisco Gate. 3/6/02 3:26 PST.

Reading Standard 2.2 Prepare a bibliography of reference materials for a report using a variety of consumer, workplace, and public documents.

Word List

Keep track of all the new words you have learned by filling out the following chart. Review these words from time to time to make sure they become part of your permanent vocabulary.

WORD	
DEFINITION: _____	
_____	

WORD	
DEFINITION: _____	
_____	

WORD	
DEFINITION: _____	
_____	

WORD	
DEFINITION: _____	
_____	

WORD	
DEFINITION: _____	
_____	

WORD	
DEFINITION: _____	
_____	

WORD	
DEFINITION: _____	
_____	

WORD	
DEFINITION: _____	
_____	

WORD	
DEFINITION: _____	
_____	

WORD	
DEFINITION: _____	
_____	

WORD	
DEFINITION: _____	
_____	

WORD	
DEFINITION: _____	
_____	

WORD

DEFINITION: _____
_____

WORD

DEFINITION: _____
_____

WORD

DEFINITION: _____
_____

WORD

DEFINITION: _____
_____

WORD

DEFINITION: _____
_____

WORD

DEFINITION: _____
_____

WORD

DEFINITION: _____
_____

WORD

DEFINITION: _____
_____

WORD

DEFINITION: _____
_____

WORD

DEFINITION: _____
_____

WORD

DEFINITION: _____
_____

WORD

DEFINITION: _____
_____

WORD

DEFINITION: _____
_____

WORD

DEFINITION: _____
_____

WORD

DEFINITION: _____

_____

WORD

DEFINITION: _____

_____

WORD

DEFINITION: _____

_____

WORD

DEFINITION: _____

_____

WORD

DEFINITION: _____

_____

WORD

DEFINITION: _____

_____

WORD

DEFINITION: _____

_____

WORD

DEFINITION: _____

_____

WORD

DEFINITION: _____

_____

WORD

DEFINITION: _____

_____

WORD

DEFINITION: _____

_____

WORD

DEFINITION: _____

_____

WORD

DEFINITION: _____

_____

WORD

DEFINITION: _____

_____

WORD		WORD
DEFINITION: _____		DEFINITION: _____
_____		_____

WORD		WORD
DEFINITION: _____		DEFINITION: _____
_____		_____

WORD		WORD
DEFINITION: _____		DEFINITION: _____
_____		_____

WORD		WORD
DEFINITION: _____		DEFINITION: _____
_____		_____

WORD		WORD
DEFINITION: _____		DEFINITION: _____
_____		_____

WORD		WORD
DEFINITION: _____		DEFINITION: _____
_____		_____

WORD		WORD
DEFINITION: _____		DEFINITION: _____
_____		_____

WORD

DEFINITION: _____

_____

WORD

DEFINITION: _____

_____

WORD

DEFINITION: _____

_____

WORD

DEFINITION: _____

_____

WORD

DEFINITION: _____

_____

WORD

DEFINITION: _____

_____

WORD

DEFINITION: _____

_____

WORD

DEFINITION: _____

_____

WORD

DEFINITION: _____

_____

WORD

DEFINITION: _____

_____

WORD

DEFINITION: _____

_____

WORD

DEFINITION: _____

_____

WORD

DEFINITION: _____

_____

WORD

DEFINITION: _____

_____

WORD

DEFINITION: _____
_____

WORD

DEFINITION: _____
_____

WORD

DEFINITION: _____
_____

WORD

DEFINITION: _____
_____

WORD

DEFINITION: _____
_____

WORD

DEFINITION: _____
_____

WORD

DEFINITION: _____
_____

WORD

DEFINITION: _____
_____

WORD

DEFINITION: _____
_____

WORD

DEFINITION: _____
_____

WORD

DEFINITION: _____
_____

WORD

DEFINITION: _____
_____

WORD

DEFINITION: _____
_____

WORD

DEFINITION: _____
_____

WORD		WORD	
DEFINITION:		DEFINITION:	

WORD		WORD	
DEFINITION:		DEFINITION:	

WORD		WORD	
DEFINITION:		DEFINITION:	

WORD		WORD	
DEFINITION:		DEFINITION:	

WORD		WORD	
DEFINITION:		DEFINITION:	

WORD		WORD	
DEFINITION:		DEFINITION:	

WORD		WORD	
DEFINITION:		DEFINITION:	

Checklist for Standards Mastery

Each time you read, you learn something new. Track your growth as a reader and your progress toward success by checking off skills you have acquired. You may want to use this checklist before you read a selection, to set a purpose for reading.

✓	California Reading Standard (Grade 8 Review)	Selection
☐	**1.1** Analyze idioms, analogies, metaphors, and similes to infer the literal and figurative meanings of phrases.	
☐	**1.2** Understand the most important points in the history of English language and use common word origins to determine the historical influences on English word meanings.	
☐	**1.3** Use word meanings within the appropriate context and show ability to verify those meanings by definition, restatement, example, comparison, or contrast.	
☐	**3.1** Determine and articulate the relationship between the purposes and characteristics of different forms of poetry (e.g., ballad, lyric, couplet, epic, elegy, ode, sonnet).	
☐	**3.3** Compare and contrast motivations and reactions of literary characters from different historical eras confronting similar situations or conflicts.	
☐	**3.4** Analyze the relevance of the setting (e.g., place, time, customs) to the mood, tone, and meaning of the text.	
☐	**3.7** Analyze a work of literature, showing how it reflects the heritage, traditions, attitudes, and beliefs of its author. (Biographical approach)	

✓	California Grade 9–10 Reading Standard	Selection
☐	**1.1** Identify and use the literal and figurative meanings of words and understand word derivations.	
☐	**1.2** Distinguish between the denotative and connotative meanings of words and interpret the connotative power of words.	
☐	**1.3** Identify Greek, Roman, and Norse mythology and use the knowledge to understand the origin and meaning of new words (e.g., the word *narcissistic* drawn from the myth of Narcissus and Echo.).	
☐	**2.1** Analyze the structure and format of functional workplace documents, including the graphics and headers, and explain how authors use the features to achieve their purposes.	
☐	**2.2** Prepare a bibliography of reference materials for a report using a variety of consumer, workplace, and public documents.	
☐	**2.3** Generate relevant questions about readings on issues that can be researched.	
☐	**2.4** Synthesize the content from several sources or works by a single author dealing with a single issue; paraphrase the ideas and connect them to other sources and related topics to demonstrate comprehension.	